The Structures and Strategies of Human Memory

The Dorsey Series in Psychology

Advisory Editors

Wendell E. Jeffrey
University of California, Los Angeles

Salvatore R. Maddi
The University of Chicago

Bruce R. Ekstrand
University of Colorado, Boulder

The Structures and Strategies of Human Memory

Leonard Stern
Eastern Washington University

1985

THE DORSEY PRESS   Homewood, Illinois   60430

© THE DORSEY PRESS, 1985

All rights reserved. No part of this publication may be
reproduced, stored in a retrieval system, or transmitted,
in any form or by any means, electronic, mechanical,
photocopying, recording, or otherwise, without the prior
written permission of the publisher.

ISBN 0-256-03250-5

Library of Congress Catalog Card No. 84–71568

Printed in the United States of America

1 2 3 4 5 6 7 8 9 0 ML 2 1 0 9 8 7 6 5

Preface

This text is intended to introduce the reader to the study of human memory. I feel that a text written for this introductory level should be as comprehensible as possible. One method I have used to help achieve this is through the organization of the material. The text is divided into two sections. The first describes the structures of the human memory system—the sensory, short-term, and long-term stores. This section is intended to familiarize the reader with the components of the memory system as well as with the terminology, techniques, and general approach used in the information-processing view of human memory. The second section deals with strategies, that is, the ways in which these memory stores can be used. This section includes a discussion of mnemonics, levels of processsing, concept acquisition, decision making, and problem solving.

One important aspect of the text's organization that contributes to its comprehensibility is the presence of a unifying theme or concept—the functioning of the memory retrieval system. The basic principles of the memory retrieval process are introduced in the chapter on the iconic store, elaborated on in discussions of the long-term store, and consistently referred to in accounting for various memory phenomena in the section of the text that deals with memory strategies. Retrieval is linked to forgetting in short-term memory, the effectiveness of mnemonic techniques, the levels-of-processing effect, the mechanism by which concepts are acquired and used, decision making, and problem solving. The constant reference to the retrieval process as a basis for various memory phenomena is intended to help integrate the text and provide the reader with general concepts by which memory phenomena other than those discussed in the text can be understood.

Understanding some new field or some experimental paradigm can be difficult. To facilitate this process, I have provided definitions for key terms and sufficient background, often historical in nature. This is intended to help the reader understand why an approach or particular study was performed. For example, in introducing Sperling's studies on iconic memory, I tell the reader why the research question was important and how the studies fit into what was known at the time. Similarly, in discussing the different approaches to concept acquisition and problem solving, sufficient historical background is provided to allow the reader to place the research into perspective. Analogies are also proposed to help explain difficult points. For instance, in explaining the memory retrieval system, I use a tuning fork analogy. Analogies are also used to explain the reasoning underlying complex experimental procedures (see the discussion on acoustic codes in the chapter on short-term memory and the discussion of memory for inferences in the chapter on concept acquisition).

In addition to providing the reader with theory and data, the text also relates this material to practical, everyday experiences. For example, the relevance of the storage properties of iconic memory to the reading process is discussed; the relevance of principles of memory retrieval is related to techniques for improving memory, and the role of concepts is related to such everyday activities as decision making and problem solving. To broaden further the applicability of the material that is presented, I have used illustrative examples drawn from a variety of disciplines within psychology, including the developmental, clinical, and social areas.

There are many aspects of human memory research and theory that are confusing. I have attempted to take a consistent position in this text on such matters as the difference between the short-term store and short-term memory, the relation between the long- and the short-term store, and the status of the levels-of-processing view of memory. I hope that the methods I have utilized in this text make study of the field of human memory stimulating and enjoyable.

Leonard Stern

Acknowledgment

I would like to acknowledge the important role played by all my teachers at the University of Oregon in helping me pursue my interest in psychology, especially Douglas Hintzman whose skill as a teacher and a researcher was vital in preparing me for the task of writing this text. Finally, I want to thank my wife Barbara for giving me the encouragement and help I needed to complete this project.

L. S.

Contents

The Structures and Strategies of Human Memory

Part 1
Structures

Chapter 1
Introduction

The Importance of Memory in Our Lives

What is 4 divided by 47? This problem was given to a Scottish mathematician, Professor A. C. Aitken, who had an extraordinary ability to perform mental calculations. Approximately four seconds after receiving the problem, Professor Aitken spoke the following digits at a rate of one every ¾ seconds: "Point 0, 8, 5, 1, 0, 6, 3, 8, 2, 9, 7, 8, 7, 2, 3, 4, 0, 4, 2, 5, 5, 3, 1, 9, 1, 4. That's about as far as I can carry it" (Hunter, 1962, p. 250).

How did he do this? An important reason for his lightning calculative ability was his having stored in memory a large number of facts about numbers. While most of us have learned that 4 is equivalent to 2 times 2 and that $144 = 12 \times 12$, Aitken had available in his memory a much richer and more complex assortment of transformations for numbers. For example, when hearing the number 1961, Aitken immediately realized that this number could be represented as 37 times 53 or $44^2 + 5^2$ or $40^2 + 19^2$. In his own words, "If I go for a walk and if a motor car passes and it has the registration number 731, I cannot but observe that that is 17×43 . . . this isn't deliberate, I just can't help it" (Hunter, 1962, p. 247). Because he had a vast store of these number facts in memory as well as a repertoire of efficient calculative methods, Aitken could perform rapid mental calculations. Observe how he used his memorized number facts to find the decimal equivalent of the fraction ⅟₈₅₁. He wrote, after doing the calculation in his head:

> The instant observation was that 851 is 23 times 37. I use this fact as follows: ⅟₃₇ is 0.027027027 and so on repeated. This I divide mentally by 23. 23 into

0.027 is 0.001 with remainder 4. In a flash I can get that 23 into 4,027 is 175 with remainder 2. And into 2,027 is 88 with remainder 3. And into 3,027 is 131 with remainder 14. And even into 14,027 is 609 with remainder 20. And so on like that. Also, before I even start this, I know that there is a recurring period of 66 places. (Hunter, 1978, p. 341)

Although Aitken's calculative capabilities were unusual, the ability that underlay his efficient performance is one that all mentally intact humans possess: the ability to remember.

The ability to memorize permits each of us to do more than manipulate numbers in our heads. We rely on our memory every time we try to understand what another person is saying to us. Imagine that you overheard the following:

The procedure is actually quite simple. First you arrange items into different groups. Of course one pile may be sufficient depending on how much there is to do. If you have go somewhere else due to lack of facilities that is the next step; otherwise, you are pretty well set. It is important not to overdo things. That is, it is better to do too few things at once than too many. In the short run this may not seem important but complications can easily arise. A mistake can be expensive as well. At first, the whole procedure will seem complicated. Soon, however, it will become just another facet of life. It is difficult to foresee any end to the necessity for this task in the immediate future, but then, one can never tell. After the procedure is completed one arranges the materials into different groups again. Then they can be put into their appropriate places. Eventually they will be used once more and the whole cycle will then have to be repeated. However, that is part of life.

This passage comes from an experiment done by Bransford and Johnson (1972). When people in the experiment heard the passage, they indicated that they had trouble understanding it, just as you perhaps did. Try rereading the paragraph, this time pretending that you overheard it while in a laundromat. When the people who participated in Bransford and Johnson's experiment heard the title "Washing Clothes" before they heard the passage, they subsequently indicated that the passage had been quite understandable.

Why does the title "Washing Clothes" or the context of a laundromat help make the passage easier to understand? Again, the answer involves memory. Whenever we hear some message, we tend to draw on our store of previous experiences to anticipate what the speaker is going to say, and to fill in details either that the speaker has omitted or that we have failed to perceive adequately. If I tell you that someone recently backed their car into mine and that it's going to cost me $150, you understand, even though I didn't specify it, that my car was damaged and that it will cost $150 to repair the damage. The reason you were able to make these inferences is because, on the basis of your learned experiences, you know that cars get dented and that dents are reparable, but that repairs cost money. These facts were available in your long-term memories. In the passage about washing clothes, you again had facts stored in your long-term memories that allowed you to fill in details that were not mentioned. However, before you knew that the passage dealt with washing clothes, you had no way of knowing that you should use those particular memorized experiences to help you understand the passage.

There are many less subtle ways that memories help us function as we do. Our understanding of such fundamental facts as where we are and why we're here depends on our ability to remember. Consider the case of an amnesic patient known by his initials, H. M. H. M. received a head injury when he was seven years old. Three years later, he began to have epileptic seizures, presumably due to uncontrolled discharges of previously injured brain cells. The seizures grew more frequent and more severe, often leading to injury, and by the time he was 27, H. M. could not hold a job or lead a normal life. When he failed to respond to all available anticonvulsive therapies, an experimental brain operation was performed. This operation intentionally destroyed much of a portion of H. M.'s brain that is known as the hippocampus. Although the operation did reduce the severity and frequency of the epileptic seizures, it also produced a serious memory impairment. It left H. M. with a nearly total inability to form new, permanent memories and, in addition, interfered with his ability to remember recent events that had occurred up to two years before the operation. Here is part of a description of what his life was like 14 years after the operation. The description was written by psychologists (Milner, Corkin, & Teuber, 1968) who observed H. M. during a two-week stay at the Massachusetts Institute of Technology's Clinical Research Center.

In social settings, H. M. is quiet, and appears at ease, except for his frequent apologies for what he fears may be considered lapses from good manners, such as forgetting the names of persons to whom he has just been introduced. It is clear that he has not lost any of the social graces he acquired in his youth. He keeps himself neat, although he has to be reminded to shave. He speaks in a monotone, but with good articulation and a vocabulary that is in keeping with his above-average intelligence.

During three of the nights at the Clinical Research Center, the patient rang for the night nurse, asking her, with many apologies, if she would tell him where he was and how he came to be there. He clearly realized that he was in a hospital but seemed unable to reconstruct any of the events of the previous day. On another occasion he remarked "Every day is alone in itself, whatever enjoyment I've had, and whatever sorrow I've had." Our own impression is that many events fade for him long before the day is over. He often volunteers stereotyped descriptions of his own state, by saying that it is "like waking from a dream." His experience seems to be that of a person who is just becoming aware of his surroundings without fully comprehending the situation, because he does not remember what went before. (pp. 216–217)[1]

The object of this book is to introduce the reader to this memory system that is so essential to our normal daily functioning. Before we begin, however, some fundamentals about our current approach to studying memory will be presented.

The Information-Processing View

The Computer Analogy

It may seem as if knowledge about a field such as human memory should progressively accumulate over time so that, once certain basic questions have been answered, a more and more detailed understanding of the field is achieved. The philosopher Kuhn (1962) has questioned whether this "accumulation model" of science is valid. He has suggested that it is true that science does go through periods during which knowledge is cumulative. However, if insoluble problems are encountered or if findings cannot be accounted for with the current theories, a discipline may go through a period of revolution during which the prevailing theories are rejected and replaced by new approaches.

The study of human memory has gone through such periods of revolution. Most recently, memory theorists have rejected the view that memory is best thought of in terms of associations that are formed between stimuli and responses. Instead, the view that is currently dominant is that human memory can be likened to a computer.

Why a computer? The analogy may at first seem strange since a computer is probably not capable of what might be termed conscious thought processes. While this incapacity may one day lead to the rejection of the computer model of memory, for the present, the computer has proven useful, for it appears to share a number of important characteristics with the human memory system. One of these characteristics is that both systems must store information. Computers generally have a number of different memory stores. There is a relatively permanent and often large capacity memory store that utilizes devices such as tapes or disks. A more temporary memory store, sometimes referred to as a working memory, is used to hold information that is being manipulated by a computer program. Additionally, infor-

---

[1] From B. Milner, S. Corkin, and H. L. Teuber, "Further analysis of the hippocampal amnesic syndrome: 14-year follow-up study of H. M." *Neuropsychologia*, 1968, 6, 215–234. Copyright 1968 by Pergamon Press, Inc. Reprinted by permission.

mation that is being entered into or read out of the computer may reside very temporarily in a rather small-capacity memory store while these "input" and "output" operations occur. In the human memory system there also seems to be a number of memory stores. These human memory stores also appear to differ according to the permanence of the information that they maintain. The following three stores have been suggested to make up the human memory system:

1. A *sensory store,* capable of storing a small amount of information for very brief periods of time.
2. A *short-term store,* also of limited capacity, but capable of maintaining information for longer periods than the sensory store.
3. A *long-term store,* having a large capacity, and capable of storing memories for very long periods of time.

Another way a computer resembles the human mind is that both may be thought of as being processors of information. That is, both take in information and then *do something* with the information before producing a response. Consider the act of driving a car. When driving, we constantly monitor the road ahead to gather information that will affect how we operate our vehicle. What happens to the information that is gathered? This is where the computer model has proven useful. It is easy to understand what happens to information that is input into a computer. The computer simply obeys the instructions prepared by the computer programmer. These instructions may be conveniently represented in diagrammatic form using a *flowchart.* As an example, Figure 1–1 shows some basic steps a computer might go through if it were programmed to simulate the behavior of a motorist who encounters a traffic signal ahead. Of course, this flowchart is not detailed enough to allow a computer actually to simulate a driver's behavior; this would require a great number of additional instructions. However, once all these instructions were provided by a programmer, one could trace the flow of information from the stage at which an input was received by the system until a response was delivered.

Psychologists interested in memory phenomena have borrowed this same method of representing the processing of information in the human mind. The resulting *human information processing system* depicts the memory system as a *combination of memory structures* and *operations* that are performed on information as it flows along specified pathways. The model shown in Figure 1–2 is typical of early human information processing models that were proposed in the 1960s (e.g., Shiffrin & Atkinson, 1969; Waugh & Norman, 1965). According to this model, when information from the environment first enters the system it is stored briefly in a sensory store. The informa-

Figure 1–1
A simple flowchart representing the sequence of steps a computer may be programmed to execute. The object of this program is to simulate the behavior of a motorist monitoring the road for a traffic signal.

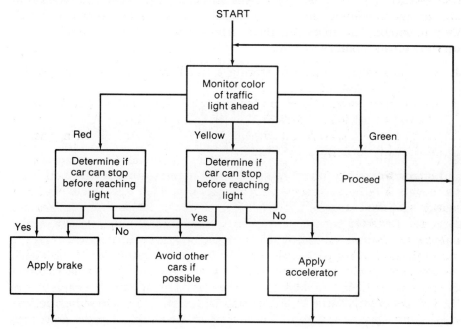

Figure 1–2
A simple model of the human information processing system.

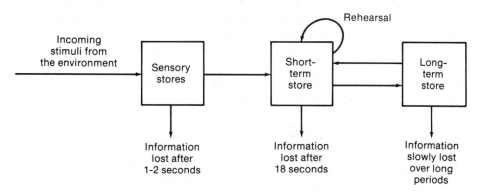

tion may either be passed along to the short-term store or it may simply be lost. Information that enters the short-term store may be maintained in the store for as long as the process of rehearsal is performed. Rehearsal refers to the act of speaking a verbal stimulus either aloud or silently to oneself. We are using rehearsal when, after looking up a phone number, we attempt to remember the number by repeating it over and over until we have finished dialing it.

In the simple memory model diagrammed here, three structures are represented. These are the three memory stores. The only operation that has been represented is rehearsal. Although we shall use this simple model as a guide for further examining human memory, it must be cautioned that this model is neither complete nor universally accepted. Note, for example, how much more complicated is the model proposed by Sperling (1970), shown in Figure 1–3. This model incorporates additional memory structures and operations.

Figure 1–3
An information-processing model proposed by Sperling (1970) for visual stimuli. The squares represent short-term memories, the rectangles represent long-term memories, and the triangles indicate scanning operations. The letters V, A, M, and R stand for visual, auditory, motor, and rehearsal, respectively.

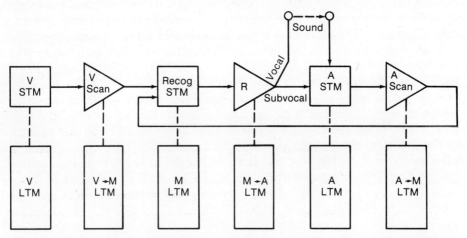

Adapted from G. Sperling, "Short-term memory, long-term memory, and scanning in the processing of visual information." In F. A. Young & D. B. Lindsley (Eds.), *Early Experience and Visual Information Processing in Perceptual and Reading Disorders,* 1970, pp. 198–215. Copyright 1970 by the National Academy of Sciences. Reprinted by permission.

Characteristics of the Memory Store

While the basic model of the human information-processing system is neither complete nor entirely satisfactory to all memory researchers, it will be useful to us as a guide in studying human memory. In the following chapters we shall examine each of the three stores shown in our basic model. To help us understand what properties the three stores have, we shall examine three general characteristics of each. The three characteristics will be referred to as *encoding, storage,* and *retrieval* properties.

Encoding. The term *encoding* has two aspects. One refers to the way information is represented in a memory store. Although it may not seem obvious, information may be represented in a number of ways. For example, when a person speaks, information is carried through the air by sound waves, which are compression patterns formed by vibrations of the vocal chords. Here, information is being represented in the air (which can be regarded as a store) in the form of compression patterns. The computer offers another example of how information may be represented. In a computer's memory, information is usually coded in terms of magnetic charges that take on one of two possible values. If we refer to these two values as 1 and 0, the letter *A* is often represented (i.e., encoded) in a computer's memory as 1100 0001, and *B* is represented as 1100 0010. In the field of human memory, questions about encoding cannot yet be answered in such a specific way. That is, we cannot specify how a concept is stored in memory. We cannot say, for example, that certain molecular configurations represent the letter *A*. Instead, this aspect of encoding is often discussed in a much more general way. Chapter 3 will present an illustration of this more general approach.

A second aspect to this issue of encoding that has been of concern to psychologists (e.g., Melton & Martin, 1972) concerns the kind of information that is stored, rather than the way the information is stored. To illustrate the importance of knowing what kind of information is stored, consider the performance of two people who had very impressive memory abilities. One is known by the initial S. He was born in Russia and was first studied in the 1920s by the Russian psychologist Luria (1968). The other person is referred to as V. P. He, too, was born in Russia. After V. P. moved to the United States, he was studied by Hunt and Love (1972). As part of these investigations, V. P. and S. were shown arrays of numbers such as the one illustrated in Figure 1–4 and asked to memorize them. V. P. and S. took several minutes to study these visual displays (3 and 6.5 minutes, respectively). Immediately after study, each was able to recall all digits in the array perfectly. Even more impressive is the ability of each of these persons to recall a column of digits perfectly both starting at the top row or in

Figure 1–4
An array of numbers typical of those used to examine the unusual memory abilities
of S. and V. P.

```
6  5  1  3  0  2
5  8  4  5  0  1
1  6  4  9  2  8
2  0  8  4  6  9
2  1  4  3  0  7
7  6  1  4  3  0
5  5  6  3  1  9
3  7  2  1  0  5
```

the reverse order, starting at the bottom row. Of relevance to the issue
of encoding is the difference between V. P. and S. in terms of information
stored. It appears as though S. tended to rely more on the visual aspects
of a stimulus than did V. P. That is, S. behaved as though he had stored
in memory a picture of the array of numbers. V. P., on the other hand,
tended to rely more on meaningful verbal translations of the stimulus. For
example, when attempting to memorize the array of numbers, V. P. reported
that he transformed the numbers into a date and then thought about what
he had done on that day. Thus, while both V. P. and S. had been presented
with the identical visual stimulus and had demonstrated similar performance
in the recall of this material, their performance was based on different
mental representations of the material.

Storage.   A second characteristic of memory stores is termed *storage.* Three
storage aspects will be of concern to us:

1. The capacity of the store.
2. The length of time information can be stored.
3. The fate of information during storage.

In a computer system, the capacity of a store can be measured in terms
of the number of memory cells (termed *bits),* each of which can take on
values of zero or one. In the human memory system we shall be quite
flexible in our choice of units we use to measure storage capacity. For example, when describing the capacity of a sensory store that is known as iconic
memory, capacity will be measured in terms of the number of individual
letters or digits. On the other hand, when measuring the capacity of the
short-term store, we may use words or even short phrases as our measurement units. It is easier to specify the units that we will use to measure
length of storage. Here we will use intervals such as milliseconds (1,000
milliseconds = 1 second), seconds, or years. Finally, when discussing the

fate of information during storage, we will be interested in determining how the passage of time affects an item residing in a particular memory store. It is possible, for example, that time may not have any effect on an item residing in a memory store. This possibility was, in fact, suggested by Waugh and Norman (1965) to be a property of the short-term store. As will be explained later, this hypothesis has not been supported (Reitman, 1971, 1974). Other possible effects of time in storage include a decay in the strength of a memory. We will soon see how this decay process plays a role in producing forgetting from various memory stores.

Retrieval. The last of the characteristics we will consider is retrieval. This is the most important property of the memory system, at least according to the view presented in this book. The term *retrieval* will be defined as the act of extracting information from a memory store. Retrieval is occurring each time we recall some event that happened in the past. Retrieval seems to play a major role in a number of memory processes. Consider the phenomenon of forgetting. If we say we have forgotten some information, we may actually still have that information in our long-term stores. The reason we cannot remember the information may be because the retrieval process does not function efficiently enough. This situation is analogous to our having some information stored permanently on a computer's magnetic tape; if we don't know which tape to request or where the desired tape is, we will not be able to extract the information from our storage device. Thus, although information may be potentially available, it is only accessible if the retrieval process works.

Looking Ahead

In the next chapter we will begin our examination of the human memory system by describing the storage, encoding, and retrieval properties of a sensory store. We begin by examining this structure because, as Figure 1–2 shows, the sensory stores are the first to receive information that enters the memory system from the environment. Although there are many sensory stores—one corresponding to each sense—our discussion in the next chapter will be limited to the store that corresponds to the visual sense, because this store has been the most extensively investigated. Subsequent chapters will examine the encoding, storage, and retrieval properties of the long-term and the short-term store.

Chapter 2
Iconic memory

Discovery of the Iconic Store

A person who is studying for a Ph.D. in psychology is usually required to write a dissertation in order to receive the degree. The dissertation is generally an account of the research that the student performs in order to arrive at an answer to some interesting question. In the late 1950s, George Sperling, a psychology graduate student at Harvard University, addressed a question that had long been of interest to psychologists. The question was "How much information can be seen in a single, brief glance?" Sperling's investigation led to the discovery of a memory store that is now known as iconic memory.

The issue that Sperling investigated is an important one because of the way our visual system works. When we look at a visual scene, our eyes tend to scan the scene in little jumps that are called saccadic eye movements. These saccadic eye movements are necessary because we can only see a small portion of a scene clearly. This small area of clear vision is detected by a region in the center of the retina called the fovea, in which the density of receptor cells is high. To observe a scene clearly, our eyes will fixate on (aim steadily at) one portion of the scene, then make a saccade (jump) to another portion of the scene and fixate on that. This process will be repeated until the scene has been adequately perceived. Figure 2–1 shows the pattern of eye movements exhibited by a person looking at a drawing. Saccadic eye movements also occur in the process of reading. The frequency of these eye movements in the reading process typically ranges between three and five per second. It has been determined that information is taken

14

Figure 2–1

A typical pattern of eye movements made by a subject viewing this drawing. The straight lines represent the path followed by the eyes during saccades. The letters indicate the order in which the fixations were made.

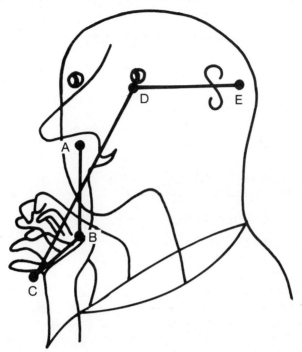

From D. Noton and L. Stark, "Scanpaths in eye movements during patern perception." *Science,* 1971, *171,* 308–311. Copyright 1971 by the American Association for the Advancement of Science. Reprinted by permission.

in for processing by the visual system only when the eyes are fixating on one part of a scene, not when they are in motion. It is this short period of time during which the eyes are stationary that Sperling referred to as a glance.

To measure how much information a person can see in a glance, Sperling flashed an array of letters and numbers on a screen and asked subjects in his experiment to try to report the identity and location of as many of these symbols as they could. By keeping the flash very brief (50 milliseconds, which is $\frac{1}{20}$ of a second), Sperling was able to ensure that subjects got only one glance. An interval that is as brief as $\frac{1}{20}$ of a second is too short a time to make two separate fixations.

At this point, Sperling's question might appear quite easy to answer. One could simply count the number of symbols that a person reports correctly. Such a procedure had, in fact, been performed previously by a number of researchers. For example, in 1933, Brigden reported that he flashed a series of cards containing stimuli to subjects and asked them to try to draw an exact copy of what they had seen. An example of one stimulus card used by Brigden is shown in Figure 2–2. Brigden noted that when the flash was very brief, as in Sperling's experiment, subjects often reported that they had been able to see all of the stimuli quite clearly. However, in the process of reporting the information, they began to forget what they had seen. Brigden mentions that a dozen or more of the 60 subjects in his study told him that this had happened to them.

Figure 2–2
An example of stimuli used in Brigden's (1933) study.

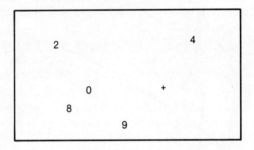

Bridgen's experiment suggests that because information is forgotten so quickly under these conditions, people can actually see more at a glance than they can report. This poses a difficulty: How can we determine how much a person can see at a glance if the information that is seen is forgotten more quickly than it can be reported?

Sperling solved this problem by utilizing a procedure that is not very different from the procedure used in testing knowledge in a classroom. When students are given an exam, they are generally not tested on everything that was learned in class. Rather, the test covers only a sample of that material. If a student gets 80 percent of the test questions correct, the teacher generalizes these results and concludes that the student knows 80 percent of all the material that was presented. In the long run, this assumption is perfectly correct.

Sperling used this same general procedure in his experiment. He asked people to report not all the stimuli they had seen during their glance, but only the stimuli in one section of the display. Specifically, Sperling used arrays consisting of three rows of four symbols (letters and numbers). He sounded one of the three tones after each stimulus array was flashed to a subject. The subjects had been told that a high tone was the signal to report the symbols in the top row, a medium tone was the signal to report symbols in the middle row, and a low tone was the signal to report symbols in the bottom row. This procedure is known as a *partial report procedure,* because subjects are asked to report only a portion of the stimuli presented to them. The procedure can be contrasted to a *whole report procedure,* which, of course, requires someone to report everything in the whole display.

Sperling tested six subjects using this partial report procedure. He found that, on the average, subjects could see 9 of the 12 symbols in the display. He arrived at this conclusion because subjects got, on the average, three out of four symbols correct in the row they were signalled to report. This is analogous to a test score of 75 percent correct. Generalizing this to all 12 items, Sperling concluded that each subject had actually seen nine symbols in their single glance.

This result was surprising. Before Sperling had publicized his study it had been found that observers could see only four to five items in a single glance. But this figure of four to five items had been obtained using a whole report rather than a partial report procedure. Evidently, prior to Sperling's study, experimenters had not been concerned enough with the problem of forgetting that can arise when a whole report procedure is used, so they had not taken measures to correct for it.

You must realize that these nine symbols that Sperling's subjects had available were being reported from memory. The reason we can say this is because Sperling found these results when he sounded the partial report cue (the high, medium, or low tone) *after* the 50-millisecond flash. Thus, when subjects received the cue telling them which row to report, the card containing the stimuli was no longer visible. We are therefore justified in claiming that the nine items that were available to these subjects were being briefly held in some memory store. This memory store has come to be known as *iconic memory,* a term coined in 1967 by Neisser.

Properties of the Iconic Store

Storage

Capacity. In describing Sperling's discovery of the iconic store, we've already answered one of the three questions dealing with the storage properties of iconic memory. That is, we know that the capacity of iconic memory is about nine items. Although more will soon be said about the capacity of the iconic store, we will deal first with another aspect of storage, the length of time that information can be held in iconic memory.

Duration.   Sperling performed an experiment as part of his dissertation that allowed him to determine the length of time information could be stored in iconic memory. The procedure simply involved delaying the partial report cue. That is, Sperling first flashed on an array of three rows, each containing three randomly chosen letters. A partial report cue in the form of a high, medium, or low tone was then sounded either immediately or after a delay of 150, 300, 500, or 1,000 milliseconds. As can be seen from Figure 2–3, Sperling found that the longer this delay was, the fewer letters the subjects could correctly report. It can be seen from this figure that when the tone was sounded immediately after the display was terminated

Figure 2–3
The total number of letters subjects had available as a function of the number of seconds the partial report cue was delayed.

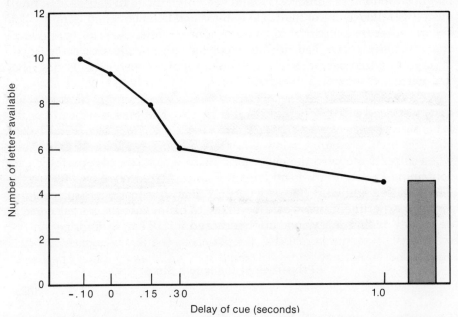

From G. Sperling, "The information available in brief visual presentations." *Psychological Monographs*, 1960, *74* (Whole No. 498). Copyright 1960 by the American Psychological Association. Reprinted by permission of publisher and author.

(zero-millisecond delay) subjects had about nine letters available. However, when the partial report cue was delayed 1,000 milliseconds, there was no longer any advantage of the partial report procedure over a whole report procedure. It may be concluded that after about a second (which is 1,000 milliseconds) there is no stimulus information available from the display in the iconic store.

One aspect of Figure 2–3 may be troubling you. If it is true that most stimulus information has decayed after 1,000 milliseconds, how could Sperling's subjects correctly identify four to five letters when the partial report cue was delayed for 1,000 milliseconds? The answer is that it is not possible for someone to do absolutely nothing while waiting for a cue. Rather, a person will immediately start to identify some letters from each row of the display. The data from this figure are consistent with the interpretation that, on the average, subjects identify 1½ letters in each row by the time 1,000 milliseconds have elapsed (1½ × 3 = 4.5, which is the total number of letters available after 1,000 milliseconds). When the partial report cue is sounded after the 1,000 milliseconds, all the stimulus information has disappeared, so no additional letters can be identified. Thus we will conclude at this point that information can ordinarily remain for no longer than one second in the iconic store.

Fate of Information in Storage. What happens to information in the iconic store over time? The experiment that was just described indicates that subjects became progressively less able to identify correctly letters in a display as the partial report cue was delayed. Thus, we can conclude that the information was fading away. This fading, or decay process as it is often called, apparently occurs at a very rapid rate. Sperling's experiment shows that after 1,000 milliseconds all information in the iconic store has decayed.

This rapid decay process is ordinarily not apparent to us, partly because we do not generally perceive our environment with single glances followed by a second or more of just dim illumination. But even if we did see a briefly exposed stimulus followed by dim illumination, as did subjects in Sperling's experiment, we would be likely to claim that the stimulus itself was rapidly fading away, not our memory of it. That is, information in iconic memory seems so real that people claim the information is still out there in the environment, even though it is no longer visible. Sperling's subjects, for example, claimed they could still see the letters for a brief period (about 150 milliseconds) after the display had actually been turned off. Eye movement studies seem to support the existence of this illusion that stimuli are still present for a brief period after their termination. Sperling originally noted that subjects in his studies tended to move their eyes to the row in the display that was signalled by the partial report cue. Hall

(1974) later confirmed this finding using a procedure similar to Sperling's, but with additional equipment to accurately measure eye movements. In Hall's study it was found that 75 percent of the time subjects' eyes moved to the row signalled by the partial report cue. These eye movements occurred after the stimuli were no longer there. Thus, when observing a fading image in iconic memory, subjects behave very much as though the stimuli are actually still present.

The Storage Properties Reconsidered

Capacity.   Let's review what has been said about the storage properties of iconic memory. It has been said that (1) iconic memory has a capacity of about nine items, (2) these nine items can be stored for no longer than 1,000 milliseconds, and (3) information that is stored in iconic memory decays rapidly over time. These three generalizations require some qualification. First, it should be emphasized that the nine-item capacity of iconic memory is a conservative estimate. It is conservative because Sperling's procedure requires that before subjects report the symbols from a display, they do a number of things that require time to perform. For example, when a subject hears a tone, the subject has to decide if the tone is a high, medium, or low tone. Then the subject has to shift attention to the appropriate row of the display. All of this takes time—not much time, but since the information in iconic memory decays so rapidly, any delay at all in beginning the reporting will decrease performance. In addition to these delays, a subject will have to postpone reporting some symbols until other symbols have been reported. For example, if a subject is signalled to report the symbols in row 2, the subject may begin by writing down the symbol in the left-most column first, then writing down the symbol to its right, and so on. Not only does this take time, but it is also possible for a memory interference phenomenon known as *output interference* to occur under these circumstances. Briefly, one experiences output interference when one has a number of items to retrieve from memory. It has been found that the very act of reporting any one of these items will lower one's chances of reporting another of them. As an example of this phenomenon of output interference, imagine that you have been shown a list of words half an hour ago, and that you are now asked to recall these words. Let's say that you now have available in memory the following words from the list: *cheese, pencil, flower, radio.* Perhaps you begin by retrieving the word *pencil* and writing it down on an answer sheet. The very act of retrieving this word will now lower your chances of retrieving any of the remaining words. This does not mean that you absolutely will not remember any of the other words, but rather that you will be a little less likely to recall any of them.

The effect will be cumulative. With each word that you recall, you will hurt your chances of recalling any of the remaining words. Thus, if you next retrieve and write down the word *radio,* you will be a little less likely to retrieve either of the remaining two words. To continue with this imaginary example, if you next are able to retrieve and write down the word *cheese,* but are unable to remember the last word from the list, a psychologist would say that you are experiencing output interference. What is important to realize is that your inability to retrieve this word under these circumstances does not mean that you do not have any memory of seeing or hearing the word half an hour ago. What it means is that the memory is there, but you are now experiencing difficulty in finding it.

All of this is relevant to Sperling's experiment. Since subjects were attempting to recall more than one symbol in response to the partial report cue (in the first experiment described here, people could recall a maximum of four), their performance was likely to be hurt by output interference. We could expect that the capacity of iconic memory would be found to be greater than nine items if output interference could be reduced.

What kind of modification in Sperling's procedure could be used to reduce output interference? A suitable procedure would be one that required subjects to report only a single symbol from a display. Such an experiment has, in fact, been performed. Averbach and Coriell (1961) flashed displays consisting of two rows of eight randomly selected letters to subjects. After these 16 letters had been displayed (the display lasted 50 milliseconds), a small mark (referred to as a bar marker) was displayed just above one of the positions where a letter had appeared. This was the signal for subjects to report the identity of the letter that had appeared there. (See Figure 2–4.) Averbach and Coriell found that subjects were able correctly to identify single letters 75 percent of the time. This means that of the 16 letters that were presented, subjects knew the identity of 12 (since 75 percent of 16 is 12). Thus, according to Averbach and Coriell's procedure, the capacity of iconic memory is 12, not 9 symbols. What shall we say is the capacity of iconic memory? Let us say that iconic memory can hold *at least* 9 symbols.

Duration.   When discussing the duration of storage, it was previously said the information can be stored in iconic memory for up to 1,000 milliseconds. This figure of 1,000 milliseconds is actually not a very good estimate of the duration of iconic storage. If you look back at Figure 2–3, you will notice that there really isn't a great deal of difference between the partial and whole report estimate of number of letters available, after partial report cue delays of about 250–300 milliseconds. What this indicates is that subjects do not get much extra information from the iconic store when they direct attention to the row signalled by a partial report cue that is delayed for

Figure 2–4
The sequence of stimuli in Averbach and Coriell's (1961) experiment. Subjects first
saw an array of 16 letters, then a blank interval, and finally a bar marker just above
one of the locations that a letter had occupied in the array.

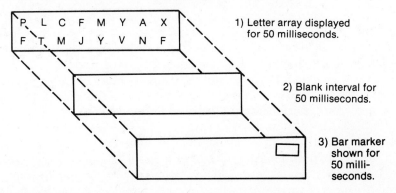

1) Letter array displayed for 50 milliseconds.

2) Blank interval for 50 milliseconds.

3) Bar marker shown for 50 milli-seconds.

250–300 milliseconds following the stimulus offset. Thus, it is more appropriate to fix the duration of iconic storage at between 250 and 300 milliseconds.
Fate.   Decay is not the only fate that may befall information in the iconic
store. Two other consequences are possible. These are known as *integration*
and *erasure.* Integration is simply the combination of two or more images.
This phenomenon produces very much the same effect as when two photographs are taken without advancing the film in a camera. Under these circumstances the second scene is superimposed on the first. Sperling showed
that this same effect occurs in iconic memory. He flashed a bright light to
subjects immediately after they had been shown an array of letters for 50
milliseconds. The subjects evidently saw a combination or integration of
the letter array and the bright light. The combination or integration of
these two stimuli made it difficult for the subjects to identify accurately
the letters in the array, since the bright light made the letters stand out
less strongly from the background. Under these conditions, subjects identified only half as many letters as when no bright light was shown. Other,
more compelling evidence for integration comes from an experiment by
Eriksen and Collins (1967). This experiment utilized a pair of stimuli. The
two stimuli in each pair appeared to be just a random series of dots. If
the two patterns were superimposed, however, they combined to form three
letters. (See Figure 2–5.) Eriksen and Collins never actually presented both
members of each stimulus pair simultaneously. Instead, they first flashed
on one member of a pair for 6 milliseconds, then waited between 0 and
500 milliseconds before flashing on the second member, which also was

Figure 2–5
An example of stimuli used by Eriksen and Collins (1967). When viewed separately, patterns A and B are meaningless; when superimposed, however, they form three letters.

Pattern A   Pattern B

Superimposed

From C. W. Eriksen and J. F. Collins, "Some temporal characteristics of visual pattern perception." *Journal of Experimental Psychology*, 1967, *74*, 476–484. Copyright 1967 by the American Psychological Association. Reprinted by permission of publisher and author.

displayed for 6 milliseconds. Integration of the two stimuli was demonstrated by subjects being able to identify the three letters at better than guessing levels even when intervals of 100–200 milliseconds separated presentations of the two stimuli. Of course, the longer the delay between the two presentations, the less effective the integration. It appears from this and other experiments (e.g., Spencer & Shuntich, 1970; Turvey, 1973) that integration will occur most effectively if the two stimuli are shown within 100 milliseconds of each other.

The other possible fate of information in the iconic store is known as *erasure*. Erasure of a stimulus may occur if a pattern is presented 50–150 milliseconds after the stimulus is presented (Kahneman, 1968). This pattern, often referred to as a *mask*, will best erase a stimulus if it surrounds the stimulus completely or flanks the stimulus on two sides (Didner & Sperling, 1980). Averbach and Coriell (1961), for example, found that when they exposed their array of 16 letters for 50 milliseconds, then, 50 milliseconds after the offset of this array, briefly exposed a circle that surrounded the location of one of the letters from the array, subjects were able to identify correctly the letter from that circled location only 10–20 percent of the time. As mentioned previously, when a bar marker was used instead of the circle, performance was correct about 75 percent of the time. Apparently, the circle erased the letter that had been stored in the corresponding location of the iconic store. The phenomenon of erasure is quite complex and has proven to be quite difficult to understand fully. One of the complexities associated with erasure has to do with the relation between the stimulus a subject is trying to identify and the pattern being used to erase the stimulus. It is often the case that one pattern will not be equally effective in erasing all stimuli. It has been found, for example, that a circle, as used in the Averbach and Coriell study, will erase the letter *C* more effectively than it will erase the letter *X*. Here we have better erasure when a mask visually resembles a stimulus. Experimenters have shown that other factors, such as phonological relations (two words that sound alike are phonologically related), also may influence the effectiveness of a mask (e.g., Naish, 1980).

The Relevance of These Storage Properties

It was previously mentioned that studies of reading have shown that a person typically makes four saccadic eye movements each second. This means that the eye is usually stationary for about 250 milliseconds. It was also mentioned that the duration of iconic storage is also about 250 milliseconds. Because the time between saccadic eye movements corresponds so closely to the duration of iconic storage, some psychologists have suggested that iconic memory plays a key role in visual perception. The suggestion made by these psychologists (e.g., Dick, 1974; Sperling, 1963) is that we let information enter iconic memory shortly after our eyes come to rest on some area of the environment, then we direct attention to some position in iconic memory and "read out" the information that is stored there. (We will deal further with this "reading out" process in the section on retrieval.) What should be noted about this suggestion is that it implies that we rely on iconic storage rather than the actual visual scene when we are doing the bulk of the information processing between saccadic eye movements. Although information from the visual scene corresponds exactly to what is stored in iconic memory, the continued presence of this physical stimulus is actually superfluous according to this view, for it is the information from the iconic store that receives the processing.

Erasure has also been proposed to serve a useful purpose. As mentioned previously, it is possible for some information to remain in iconic memory for longer than 250 milliseconds. Imagine how confusing the world would look if a person made a saccadic eye movement before all information had decayed from the previous glance. One might see two scenes superimposed on each other. Sperling (1963) has suggested that erasure helps prevent this from happening. That is, information from one's present glance erases information remaining from the previous glance.

Finally, one might ask why it is necessary to store more information from a glance than can be reported. That is, since we can only report four to five items from each glance, what purpose is served by our ability to store nine or more items? One answer is that this relatively large storage capacity increases our flexibility and efficiency in processing information from our environment. These benefits are due to our ability to process superficially some of the unattended information in the iconic store. This superficial processing of these supposedly ignored stimuli can affect our behavior. A demonstration of this comes from an experiment on reading conducted by Rayner (1975). Rayner had subjects read various sentences that were displayed on a TV screen controlled by a computer. As mentioned previously, when we read, our eyes fixate on one portion of a sentence. After we process the information we observe there, our eyes make a saccade to another portion of the sentence to process information found there. Rayner included the following sentence in his experiment:

"The king watched the fcaobcn from his throne."

Reading this sentence, how soon did you notice that the letters *fcaobcn* were present? This is basically the issue that Rayner was investigating: he wanted to know "the size of the area from which a person picks up information during a fixation in reading" (p. 65). Of course, it is difficult to answer this question accurately. Rayner, however, arrived at an answer using a technique made possible only by modern technology. He used a computer that was capable of tracking a person's eye movements. In the above sentence, when the computer detected that a reader was about to move his eyes to focus on the letters *fcaobcn*, the computer abruptly substituted the word "traitor" in place of *fcaobcn*. This substitution was made when subjects were making a saccadic eye movement. It has been found that during these movements nothing is visible to a person, so these subjects never actually observed the substitution taking place. Instead, as the reader's eyes reached the location of the letters *fcaobcn*, they were suddenly confronted by the new sentence: "The king watched the traitor from his throne."

What do you think you would do if you believed you were going to read one word, and then suddenly were shown another word? Rayner reasoned that this conflict would cause a person to slow down and use more time to process the unexpected word. Thus, if you expected, even at an unconscious level, that you were about to encounter a word that looked something like *fcaobcn* and then were actually shown the word *traitor*, you would require extra processing to read the word *traitor*. Rayner found evidence that this expectation was formed when a person was fixating as far away as 10–12 character spaces before the beginning of the letter string *fcaobcn*. He concluded this because a substitution (e.g., *traitor* for *fcaobcn*) led to a 50-millisecond average increase in processing time when the glance immediately preceding fixation on some critical word (the word *traitor* in our example) was centered 10–12 spaces before the critical word. In our example, 10–12 spaces before the word *traitor* falls on the letters *wat* in the word *watched*.

What all of this indicates about iconic memory is that even though we cannot fully utilize all the information that is in our iconic store at any one time, that information may be processed to some degree and may be capable of exerting an influence on our behavior. This can increase the efficiency of our processing when partially processed information from one glance conforms to the attended information from the subsequent glance (e.g., Rayner, 1975); it allows us to be flexible by permitting our attention to be attracted by information that is not the present focus of our attention.

Encoding in the Iconic Store

It should come as no surprise that the information stored in iconic memory is visual. That is, the information consists of the lines and angles that define a visual stimulus. What is more surprising is the type of information that is not represented in iconic memory. This type of information is semantic information.

The implications of these encoding properties of iconic memory may not seem obvious at first. But think of what it means to have only visual and not semantic information available. Since semantic information consists of meaning, the absence of this information leaves a person without any idea of the identity of a stimulus. To get a better idea of the type of information that is missing from the iconic store, consider the meaningful properties of the symbol *A*. This symbol is a letter, it is the first letter of the alphabet, and it functions as an English word. It is just this type of information that is not present in iconic memory. Thus, when some symbol is stored in the iconic store, all that is represented is a visual configuration.

Evidence for the claim that semantic information is absent from this store comes from an experiment done by Sperling (1960). In Sperling's experiment, subjects were presented with arrays made up of letters and digits, such as the one in Figure 2–6. These arrays were presented for 50 milliseconds and were followed by partial report cues. In one experimental condition the partial report cues signaled subjects whether to report the top or the bottom row of the array. The results were just as expected from Sperling's other studies. When the partial report cues were presented immedi-

Figure 2–6
An array of stimuli typical of that used by Sperling (1960) in investigating the nature
of the encoding properties of the iconic store.

```
X   4   N   8
S   R   7   2
```

ately after the array was terminated, subjects' performance indicated that
they had most of the eight symbols from the display available. This was
shown by their getting nearly 100 percent of the symbols in the signalled
row correct. Now let's consider the other experimental condition in which
on half the trials the partial report cue signalled subjects to report just
the four letters, and on the other half of the trials the partial report cue
signalled subjects to report just the four numbers. What prediction would
be made if it were true that no semantic information was present in iconic
memory? The answer is that these semantic partial report cues would be
much less effective than those indicating which row to report. The reason
is that the absence of semantic information in iconic memory would prevent
a person from knowing which symbols in the memory store were letters
and which were numbers. Thus, upon receiving a partial report cue signalling that numbers were to be reported, a person would not know where
in the array the four desired symbols were located. Under these circumstances, a person might resort to guessing. Since there will only be time
to report the identity of a total of four to five of the symbols in iconic
memory, and since half the symbols in this array are letters and half are
numbers, we can expect that in the long run half of these four to five
symbols that a subject reports (i.e., two to two and one-half) will be of the
desired semantic catagory. For example, if a person were shown the display
shown in Figure 2–6 for 50 milliseconds and then received a cue to report
just the letters from the display, the person might guess that the desired
symbols were located in the two middle columns and start to report the
symbols 4, N, R, and 7. By the time this subject had reported these four
symbols, little additional information from the display would be accessible.
Since the partial report cue has called for just letters, only two of these
four symbols would be counted as correct. This score of two correct represents a performance of 50 percent correct, which is only half as high a
score as is obtained when the partial report cue signals which row of the
display to report. Sperling's results did, in fact, turn out like this. When
subjects received a partial report cue indicating which row of symbols to
report, they correctly reported close to 100 percent of the signalled symbols.
When a semantic partial report cue was delivered, the performance was

close to 50 percent correct. Thus, it appears as if semantic information is not encoded in the iconic store.

Obtaining Semantic Information from Visual Encoding.   You may be wondering how it is possible for anyone to identify a symbol if semantic information is not present in the iconic store. That is, in this experiment of Sperling's, how could subjects report the identity of the symbols in any one row if only visual information was present in the iconic store? The answer to this question requires some understanding of the process of retrieval from the long-term store. One important thing to know about the long-term store is that it contains a great deal of semantic information as well as other forms of information. Thus, in the long-term store, in addition to the visual information that corresponds to a symbol such as the letter A, there will also be a great deal of semantic information stored with (we often say it is associated with) this visual information. In order for us to identify a symbol that is stored in iconic memory, the following two steps must occur:

1. The visual information in the iconic store must find (i.e., retrieve) the matching visual information in the long-term store.
2. The visual information in the long-term store that has been retrieved must activate the semantic information that is associated with the visual information.

To see how this whole process fits in with Sperling's experiment, let us reconsider the spatial partial report cue condition in which one tone signalled subjects to report from the top row and another signalled subjects to report from the bottom row. When a tone is sounded, a subject begins the long-term memory retrieval process on the symbols in the signalled row. The subject may perhaps choose to conduct this retrieval process in a left-to-right order, or may choose to conduct this retrieval process first on one and then on the other of the two symbols on the extreme ends of a row before moving to the two middle symbols. Although this second strategy may sound a bit odd, there is evidence that people use it both in experimental situations and in the process of reading (Merikle, Coltheart, & Lowe, 1971). In any case, as each symbol that is stored in iconic memory retrieves its matching visual representation in the long-term store and then activates the associated semantic information, a person will be able to become conscious of the semantic properties of each of these symbols. You should realize that it is only after this retrieval from the long-term store that a person can be aware of the identity of a symbol.

Imagine now that you are a subject in Sperling's experiment and have just received a semantic partial report cue signalling you to report all the letters in the display. Which symbols are letters? You won't be able to tell until you perform a retrieval operation on each symbol. Unfortunately, you won't have time to do the retrieval and report the identity of all eight symbols. You'll only be able to complete both of these operations on about four to five of the symbols. In the long run, half of these symbols (i.e., two to two and one-half) will be letters. Thus, you will probably achieve a partial report score of about 50 percent (or slightly higher) when semantic partial report cues are used.

As you can see, the retrieval process is crucial in this task. It is only after one has performed this retrieval of information from the long-term store that an awareness of the identity of the contents of the iconic store is possible. But how does this retrieval process actually occur? Of all the information stored in the long-term store, how is it possible to find the correct, matching information? Not a great deal is known about the retrieval process. However, because it is one of the most important processes in the human memory system, we must attempt to understand it better. In the next section additional information about the retrieval process is presented.

Retrieval and Iconic Memory

One way to understand some process is to compare it with something similar that occurs in another context. If this second similar process is much more concrete and accessible than the one we are attempting to understand, we may be able to conceptualize better our little-understood process. In the case of memory retrieval, then, we would like to say that the retrieval process is just like some other process that occurs in nature.

The process that is comparable to memory retrieval will be referred to here as the *tuning fork analogy of retrieval.* A tuning fork is a U-shaped piece of metal mounted on a handle. When a tuning fork is struck, it begins to vibrate and to make an audible hum. Piano tuners use tuning forks to help determine a note's correct pitch. The frequency at which a tuning fork vibrates will depend on the thickness and height of the tuning fork. Small, thin forks will vibrate at high frequencies and consequently sound like high notes on a piano.

The tuning fork analogy of retrieval is exhibited in the following situation. Let us imagine that someone has a collection of tuning forks, each of which is labeled according to the frequency at which it is set to vibrate. Suppose that another individual has a tuning fork that is unlabeled and that this person wishes to determine the vibration frequency of this unlabeled tuning fork. One way he could do this would be to strike the unidentified tuning fork and to hold it before the collection of labeled tuning forks. Something

Figure 2–7
A vibrating tuning fork will cause another tuning fork that is capable of vibrating at the identical frequency to begin to hum. In the tuning fork analogy of memory retrieval, this process allows the identity of the unlabeled tuning fork to be determined from the label attached to the tuning fork in the labeled set that has begun to hum.

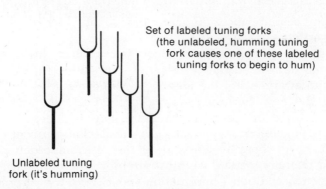

Set of labeled tuning forks
(the unlabeled, humming tuning
fork causes one of these labeled
tuning forks to begin to hum)

Unlabeled tuning
fork (it's humming)

rather surprising would happen. The unidentified tuning fork would cause one of the labeled tuning forks that is set to vibrate at the same frequency as the unknown tuning fork to begin to hum. Now, simply by reading the identifying label on this tuning fork that has begun to hum, the person could ascertain the vibration frequency of the unlabeled tuning fork. (See Figure 2–7.)

Do you see the analogy between this process and memory retrieval? Think of the collection of labeled tuning forks as being information in the long-term store. Each tuning fork represents a concept in the long-term store. The label attached to a tuning fork is analogous to semantic information that is associated with each concept. The unlabeled tuning fork can be regarded as being information in the iconic store. The act of striking the unlabeled tuning fork is analogous to directing attention to the location in the iconic store in which some information is stored. The process by which the vibrating, unlabeled tuning fork causes a matching labeled tuning fork to vibrate is analogous to the process by which unidentified visual information in iconic memory contacts matching visual information in the long-term store. We can consider the vibration of a labeled tuning fork as being similar to an activation or a feeding of energy into some location in the long-term store in which the appropriate matching concept is stored. This activation, in turn, will be regarded as causing a person to become conscious of the concept and its associated information. This entire process can be summarized as follows:

Human Memory System	Tuning Fork Analogy
1. A person directs attention to some location in the iconic store in which unidentified visual information is stored.	1. A person strikes an unlabeled tuning fork.
2. Visual information in the long-term store is contacted that matches the information in the iconic store. This process activates not only the visual information in the long-term store, but associated semantic information as well.	2. A tuning fork that is set to vibrate at the same frequency as the unlabeled tuning fork begins to hum.
3. A person becomes conscious of the existence of and identity of the information in the iconic store.	3. A person identifies the vibration frequency of the unlabeled tuning fork by reading the label on it.

This tuning fork analogy of memory retrieval does not, of course, explain exactly how the retrieval process works. It does, however, make the retrieval process easier to discuss by allowing us to conceptualize it in concrete, easily visualized terms. This analogy and the process of memory retrieval will be of great importance in much of the material that will be presented.

The Locus of Iconic Memory

A question about the iconic store that has not yet been settled is its location. In general, psychologists who study memory are not terribly concerned with the exact physiological structures that correspond to any proposed memory stores. It has not been considered essential, for example, for a psychologist to know exactly where in the brain long-term memories or short-term memories are stored. Rather, the focus of attention has been on ascertaining the characteristic properties of each store.

Even though there is no great emphasis on establishing the precise locus of a memory store in the brain, psychologists often attempt to make general statements about location by distinguishing between what are called *central* and *peripheral* stores. This distinction parallels that between the central and peripheral nervous system. Generally, the peripheral nervous system is located outside the skull and vertebral column, while the central nervous system lies within these protective bony structures. Since signals that are first received from the environment by the sense organs become more analyzed and abstract as they proceed into the central nervous system, psychologists also use the criterion of extent of abstraction of a memory representation to distinguish between central and peripheral structures.

Thus, a peripheral store would be one that is located in or close to the sense organs and holds information in an unanalyzed, unrefined form. A central store would be located at higher levels in the nervous system; the information stored there would be in a rather abstract, highly processed form.

At present, psychologists have not been able to determine conclusively whether iconic memory is purely a peripheral or a central phenomenon. The issue is unsettled because there seems to be good evidence for both of these possibilities. Barbara Sakitt and her co-workers (e.g., Sakitt, 1976; Sakitt & Long, 1979) are responsible for gathering much of the evidence for the peripheral interpretation of iconic memory. Sakitt has claimed not only to have demonstrated that iconic memory is a peripheral phenomenon, but that more specifically, the locus of this store is in the photoreceptors of the retina. The retina is a net of nerves on the back of the eyeball on which the light that enters the eye is focused. The first layer of cells in the retina that detect light consists of rods and cones. These cells are known as photoreceptors.

Evidence for Peripheral Iconic Storage.   Normally, a person has both rods and cones in their retinas. However, very occasionally a person is born with just rods, but no cones. Such people are called rod monochromats, and have special vision problems. One problem is that they are color-blind because they lack cones. (Cones are responsible for color vision.) Another problem is that it is difficult to see in bright light. This results because rods function best in dim light. (A person normally has to rely on cones for vision in bright light.) This does not mean, however, that a rod monochromat will be totally blind in bright light. One trick such a person can use is to shut the eyes after looking at a bright scene. This will allow the rods to recover from the overstimulation and soon give the rod monochromat a view of the scene.

Sakitt (1976) performed an experiment like Sperling's (1960) on a rod monochromat. Sakitt first investigated whether a rod monochromat would show the usual advantage in number of letters reported when a partial report procedure rather than a whole report procedure was used. Sakitt's experiment showed that there was indeed an advantage of partial report over whole report and that, as with subjects who have normal vision, the advantage of partial report over whole report decreases as the partial report cues are delayed. Thus, a person who has only rods demonstrates normal iconic memory. In a second experiment Sakitt shined a bright light in the rod monochromat's eyes before flashing on the array of letters. This bright light essentially blinded this person. Consequently, the subject did not see the even brighter array of two rows of four letters that was subsequently flashed on. Sakitt, of course, expected that this would happen: she expected that the rod monochromat would not be able to see any of the letters in the array under these circumstances. The interesting finding in this experiment came as a result of another manipulation Sakitt included. Sakitt instructed the rod monochromat to shut her eyes immediately after the array had flashed on and off. When this instruction was carried out, the subject was soon able to demonstrate the usual iconic memory for the arrays of letters; that is, she was able to report more letters using a partial report procedure than a whole report procedure. (See Figure 2–8.) This demonstrated to Sakitt that the information about the letters was being stored by this person's rods. If the rods had been unable to store the information, then no letters could have become visible after the rod monochromat shut her eyes and let the rods recover from their overstimulation.

Figure 2–8
The difference, in terms of number of letters available, for partial and whole report procedures when a rod monochromat was instructed either to close her eyes after the display terminated (top line) or to keep them open (bottom line).

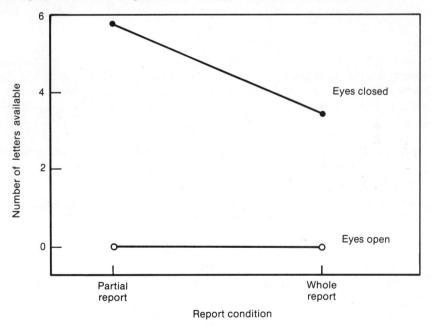

Adapted from B. Sakitt, "Iconic memory," *Psychological Review,* 1976, *33,* 257–276. Copyright 1976 by the American Psychological Association. Reprinted by permission of publisher and author.

Evidence for Central Iconic Storage.   Other experimenters have found
evidence that suggests that iconic memory is located at a level more central
than the rods. McCloskey and Watkins (1978), for example, claim to have
demonstrated this using the following task. They cut a narrow slit in a
screen and had subjects look through the slit from about six inches away.
Subjects attempted to report the identity of the stimuli that moved rapidly
behind the slit. (See Figure 2–9A.) You'll notice from Figure 2–9A that
each stimulus object or set of objects was longer than the width of the
slit. Thus, it was not possible for each stimulus object or set of objects to
be completely in view at any one time. The surprising outcome of the
experiment was that subjects viewing the drawings being rapidly passed
behind the slit in the screen believed they actually saw most of the figure
appear through the opening at once. This illusion McCloskey and Watkins
call the seeing-more-than-is-there phenomenon. Figure 2–9B shows drawings made by subjects who were instructed to sketch what they had observed.

McCloskey and Watkins claim that the seeing-more-than-is-there illusion
can be easily demonstrated outside the laboratory:

> The effect may be observed by using a partially open door as the slit and a
> person as target figure.
> Arrange the door so that it is not open quite enough to allow full view of the
> person on the other side. Then have the person shuffle rapidly back and forth,
> clearing the opening on each side, and he or she will be slimmed to fit the
> opening! (p. 563)

Iconic memory is thought to underlie this illusion. McCloskey and Watkins
suggest that iconic memory stores and integrates successive sections of each
drawing that come into view at different times. They argue, however, that
such a storage and integration process is too complex to occur in the rods.
To help understand why the rods could not perform these functions, regard
the rods as being analogous to photographic film. If a camera were substituted for an observer in this experiment, and the camera shutter were
held open as the object passed rapidly behind the slit, the picture that
appeared on the film would resemble a blur formed by a superposition of
various segments of the object. A similar image would be registered in
the rods. Since a person sees the stimulus object and not a meaningless
blur, McCloskey and Watkins conclude that iconic memory is not located
in the rods but in a more central locus. At this more central level in the
nervous system, it is assumed that processing is sufficiently sophisticated
to allow successive segments of the stimulus object to be sorted out and
integrated.

Figure 2–9
Part A shows the stimuli used by McCloskey and Watkins (1978). The vertical lines represent the slit through which subjects viewed the moving objects. Part B shows representative drawings of subjects who were instructed to sketch what they had seen through the slit.

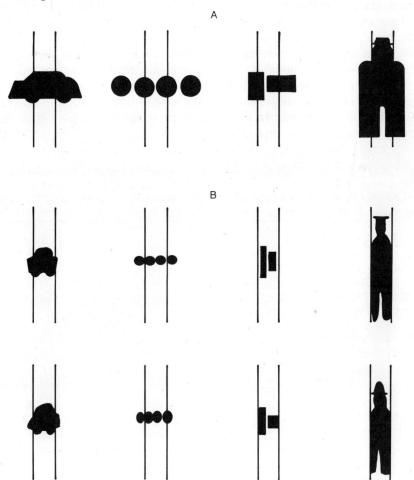

From M. McCloskey and M. J. Watkins, "The seeing-more-than-is-there phenomenon: Implications for the locus of iconic storage." *Journal of Experimental Psychology: Human Perception and Performance,* 1978, *4,* 553–564. Copyright 1978 by the American Psychological Association. Reprinted by permission.

More than One Storage Locus?   The controversy about iconic memory's location has most recently centered on whether the rods alone are responsible for iconic storage. It has been argued (Banks & Barber, 1977) that if the rods are the locus of iconic memory, iconic memory could not store color information since color vision is the function of the cones. Sakitt and her co-workers (Sakitt, 1976; Sakitt & Long, 1979) have pointed out that some color information is available to rods. Rods are able to distinguish colors in terms of their different light intensities. Blue and red, for example, appear to a rod monochromat as different shades of gray. As a result of further investigation of the function of cones in iconic memory, Sakitt and Long (1979) and Long and Sakitt (1980) have shown that cones do play a part in iconic storage, but that their role is much briefer than that of the

Figure 2–10
The decrease in number of letters available as a partial report cue is delayed. The dotted line shows performance for stimuli that were visible to both rods and cones; the solid line shows performance for stimuli visible just to cones.

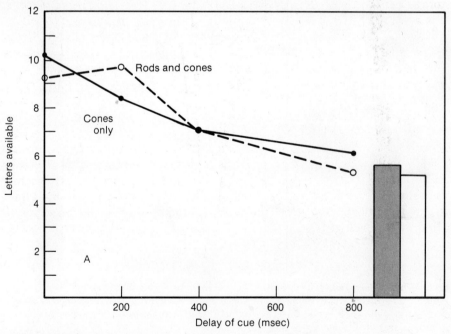

Adapted from E. H. Adelson, "Iconic storage: The role of rods." *Science,* 1978, *201,* 544–546. Copyright 1978 by the American Association for the Advancement of Science. Reprinted by permission.

rods. Their evidence indicates that cones store information for only about 100 milliseconds. Adelson (1978), however, has found evidence that contradicts these conclusions. Using a procedure similar to that of Sperling (1960), Adelson flashed arrays of letters to subjects and delivered partial report cues after various delays. Adelson's procedure differed from Sperling's in that it employed arrays of letters made up of specially selected colors that, for the rods, were totally indistinguishable from the background. Thus, only the cones could detect that letters were present. If it were true that most of iconic storage occurs in the rods, then this specially colored display should have produced a much briefer memory than a display that was visible to both the rods and the cones. Adelson's results did not support this. As shown in Figure 2–10, there was little difference in the duration of iconic storage when the display was visible just to the cones than when it was visible to both the rods and the cones.

Where is iconic memory? Perhaps it is most reasonable to conclude at this point that iconic memory has more than one locus (Adelson, 1978; Wickelgren, 1979a, p. 198). The evidence as a whole suggests that peripheral storage can occur in the rods and the cones. At this photoreceptor level it is likely that the stored information is much like a photograph of the stimulus in the sense that it duplicates the stimulus quite closely. Other storage sites may exist at more central locations in the nervous system. At these higher levels, information may exist in a more abstract form. Additional experimentation may help us to distinguish between a peripheral and a central iconic store.

This completes the discussion of the iconic store. The reader should realize that the iconic store is just one of several sensory stores, each of which appears to have somewhat different characteristics. For example, the sensory store known as echoic memory holds auditory information for durations that appear to be slightly longer than that of iconic storage—approximately two seconds by one estimate (Crowder, 1976). We have concentrated here on iconic memory because it is the store that has been most intensely investigated by psychologists.

Chapter 3
Encoding in the long-term store

In the previous chapter it was demonstrated that the long-term store plays an important role in processing information in the iconic store. Specifically, it was shown that to identify information in the iconic store, the visual information that is held there must contact matching visual information in the long-term store and arouse associated semantic information. Thus, the flow of information appears to be from the iconic store to the long-term store. Later chapters will show that information appears to flow next to what will be termed the short-term store. This theoretical sequence of information flow from sensory to long-term to short-term store is a departure from the basic model of the information processing system presented in chapter 1. There it was specified that information from the iconic store flows first to the short-term store before entering the long-term store. However, as will be explained in the chapter on the short-term store, the modification proposed here provides a better, more logical description of the human information processing system. In accord with this revised view, the memory store to be examined next is the long-term store.

This chapter will begin our investigation of the long-term store with an examination of the store's encoding properties. The issue of encoding deals with the question of information representation. As explained previously, this question has two concerns. One deals with the kind of information that is stored—this can be thought of as the "what" aspect of encoding; the other deals with the way information is represented—this can be thought of as the "how" aspect of encoding.

38

To get a better understanding of these questions, imagine that you encounter a robot-like device in a science class. When spoken to, the device responds in what seems like a reasonable way. To determine better the capabilities of the machine, you ask it to perform various tasks, one of which is to repeat back a list of 20 words that you read aloud. The machine reports all the words correctly. At this point you may wonder how the device is performing this task. More specifically, you may wish to know whether the machine is actually storing the meanings of the words—does it really understand what you're saying—or whether it is storing just the sounds that make up the words. This question corresponds to our "what" aspect of the encoding issue, for you are trying to find out what aspects of the stimuli—their meanings or their sounds—are being stored. A second question you may wish to address might deal with the way the device is storing the information. For example, if the machine is storing just the sounds of the words, it could be storing these sounds in the same way that sounds on a tape recording are stored or it could be storing the sounds using the methods employed by digital recording devices. This question corresponds to the "how" aspect of encoding.

We will start by addressing the "what" aspect of encoding. As you might suspect from your own experiences, the long-term store can hold information conveyed by each of our sense organs (e.g., visual, acoustic) as well as information about the meaning of stimuli. What might not be so obvious are the techniques for demonstrating the presence of these encodings. The first part of this chapter will deal with some of the techniques used to detect semantic, visual, and acoustic encodings. The second part will examine the "how" aspect of encoding, concentrating on theories of how semantic and visual information is represented.

Determining What Information Is Stored

Evidence for Semantic Encoding

How can it be demonstrated that an information-processing system has stored the meaning of some stimulus? For example, if a person correctly recalls that the word *car* was included in a list of previously presented words, how can it be determined that the person has stored the meaning of this word?

The False Recognition Technique. A procedure that has been used to demonstrate the existence of semantic encodings is known as the *false recognition technique*. It involves testing a subject's memory with a stimulus that resembles the memorized stimulus in some way. For example, if I wanted to know whether you had stored the meaning of the word *car*, I might later present you with the test word *auto* and ask you whether that was the word you had previously been shown. The word *auto*, of course, is semantically nearly identical to the word *car*. Thus, if a person falsely recognized the word *auto*, it is reasonable to conclude that the semantic properties of the word *car* had been stored in the long-term store.

This logic has been the basis of a number of memory experiments (e.g., Anisfeld & Knapp, 1968; Grossman & Eagle, 1970). In the Grossman and Eagle study, subjects were read a list that contained 41 different words. Five minutes later, the experimenters gave the subjects a recognition test. Of particular interest to us is the response of subjects to nine words on this recognition test that were synonyms of nine words on the study list. It was found that on the average, subjects falsely recognized 1.83 of these synonyms. This can be compared with an average false recognition rate of only 1.05 for nine words on the recognition test that were unrelated to words on the study list. Thus, if a subject had actually heard the word *car* in the study list, the subject would have been significantly more likely to incorrectly recognize having heard the word *auto* as opposed to a semantically unrelated word such as *hat*.

Clustering.   Other evidence that also supports the existence of semantic encodings in the long-term store comes from a phenomenon known as *clustering*. One can observe clustering when a person is *free-calling* information from memory. In a free-recall procedure a person is asked to report previously memorized items in any order the person desires. Clustering is exhibited as a tendency for items sharing certain properties to be grouped together, that is, reported in close succession. For example, if the following words are presented for study, one at a time, *muskrat, blacksmith, Jason, panther, baker, wildcat, Howard,* and *printer,* a person who is later asked to free-recall the words might produce some of them in the order *panther, wildcat, baker, blacksmith, Howard, printer.* You can see that the order in which these words are recalled differs from the order in which they were presented. Furthermore, the order of recall reflects some organization according to semantic categories. That is, animal words are reported in close succession, as are profession words.

Bousfield (1953) performed an experiment to examine this clustering phenomenon. He read subjects a list of 60 words at a three-second rate. The list consisted of 15 animal names, 15 professions, 15 vegetables, and 15 names of people. After subjects heard these words, which were read in a random order, they began to write down as many of them as they could. On the average they recalled 24.97 words. More important than the number correct, however, was the order in which subjects recalled words that be-

Table 3–1
Incidence of single items and clusters of varying size for subjects and for artificial experiment.

	1s	2s	3s	4s	5s	6s	7s
Subjects	810	261	164	85	38	18	5
Artificial experiment	1,452	343	87	18	4	1	—

From W. A. Rousfield, "The occurrence of clustering in the recall of randomly arranged associates." *Journal of General Psychology*, 1953, *49*, 229–240. Copyright 1953 by the Journal of General Psychology. Reprinted by permission.

longed to the same category. It was found that they tended to recall them in groups.

To demonstrate that this tendency to group words together according to semantic category was not due just to luck (or chance, as it is usually termed), Bousfield performed an experiment using colored balls. Bousfield used these balls to simulate the recall process of subjects whose choice of recall order was purely random or due to chance. From a box containing 15 blue, 15 green, 15 orange, and 15 white balls, Bousfield randomly selected 1 ball for each word a subject had recalled. Thus, if a subject had recalled 20 words, Bousfield would have drawn 20 balls from the box. The process was repeated for all 100 subjects in the experiment. The color of each ball represented the category of a word. By counting the number of times he had drawn sequences of similar-colored balls, Bousfield was able to estimate how often his subjects would have recalled strings of words from the same categories if their choice of words was due just to chance. The data are presented in Table 3–1. It can be seen from this table that subjects showed a tendency to recall sequences of three or more words from a category more often than would be expected just by chance. This is a clear demonstration of clustering.

The clustering exhibited by Bousfield's subjects indicates that semantic encodings exist in the long-term store. If subjects did not store semantic information in the long-term store, they could not have realized that words such as *muskrat* and *panther* were related to each other.

Evidence for Visual Encodings

It might seem obvious to you that as a result of your having encountered a visual stimulus, you will store visual information in your long-term store. For example, you may think that when you look at a photograph of some scenery you will start to form a memory trace consisting principally of visual information. Consider another possibility, however. When you see some visual stimulus you may produce an abstract verbal label for it. Thus, you may store the information that you have encountered a photograph of mountain scenery.

Although it has been shown that children as young as three years old spontaneously produce and store verbal labels when they are shown pictorial stimuli (Luszcz & Bacharach, 1980), there is also evidence that both children and adults encode visual information from a visual stimulus. Such evidence has been obtained, in part, from a false recognition procedure.

False Recognition. In the preceding discussion of semantic encoding, the false recognition procedure supported the presence of semantic information in the long-term store by demonstrating that subjects tend to incorrectly recognize synonyms of previously studied words. To demonstrate the existence of visual encodings with this procedure, it must be shown that subjects tend to falsely recognize stimuli that visually resemble previously studied stimuli. The outcome of an experiment by Bahrick, Clark and Bahrick (1967) is consistent with this requirement. These experimenters presented subjects with drawings of 16 common objects. Each drawing was displayed for two seconds. Memory for the drawings was tested immediately or after delays of two hours, two days, or two weeks. Each question in the recognition memory test consisted of a randomly ordered sequence comprised of 1 previously shown object (often refered to as an *old* stimulus) and 10 objects that visually resembled the old stimulus to varying degrees. Much care had gone into selecting these 10 alternative stimuli (often referred to as *new* stimuli). Before conducting the experiment, the experimenters had drawn 100 variations of what was to be each old stimulus and had asked 10 people to use a nine-point scale to rate how closely each of these 100 drawings resembled the old stimulus. From these ratings the experimenters had selected 2 drawings that were highly similar to each old stimulus, 2 that were less similar, and so on, until 10 drawings had been selected that represented the old stimulus with five degrees of similarity. An example of one set of drawings—the old stimulus and the 10 new versions of it—is shown in Figure 3–1. The results of the recognition test are shown in Table 3–2. These data support the view that subjects in the experiment stored visual information in their long-term stores, since recognition errors were most frequently made to stimuli that were visually highly similar to the old stimuli. That is, subjects tended to falsely recognize stimuli that had been rated as most closely resembling the stimuli in the study list.

Clustering. Visual codes have also been demonstrated using a clustering measure. Frost (1972) presented subjects with 16 drawings of various objects. These included four clothing items, four animals, four vehicles, and four

Figure 3–1

An example of a set of items in the recognition test of Bahrick, Clark, and Bahrick's (1967) study. The old stimulus has the label 0; the 10 new stimuli in order of degree of similarity to the old stimulus are labeled with the numbers 1–5.

5   3   1   4   2   5   1   3   4   0   2

From H. P. Bahrick, S. Clark and P. Bahrick, "Generalization gradients as indicants of learning and retention of a recognition task." *Journal of Experimental Psychology*, 1967, *75*, 464–471. Copyright 1967 by the American Psychological Association. Reprinted by permission of publisher and author.

items of furniture. The drawings differed not only on this semantic dimension but also on a visual dimension: four objects were drawn angled to the left, four were angled to the right, four were horizontal, and four were vertical. (See Figure 3–2.) Subjects were told to study the drawings that were presented to them one at a time in a random order. After seeing all 16 drawings, subjects attempted to free-recall the names of these objects. As expected from previous studies of categorical clustering, there was a tendency for subjects to cluster the object names according to the four semantic categories represented. However, of relevance to the question of visual encodings was the finding that subjects also showed a significant tendency to cluster according to a stimulus' angle of presentation. For example, there was a greater-than-chance tendency to recall, in a sequence, the objects that were presented angled to the right. Since angle of presentation is a visual property, this clustering phenomenon indicates that subjects had visual information stored in memory.

Table 3–2

Frequency distribution of recognition responses as a function of retention interval.

Retention Interval	Error Magnitude					
	0	1	2	3	4	5
0	77	39	28	6	5	5
2 hours	48	39	30	16	14	13
2 days	47	34	31	19	21	8
2 weeks	41	47	35	21	8	8

Adapted from H. P. Bahrick, S. Clark and P. Bahrick, "Generalization gradients as indicants of learning and retention of a recognition task." *Journal of Experimental Psychology*, 1967, *75*, 464–471. Copyright 1967 by the American Psychological Association. Reprinted by permission of publisher and author.

Figure 3–2
Examples of stimuli used by Frost (1972).

From N. Frost, "Encoding and retrieval in visual memory tasks." *Journal of Experimental Psychology,* 1972, *95,* 317–326. Copyright 1972 by the American Psychological Association. Reprinted by permission of publisher and author.

A Reaction Time Measure. Other measures besides clustering and false recognition allow us to determine what information is being stored. One such measure utilizes reaction times. To illustrate this process, imagine that you are in a psychology experiment and that the experimenter tells you to study a series of 16 drawings that you will be shown, 1 at a time. Included in these drawings is the one shown in Figure 3–3A. Fifteen minutes after the last drawing is shown, the experimenter explains to you that your memory will be tested in the following way. A picture will be presented to

Figure 3–3
Part A shows an example of a drawing subjects studied in the first phase of Frost's (1972) experiment. Part B shows two test stimuli.

A   B

From N. Frost, "Encoding and retrieval in visual memory tasks." *Journal of Experimental Psychology,* 1972, *95,* 317–326. Copyright 1972 by the American Psychological Association. Reprinted by permission of publisher and author.

you. You will have to decide whether the object shown was included in the list you studied 15 minutes ago. As fast as you can, you must press a "yes" key or a "no" key to signal your answer. A crucial point in these instructions is that you must answer "yes" even if the object you see in the test is drawn differently than it was in your study list. Look now at the drawings shown in Figure 3–3B. To which do you think you would react faster?

Frost (1972) did just such an experiment. She reasoned that if subjects store visual information when they study the picture list, they will react faster to the test picture that is identical to the study stimulus. On the other hand, if a person stores just semantic information, reaction time to these two kinds of stimuli will not differ. Frost's results showed that subjects could, in fact, store visual information. On the average, they reacted about 180 milliseconds faster to old stimuli that were tested with an identical version rather than a different version of the object.

Flexibility in Encoding Information.   I would like to digress for a moment to emphasize that people are capable of encoding a stimulus in a variety of ways. In response to a visual stimulus, for example, an observer can encode information about the stimulus' semantic properties. Alternatively, if the visual stimulus consists of letters, a person can store information about its sound. It is interesting to note that S., the Russian man with the extraordinary memory, would often *recode* a stimulus. That is, he would transform information from one form to another. He once described a person's voice as sounding crumbly and yellow. Here an auditory stimulus has been recoded into a visual and tactile form. On another occasion he described a tone as having a taste of sweet and sour borscht.

What determines how we encode a stimulus? One general rule seems to be that people tend to store the type of information that they think will be of most use to them in the future. Evidence of this can be seen in the two experiments of Frost's described in the preceding sections. In the first experiment that was described, it was mentioned that visual encodings were demonstrated by the tendency of subjects to cluster object names according to a visual property, angle of presentation. What was not mentioned in this discussion was that Frost had deceived her subjects. Before showing them the series of 16 drawings, she had led the subjects to believe that their memory would be tested using a recognition (rather than a free-recall) procedure. Since a recognition test involves responding to a visual stimulus, it is to a subject's advantage to store visual information during the study phase.

One of Frost's experiments revealed that this is just what occurs. Frost had two groups of subjects in this new experiment. One group was again deceived into thinking that their memory for 16 drawings would be tested with a recognition procedure. The other group of subjects was told that they would be asked to free-recall the object names. Since this second group was led to believe that visual information would not be of help to them on the test, they should not have tried to store a great deal of visual information about each drawing. The results confirmed this. Only the group expecting a recognition test clustered according to angle of presentation of the objects. An analogous result was obtained with the reaction time measure: only the group expecting a recognition test responded faster to identical test drawings (i.e., if the drawing shown in Figure 3–3A was in the study list, a faster "yes" response was made when memory was tested with the drawing shown on the left rather than the right of Figure 3–3B). Thus, the type of information stored was affected by how the subjects expected to use the information. We will find more evidence for subjects' flexibility in encoding stimuli when the levels-of-processing view is discussed.

Evidence for Acoustic Encodings

When a person encounters a stimulus, a variety of information about the stimulus can be encoded. For example, in the process of learning a list of words, information about the visual properties of the word can be stored in addition to information about the meaning of the word. There is also evidence that people store the sounds of words in memory.

The Transfer Technique.   An experiment performed by Nelson and Rothbart (1972) provides a demonstration that people store the sounds of stimuli they encounter in a laboratory learning task. Nelson and Rothbart demonstrated this using a *transfer technique.* The principle underlying this technique is quite simple: it is easier to relearn old information than to learn new information. The reason for this is, of course, that once something has been learned, that knowledge can be transferred to the relearning of either the same information or similar information. This rather elementary principle, when skillfully applied, can allow an experimenter to determine the kind of information a person is storing in memory.

In the transfer technique, an experimenter generally has subjects learn two sets of stimuli. An interval of time, which varies from experiment to experiment, usually separates the learning of the two sets of stimuli. By carefully controlling the similarity of the set-2 to the set-1 stimuli, and by noting what kind of similarity relations (e.g., semantic, visual, acoustic) lead to transfer, an experimenter can establish what information has been stored for the set-1 items. The specific procedure used by Nelson and Rothbart will help convey the essence of this approach.

As is generally the case with experiments using the transfer procedure, the two sets of stimuli used by Nelson and Rothbart consisted of *paired associates*. A paired associate is any two stimuli that are intended to belong together. In Nelson and Rothbart's experiment, the first item in each paired associate (generally referred to as the *stimulus* term) was a two-digit number, and the second item (generally referred to as the *response* term) was a common word. Examples are 27-*tacks* and 81-*jury*. Subjects in the experiment first learned the set-1 items, which consisted of 24 different paired associates. The learning process entailed subjects' attempting to supply the correct response term when they were shown each stimulus term. After mastering this first paired associate list, subjects were dismissed from the experiment without being told that they were going to be tested again one month later. One month after learning this first list, subjects were asked to return. They were first tested to see how many of the set-1 response terms they could correctly provide when shown the set-1 stimulus terms. Then, they were asked to learn the set-2 paired associates. The same two-digit numbers used in set-1 were reused as stimulus terms in set-2. Some of these numbers were paired with exactly the same response words as used in set-1. These paired associates in set-2 will be referred to as the "identical" items. Other of the numbers in set-2 were paired with a word that sounded like the word used in set-1. For example, if subjects had studied 27-*tacks* in set-1, they might have seen 27-*tax* in set-2. These paired associates will be referred to as "acoustically similar" items. Finally, some numbers in set-2 were paired with words that were unrelated to the set-1 words (e.g., 63-*prey* in set-1, 63-*dough* in set-2).

To determine whether subjects had stored acoustical information from list-1, Nelson and Rothbart simply determined whether there was any transfer of learning for the acoustically similar items in list-2. That is, they determined whether, in set-2, subjects learned response terms that were acoustically similar to the set-1 responses faster than they learned response words that were unrelated to those from set-1. As an illustration of this, for subjects who saw 39-*heal* in set-1, those who learned 39-*heel* in set-2 faster than those who learned 39-*ant* in set-2 would be exhibiting transfer. The data for the experiment are shown in Figure 3–4. One important fact about these data is that they apply just to the response terms that subjects had forgotten from set-1. Thus, the data show that even though a subject had forgotten what word had previously been paired with a number in set-1, the subject learned words that sounded like the forgotten word faster than words that were acoustically unrelated to the forgotten word. Nelson and Rothbart concluded from these data that subjects must have stored the sounds of the words in the long-term store.

Figure 3–4
The proportion of correct responses in relearning identical, acoustically similar, and unrelated items.

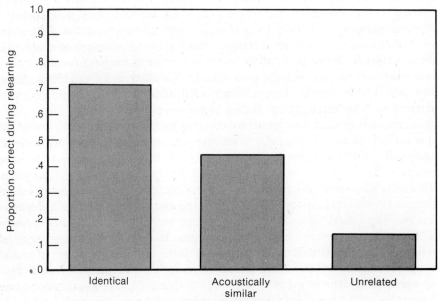

T. O. Nelson and R. Rothbart, "Acoustic savings for items forgotten from long-term memory." *Journal of Experimental Psychology*, 1972, *93*, 357–360. Copyright 1972 by the American Psychological Association. Reprinted by permission of publisher and author.

Some Practical Applications

Although these experimental techniques may seem to be demonstrating the obvious, there are many situations in which it is very useful to know what information a person is and is not storing from encounters with stimuli. For example, when studying people who have exceptional memory abilities, psychologists have found it important to determine the kinds of information that the memory experts tend to store.

Hunt and Love (1972) have addressed this issue in their examinations of the unusual memory abilities of the person known as V. P. To determine what kind of information V. P. based his extraordinary memory performance on, Hunt and Love chose a technique that was designed to detect the presence of visual and semantic information. One reason for checking for the presence of visual information was that another famous memory expert, S., was known to have often encoded stimuli visually. Semantic encodings were also a possibility, for, as will be shown later, information that is encoded in terms of its meaning is remembered much better than if it is encoded in terms of a property such as its sound. Although the sound of a stimulus is often stored (as Nelson and Rothbart's study showed), this acoustic information is usually found to be a much less effective basis for long-term memory performance than is semantic information (Craik & Tulving, 1975). Thus, Hunt and Love chose to disregard acoustic information and to determine whether V. P. relied more on semantic or visual encodings.

The procedure that Hunt and Love used to examine this was based on Frost's (1971) clustering studies. As you'll recall, this entails showing subjects a series of line drawings oriented at one of four angles and leading them to expect that memory will be tested using a recognition procedure. The memory test actually requires that the names of the objects represented by the line drawings be free-recalled. Order of recall is analyzed for visual and semantic clustering. As previously mentioned, visual clustering is manifested as a tendency to recall in a sequence objects that were presented at the same angle; this form of clustering indicates the presence of visual encodings. Semantic clustering is manifested as a tendency to recall in a sequence words from the same conceptual category; this indicates the use of semantic encodings. Hunt and Love described the outcome of their study in this way:

> The results were simple and dramatic. The control subjects consistently clustered by visual orientation. VP's clustering scores indicated only chance visual organization, but a high degree of semantic organization. In fact . . . his semantic clustering was perfect. (p. 254)

Other techniques have proven to be useful in other situations. The encoding preferences of persons who have developed memory problems are often studied in order to find out more about the characteristics of the memory deficits as well as to discover possible ways to alleviate the problems. Cermak, Butters, and Gerrein (1973) have used a false recognition procedure to understand better how Korsakoff amnesic patients encode words. A person who has Korsakoff's syndrome will, as a result of many years of alcohol abuse, have developed a number of mental disabilities. These disabilities can include memory impairments that make it difficult to learn certain new information. It is not uncommon, for example, for a Korsakoff amnesic to remember almost nothing of his current experiences when tested by recall or recognition (Zangwill, 1966). Cermak and his co-workers used a false recognition procedure to help determine what information a group of Korsakoff patients were storing when they read and tried to remember a list of words. The results of a recognition test revealed that the amnesics made significantly more acoustic false recognitions than control subjects who were not amnesic. These two groups of subjects did not differ in terms of the number of false recognitions made to synonyms of previously studied words. Cermak et al. concluded that Korsakoff amnesics rely more on acoustic encodings and less on semantic encodings than do unimpaired persons. This preference for storing acoustic information rather than semantic information leaves an amnesic patient without the ability to correctly reject words on the recognition test that sound like a previously studied word but do not share its meaning. Thus, an amnesic patient may have difficulty in distinguishing between his memory of the word *bear* and his present encounter with a word such as *hair*.

Other studies (e.g., Cermak & Reale, 1978) have attempted to determine whether it is possible to improve the memory performance of Korsakoff amnesics by encouraging them to store information about a stimulus' semantic properties. The results of such attempts have not been encouraging. Thus, it seems most appropriate at this point to regard the tendency of Korsakoff amnesics to rely on acoustic encodings as being a symptom rather than the cause of their memory deficiencies.

Other Techniques for Assessing Encodings

The procedures mentioned in this chapter for characterizing encoding in the long-term store are by no means the only methods employed. A very useful collection of procedures is based on mechanisms that underlie forgetting. These will be presented in upcoming chapters.

This completes the discussion of the kinds of information that can be encoded in the long-term store. We turn now to a second aspect of encoding, one referred to earlier as the "how" aspect of encoding. In the remainer of this chapter discussion of this issue will be limited to the question of how semantic and visual information is represented in the long-term store.

How Semantic Information Is Encoded

Although it is relatively easy to ascertain that the long-term store contains semantic information, it is difficult to determine just how this information is represented in memory. A basic assumption made by psychologists investigating this issue is that meaning is derived from relations. That is, it is assumed that a concept's meaning is established from the way the concept compares with other concepts. Thus, the concept of "bird" may be understood in terms of its relation to the concept of "living thing." This relational information may include the specification that a bird is similar to other instances of living things yet is different in that it usually has the ability to fly. The concept of living thing and flying may, in turn, be made meaningful by their relations to other concepts. In general, while theories of semantic representation share this basic assumption that meaning is based on relations, they differ most fundamentally on how these relations are represented in memory.

Network Models

Structural Assumptions. In one class of memory models, the relations that give meaning to concepts are assumed to be directly represented in memory in the form of pathways that connect information about concepts. A memory model proposed by Quillian (1967) examplifies this approach. In Figure 3–5 a portion of Quillian's proposed semantic network model is depicted in a simplified form. It can be seen that information about each concept, that is, each concept node, is connected to other concept nodes by pointers. In this figure the pointers are meant to represent one of two

Figure 3–5
A simplified representation of the heirarchical network model proposed by Quillian (1967).

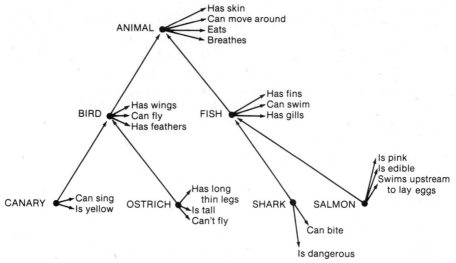

From A. M. Collins and M. R. Quillian, "Retrieval time from semantic memory." *Journal of Verbal Learning and Verbal Behavior,* 1969, *8,* 240–247. Copyright 1969 by Academic Press. Reprinted by permission.

possible relations: either that a concept is an example or instance of a more general concept (this is often referred to as an "isa" relation), or that the concept possesses certain properties. While Quillian's model is actually more complicated than this (Collins and Loftus, 1975), the simplified representation allows certain implications of the model to be most apparant.

Processing Implications.   One important implication of this network model is based on the location of a concept's property relations. To understand this one must first observe that the model allows concepts to be represented hierarchically. That is, in this model particular instances of a concept (e.g., canary is a particular instance of the concept of bird) are all connected to the more general concept. This concept, in turn, is connected to an even more general concept (e.g., a bird is an instance of the more general concept of animal). This hierarchical arrangement, Collins and Quillian (1969) point out, allows for a very economical storage of information, because properties common to instances of a concept need not be stored directly with each instance, but can instead be stored just with the more general concept. Thus, since most birds have beaks and wings, these properties can be connected to the concept of bird rather than with each particular instance of a bird.

Does this model suggest anything to you about the relative speeds with which different information can be accessed in memory? Imagine, for example, that you were asked to judge as rapidly as possible whether or not each of the following sentences was true or false.

1. A canary can sing.
2. A canary has skin.

According to this model, which judgment should be faster? Collins and Quillian (1969) proposed that the information contained in sentences such as that shown in example 1 should be accessed more rapidly than the information contained in sentences such as that shown in example 2. Collins and Quillian based this prediction first on the assumption that property relations will tend to be stored at the most general level of a concept (i.e., the property "has skin" will be stored at the "animal" node rather than at the nodes representing each lower level instance of the concept), and, second, on the assumption that it takes time to traverse each relational pathway. Thus, Collins and Quillian assumed that when given the task of verifying a sentence such as that shown in example 1 above, a person will enter the semantic network at the canary node and search for the stated property. If the property is not found at the concept node, the person will have to proceed up the "isa" relational link to the next node and search there for the stated property. On the basis of these assumptions it can be seen that verifying that a canary has skin will require traversing more relational links and thus require more time than will verifying that a canary can sing.

Collins and Quillian tested this prediction by asking subjects to verify the truth of various sentences that expressed a relation between a concept and a property. The sentences that expressed true relations differed in that some properties tended to be applicable to the named concept itself but not to the concept that was one step higher in the hierarchy (e.g., a canary can sing), some properties were applicable to a concept that was one step more general than the named concept (e.g., a canary can fly), and some properties were applicable to a concept that was two steps more general than the named concept (e.g., a canary has skin). Collins and Quillian also tested verification reaction times for sentences that expressed "isa" relations between concept names. Here again, the sentences that expressed true relations differed in that some related concepts at the same level of generality (e.g., a canary is a canary), some related concepts that differed in generality by one step (e.g., a canary is a bird), and some related concepts that differed in generality by two steps in the hierarchy (e.g., a canary is an animal). Again, the prediction for these sentences was that more time would be required to verify sentences that expressed relations between concepts that were separated by more relational links in the semantic network model.

Figure 3–6 shows the results of the study. It can be seen that for both types of sentences used in the study—those expressing property relations and those expressing "isa" relations—verification times for true sentences turned out very much as predicted. On the average, the traverse of each "isa" relational link appeared to require 75 milliseconds, and the search for properties at each node appeared to require 255 milliseconds.

Reactions to this Network Model. The successes of Quillian's model led other psychologists to extend and refine the network approach. Some psychologists (e.g., Anderson & Bower, 1973; Rumelhart, Lindsay, & Norman, 1972) designed memory models to represent not only a person's general knowledge of the world but also the learning of new events and experiences. (The memory of what was eaten for breakfast yesterday morning is an example of the learning of a new event. The distinction between general information about the world—known as *semantic* information—and information about particular episodes or events a person experiences—known as *episodic* information—will be further discussed in a later chapter.) Other psychologists (e.g., Collins & Loftus, 1975; Glass & Holyoak, 1975) elaborated on Quillian's basic network model of semantic representation. Collins and Loftus (1975), for example, specified that in a heirarchical network, all the links representing relations will not necessarily be equally strong. For exam-

Figure 3–6
The average times required to verify sentences as a function of the number of relational links separating concepts.

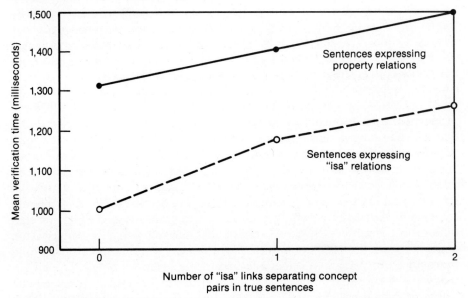

From A. M. Collins and M. R. Quillian, "Retrieval time from semantic memory." *Journal of Verbal Learning and Verbal Behavior*, 1969, 240–247. Copyright 1969 by Academic Press. Reprinted by permission.

ple, the relation between bird and chicken might not be as strong as that between bird and robin. As a result, the time to traverse the link between bird and robin should be faster than that between bird and chicken. This specification accommodated a frequent finding that people are faster to verify that typical instances are members of a category than to verify that atypical instances are members of a category (Rips, Shoben, & Smith, 1973; Rosch, 1973). Collins and Loftus also specified that concepts that are similar will have many links connecting them. These connections, Collins and Loftus proposed, will be formed via the properties that the concepts have in common. For example, since cars and trucks share many properties, such as having wheels, engines, and cargo spaces, there will be numerous links between them in addition to an indirect link via the more general concept of "vehicle." This specification allows the model to represent degrees of similarity among concept instances: Concepts that are very similar will have a great number of connections, while those that are dissimilar will have few or no connections via their properties. It should be noted that although this proposed interconnection among concept instances helps account for certain psychological phenomena (e.g., priming, which will be discussed in chapter 5), it represents a move away from the strictly hierarchical representation of concepts that Collins and Quillian (1969) had previously portrayed in their article. This loosening of the strict hierarchical structure is evident in the graphical representation of a portion of Collins and Loftus' (1975) proposed memory network that is shown in Figure 3–7.

Set Models

Structural and Processing Assumptions. One property of Quillian's network model that has not been well received by all psychologists is the degree to which the relations among concepts are proposed to be built into memory. That is, in Quillian's model, concepts are proposed to be joined to each other by labeled pathways (using labels such as "isa" or "has"). Although these relations presumably become established through learning, they are assumed to be already present in an adult's memory when the adult is called on to verify a statement such as "a robin has a beak." In a sense, then, according to Quillian's model, the answer to such questions will be clearly specified in memory even before the question is posed. The process of verifying such a statement involves merely traversing the pathways that specify the relations between these concepts to arouse the information in the labeled relational link.

Smith, Shoben, and Rips (1974) have proposed a different model of semantic encoding. They rejected the idea that hierarchical relations among concepts are clearly specified in memory. Instead, they suggested that each concept in memory is represented by a set of information that specifies the properties of the concept. For example, the concept "robin" could be represented by information such as "has wings," "is small," and "has distinctive colors."

Smith et al. were careful to specify that the information that is stored about each concept can vary in how necessary it is to the definition of the concept; that is, some information (or features, to use the terminology of Smith et al.) will be more essential to the definition of a concept, while other features will be more "accidental or characteristic" (Smith et al., 1974, p. 216). McCloskey and Glucksberg (1979) express the distinction between these two types of features in the following way: "Features that must be possessed by all members of a category (e.g., *has wings* and *has feathers* for the category *bird*) are considered to be defining, while those shared by many but not all category members (e.g., *can fly, eats berries*) are said to be characteristic" (p. 4).

Figure 3–7
A representation of the Collins and Loftus model of memory. Shorter lines are meant to represent higher relatedness between concepts.

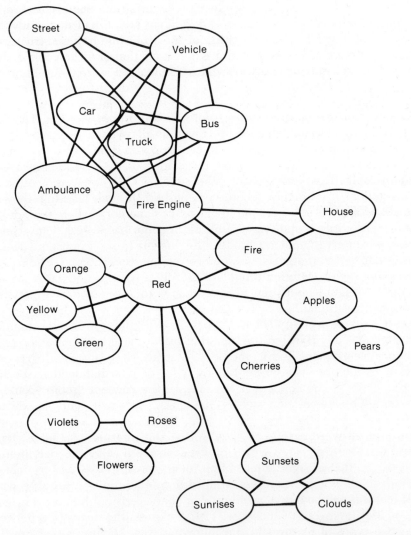

From A. M. Collins and E. F. Loftus, "A spreading-activation theory of semantic processing." *Psychological Review,* 1975, *82,* 407–428. Copyright 1975 by the American Psychological Association. Reprinted by permission of publisher and author.

If each concept is represented only by a set of defining and characteristic features, how then are the relations among concepts established? According to Smith et al., relations are derived by assessing the information overlap among concepts' feature sets. Consider, for example, the process of verifying a sentence such as "A robin is a bird." According to Smith et al., this involves a retrieval of the feature sets for the concepts robin and bird and a comparison of the two sets to determine how extensively their information matches. The high degree of similarity between the feature sets representing the concepts bird and robin will produce a positive response to the statement. On the other hand, for statements such as "A robin is a car," the low degree of similarity between the feature sets that represent these concepts will produce a negative response. In this model, then, relations among concepts are not represented explicitly in memory but are derived during the retrieval process.

Advantages of this Set Model. What advantages does this representation have over network models? Smith et al. (1974) have emphasized that their model readily accounts for the finding that people perceive instances of a category (e.g., robin, chicken) to differ in how representative they are of the category ("bird" in this example). The set model accounts for this with the assumption that concept instances that are highly representative of a category possess both the defining features of the category and a great number of characteristic features of the category. On the other hand, instances that are not typical of a category are proposed to possess just the defining features of the category. Thus, when the feature overlap between a pair of concepts such as chicken and bird is evaluated, fewer matching features will be found than when the overlap between a pair of concepts such as robin and bird is evaluated.

Another advantage claimed for this model is its ability to easily account for what has become known (Collins & Loftus, 1975) as the *typicality effect,* the finding that increased semantic similarity between two concepts named in a sentence decreases verification time when the sentence is true (e.g., "A chicken is a bird" versus "A robin is a bird") but increases verification time when the sentence is false (e.g., "Magnesium is an animal" versus "A tree is an animal"). According to the Smith et al. model, this effect can be accounted for by making certain assumptions about the way similarity is evaluated in memory. The process is proposed to proceed as follows: When two concepts are to be evaluated for similarity, the feature sets that represent the concepts in memory are retrieved, and a determination is made of the number of features shared by the two concept representations. Smith et al. suggest that this comparison process, which is the first of two possible comparison processes, is fairly crude in the sense that it distinguishes only whether there is extensive similarity or very low similarity between the concepts. It bases this overall similarity judgment on both defining and characteristic features; that is, the comparison process does not make any distinction between these two kinds of features. If, on the basis of this comparison process, the two concepts are found to have extensive similarity, a positive response is made in the verification task; if the two concepts are found to have low similarity, a negative response is made. What is important to note is that these responses will be relatively rapid because they are based on just a single comparison process rather than on two comparison processes (as described below).

What kinds of sentences will be verified with this single-stage comparison process? Sentences such as "A robin is a bird," according to Smith et al., because a highly typical instance of a category and the category name are presented. Under these circumstances, because the highly typical instance shares both the defining and many characteristic features of the category, the feature sets will have extensive similarity. Sentences such as "Magnesium is an animal" will also be verified by this single-stage process, according to Smith et al. In this case, because the concepts have so little in common, a negative response will be made. Thus, this model predicts fast responses for highly typical instances of a category and for very dissimilar concepts that represent different categories.

What happens when concepts are compared that are neither highly similar nor of very low similarity? According to Smith et al., this requires that a second, more discriminating comparison process be conducted after the first comparison process. In this second comparison process, just the sets of defining features of the two concepts are evaluated. If there is a sufficient match between the two sets of defining features, a positive response can be made; otherwise, the response will be negative. In accord with the typicality effect, the result is that sentences expressing valid relations between atypical instances and their categories will require this second comparison stage and thus additional processing time. Thus, sentences such as "A chicken is a bird" will take longer to verify than will sentences such as "A robin is a bird," because two comparison stages, not one, are utilized. On the other hand, sentences that express invalid relations involving two concepts that are nevertheless similar in certain respects (for example, in the sentence "A tree is an animal," two living things are described) will require more processing time than sentences expressing invalid relations between two very dissimilar concepts (e.g., "Magnesium is an animal"). The reason, again, is that two, not one, comparison stages will have to be utilized.

Choosing between Network and Feature Set Models

Similarities between the Models. It is difficult to choose between these two models of semantic representation, because both can be developed to account for many of the same experimental outcomes. Consider, for example, the finding that was taken to be strong evidence for Collins and Quillian's (1969) network model, the finding that a person is faster to verify relations between an instance and its direct superordinate (e.g., between robin and bird) than between an instance and its more remote superordinate (e.g., between robin and animal). According to Collins and Quillian, this finding can be accounted for easily with a hierarchical network model, because such a model suggests that the more links there are between concept nodes in the network, the longer it will take to verify the relation between the concepts. According to Smith et al., however, this same finding can be accounted for in terms of the overall similarity between an instance and its superordinate. Specifically, Smith et al. suggest that in the Collins and Quillian (1969) study, the instances shared more characteristic features with their direct superordinate than with their more remote superordinate; that is, a concept such as robin shared more characteristic features with bird than with animal. Consequently, verification times were faster for sentences such as "A robin is a bird" than for sentences such as "A robin is an animal," because one comparison stage, not two, tended to be utilized.

On the other hand, network models have been able to account for the typicality effect. According to the Collins and Loftus (1975) model, one important reason that typical instances of a category are verified as belonging to the category faster than are atypical instances is that typical instances are more strongly connected to the category representation in memory. The reason that false statements may be rejected faster when the two concepts are weakly rather than strongly related is because weakly related concepts will have few shared connections. Thus, there will be less evidence that will conflict with the information that the stated relation between the two concepts (e.g., that magnesium is an animal) is false.

In addition to being able to account for many of the same findings, network and feature set theories of semantic representation are, or can be made to be, structurally quite similar (Hollan, 1975). For instance, one could suggest that in a feature set model, the features that make up a concept are connected to the concept node by links or associations. Furthermore, one could suggest that some of this information associated with a concept consists of superset information (e.g., that a canary is a bird). This suggestion was, in fact, made in a set model that predated the Smith et al. model. Rips,

Shoben, and Smith (1973) suggested that "in set models, concepts . . . are represented by a set of elements where these elements might be exemplars, attributes, or supersets of the concept" (p. 2). Given these assumptions, a model similar to the network model of Collins and Loftus (1975) results.

Are Both Models Valid?   In spite of the similarities between the two classes of models in terms of their abilities to account for major experimental findings and their potential for being structurally represented in much the same way, those who have sought to choose between the models have emphasized certain aspects of particular models that they feel lead to different testable predictions. Perhaps the most fundamental difference between the Smith et al. (1974) version of the set model (see also McCloskey & Glucksberg, 1979) and the various network models is that the Smith et al. model specifically excludes the possibility that superset information is directly represented in memory, whereas network models do not. According to the Smith et al. model, then, information such as "a robin is a bird" is not supposed to be present in memory, or at least is not supposed to participate in a decision about the relation between the two concepts. Smith et al. propose, instead, that people derive this superset relation by comparing the feature sets of the concept "robin" with that of the concept "bird." In network models, on the other hand, this relation is assumed to be directly represented in memory by an "isa" link between the concepts of robin and bird. The act of verifying the relation in network models involves having energy from the two concept nodes under consideration converge via the "isa" link and activate the information that specifies that, in this case, a robin is a bird. Thus, these particular structural assumptions of the two models lead to different predictions about how people process information: In one class of set models certain information must be derived or computed from a feature comparison process, while according to network models, this information will be readily aroused from existing information in memory.

Lorch (1981) has tested this and other processing implications of these two classes of memory models and has found that people seem capable of using processes predicted by both models. For example, Lorch found that under certain circumstances his subjects appeared to retrieve relations directly from memory, while under other circumstances they appeared to derive relations using a comparison process. Whether one or the other process seemed to be adopted depended on the makeup of the stimulus lists the subjects were processing.

If future research confirms that people are capable of adopting processing strategies consistent with set and network models, it may indicate that a model based on some form of compromise between set and network models is appropriate. This compromise model may have superset information associated with concept nodes (as in network models) and also feature sets representing each concept, which are capable of being compared with each other to assess overall similarity (as in set models).

It may be useful to note that the fast, first-stage comparison process of the Smith et al. set model is conceptually similar to the retrieval process embodied in the tuning fork analogy of memory introduced in the chapter on the iconic store. In this tuning fork analogy, communication between elements is based on shared properties rather than on fixed transmission channels that link elements in the system. As mentioned in the discussion of the iconic store, this tuning fork analogy provides a useful model for describing the process by which information that is received by the visual system makes contact with the matching visual information stored in the long-term store. It seems reasonable to suppose that a retrieval mechanism that has this remarkable ability to contact information in memory that shares similar features with newly encountered information will play some part in making decisions about the relations between concepts named in a verification task. Information in upcoming chapters will provide a further insight into the role that such a retrieval mechanism might play in processing information.

How Visual Information Is Encoded

We all have a great deal of visual information stored in memory. Thus, if asked to, we could probably picture such things as the faces of people we know, the places we visited on our last vacation, or the main street of our hometown. Of concern to us now is how this visual information is represented in the long-term store.

This question could probably be settled if it were possible to peer unobtrusively into the intact human brain and observe the neural processes occurring there as visual memories were established and retrieved. As Anderson (1978) has pointed out, however, no neuroscientist has been able to find any direct indication of the format in which visual information is stored in memory. Thus, to investigate this "how" aspect of visual encoding, psychologists have had to resort to more indirect methods, ones that generally rely on behavioral data. A better understanding of this behavioral approach can be achieved by first considering possible ways in which visual information may be represented in memory.

Analog and Propositional Encodings

One possible way that visual information can be represented in memory is in a picture-like format. Psychologists who adhere to this general point of view, however, do not necessarily believe that visual information is represented in memory in exactly the same way as the viewer perceives some stimulus; that is, they do not believe that visual information is stored in the form of a mental photograph. Rather, adherents to this view allow that visual information may be represented more abstractly. For example, Kosslyn and Pomerantz (1977) have specified that the representations of visual information in memory may be *analogous* to, rather than identical to, the physical features of the visual information. This conception of visual encoding is often referred to as the *analog* view.

What alternative is there to the analog view? One possibility that has been considered (Pylyshyn, 1973; Anderson & Bower, 1973) is that visual information may be represented in the form of some sort of description. To understand better how this is possible, consider the way information about a visual display may be stored in a computer's memory. As a specific example, consider one possible way of representing the letter *A*. For the sake of this demonstration, let us pretend that this pattern must be displayed on an imaginary grid five units high by five units wide. (See Figure 3–8.)

Figure 3–8
The letter *A* displayed on a five-by-five grid. Each segment of the grid is identified by a number.

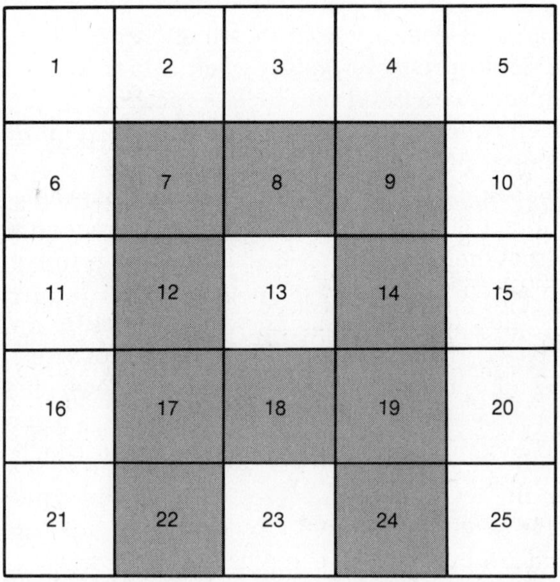

Under these circumstances, the letter *A* may be represented as a series of specifications as to whether each grid area in this five-by-five matrix is colored either light or dark. Thus, if each area of the grid were referred to using a number from 1 to 25, the letter *A* could be represented as a set of 25 descriptions specifying the shading of each grid area. (See Table 3–3.) Here, visual information is being stored in a representation that does not resemble the pattern in the sense that a photograph resembles some scene. Rather, the memory representation captures the essence of the visual information through description.

Table 3–3
Several of the 25 descriptive statements that could be used to represent the visual display of the letter *A* on a 5 × 5 grid.

Area 1	Shade light
Area 2	Shade light
Area 3	Shade light
Area 4	Shade light
Area 5	Shade light
Area 6	Shade light
Area 7	Shade dark
Area 8	Shade dark
Area 9	Shade dark
Area 10	Shade light
etc.	

It should be understood that those who suggest that visual information is represented in memory in a descriptive format do not necessarily mean that people store a verbal description of this information in memory. Rather, they believe that some abstract symbolic code fulfills this function. According to this view, visual information about a stimulus such as the letter *A* may be represented with a series of abstract statements, often termed *propositions,* that concisely describe both the visual features that make up the stimulus and the relations among these features. To summarize, then, the two opposing views of the representation of visual information in memory are the analog view and the symbolic (often called propositional) view. The analog view holds that the representation of visual information resembles the information in some important way, whereas the symbolic or propositional view holds that the memory representation does not resemble the information at all, but describes it in some abstract way.

Evidence for Analog Encodings

Image Scanning. What kind of evidence could be used to support the analog view? One general approach to this issue has been to attempt to determine if subjects who are consulting some representation of visual information in memory behave as though this representation were analogous to the visual scene that is being depicted. To understand better how this may be assessed, imagine that a person has retrieved a mental representation of an object from memory. Imagine, further, that the person has been induced to shift attention from one end of this object in memory to the other end of the object. Proponents of the analog view have suggested that if the mental representation is analogous to the imagined object, then it is reasonable to assume not only that it will take some time to shift attention from one point in the imagined object to another point, but, more important, the larger the imagined separation between the original and final point of focus, the longer it should take to complete this operation. Thus, the assumption being made in this approach is that the processing of a visual representation in memory is much the same as the processing of a visual stimulus with the eyes. That is, just as it will take the eyes longer to scan from the bottom to the top of an object than halfway up the object, so too will it take the "mind's eye" longer to scan between two distant rather than two close points in an analog representation of an imagined visual scene. An experiment by Kosslyn, Ball, and Reiser (1978) illustrates this approach. Subjects in the study were shown a map of a fictional island. As can be seen in Figure 3–9, the map showed the locations of various objects, such as a hut, a tree, and a lake. Subjects studied the map until they could draw it accurately from memory, placing the locations of each of the six objects no more than one quarter inch from their correct positions. At this point, the critical part of the experiment was begun. The experimenter read subjects the name of one object. Subjects had previously been told that upon hearing the name of this first object they should mentally picture the whole map and then focus in on the location of the named object. Five seconds later the experimenter read the name of a second object. Subjects had been instructed that as soon as they heard the name of this second object, they were to mentally scan directly to it and press a response key as soon as they had arrived at this location on their mental map. The procedure was repeated a number of times using a variety of pairs of locations (e.g., lake–grass, rock–tree). For each location pair, the experimenters kept track of the time it took subjects to complete the scan between the named objects. The data, averaged over all subjects, is shown in Figure 3–10. It can be seen that, in accord with the processing assumptions of

Figure 3–9
The map of an imaginary island used in an experiment by Kosslyn, Ball, and Reiser.

From S. M. Kosslyn, T. M. Ball, and B. J. Reiser, "Visual images preserve metric spatial information: Evidence from studies of image scanning." *Journal of Experimental Psychology: Human Perception and Performance*, 1978, *4*, 47–60. Copyright 1978 by the American Psychological Association. Reprinted by permission of publisher and author.

the analog view, the more distant the separation between two points on the map, the longer the subjects' scanning times.

Feature Verification.　Kosslyn (1975) has obtained other evidence that people can process imagined stimuli in memory in much the same way that they process visual stimuli. This evidence shows that just as it is more difficult to detect and identify the components of very small objects that are presented for visual inspection, so too is it more difficult to recognize the components of small rather than large images generated from memory. In one demonstration of this (experiment 1), Kosslyn (1975) manipulated the size of imagined objects in subjects' minds indirectly, by requesting that they visualize a particular animal—a duck, for instance—standing next to either

Figure 3–10
The scan times of subjects in the Kosslyn, Ball, and Reiser study. The figure shows
scan times as a function of the distance between pairs of locations.

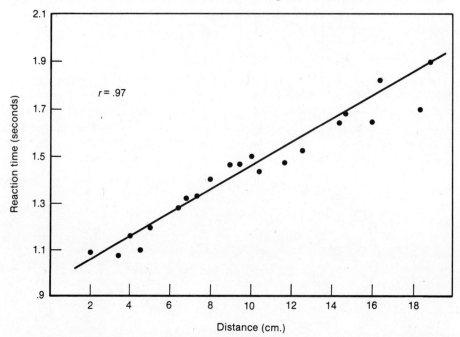

From S. M. Kosslyn, T. M. Ball, and B. J. Reiser, "Visual images preserve metric spatial informa-
tion: Evidence from studies of image scanning." *Journal of Experimental Psychology: Human
Perception and Performance*, 1978, *4*, 47–60. Copyright 1978 by the American Psychological
Association. Reprinted by permission of publisher and author.

an elephant or a fly. Kosslyn expected that this instruction would affect
the size of this animal in a subject's imagination. That is, Kosslyn expected
that when a duck was imagined standing next to an elephant, the duck
would be pictured as being much smaller than when it was imagined standing next to a fly. To determine what effect this manipulation of size had
on subjects' abilities to process the visual image, Kosslyn next presented
subjects with the name of a possible property of the imagined animal. For
example, if a subject had been asked to imagine a duck standing next to
an elephant, Kosslyn might next have read the word *wing* to the subject.
The subject's task was to determine as quickly as possible, on the basis of
the imaged animal, whether the property named by the experimenter was
appropriate to the animal. Kosslyn found that, just as in the case of visual

perception, it took subjects longer to verify a property of smaller rather than larger imagined objects. Overall, the subjects verified properties of the 20 animals that were used in the study 211 milliseconds faster when each animal was imagined standing next to a fly rather than next to an elephant.

Alternative Interpretations of the Evidence

The Propositional View.   Although there is no one startling piece of evidence to contradict the analog view, its validity has been undermined by possible alternative accounts of the evidence, accounts based on propositional (i.e., symbolic) approaches. For example, consider some evidence that Shepard and his co-workers (Shepard & Metzler, 1971; Cooper & Shepard, 1973) have gathered in support of analog mental encodings. Shepard and Metzler (1971) presented subjects with drawings of pairs of three-dimensional objects. Examples are shown in Figure 3–11. As soon as subjects saw a pair of objects, they were to decide, as quickly as possible, whether the two drawings showed the same three-dimensional shape. Try this yourself with the three stimulus pairs shown in Figure 3–11. Do you have any idea how you arrived at your decisions? In each case, you might have found it necessary to mentally transform one of the objects so that it was in the same orientation as the other before you could adequately compare them. It was with this mental transformation process that Shepard and Metzler were most concerned. Their data showed that the greater the angular separation between the two orientations, the longer it took subjects to make their decisions. This was true both when the transformation required rotation in the plane of the picture (as is true for pair A in Figure 3–11) and in depth (as is true for pair B). Figure 3–12 shows the reaction time data. Shepard and Metzler considered these data to support the analog view, for the data were strikingly similar to what would result if a person were physically rotating an actual object in order to line it up with another object. Thus, it appeared to Shepard and Metzler that subjects were behaving as if they had an analog representation of the objects in memory.

Critics of the analog view have suggested that there are other ways to account for this increase in reaction time as the angular separation between two comparison items increases. Anderson (1978), for example, has noted that a propositional description of some object can include information about the orientation of the object in space. Given such a representation, it is not inconceivable, Anderson suggests, that an information-processing system could calculate a series of small changes in the angular orientation. If the orientation information were changed in incremental steps, it would take longer for such a system to reach a desired orientation the greater the

Figure 3–11
Pairs of stimuli used in the Mezler and Shepard (1971) study. Subjects were required to determine whether each pair of objects had the same three-dimensional shape.

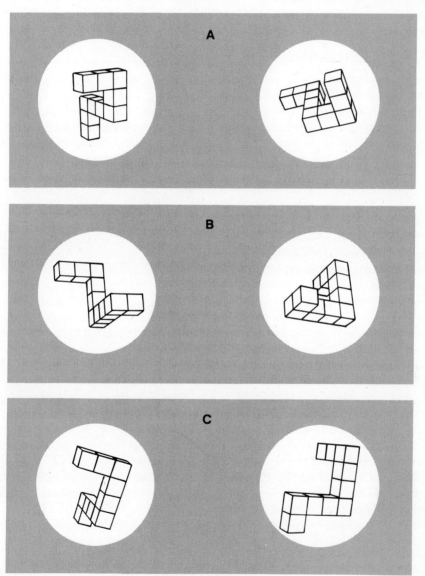

From R. N. Shepard and J. Metzler, "Mental rotation of three-dimensional objects." *Science,* 1971, *171,* 701–703. Copyright 1971 by the American Association for the Advancement of Science. Reprinted by permission.

Figure 3–12
Mean reaction times as a function of the angular difference in the orientations of
two comparison stimuli. The data are from Metzler and Shepard's (1971) study.
Part A depicts the data for rotations that had to be made in the plane of the picture.
Part B depicts the data for rotations that had to be made in depth.

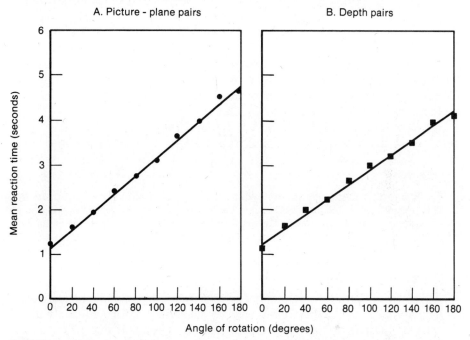

From R. N. Shepard and J. Metzler, "Mental rotation of three-dimensional objects." *Science,*
1971, *171*, 701–703. Copyright 1971 by the American Association for the Advancement of
Science. Reprinted by permission.

angular separation between the original and target orientations. Thus, according to Anderson's proposal, a propositional model of visual information
representation could account for Shepard and Metzler's mental rotation
data.

Other evidence that has been taken to support the analog view of visual
information can also be accommodated within the propositional view by
making certain assumptions about how propositional representations are
processed. For example, Anderson (1978) suggests that Kosslyn's (1975) findings that subjects take longer to verify properties of objects that are imaged
small rather than large can be accounted for with a theory of propositional

representation that makes the following assumption: A subject who is asked to image an object small activates fewer propositions to depict the object than when asked to image it large. For example, if asked to image a house very small, a subject might just activate propositions that describe the house as having a rectangular shape, a roof with sloping sides, some windows, and a front door. On the other hand, when constructing a large image of a house, a subject might activate much more detailed information, information that includes the fact that the house has basement windows, shutters, gutters, and a front porch. When asked to verify that the property "porch" fits the concept of a house, a subject who has generated this more detailed list of properties will react faster because the appropriate information will be highly available in memory.

In defense of the analog view, Kosslyn and Pomerantz (1977) have suggested that these propositional accounts are less plausible than analog accounts. With regard to the mental rotation data, Kosslyn and Pomerantz specify that:

> The imagery account seems somewhat plausible and relatively straightforward. The propositional account seems less satisfactory: Aside from the problem of not knowing how to represent the [stimuli] in the first place, it is not clear why rotation is gradual in such a system. . . . It appears that people do not (or cannot) skip from one orientation of an image directly to another, but must proceed gradually. Such a prediction does not follow from basic concepts of propositional representation. (p. 69)

With regard to the propositional account of the image size results, Kosslyn and Pomerantz ask, "Why should people access less information about an object when asked to 'image it small'?" (p. 71). They add that "This seems ad hoc; a propositional model would not lead one to expect such effects" (p. 71).

It is interesting to note that Anderson (1978) has levelled this same criticism at analog accounts of the data, the criticism that these accounts are ad hoc. For example, in considering the analog account of the mental rotation data, Anderson writes:

> One can ask why rotation of the image must be gradual. Why should it be computationally harder in the image model to calculate a 180° step than a 1° step? It is no less ad hoc to propose this limitation on the [analog] model than it is to propose it for the propositional model. (p. 260)

Thus, Anderson wonders why, when a stimulus has an analog representation, this necessarily means that the representation cannot be transformed 180 degrees as quickly and as effortlessly as it can be transformed 1 degree. Similarly, it can be asked whether an analog representation necessarily requires that a mental traverse of the distance between two close points in the represented object should take less time than one between two more distant points. That is, couldn't an analog model be proposed that did not make this assumption? These ambiguities have led Anderson to specify that in general one cannot evaluate a theory of mental representation on the basis of behavioral data alone; the theory must specify both how information is represented and the kinds of processes that operate on the information. Thus, it is not enough, according to Anderson, that a theory proposes an analog representation of visual information. The theory must also specify such matters as how the information is accessed in memory and how different information is compared. Without such specifications, Anderson asserts, "any claim for a particular representation is impossible to evaluate" (p. 250).

Covert and Overt Signals in Experiments. There are other grounds on which the evidence for analog encodings has been challenged. These have to do with the possibility that experimenters may be inadvertently signalling subjects as to how to behave in the experiment. Consider, for example, the mental scanning evidence for analog encodings obtained by Kosslyn et al. (1978). As you will recall, the results of this study were that subjects who were given the names of two locations on an imaginary island took longer to scan between the two locations the more distant the two points were. Pylyshyn (1981) has argued that such evidence may be due simply to subjects' knowledge that, in the real world, it takes longer to travel between two points the more distance separates the points (assuming, of course, that all travel takes place at the same speed). Pylyshyn maintains that the instructions and training given to subjects before the experiment was begun served to inform the subjects about what kind of behavior was expected of them. To understand Pylyshyn's point better, consider the instructions given by Kosslyn et al. (1978, experiment 2). Subjects in the study were told that they would hear the names of two objects, and that if the object named second was on the map, the subjects

> Were to scan to it and depress one button when they arrived at the dot centered on it. The scanning was to be accomplished by imagining a little black speck zipping in the shortest straight line from the first object to the second. . . . We [the experimenters] interviewed subjects in the course of the practice trials, making sure that they were following the instructions about imagery use. (p. 52)

Pylyshyn observes that subjects know from experience that it takes a moving object longer to cover greater distances, so that findings such as that of Kosslyn et al. (1978) "may represent a discovery about what subjects believe and what they take the goal of the experiment to be, rather than a discovery about what underlying mechanisms of image processing are" (p. 23).

The effects of more subtle signals sent by experimenters to subjects in imagery studies have been demonstrated by Intons–Peterson (1983). In her study, Intons–Peterson did not serve as the experimenter herself. Rather, she trained two students "known for their intelligence, dependability, good judgment, and maturity" (p. 396) for this purpose. The task that these student–experimenters were to present to subjects was modelled after a mental rotation task used by Cooper and Shepard (1975). In one condition of this experiment (experiment 3), a subject was first presented with a drawing of either a right hand or a left hand in an upright position. This first drawing will be referred to as the priming stimulus. The subject was next presented with a drawing of either a right or a left hand oriented at 0, 120, or 240 degrees from the upright position. Subjects had to determine whether this second stimulus matched the priming stimulus in terms of its being either a right or a left hand. A second condition in the experiment differed from the first only in that the subjects were asked to generate the priming stimuli from memory. That is, in this condition, subjects were not shown the left or right hand in the upright position but instead were signalled to imagine a left or a right hand in this position. The crucial manipulation in this experiment was the expectation of each student–experimenter. Some student–experimenters were led to expect faster decisions when the priming stimuli were actually presented and other student–experimenters were led to expect faster responses when the priming stimuli were imagined. As shown in Figure 3–13, both expectations affected subjects' performances. That is, at all orientations of the comparison stimuli, when the experimenter expected faster responding with imagined rather than visible primes, the subjects exhibited this behavior, and when the experimenter expected faster responding with visible than imagined primes, the subjects exhibited this pattern of behavior.

What signals did the student–experimenters give to induce this behavior from their subjects? To investigate this, Intons–Peterson repeated the experiment, this time with four observers behind a one-way mirror. After the experiment was over, the observers were questioned about the student–experimenters' behaviors and attitudes. The observers were unable to detect any differences in the way different student–experimenters spoke or behaved with their subjects. Yet, the observers could all categorize the student–experimenters according to which expectations the experimenters held. Further examinations were made of tape recordings of the experimenters reading instructions to their subjects. These analyses revealed that experimenters emphasized their point of view by speaking more slowly and pausing longer before and after reading key parts of the instructions. It is difficult to know, however, whether this was the only aspect of the experimenters' behavior that cued subjects to respond the way they did, or whether this

Figure 3–13
Mean judgment times for decisions about target items rotated 0, 120, or 240 degrees from the upright priming stimulus. The dashed lines shown the responses for perceptual primes; the solid lines show responses for imaginal primes. Panel A shows the data obtained by an experimenter who expected faster judgments with imaginal than perceptual primes. Panel B shows the data obtained by an experimenter who expected slower judgments with imaginal than perceptual primes.

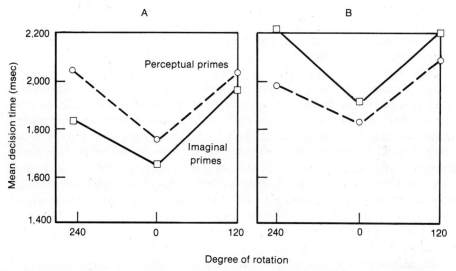

From M. Intons–Peterson, "Imagery paradigms: How vulnerable are they to experimenters' expectations?" *Journal of Experimental Psychology: Human Perception and Performance*, 1983, 9, 394–412. Copyright 1983 by the American Psychological Association. Reprinted by permission.

was even a relevant factor. Further investigation is required to determine this. What can be concluded, though, is that experimenters are capable of unintentionally conveying their expectations about a subject's behaviors and that this communication can be done so subtly that it may be difficult to discern consciously.

Counterevidence

These findings do not mean that the results of all psychological studies can be produced by or even affected by an experimenter's expectations. (Anyone who has conducted psychological experiments that have not turned out as expected can attest to this.) Rather, these results suggest the need for caution when interpreting the results of studies that are particularly

vulnerable to experimenter effects. As Intons–Peterson points out, the procedures used to investigate mental images are "often vague, unfamiliar, and
subjective" (p. 411) and thus very susceptible to these experimenter effects.

It should be understood that demonstrations of the susceptibility of imagery paradigms to experimenter effects do not prove that all the evidence
offered to support the analog view is irrelevant. Rather, such demonstrations
only weaken the analog position by raising the possibility that reasonable
alternative accounts of the data are possible. To counter these attacks on
the analog view, some researchers have looked for evidence of image scanning in experimental situations that are less vulnerable to these experimenter effects. For example, Finke and Pinker (1982) devised a task in which
a pattern made of four dots was first presented to subjects. The pattern
was displayed on a screen for five seconds, during which time subjects were
to attempt to remember the positions of the dots. Then, after a blank interval
of one second, an arrow was displayed on the screen. (See Figure 3–14.)
Subjects were asked to signal whether or not the arrow pointed to any of
the dots that had been shown in the pattern. Finke and Pinker attempted
to make the task easier by telling subjects that the arrow either would
point right at a dot or would clearly be pointing in another direction; thus,
no "near misses" would occur. What is important to realize about this study
is that the experimenters made no mention of how subjects were to perform
the task. That is, the experimenters did not instruct subjects to generate
a mental image. In spite of this, the subjects' responses were very much
like those observed in studies that requested subjects to scan mental images.
Specifically, subjects took longer to respond the greater the distance between the arrow and the dot to which it pointed. In addition, 11 of the

Figure 3–14
An example of stimuli used in the Finke and Pinker (1982) study.

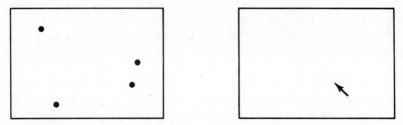

From R. A. Finke and S. Pinker, "Spontaneous imagery scanning in mental extrapolation."
Journal of Experimental Psychology: Learning, Memory and Cognition, 1982, *8,* 142–147.
Copyright 1982 by the American Psychological Association. Reprinted by permission.

12 subjects in the study reported that they either made use of images of the patterns when performing the task or that they both formed mental images and scanned these images when making their judgments. Other evidence obtained by Reed, Hock, and Lockhead (1983) offers additional support to the analog view by showing that subjects can exhibit appropriate image scanning behavior even when they are not aware of what scanning behavior is appropriate.

Conclusion

What conclusions can be drawn about the analog representation of visual information? It seems that there *is* evidence that people behave as though information in memory were represented in an analog form. But the point can still be made that this evidence is more appropriate to the contents of a person's conscious awareness (what we shall later refer to as the short-term store) rather than the long-term store. That is, in the experimental tasks we have considered, when subjects have behaved as though they were processing information that was represented in an analog form, that information was no longer being stored just in the long-term store but had been retrieved and "placed" in the short-term store. (This process will be more fully dealt with in the chapter on the short-term store.) Thus, it could be argued that the evidence still is ambiguous with respect to the representation of information in the long-term store. It is interesting to note that Kosslyn (1980) considers it possible that information in the long-term store has a propositional format that when activated is "displayed" much like information is displayed on a TV screen. According to Kosslyn, "the underlying data-structures *may* be decidedly nonpictorial in form; an image could be generated from sets of descriptions, lists of vectors, or the like" (p. 7). Thus, what Kosslyn is most concerned with is demonstrating that analog codes occur somewhere in memory, not necessarily in the long-term store. Of course, a clear demonstration that analog codes are present in any central memory store would make the claimed existence of long-term analog codes more plausible. This would strengthen the proposals made by psychologists such as Allan Paivio (1971, 1977), who argues that information in the long-term store has a dual representation—both a descriptive and an analog code.

I often think that the issue of analog versus propositional encoding could be presented in the format of a court case. The prosecution could open by considering some of the evidence for analog codes. This data could then be seriously questioned, even ridiculed, by pointing out how alternative accounts of the findings are possible, accounts based on propositional encodings or on demands imposed overtly or covertly by experimenters. The defense for analog encodings could counter with more evidence that people can process information in an analog fashion, even when no explicit imagery instructions are given or when subjects have no tacit knowledge of how the experimenter wishes the results to turn out. Additional considerations pertinent to the issue could be brought up. Pylyshyn (1973), for example, has attacked the analog position on a theoretical basis by pointing out that the constant storage of information in a picture-like format would require a vast amount of storage space, that introspective evidence for mental images—the subjective impressions that a mental picture has been formed—can be misleading and should be discounted, and that the presence of dual picture and descriptive encodings would, in any case, require a more abstract, perhaps propositional code to mediate between the two representations and allow their intertranslation. Responses to these and other points have been made by Kosslyn (1980) and Paivio (1977).

How would such a trial turn out? It does not appear that the current evidence is sufficiently compelling to produce a clear victor. Perhaps a resolution to this issue will eventually come from progress in our understanding of the neurological basis of memory.

Overview

Unlike the iconic store, the long-term store is not limited to encoding primarily one form of information. In the first part of this chapter some experimental techniques were described that have been used to demonstrate the existence of semantic, visual and acoustic information in the long-term store. It should be understood that other forms of information including olfactory (smell), gustatory (taste), and tactile (touch) information can also be encoded in this store. Discussion concentrated on semantic, visual, and acoustic encodings because these have been studied most often by cognitive psychologists.

The discussion of how information is represented in the long-term store contrasted network and set models of semantic information representation and analog and propositional theories of visual information representation. In spite of the many experiments that have been conducted to investigate these views, it does not yet seem possible to declare one of the opposing approaches to either semantic or visual information representation as clearly superior.

Chapter 4
Storage properties of the long-term store

Measuring Information

The first of three questions to be asked about storage is "How much information can the long-term store hold?" One difficulty in answering this question
lies in defining information quantitatively. For example, it is not clear how
much information a person will have received from a list of 10 unrelated
words. Perhaps we could specify that one word is equivalent to one unit
of information. But if the 10 words are written in a foreign language that
the reader does not speak, would it be appropriate to say that 10 units of
information had been transmitted? Alternatively, since words are composed
of letters, perhaps it would be more appropriate to equate amount of information with the number of letters.

Shannon (1948) proposed a better system for quantifying information.
According to Shannon's system, a person is receiving information only when
finding out something that is not predictable. For example, if you invite
one guest to dinner, and at dinner time you hear the doorbell ring, you
can be almost positive that the person ringing the bell will be your guest.
Thus, your opening the door will not produce a great deal of information.
However, if you invite a dozen people for dinner, then you will be much
more uncertain about who is ringing your bell. In this situation, you will
gain a great deal more information when you open your door.

Shannon defined the basic unit of information to be a *bit*. A single bit
is the amount of information that is gained when a person discovers which

77

of the only two equally likely alternatives is the correct one. For example, if you invite two people for dinner, and you know both are equally likely to arrive on time, then you will gain one bit of information when you answer the first ring of your doorbell. If you invite four people, perhaps two men and two women, then you will gain two bits of information by opening your door the first time your bell rings. In this case you will resolve whether your guest is a male or a female, and find out which of the two guests of that sex your first caller is. With eight guests invited, you will gain three bits from opening your door to the first caller.

In general, the amount of information (which we will symbolize using the letter I) that you gain will be dependent on the number of equally likely alternatives (N) in accordance with the formula: $I = \log_2 N$. Another way of stating this relation is to say that the amount of information is equal to the power to which the number 2 must be raised to get the number of equally likely alternatives, or: $2^I = N$. Thus, if there are 4 equally likely alternatives, 2 must be squared to get 4, so that the amount of information is 2 bits. If there are 8 likely alternatives, 2 must be cubed to get 8, so $I = 3$.

Although Shannon's ideas made an important contribution to the information-processing view of memory, his method for calculating the information value of complex stimuli has proven impractical (Lachman, Lachman, & Butterfield, 1979, pp. 74–75). The reason is that to be able to calculate the amount of information, one has to be able to specify the number of possible alternatives and how probable each alternative is. This is ordinarily very difficult to do. Imagine how difficult it would be for you to list every possible event that could occur at every point in your day, and to assess how likely every one of these potential occurences was.

A Physiological Approach.   Since it is difficult to accurately quantify information in a nonlaboratory situation, we might have to be satisfied with addressing a weaker version of our question concerning storage capacity. Instead of asking how much information can be stored, we could ask whether there's an upper limit to the capacity of the long-term store. That is, we could ask whether we can ever learn enough to completely fill our memories.

One way to answer this question is to estimate the number of nerve cells in the human cortex, then to estimate how many nerve cells we "use up" in a typical life span. Even though it's possible to arrive at an estimate of the number of cortical cells—there are perhaps as many as 5–7 billion (P. Milner, 1970, p. 112)—it is not yet possible for us to specify with any confidence the neural mechanisms that produce memory. We do not know, for example, what kinds of changes occur in the brain when we learn to recognize a word or a picture.

Although highly speculative, a number of theories have been proposed to help explain the kinds of neural changes that might be involved in learning. One such theory has been proposed by Hebb (1949). According to Hebb, when we first perceive some novel stimulus, electrical activity in a series of cells form what Hebb terms a *cell assembly.* Hebb proposes that when a person continues to perceive a stimulus, electrical activity will continue to flow along the chain of cells that make up the cell assembly, and the continued electrical activity will produce physical changes in the chain of cells that facilitate the flow of electrical current. In addition, repeated electrical activity can cause new nerve cells to join the assembly. Because each nerve cell in the cortex has so many weak connections to other nerve cells, it is possible for a closed loop of cells to develop eventually. In such a *reverberatory circuit,* electrical activity can be maintained beyond the period of time that the stimulus is perceived. (See Figure 4–1.)

Hebb suggests that a person must learn to perceive stimuli. In the process of learning to recognize a triangle, for example, it is proposed that a number of cell assemblies must be developed in the brain, perhaps one for each of the three sides of the figure and one for each of the three angles. These six cell assemblies are proposed to become linked together eventually, since the perception process will tend to activate them concurrently. The linked cell assemblies that correspond to a complex stimulus Hebb calls a *phase sequence.*

There is some evidence that conforms to Hebb's theory (e.g., Burns, 1958; Hebb, 1963). However, since the theory is quite general, it has not proven to be of great use to memory theorists. With regard to the question of

Figure 4–1
A simplified representation of a reverberatory circuit. The arrows show the direction of travel of electrical activity.

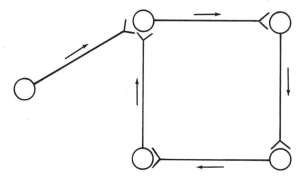

long-term storage capacity, for example, Hebb's theory is not very informative because it doesn't allow us to estimate the number of nerve cells required to represent the stimuli we encounter.

Even if Hebb's theory allowed a precise estimate of the number of nerve cells required to form a typical cell assembly, it would still be difficult to use this physiological approach to answer questions about storage capacity. One difficulty has to do with the way we mentally represent encounters with familiar stimuli. Much of the time, what we are remembering is not completely new events, but familiar stimuli that we encounter in new contexts. For example, when a subject in a memory experiment is asked to learn a series of words, the words are probably known to the subject long before the experiment begins. Thus the subject will not be learning the words themselves, but rather that the words were encountered in the context of the experiment. This latter kind of learning may require much less mental work than the former. That is, fewer new connections among nerve cells may have to be made to remember that some familiar stimulus was encountered, as opposed to the connections required originally to learn to recognize that stimulus. This distinction further complicates any attempt to assess the capacity of the long-term store.

If you are beginning to suspect that you are not going to get a definite answer to the question of long-term storage capacity, you are correct. Psychologists often deal with this question by suggesting that the capacity may be infinite (e.g., Hintzman, 1978) or by not specifying what the limits may be (e.g., Atkinson & Shiffrin, 1968). At present, there are too many unknowns for any more definite answer to be proposed.

Duration of Storage

When the material on the iconic store was presented, precise estimates of both the capacity and the duration of storage were made. As was just demonstrated in the preceding discussion, this sort of precision is not possible in estimating long-term storage capacity. The ensuing material will show that it is also difficult to fix precisely the length of time that information will reside in the long-term store.

This may seem puzzling to you. It may seem as though an estimate of long-term storage duration is easy to determine: Simply present stimuli to a person or group of people and keep testing subsets of the material year after year to see how long the stimuli are remembered. Experiments such as this have been done. In the early 1920s an American psychologist named Harold Burtt (1941) began to read his 15-month-old son passages from Sophocles' *Oedipus Tyrannus* in its original form. Each 20-line passage was read

90 times over a three-month period. This process was continued, using different Greek passages, until the child was three years old, by which time 21 different passages had been read. Burtt tested his son's memory for these Greek passages when the boy was 8½, 14, and 18 years old.

Before you are presented with the results of this experiment, the method used to test the boy's memory must be described. Burtt evaluated his son's memory using a *savings* measure. A savings score reflects how much easier it is to relearn previously studied material as opposed to learning new material. For example, if you learned a song two years ago, you may not now be able to sing it perfectly. You may have to listen to someone else sing the song twice before you get it perfect once again. To turn your memory performance into a savings score, it would have to be determined how long it would take for you to learn a completely new song of comparable difficulty. Let's say that to learn a new song you had to listen to it eight times. Your savings score for the song you learned two years ago can be calculated from this formula:

$$\text{Percent savings} = 100 \left(\frac{\begin{array}{c}\text{Number of trials to} \\ \text{learn new song}\end{array} - \begin{array}{c}\text{Number of trials to} \\ \text{relearn old song}\end{array}}{\text{Number of trials to learn new song}} \right)$$

The above example results in a 75 percent savings score.

In Burtt's experiment, the boy was asked to try to learn to recite Greek passages, some of which had been presented to him as an infant, and others that were new. (He wasn't told which were which.) The savings score was calculated to be 27 percent when the boy was 8½, 8 percent when he was 14, and 0 percent when he was 18.

The results may seem to indicate clearly that information was stored for up to 15–16 years. Thus, it may seem reasonable to conclude that 15 years is the duration of long-term storage. However, there is another possibility. It is possible that information may be stored for much longer periods. Would it surprise you to know that some psychologists might even consider Burtt's experiment to be consistent with the hypothesis that information is stored permanently?

The reason for this alternate conclusion is that forgetting may be due to either or both of the following two factors: (1) Information is no longer stored in memory; (2) the stored information is still in memory, but it cannot be retrieved. An experiment by Tulving and Psotka (1971) shows the importance of this second factor in the forgetting process. It is well-known in memory research that a person's ability to remember an event will be best if no similar events are encountered afterwards. If, for example, you are introduced to someone named Maureen, your chances of remembering her name will diminish if you are subsequently introduced to Myrtle, Mavis, Mitzy, and Marie. This decrement in memory performance that comes from later learning is termed *retroactive interference*. To investigate the cause of this form of forgetting, Tulving and Psotka presented subjects, not with lists of people's names, but with lists of 24 words drawn from various conceptual categories. One list consisted of the words *hut, cottage, tent, hotel, cliff, river, hill, volcano, captain, corporal, sergeant, colonel, ant, wasp, beetle, mosquito, zinc, copper, aluminum, bronze, drill, saw, chisel,* and *nail.* All six lists used in the experiment were similar in structure to this one. They all contained blocks of four words from six conceptual categories. The six lists differed in that six different catagories were represented in each.

Subjects studied words from a list and then free-recalled the words immediately. Some subjects studied and free-recalled words from just one list, while other subjects repeated this process with as many as six lists. Subjects were then occupied with an irrelevant task for 10 minutes, after which they were asked to free-recall words from all the lists they had seen. Up to this point, Tulving and Psotka's procedure is analogous to introducing subjects to between one and six people (and having them immediately repeat each name after hearing it) and then, after a 10-minute distraction, having them repeat all the names of people they were introduced to. It should be readily apparent what Tulving and Psotka found from the delayed, comprehensive test in this first part of the experiment. Their data showed that, in accord with the concept of retroactive interference, the more lists a person had studied, the fewer words the person could recall from the first list. This is shown by the line marked with solid circles in Figure 4–2. As can be seen from the figure, when subjects learned only one list, they recalled about 70 percent of the words from it after the 10-minute break. Progressively fewer list-1 words were recalled as subjects studied more lists. After learning five additional lists, subjects recalled only 30 percent of the words from their first list.

These results clearly demonstrate the phenomenon of retroactive interference. Producing retroactive interference, however, was not the main purpose of the experiment. Tulving and Psotka were most interested in determining whether the forgetting produced in this way was due just to a loss of the list-1 words from memory or whether the list-1 information was still in memory but simply could not be retrieved. They attempted to resolve this question by giving subjects one additional memory test. This test involved providing subjects with hints, or, to use more formal terminology, *cues.* The cues were the names of categories represented in each list. To get some idea of the effect of these cues, try now to recall the words from

Figure 4–2
Percent of words recalled from list 1 as a function of the number of subsequently learned, interfering lists. The open circles represent cued recall, the closed circles represent free recall, and the triangles represent immediate free recall after learning list 1.

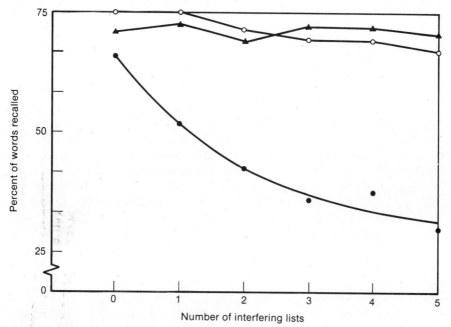

Adapted from E. Tulving, "Cue-dependent forgetting. *American Scientist,* 1974, *62,* 74–82. Copyright 1974 by Sigma Xi. Reprinted by permission.

the sample list that was just provided. Do the following cues help you recall some words you missed? types of buildings; earth formations; military titles; insects; metals; carpenter's tools. In Tulving and Psotka's experiment, these cues had a dramatic effect. They removed practically all the retroactive interference produced by the later lists. (See Figure 4–2.) Tulving and Psotka interpreted this as clear evidence that the previous forgetting was not due just to loss of information from the long-term store. If this information had been lost, the retrieval cues could not possibly have restored performance. Instead, these results were considered to support the retrieval failure view of forgetting (Tulving & Pearlstone, 1966).

This finding is relevant to the discussion of duration of long-term storage. Any attempt to assess storage duration from the interval that begins when the information is originally learned and ends when the information seems to be completely forgotten is potentially an underestimate. The interval underestimates storage duration because forgetting may be due not just to information loss, but also to the failure to retrieve potentially available information. In the case of Burtt's experiment, the Greek passages may still have been in the boy's long-term store when he reached 18; the reason he showed no savings may have been because the information was unable to be successfully retrieved. Thus, this sort of experiment does not give a good estimate of long-term storage duration.

The Permanent Storage View

One possibility may have occurred to you while reading the preceding section: Perhaps information is stored permanently in the brain. The reason we cannot remember absolutely everything that has happened to us and that we have committed to memory is because that information cannot be retrieved. This possibility has been considered by psychologists. The evidence used to support this permanent memory hypothesis, however, is not very convincing (Loftus & Loftus, 1980).

One of the most startling demonstrations that has been taken as evidence for permanent memory storage comes from brain operations reported by Wilder Penfield (1955, 1969). These operations were performed on patients with epilepsy caused by some localized abnormality of the cortex. Surgical removal of the afflicted portion of the cortex is sometimes resorted to if the epileptic seizures cannot be controlled with medication and if the abnormal area of the cortex is not required for some essential function, such as speech. To help determine both the locus of the epileptogenic abnormality and the kinds of functions that are controlled by the area of the cortex surrounding this site, the surgeon may use an electrode to stimulate regions of the exposed cortex with a gentle electric current. Penfield (1969), in commenting on this procedure, mentions that the surgeon:

> Must, of course, protect the patient from pain by local anaesthesia and from anxiety by carrying on a calm running conversation with him. . . . The neurosurgeon can use electrical stimulation to reproduce any fit that ordinarily begins in an abnormal epileptogenic area of the cerebral cortex. (The patient will often say, "That is the way they begin.") But, if the surgeon is careful to use a mild stimulus, no after-discharge occurs, and no fit follows. The surgeon can also use an electrode to map out the normally responsive functional areas, thus increasing the accuracy and safety of proposed surgical excision of the epileptogenic areas of cortex. The patient, who is inevitably well aware of the need for accuracy, can talk with him and guide his hand. (pp. 137–138)

It is through this process of stimulating regions of the cortex and having patients report their experiences that Penfield has obtained evidence of what he feels is permanent long-term storage. Following is a transcript of one interaction between Penfield and a patient. The numbers in the beginning of sentences refer to arbitrarily labeled locations marked by Penfield on the cortex of the patient. Each time a number is mentioned, it means an electrical current has been applied at that location.

11: "I heard something familiar, I do not know what it was."

11 [*repeated without warning*]: "Yes sir, I think I heard a mother calling her little boy somewhere. It seemed to be something that happened years ago." [*When asked to explain, she said,*] "It was somebody in the neighbourhood where I live." [*She added that it seemed that she herself*] "was somewhere close enough to hear."

[*Warning without stimulation*]: "Nothing."

11 [*repeated*]: "Yes, I hear the same familiar sounds, it seems to be a woman calling, the same lady. That was not in the neighbourhood. It seemed to be at the lumber yard." [*Then she added reflectively,*] "I've never been around the lumber yard much. . . ."

12: "Yes. I heard voices down along the river somewhere—a man's voice and a woman's voice calling."

[*When she was asked how she could tell that the calling had been "along the river," she said,*] "I think I saw the river." [*When asked what river it was, she said,*] "I don't know. It seems to be the one I was visiting when I was a child."

[*Warning without stimulation*]: "Nothing."

[*Three minutes later without any warning stimulation was carried out again, probably near 13. While the electrode was held in place, she exclaimed*]: "Yes, I hear voices. It is late at night, around the carnival somewhere— some sort of traveling circus." [*Then, after removal of the electrode*]: "I just saw lots of big wagons that they use to haul animals in." (Penfield, 1955, p. 54)[1]

A number of objections have been raised to Penfield's conclusion that reports such as this are indicative of permanent memory. One objection is that these flashbacks have been elicited just when stimulation is applied in the region of an epileptic focus. Penfield accounts for this by saying that the years of abnormal electrical discharges in the afflicted areas of the cortex have merely sensitized these regions, making them more responsive to externally applied stimulation. Penfield (1955) notes that this phenomenon is not unusual: "Sensitization of the cortex, so that it reveals its function with greater ease when stimulated, is the common result of the presence of

---

[1] From W. Penfield, "The permanent record of the stream of consciousness." *Acta Psychologica*, 1955, *11*, 47–69. Copyright 1955 by North Holland Publishing Co. Reprinted by permission.

local epileptogenic process in other areas of cortex as well as in the temporal lobes" (p. 49). Hintzman (1978), however, has suggested that the abnormal electrical activity around the epileptic focus may have altered memory storage processes, perhaps by keeping stored memories more active than they ordinarily would be. Any such process would, of course, prevent one's drawing generalizations about memory storage in nonepileptic populations from Penfield's reports.

A second problem with using these stimulation-induced flashbacks to support a permanent memory hypothesis is that alternate explanations of the patients' reports are possible. Some psychologists (Hintzman, 1978; Loftus & Loftus, 1980; Neisser, 1967) suggest that these reports may not reflect highly accurate memories of actual past events; instead, they may be hallucinations or dream-like states in which a variety of sensations and memories are activated. An important part of this alternate interpretation is the finding, reported by Penfield, that a feeling of familiarity is often produced by the externally applied stimulation. The following comments were made by the same patient previously quoted, this time at a later point in the operation.

14   [*just posterior to 15, this stimulation caused her to say*]: "The whole operation now seems familiar."

[*Warning without stimulation*]: "Nothing."

15: "Just a tiny flash of familiarity and a feeling that I knew everything that was going to happen in the near future." [*Then she added,*] "as though I had been through all this before and thought I knew exactly what you were going to do next."

[*At point 17, an electrode, covered with an insulating coat except at its tip, was inserted to different depths and the current switched on so as to stimulate in various buried portions of the first temporal convolution and uncus.*]

17c [*1 cm deep*]: "Oh, I had the same very, very familiar memory, in an office somewhere. I could see the desks. I was there and someone was calling to me, a man leaning on a desk with a pencil in his hand."

[*Warning without stimulation*]: "Nothing."

11 [*40 minutes after first stimulation of this point*]: "I had a flash of familiar memory. I do not know what it was." (p. 55)[2]

Hintzman (1978) suggests that when this familiar feeling is produced at the same time that a patient imagines something, that imagined event will, on account of its familiarity, seem to have occurred sometime in the patient's past. Loftus and Loftus (1980) make a similar point. They suggest that Pen-

---

[2] From W. Penfield, "The permanent record of the stream of consciousness." *Acta Psychologica*, 1955, *11*, 47–69. Copyright 1955 by North Holland Publishing Co. Reprinted by permission.

field's patients may have been combining a number of imagined or actual past events, some of which may be quite recent. After reviewing the evidence, Loftus and Loftus conclude that the reports of Penfield's patients "appear to consist merely of the thoughts and ideas that happened to exist just prior to and during stimulation" (p. 414).

The Reconstructive View. These alternative interpretations of the patients' reports may strike you as being no more plausible than Penfield's permanent memory view. You must realize, however, that the objections raised to the permanent memory hypothesis are being based not just on Penfield's patients' reports, but on approaches and viewpoints developed through other memory studies. One such approach to memory proposes that the recall process entails a *reconstruction* rather than an exact reproduction of some event. According to this view, when a person is asked to recall some information, the recall is based not just on specific information stored from the previous encounter with the event, but also on relevant memories formed on other occasions. It is often difficult to tell from just a person's recall response whether or not the response is based on a reconstruction. For example, if someone asks you to recall what color shoes you put on this morning, and without looking you supply the correct answer, it is possible that you may be basing your response on information about your shoe color that you actually did encode into memory earlier today. This would constitute a reproductive process. On the other hand, you may have reconstructed this information from other events you remember. For example, you may remember that you have only two pairs of shoes that you find comfortable and that one of them is being repaired. Or, you may remember what color your other clothes are and recall which pair of shoes you usually choose to coordinate with that color. In these reconstructive processes, a person often makes use of general knowledge (such as what colors go with other colors) in order to fill in details that were not actually stored.

One source of evidence for the reconstructive view of memory is studies of eyewitness testimony. These experiments sometimes present subjects with a simulated crime or accident and later test subjects' memory for the incident. A study by Buckhout and his co-workers (1974) was conducted in the following manner:

> The incident was staged in two Brooklyn College classes, midway through a lecture period. A male student appeared at the door and stated that he thought he had left a book in the room during the preceding class and that he would like to look for it. The instructor, who was aware that the incident was staged, agreed to the student's request. The male student (the assailant) then walked to a chair where a confederate was seated and bent over as if to look for a book. He grabbed the confederate's pocketbook and fled out of the class. The instructor cautioned the class to remain seated, and ran after the assailant. A

few minutes later, the instructor and the Es [experimenters] returned and informed the students of the experimental nature of the incidents, and distributed questionnaires. Three weeks later, the Es again returned to the classes and distributed another set of questionnaires which asked the Ss [subjects] to indicate their confidence in their ability to correctly identify the purse snatcher. The Ss were then shown the two videotaped lineups and asked to pick out the assailant. (p. 191)

The two videotaped lineups each were comprised of five male college students. The students in these lineups bore some resemblance to the assailant, who was included in only one of the lineups. The other lineup included a person who closely resembled the assailant. The recognition performance of the 52 witnesses who viewed the lineups was not impressive. Only 13.5 percent of the witnesses picked just the assailant alone from the lineups. Of interest to the reconstructive view of memory is the recall data supplied in the questionnaire. From the description of this performance, summarized below, it is clear that subjects were basing recall of the assailant's description principally on their knowledge of what a typical college student looks like.

Our eyewitnesses gave typically poor descriptions of the suspect, showing a general tendency to approximate the norm for a male college student as evidenced by the higher age estimate (matching the age of the witnesses) and the idealized height to weight proportions (5 ft. 10 in., 168 lbs.) which match the data on a life insurance company chart. These convenient frames of reference may be turned to by witnesses who really don't recollect what they saw. (p. 192)

Returning to Penfield's evidence, it seems likely that reconstructive processes must have contributed to certain reports that were produced by the electrical stimulation. For example, Loftus and Loftus mention that one of Penfield's patients claimed that she reexperienced her own birth when she received a stimulation. It is probable that this patient did have memories that dealt with childbirth, perhaps those of her own children or births that she had witnessed. Her reexperiencing her own birth could be the product of combining these memories with the hallucination, perhaps triggered by feelings of helplessness while on the operating table, that she was once again an infant.

There are other findings, besides those that support the reconstructive view of memory, that may have contributed to skepticism for the permanent memory hypothesis. These must include studies that indicate that memories in the long-term store undergo certain changes. It is to this evidence that we turn next.

Changes in Storage

Strength

A number of memory theorists (e.g., Atkinson & Juola, 1973; Morton, 1969) have suggested that when a person perceives some stimulus, the representation of that stimulus in the long-term store will be activated. Repeated exposure to a stimulus is assumed to lead to an accumulation of this activation, so that frequently encountered stimuli will have the strongest representations in memory. Crowder (1976, p. 374) has suggested a hydraulic analogy for this view. He says that one can think of the memory representation of each concept as being like a bucket that collects liquid whenever that concept is aroused. Since the level of liquid will rise each time the concept is encountered, common concepts will be associated with higher levels of liquid. Psychologists usually refer to this property of a memory trace as its strength or familiarity.

Evidence for this accumulation of trace strength comes from an experimental task known as *lexical decision.* In this task, a subject is shown a string of symbols and must decide as quickly as possible if the symbols spell a word. For example, a subject may be shown the string *veath* or the string *hair.* Typically, subjects make very few errors in this sort of task, and the main interest is in the speed with which the person produces a response (McKoon & Ratcliff, 1979). Of relevance to the issue of memory strength is the finding that common English words are responded to more rapidly than uncommon words. This has been demonstrated in an experiment performed by Rubenstein, Garfield, and Millikan (1970). Subjects in this experiment were informed that strings of letters would be shown to them on a screen, and that some of the letter strings would spell words and others would spell words that looked like English but were actually nonsense. The subjects were told to press a response key marked "yes" as soon as they decided an English word had been presented, and to press a key marked "no" if the string was a nonsense word. The experiment included English words that occurred with low, moderate, or high frequency in the English language. It was found that reaction times were fastest for high frequency words, such as *chair* (740 milliseconds), were intermediate for moderate frequency words, such as *wine* (802 milliseconds), and were slowest for low frequency words, such as *foyer* (899 milliseconds).

Strength and Memory Models. The exact physiological basis of a memory's strength is not certain. According to our hydraulic analogy, we might expect strong memories to be more active or energetic on some sense. In terms of Hebb's model, which describes memories in terms of reverberatory loops in cell assemblies, this heightened activity may take the form of an increased level of electrical activity in an unstimulated reverberatory loop. If we assume that electrical activity must exceed some critical threshold level for a stimulus to be consciously perceived, then reverberatory loops that have a high level of activity in their unstimulated state will require less stimulation from the environment to trigger conscious perception than will loops that have low levels of activity.

There is another way that strength may be represented. Instead of altering the resting level of activity in a series of cells that forms a reverberatory loop, increased exposure to a stimulus may lower the threshold for triggering electrical activity. This suggestion is, in fact, more in line with Hebb's own views of the physiological basis of learning, for Hebb suggests that prolonged electrical activity stimulates the development of connecting pathways between cells, which facilitates the ability of a cell assembly to become active. Thus, instead of our hydraulic analogy having buckets becoming increasingly more full as a stimulus is repeatedly encountered, it may be more appropriate to liken the long-term effects of repeated stimulation to a process of lowering the rim of a bucket. Under these conditions, less input (i.e., stimulation from the environment) is required for the contents to overflow (i.e., to achieve awareness of the stimulus).

Morton (1969) has proposed a model of memory that is in accord with this latter conception of memory strength. Morton suggests that information is represented in memory units that he calls *logogens*. A logogen is just a collection of information that defines a concept. For example, the logogen representing the word *cat* includes information about the meaning as well as the visual and acoustic properties of the word. An important characteristic of logogens is their ability to keep a count of the number of times their information has been contacted. That is, a logogen will keep track of the amount of information from the environment that matches any of the information it stores. Environmental information does not have to match all information stored in the logogen for a count to be incremented. For example, if the word *cap* is encountered, there will be some matching information in the logogen representing the word *cat*, so the count in the *cat* logogen will be incremented to a small extent. Morton suggests that when a count in a logogen exceeds some threshold value, the concept will become available to a person; that is, a person will become conscious of the information. Soon after the logogen has been triggered, the count returns to its original value. Morton further suggests that when a logogen has been repeatedly activated in this way, the threshold necessary for activating the logogen will be lowered.

This notion that there is a decreased threshold could readily be used to account for the finding that high-frequency words are recognized more rapidly in a lexical decision task than are low-frequency words. The lexical decision process might proceed in the following manner. Very soon after a person begins to attend to a word, counts begin to accumulate in any logogens that contain information that matches information conveyed by the stimulus. According to a hydraulic analogy, this may be conceived as a process of liquid being poured into buckets that represent appropriate concepts. Since logogens of high-frequency words have a lower threshold than logogens of low-frequency words, the logogens of high-frequency words will exceed their thresholds sooner. Thus, a person will be able to decide about a high-frequency word faster than about a low-frequency word.

Changes in Strength. This information about logogens and the lexical decision task is intended to familiarize you with the concept of memory strength. More will be said about this concept in other sections of this text. For the present, however, memory strength is of interest principally because of the changes it is believed to undergo over time.

Ever since the late 1800s, when the German philosopher Ebbinghaus began to investigate experimentally the process of forming mental associations, the idea that over time, memory strength decays, has been considered a possible mechanism for forgetting. More recently, Wickelgren (1974) has proposed a theory of forgetting that incorporates this concept of decay.

Finding experimental support for a decay process has proven difficult, however, because decay is not the only mechanism that contributes to forgetting. As mentioned previously, forgetting can also result from interference produced by subsequently learned information. Thus, any observed forgetting can be attributed to either or both of these mechanisms. How can one demonstrate that some of the forgetting that occurs is due just to decay? A situation is required in which retroactive interference is eliminated. This means that a person must learn some information and have a memory test after a delay, but during this delay, no new information must be encountered. In addition, the person must not think about (i.e., rehearse) the information.

In 1924, Jenkins and Dallenbach performed an experiment that they believed satisfied these requirements. Two subjects learned lists of 10 nonsense syllables either in the morning or at night, just before going to sleep. Jenkins and Dallenbach reasoned that while a person is asleep no new material will be memorized and little or no rehearsal of the list words will occur. Thus, if retroactive interference is the principal cause of forgetting, memory should be much better when subjects fall asleep after learning than when they stay awake. On the other hand, if decay is the principal cause of forgetting, the forgetting rates of the two learning conditions should be equivalent. The results of the experiment are shown in Figure 4–3. It can be seen that when the subjects stayed awake they forgot the nonsense syllables much more rapidly than when they fell asleep. This finding was interpreted by Jenkins and Dallenbach to show that interference from subsequent learning is the chief cause of forgetting.

The results of this experiment were influential in changing the focus of psychologists' attention from decay to retroactive interference as a mecha-

Figure 4–3
The average number of nonsense syllables recalled by subjects after sleeping or
staying awake for varying intervals of time.

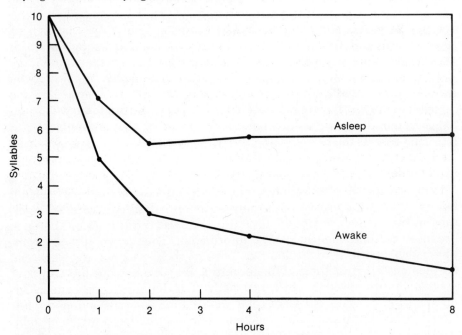

Adapted from J. G. Jenkins and K. M. Dallenbach, "Obliviscence during sleep and waking."
American Journal of Psychology, 1924, *35*, 605–612.

nism for forgetting. Retroactive interference has, in fact, proven to be a
very important contributor to forgetting. But it is possible that more than
one factor contributes to forgetting. Recently, Wickelgren (1974, 1977) has
helped to redirect attention once more to the process of decay of strength
in the long-term store. Wickelgren has proposed that both interference
from extraneous learning and decay over time affect forgetting. He has
described the relation of these two factors to strength of the memory trace
with the following rather complex formula:

$$m = Lt^{-D}2.72^{-It}$$

where m = memory strength, t = time after learning, L = initial strength
of a memory trace immediately after learning, I = rate of loss due to interference, and D = rate of decay. It is with the parameter D that we will
presently be concerned. Wickelgren has shown that the value of D can

remain constant at a nonzero value over a wide range of learning situations and still allow the equation to accurately describe the rate of forgetting. For example, Wickelgren (1975a) has shown that this equation fits data produced by groups of children (average age, 9½ years), young adults (average age, 21 years), and older persons (average age, 68 years) who learned a list of words and subsequently were given a recognition test for the words after delays of up to two hours after learning. The data are shown in Figure 4–4. It can be seen that the three lines that summarize the changes in memory strength of the three groups of subjects all have almost the same slope. Thus, all three groups show similar rates of forgetting. Of most importance to our discussion of strength is the value of the parameter *D*. *D*, which represents the rate of decay, was established to be .26 for the children, .26 for the young adults, and .24 for the elderly, values which are not significantly different. The value of this parameter is similar for other learning conditions. Wickelgren (1975b) has found that his equation fits recognition data obtained from groups of sober subjects and subjects who learned words

Figure 4–4
Memory strength for three age groups as a function of delay of memory test.

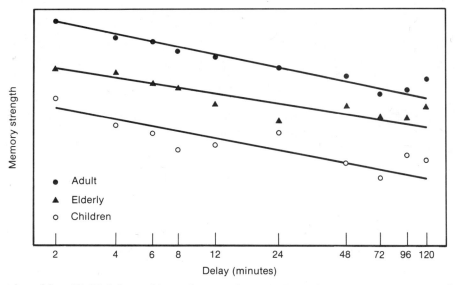

Adapted from W. Wickelgren, "Age and storage dynamics in continuous recognition memory." *Developmental Psychology*, 1975, *11*, 165–169. Copyright 1975 by the American Psychological Association. Reprinted by permission of publisher and author.

while intoxicated with alcohol. These results are shown in Figure 4–5. Again, similar rates of decay are apparent as reflected in all groups of subjects, both sober and intoxicated, being assigned a *D* value of .25. These results add credibility to the existence of the decay process. It is interesting that according to Wickelgren's theory, any differences in memory strength among the subject groups he tested are due to degree of initial learning. Thus, it appears that any memory impairments due to age or alcohol intoxication are due to how well the information is encoded and not to how rapidly the information decays or becomes inaccessible.

Decrease in Fragility. Wickelgren has suggested that there is another property of the memory trace that changes over time. This property Wickelgren calls *fragility*. It indicates how susceptible a memory is to the process of decay. A fragile trace is suggested to be one that will decay most rapidly. A less fragile trace will be more resistant to the decay process. According to Wickelgren, the fragility of a memory decreases over time. In the first few seconds after a memory is established, it is in its most fragile state, so during this period the memory will decay most rapidly. Over longer periods of time, fragility will continue to decrease, but ever more slowly. You will notice that in the previously mentioned equation for memory strength, there was no term for this fragility factor. The reason is that a calculation of memory strength, according to Wickelgren's theory, will be most affected

Figure 4–5
Memory strength for sober and intoxicated subjects as a function of delay of memory test.

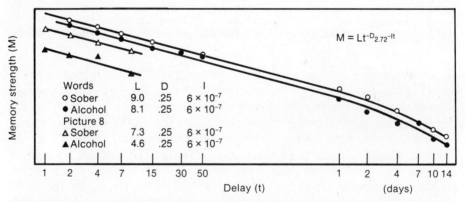

Adapted from W. Wickelgren, "Alcoholic intoxication and memory storage dynamics. *Memory & Cognition*, 1975, *3*, 385–389. Copyright 1975 by the Psychonomic Society. Reprinted by permission.

by fragility during the first few seconds after learning has occurred. In the two studies just described, memory was tested after no less than one minute following learning. Wickelgren has determined that an inclusion of a fragility term for these studies would not have substantially altered the calculation of memory strength. Equations that incorporate a fragility term are available (Wickelgren, 1974).

Evidence that memory traces become less fragile over time comes from studies of amnesia. When a person receives a head injury, it is often found that, in addition to having problems with new learning, the person is unable to remember events from the more recent past. This loss of previously formed memories is known as *retrograde amnesia*. If memories are most fragile after they have just been formed, it should be the very recent memories that are most affected by a head injury. This is just what is usually observed. Here is an account of a patient who was thrown off a motorcycle in 1933 when he was 22 years old:

> A week after the accident he was able to converse sensibly, and the nursing staff considered that he had fully recovered consciousness. When questioned, however, he said that the date was in February [1922], and that he was a schoolboy. He had no recollection of five years spent in Australia, and two years in this country working on a golf course. Two weeks after the injury he remembered the five years spent in Australia and remembered returning to this country; the past two years were, however, a complete blank as far as his memory was concerned. Three weeks after the injury he returned to the village where he had been working for two years. Everything looked strange, and he had no recollection of ever having been there before. He lost his way on more than one occasion. Still feeling a stranger to the district, he returned to work; he was able to do his work satisfactorily, but had difficulty in remembering what he had actually done during the day. About 10 weeks after the accident, the events of the past two years were gradually recollected; and finally he was able to remember everything up to within a few minutes of the accident. (Russell & Nathan, 1946, p. 291)[3]

Occurrences such as this, in which a person initially loses memory for a period of the past, and then the memory gradually returns with the oldest memories recovering first, is known as *shrinking retrograde amnesia*. As in the case described above, it is generally found that the most recent memories are most likely to be irrecoverable. Russell and Nathan (1946) report that in a sample of 1,029 cases of amnesia, 707 involved retrograde amnesia for memories formed less than 30 minutes prior to the accident, and, although the figures are only approximate, for 60 percent of these 707 cases,

---

[3] From W. R. Russell and P. W. Nathan, "Traumatic amnesia." *Brain*, 1946, *69*, 280–300. Copyright 1946 by Oxford University Press. Reprinted by permission.

the retrograde amnesia extended for a period of less than 1 minute before the accident.

Although it has been suggested that the fragility of a memory trace undergoes its greatest decline just after learning has occurred, the fragility is thought to decrease continuously throughout a person's lifetime. Evidence of this comes from an experiment by Squire, Slater, and Chace (1975). The subjects in this study were psychiatric patients suffering from severe depression. The patients had been prescribed to receive a program of electroconvulsive shocks, delivered through electrodes temporarily placed against both sides of the head. If you've read Ken Kesey's novel *One Flew Over the Cuckoo's Nest* or seen the movie, you are aware of some of the effects produced by these shocks. They include a *grand mal* seizure, from which the patient must be protected by relaxant medication, and memory impairments. (The treatment is also claimed to relieve depression.) Squire and his co-workers wanted to better determine the retrograde amnesic effects of the electroconvulsive therapy. To do this they administered a newly developed memory test to the patients both before and after they received the program of shocks. The memory test was designed to test distant memories formed within the last 16 years of a person's life. Designing such a test is difficult because events must be found that each occurred for just a short time and were not subsequently mentioned or re-presented. The events used in the test were the names of TV shows that had appeared on the air for just one season. These TV programs had been equally popular, and had all been aired between 6 and 11 P.M. The test required subjects to pick the name of one of these old TV shows from a list of four program names. Of the four program names in each question, three were fabricated. Here are three sample questions:

Which of the following was a TV show?

(a) Bloody Noon, (b) Latest Thing, (c) Fair Exchange, (d) Red River Road

(a) Bluegrass Country, (b) Garrison's Gorillas, (c) Navajo Country, (d) Divorce Lawyer

(a) The Cathan Boys, (b) Crime Haters, (c) Banyon, (d) Monkey Business

The answers are c (from 1962), b (from 1967), and c (from 1972).

Patients in the experiment were given 40 questions before the shock treatments and 40 different questions after the last shock session. The percent correct responses are shown in Figure 4–6. From this figure it can be seen that shock treatment disrupted only the more recent memories, that is, the memories formed one to three years previously. The shocks had no effect on memories that were formed before that time. These results

Figure 4–6

Proportion of correct responses as a function of the year the event occurred. The test was administered to patients both before and after receiving a program of electroconvulsive therapy.

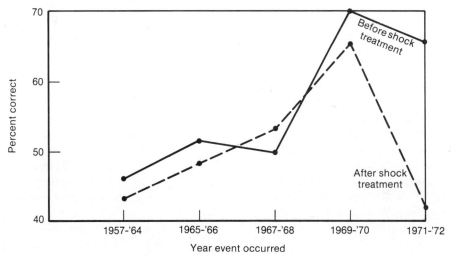

Year event occurred

Adapted from L. R. Squire, P. C. Slater and P. M. Chace, "Retrograde amnesia: Temporal gradient in very long term memory following electroconvulsive therapy. *Science,* 1975, *187,* 77–79. Copyright 1975 by the American Association for the Advancement of Science. Reprinted by permission.

conform to the idea that memories are initially highly fragile but that they decrease in fragility over a period of years. In a fragile condition a memory will be most susceptible to the natural process of decay as well as to traumatic events, such as electric shocks or blows to the head.

Consolidation Theory and Fragility.   Wickelgren's proposal that memories become less fragile as they age is very much like a theory that was introduced in 1900 by the German psychologists Müller and Pilzecker. Their *consolidation* theory was based on the idea that the learning process produces neural activity that continues even after the actual learning period has ended. It is suggested that this continuing or perseverating neural activity, as it is called, produces a more permanent, more secure memory. Consolidation theory has been used to explain retrograde amnesia. According to the consolidation view, retrograde amnesia most strongly affects recent memories because these memories have undergone the least consolidation and thus are the least secure.

The consolidation theory is rather vague. There is no specification of such matters as how long the perseverating neural activity may last or of the kinds of changes produced by this perseverating activity. To remedy this, a number of elaborations and extensions of the consolidation view have appeared since it was introduced in 1900. Hebb's theory is, perhaps, an example. The perseverating activity in the consolidation process can be considered to correspond to Hebb's suggested persistance of electrical activity in reverberating loops. This perseverating activity leads to more permanent changes by stimulating the growth of additional connections among nerve cells in a cell assembly. Adaptations of the consolidation view to other memory models have also been proposed (see Wickelgren, 1979a, pp. 366–376). Wickelgren's theory can be regarded as another refinement of the consolidation approach, this time interpreting the more permanent, structural changes of the consolidation process as being a decrease in memory fragility. An advantage of Wickelgren's approach is its quantitative nature. This allows one to make numerical predictions about changes in memory fragility over time.

Summary

Three questions about long-term storage have been discussed. The *capacity* of this store can be described as very large and, for all practical purposes, unlimited. A more precise description of storage capacity is hampered by difficulties in quantifying information and by uncertainty about the neural changes that underlie learning. The *duration* of storage is also difficult to specify accurately, principally because information that appears to be forgotten may still actually be present in the long-term store. Although it has been claimed that information may be stored permanently, a consideration of the relevant evidence and a discussion of the third storage issue, that of *changes* that occur over time, strongly suggest that memories do not remain fully intact. Instead, it appears that memories decay in strength and also become less fragile. These two changes are believed to occur simultaneously so that even though a memory will be less strongly represented in time, what does remain will be more resistant to disruption.

Chapter 5
Retrieval

Properties of the Retrieval System

The memory retrieval process is remarkable. When we perceive a stimulus the retrieval process seems to automatically find a matching set of stimuli in memory from the vast number of stimuli that are represented there. The taste or smell of something we have not encountered since childhood, an emotion that we have not recently felt, or a voice of a person we once knew can suddenly cause us to remember our previous experiences with these things.

Serial versus Parallel Retrieval

How might some mechanical or electrical system be designed to accomplish a similar act of retrieval? One possibility is to have a system search a memory store sequentially, item by item. For example, suppose that we have decided to simulate the memory retrieval process using a computer. Let us assume that in the computer's memory is a series of words, each associated with a definition, just as in a dictionary. The problem now is to design a process that will allow the meaning of a string of letters, newly entered into the computer, to be identified. According to the sequential scheme mentioned above, this could be accomplished by having the computer compare the newly entered letter string to every letter string in memory that has been defined. When a match is found, the meaning of the new string can be determined by referring to the associated definition. Such a process in which an item is compared individually with a series of other items is known as a *serial* scanning process.

One drawback of using a serial scan to simulate memory retrieval is that it may be too time-consuming. Even if each comparison can be made very quickly, it would take a considerable amount of time and be rather inefficient. Such a process would be equivalent to a person beginning with the first word in a dictionary and looking at each word in the order listed in the dictionary when attempting to find the definition of some word.

How might the efficiency of a serial scanning process be improved? One way is to shorten the list of items that must be scanned. In effect, this is what we do when we use a dictionary. To look up the meaning of the word *xylophone,* for example, we would open the dictionary not to page 1, but to somewhere near the end. A similar suggestion has been applied to some models of memory retrieval (e.g., Broadbent, 1966). To implement such a suggestion, however, it is necessary that information in memory be organized. In terms of our example of identifying and retrieving the definition of a letter string, a suitable organization scheme is one that has words arranged alphabetically in memory, just as in a dictionary. This allows a retrieval system initially to restrict the scanning process to just the words in memory that begin with the first letter in the unidentified letter string.

Of course, in order for this abbreviated serial scan to occur, it is necessary to identify the first letter in the letter string. This, again, requires a retrieval operation. For a simple task such as the one being considered here, this operation is fairly easy and fast, for no more than 26 letters of the alphabet need to be serially scanned to make an identification. However, in the real world, we do not always know exactly what kind of a stimulus we are trying to identify. The stimulus might be a living thing, an article of clothing, or a piece of furniture, not a letter string. Thus, in order to abbreviate the list of items that has to be inspected, a serial scan through a large number of representations in the long-term store might have to be initiated anyway. The point being made here is that a retrieval system that relied totally on a serial scanning process, even when modified to enhance efficiency, would still require that a great deal of "work" be done in making each retrieval.

Although evidence to support a serial memory scanning operation in humans has been offered (Sternberg, 1966), it seems that the retrieval operations needed for identification of stimuli are more like a *parallel* scanning process rather than a serial process (Sperling, 1970; Wickelgren, 1977, p. 15). In a parallel scan, all items are inspected at the same time rather than one after another. The tuning fork analogy of retrieval introduced in chapter 2 illustrates a parallel scanning process. According to this analogy, a vibrating tuning fork, when held before a set of motionless tuning forks, will cause a tuning fork that is designed to vibrate at the same frequency to begin to hum. Here, it is as if the entire set of motionless tuning forks is being scanned or inspected at the same time. If the set of silent tuning forks is envisioned to be arranged in a circle around the vibrating fork, it takes no longer for the matching tuning fork in this set to begin to hum if the same circle contains 10 or 100 different tuning forks. This is a distinctly different outcome than would be expected from a serial scanning process. In a serial scan, because items are inspected one after another, the more items there are to scan, the longer the process takes.

Experimental Evidence: Sternberg's Study.   Experiments that are intended to discover whether memory retrieval utilizes a parallel or a series scan often measure a subject's recognition reaction time. The logic underlying such experiments is that a parallel scanning process will not be affected if a subject has more items in memory to scan, whereas a serial process will. An experiment by Sternberg (1966) illustrates this approach. Subjects were first shown a short series of single numbers between zero and nine. The numbers were displayed for 1.2 seconds each and appeared in a random order. A list could consist of between one and six different digits. After each list had been shown, subjects' memory for the list was tested with a probe digit. In this testing procedure, a subject first heard a warning signal that indicated the test was going to begin and then was shown a single number, the probe digit. As soon as possible, the subject had to decide whether or not the probe digit had been included in the list that had just been presented and press a "yes" or "no" response key. (See Figure 5–1.) Subjects received a number of practice trials before beginning the task and then received 144 test trials in which digit lists of various lengths were presented in a random order and each tested immediately with a probe digit that either had or had not been included in the immediately preceding list (these are referred to as positive and negative probes, respectively). The reaction times for trials with positive probes are shown in Figure 5–2. What is important here is the finding that reaction time increased with the length of the list. Each additional digit in the list lengthened processing time by an average of 37.9 milliseconds.

Alternate Interpretations of Sternberg's Data.   Sternberg (1966) interpreted his data as offering evidence of serial scanning. The view to be adopted here, however, is that this type of experiment is incapable of conclusively discriminating between a serial and a parallel scanning process. A parallel scanning process could also account for these data if some additional assumptions were made about the scanning operation. For example, if the scanning process were conducted more slowly the more items there were to be scanned, then, in accord with Sternberg's (1966) data, reaction time would increase as a function of the number of memory items. In terms of

Figure 5–1
An illustration of the sequence of events occurring in Sternberg's (1966) experiment. In this example, a series of four digits is displayed on a viewing screen one at a time, followed by a warning signal and a probe.

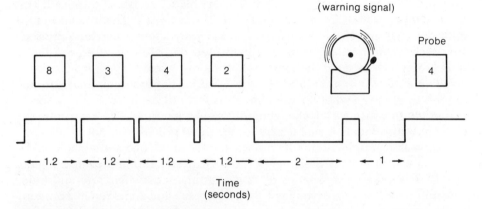

Figure 5–2
Reaction time to positive probes as a function of number of digits in the list.

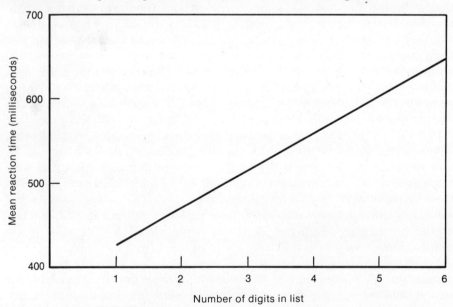

Adapted from S. Sternberg, "High-speed scanning in human memory." *Science*, 1966, *153*, 652–654. Copyright 1966 by the American Association for the Advancement of Science. Reprinted by permission.

the tuning fork analogy, this could be modeled by having the diameter of the circle of scanned tuning forks be enlarged as the number of items in the memory set increased. This would increase the distance between the humming tuning fork and the set of motionless tuning forks. Since it takes sound longer to travel greater distances, the identification process would be slowed. A more general approach to the issue has been taken by Anderson (1976). Using mathematical equations, Anderson has shown that modifications in the assumptions about serial and parallel processes allow either to account for the same behaviorial data, so that "it is never possible to decide whether a process is parallel or serial" (p. 6).

Another problem with Sternberg's experiment concerns the generality of his findings. Even if it is assumed that the subjects in his experiment were scanning memory serially, can it be said that other memory retrieval tasks will also entail a serial scan? Perhaps memory retrieval can be based on either a parallel or a serial process depending on the nature of the retrieval task. This possibility has been discussed by Atkinson and Juola (1973, 1974). They have proposed that a serial search is resorted to in the kind of task used by Sternberg, that is, when a subject is asked to detect the presence of some stimulus that has been used repeatedly in the same experiment. Recall that subjects in Sternberg's experiment were being retested with subsets of the digits zero to nine throughout the experiment and that they received practice trials with these same stimuli before the actual experiment was begun. Atkinson and Juola suggest that when a set of stimuli has not been used repeatedly in this way, subjects will rely instead on just a parallel scan.

The two situations described by Atkinson and Juola are really quite different because different kinds of information are required in order for correct responses to be made. In Sternberg's experiment, the subject has to take context carefully into account. The subject must answer "yes" only if the digit occurred in the context of the most recently presented memory set. In the other case, it is not quite as important for a subject to make a discrimination based on a stimulus' occurrence context. To get a better understanding of these two different situations, consider the following questions:

1. Does the number *three* appear in your social security number?
2. Is the following an English word? *rain*

The first question requires a stimulus' presence in a particular context to be determined. The second question simply requires a match to be found in memory.

It should be noted that in order to comprehend the first question a retrieval of the sort required in question 2 is necessary. That is, a person must identify the meaning of each word in question 1 by finding a match in memory. However, this retrieval operation is insufficient to allow question 1 to be answered. Because question 1 demands a more complex form of processing than does question 2, it seems reasonable to suspect that different retrieval methods may be called for. The assumption to be made here is that the more basic form of retrieval, that required for the identification of stimuli, is a parallel process as exemplified by the tuning fork analogy.

Retrieval Is Automatic

According to the tuning fork analogy of retrieval presented in chapter 2, when attention is directed to a stimulus that is represented in a sensory store, a matching representation is contacted in the long-term store. An important property of the retrieval system is that contact with the matching information in the long-term store appears to occur automatically. Evidence of this comes from a task originally described by Stroop (1935). The so-called Stroop task simply requires a subject to identify a color as quickly as possible. Thus, if a subject is shown a patch of blue ink on a white card, the subject should immediately call out the word blue. Although this may seem like an absurdly simple task, something rather startling occurs when the patch of colored ink takes the form of letters that spell a color name, for example, when the word *red* is written in green ink. Typical reactions to this task have been described by Klein (1964): "Volume of voice goes up; reading falters; now and then the word breaks through abortively; and then there are embarrassed giggles" (p. 576).

In Stroop's (1935) experiment subjects were given lists of words printed in various colors; the words always spelled the name of a color other than that of the ink. The subjects' task was to call out the color of the ink used in each of these stimuli. Stroop found that it took subjects an average of 110.3 seconds to call out the 100 colors. This can be compared with an average time of only 47.0 seconds that these subjects required to call out the names of the same colors when the ink did not spell a word but instead formed a solid square.

It must be emphasized that subjects in this experiment were aware that they should ignore the meaning of each word on their stimulus list and report only the color of the ink. It is evident, however, that Stroop's subjects were unable to do this. Rather, the meaning of each word seems to have been automatically retrieved and to have interfered with the process of naming the ink, which was always some color other than that spelled by the word. Other researchers have confirmed and extended Stroop's finding (see Dyer, 1973 for a review). Klein (1964), for example, has demonstrated that words such as *lemon, grass, fire,* and *sky,* each of which is associated with a color, also produce a Stroop effect, though not quite as sizeable an effect as with color words themselves. Sichel and Chandler (1969) have shown that color naming can be speeded when the meaning of a word is the same as the color of the ink, for example, the word *red* written in red ink.

The Stroop effect demonstrates that retrieval is automatic. When a person pays attention to some environmental stimulus, matching information in the long-term store can be retrieved without the person actually willing this retrieval operation to occur. In fact, the Stroop effect demonstrates that people cannot halt this retrieval process even when it is to their advantage to attempt to do so.

Retrieval and Activation

When retrieval was introduced in chapter 2, it was mentioned that in the retrieval process energy gets fed into representations in the long-term store that match those being attended to in the sensory store. In the tuning fork analogy of retrieval, this activation was said to be manifested by a previously silent, labeled tuning fork beginning to vibrate. It is being assumed here that when a memory location is sufficiently activated, a person will become conscious of the information represented in that activated representation. In this section, evidence for this activation process will be presented.

The activation being considered here is a temporary one. That is, it is being assumed that when energy is fed into some memory representation in the long-term store, that representation will become activated, but the activation will soon die down. This same process is manifested in the tuning fork analogy: A tuning fork that is either struck once or caused to vibrate by an identical vibrating tuning fork briefly placed in its vicinity will initially hum loudly, but will soon return to silence. In the human information processing system, one source of evidence for this temporary activation comes from lexical decision studies. As you will recall, in a lexical decision task a subject must decide as quickly as possible if a series of symbols spells an English word. One version of this task (Meyer, Schvaneveldt, & Ruddy, 1975) has been concerned not so much with whether the retrieved word itself is activated, but with the effect of retrieval on words that are associated with the retrieved word. If it is assumed that words in the long-term store are linked or associated with other words (for example, the word *sky* linked to the word *blue*), then the following prediction can be made. Activation of one of these representations should allow energy to spread to associated representations.

A task used by Meyer and his co-workers (1975) to demonstrate this required subjects to make lexical decisions for a series of letter-string pairs. We will be concerned here with trials in which the letter strings spelled real English words. The two words in each pair in this experiment were either associated semantically (e.g., *bread–butter*) or unassociated (e.g., *wine–glove*). For each trial in the experiment, subjects were first presented with one member of each stimulus pair. After the subject had decided whether or not this first letter string was a word, the second member of the stimulus pair was presented. The subject then made a decision about this second letter string (see Figure 5–3). The critical response measure in this task was reaction time to the second member of each stimulus pair. Meyer and his co-workers found that subjects were significantly faster in responding to a word that was associated with the immediately preceding word than to words that were not associated. On the average, it took a subject about 525 milliseconds to respond to a word such as *butter* if it followed a related word, such as *bread*. However, if a word such as *butter* followed an unrelated word, such as *glove,* it took subjects about 570 milliseconds to respond. These researchers concluded that "accessing information from a given memory location produces residual neural activity that spreads to other nearby locations." (p. 102) Under these conditions, faster responding occurs because less activation from the environmental stimulus

Figure 5–3
An illustration of the procedure used by Meyer et al. (1975) in a lexical decision task.

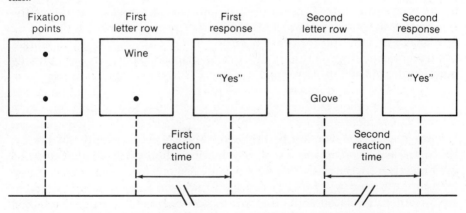

Adapted from D. Meyer, R. Schvaneveldt and M. Ruddy, "Loci of contextual effects on visual word-recognition." In P. M. A. Rabbitt and S. Dornic (Eds.), *Attention and Performance V.* Copyright 1975 by Academic Press. Reprinted by permission.

itself is required in order to energize the representation sufficiently to bring it to consciousness.

This phenomenon in which some stimulus activates its representation in the long-term store as well as the representation of semantically related stimuli (Fischler, 1977) is often referred to as *priming*. Studies have indicated that priming occurs automatically (Fischler & Goodman, 1978) and that the priming effect is temporary. The transient nature of priming has been shown by the rapid disappearance of the reaction time facilitation in this lexical decision process as the interval between presentation of a priming word (e.g., *doctor*) and a semantically associated word (e.g., *nurse*) is increased from zero to four seconds (Meyer, Schvaneveldt, & Ruddy, 1972).

Activation and the Stroop Task.   The notion that retrieval is automatic and that it activates representations in the long-term store that match the environmental stimulus can contribute to an explanation of the cognitive mechanism underlying the Stroop effect. A key assumption in the following proposal is that activation energy that contributes to making a memory representation available to consciousness can accumulate simultaneously in a number of memory representations (Morton, 1969). For example, in the Stroop task, if a subject is presented with the word *red* written in green ink, this stimulus may activate memory representations of both the concepts red and green. The subject, however, is required to speak only a single response. Compared with when only a single mental representation is strongly activated, the present situation will require a subject to engage in some extra mental processing. Whether the additional processing is devoted to inhibiting the inappropriate response (Wickelgren, 1979a, p. 280), to seeking additional information from the stimulus (Klein, 1964), or to waiting until the conflict between activated representations that are competing for a limited capacity "output buffer" is resolved (Warren, 1972), the subject's response will be delayed since mental processing takes time.

Retrieval Cues

Up to now it has been implied that retrieval is triggered only by information in the sensory stores. It will be proposed here, however, that information in the long-term store can also be retrieved by information that is being held in the short-term store. Since the short-term store is being treated as equivalent to consciousness, the proposal being made is that information that a person is conscious of will be capable of retrieving matching information from the long-term store.

Such a process may at first seem to be of little consequence, for if a person is conscious of a stimulus, the long-term representation must already have been retrieved; what good could it do to keep retrieving it? To see the value of such a mechanism, attempt the following task. Name three words that begin with the letters *gl*. Perhaps in a first attempt to do this you generate the sounds of these two letters to yourself. If no words come to mind perhaps you then make up some other sounds and add these onto the *gl* sound. For example, you may add the sound *uh* to *gl* to produce *gluh*. When you do this, the word *glove* might come to mind. Gruneberg (Gruneberg & Sykes, 1978) has reported the use of a similar strategy by subjects who have developed memory blocks in memory experiments. When a subject is unable to recall some information that he feels he knows—for example, the name of a relative or the capital of a country—one method used to counteract the memory block is to generate letters of the alphabet and thus "trigger off the missing word" (Gruneberg & Sykes, 1978, p. 190). Harris (1980) similarly reports that in a questionnaire study of memory aids people use, this strategy of producing letters to help trigger retrieval is one of the two most popular memory aids.

The strategy of consciously generating information is useful because one can end up with more than one starts with. In the above example, starting with an awareness of just the first letters of a word or with some of its sounds, an entire word was obtained from memory. This occurred because there are associations in the long-term store. What we think of as being a single stimulus, the word *glove,* for example, may instead be considered a series of sounds that have become associated together in the long-term store. Hebb (1949) was making a similar assumption when he described the mental representation of a triangle as consisting of several cell assemblies, each representing a feature of the triangle. In the retrieval process, activation of just a portion of such an associative network in the long-term store may cause closely associated information also to become activated. Information in the short-term store that retrieves information from the long-term store this way will be referred to as a *retrieval cue.*

Factors That Affect a Retrieval Cue's Effectiveness

An important prerequisite for successful retrieval must be mentioned before presenting the three factors that determine a retrieval cue's effectiveness. The prerequisite is that the information contained in the cue be present in the long-term store and be associated there with the to-be-recalled stimulus. For instance, if someone is to use the information "a tool used to drive nails" as a retrieval cue for the word *hammer,* the long-term store must contain a representation of the word *hammer* to which is attached the information that a hammer is a tool and that it is used to drive nails. Similarly, if a subject in an experiment is to use the contextual information "words learned at the beginning of the experiment" as a retrieval cue, the subject must have associated this learning context with the representation of the words in the long-term store.

This can be stated more abstractly. Let us say that a person has stored information in the long-term store, and let us refer to this information with the letter A. Let us also assume that associated with information A in this person's long-term store is other information that we will label with the letter B. According to the proposals made in the preceding section, information B can be retrieved by presenting this person with information A. Here, information A is acting as a retrieval cue for information B.

The Match between Information in the Cue and Information in Memory

Let us assume now that a person has information A and B associated together in the long-term store. An important factor that will influence the effectiveness of a retrieval cue is the extent to which information contained in the retrieval cue matches information associated with the to-be-remembered information. In terms of our abstract notation, if information B must be retrieved, then retrieval will be more probable when the retrieval cue consists of information A rather than information A'. (Information that resembles A but is not identical to it will be referred to as A'.)

People often make use of this principle when they have lost something and are trying to remember what they did with it. For example, if you find your wallet is missing, you may at first have absolutely no idea where you could have left it. To help you remember, you may resort to mentally retracing your actions during the day. In this process you may perhaps remember having gone into a bank to get money. This information may remind you that you opened your wallet on the way out of the bank and that you thought how worn and shabby your wallet was getting. Information such as this is being retrieved now because you have a retrieval cue that matches information associated with a particular encounter with your wallet. In terms of our notational scheme, this strategy of retracing actions can be conceived of as a process of generating information A that has previously been associated with information B, the information whose retrieval is now being attempted. The effectiveness of this strategy is attested to by its popularity. Harris' (1980) survey data shows that this memory aid was used at least once by nearly all persons interviewed, and was used more than once a week by about 30 percent of these people.

State-Dependent Remembering.   Another illustration of how retrieval is enhanced when the information in the cue matches the information associated with a desired memory comes from the phenomenon of *state-dependent remembering*. An assumption often made by memory theorists (e.g., Anderson & Bower, 1973) is that when a person stores information in the long-term store, information about the learning context is also stored with, that is, associated with, that information. Thus, if a person is attempting to learn a list of words on a sunny day while feeling happy, not only will information about the words be stored, but also information about the person's mood and surroundings. This contextual information will be attached to the information about each word. Studies of state-dependent remembering have confirmed this by showing that recall of information is enhanced when the retrieval cue contains contextual information that matches the contextual information that prevailed when the material was learned. The following case illustrates this phenomenon. It describes the conditions under which Sirhan Sirhan, Bobby Kennedy's assassin, recalled the events of the murder.

> Interestingly, Sirhan had absolutely no recollection of the actual murder, which occurred in the small kitchen of the Ambassador Hotel where he pumped several bullets into Kennedy. Sirhan carried out the deed in a greatly agitated state and was completely amnesic with regard to the event. Diamond [a forensic psychiatrist], called in by Sirhan's attorneys, hypnotized Sirhan and helped him to reconstruct from memory the events of that fateful day. Under hypnosis, as Sirhan became more worked up and excited, he recalled progressively more, the memories tumbling out while his excitement built to a crescendo leading up to the shooting. At that point Sirhan would scream out the death curses, "fire" the shots, and then choke as he reexperienced the Secret Service bodyguard nearly throttling him after he was caught. On different occasions, while in a trance, Sirhan was able to recall the crucial events, sometimes speaking, other times recording his recollections in automatic writing, but the recall was always accompanied by great excitement. (Bower, 1981, p. 129)

An experimental investigation of state-dependent remembering has been reported by Bower (1981). Using hypnosis to induce a happy or sad mood in his subjects, Bower demonstrated that recall of an incident is facilitated when the subject's mood during retrieval is the same as the mood that prevailed when the incident occurred. In one experiment, subjects were asked to keep a diary of their important emotional experiences. Each day for one week, subjects recorded these events and rated each on a 10-point scale that ranged from pleasant to unpleasant. Seven days after turning the completed diaries over to the experimenters, the subjects returned to the experiment. All 14 subjects were hypnotized. A good mood was induced in half of these subjects by having them remember or imagine a scene in which they were very happy. The other subjects were asked to imagine or remember a scene in which they were very sad. After reexperiencing the mood for one minute, subjects were asked to maintain that disposition while recalling as many incidents as possible from their diaries. The subjects' mood had a sizeable effect on the type of incident recalled. When subjects were in a sad mood, they recalled about 12 percent more unpleasant than pleasant incidents. On the other hand, when subjects were in a happy mood, they recalled about 30 percent more pleasant than unpleasant incidents.

The subjects in this experiment of Bower's were a bit unusual in that they were among the 20–25 percent of the population that is highly susceptible to hypnosis. Other experiments indicate, however, that the phenomenon of state-dependent remembering is not restricted to just highly hypnotizable people. For example, in an experiment by Rand and Wapner (1967) subjects were required to learn a list of six nonsense syllables, such as DAX and NIR, while in one of two positions—either standing up or lying down. After completing this task, subjects performed another unrelated task for 15 minutes. As the experimenters had expected, some forgetting of the six nonsense stimuli took place during this 15-minute period. Subjects were then asked to relearn the same set of six nonsense syllables. The crucial manipulation in this experiment was the position the subjects assumed in these relearning trials. When they relearned the lists in the same body positions they had assumed during the first learning session, fewer relearning trials were required. Thus, if subjects first learned the list lying down, they relearned the words faster when they were lying down rather than standing up during the relearning session. On the average, when a list was relearned in the same body position that had been assumed during original learning, 3.25 trials were required. However, when body position differed during original learning and relearning, 4.45 relearning trials were required. This finding is consistent with the view that subjects were associating the learning context with information about the nonsense syllables. Retrieval of these nonsense syllables was consequently facilitated when the context during the relearning task matched the context of the original learning.

A number of other studies have indicated that some drugs can produce a similar effect on recall. For example, if a person consumes alcohol, recall for information learned under intoxication will be better when the person is intoxicated during the recall attempt rather than sober. The same, of course, applies to a person who learns material while sober: The material will be most successfully retrieved when the person is in a sober rather than an intoxicated state. A study by Eich (1976, cited in Eich, 1980) illustrates this drug-induced effect. The subjects in Eich's study were male college students. All students studied a list of 24 common English words shortly after smoking a marijuana cigarette containing 15 milligrams of THC (the active ingredient in marijuana). A free recall test for these words was subsequently given to these subjects, half of whom were again in a state of marijuana intoxication and half of whom were not. Subjects who were intoxicated both at study and test recalled an average of about 32 percent of the words. Those who were not intoxicated during the test recalled only about 20 percent of the words. These results, again, conform to the principle that retrieval is most successful when the information in the cue matches the information in the memory trace. It is generally acknowledged that state-dependent remembering can be accounted for using this principle (Eich, 1980; Swanson & Kinsbourne, 1979).

Environmental Context Effects. In experimental studies that investigate the phenomenon of state-dependent remembering, subjects' internal states are manipulated using methods such as hypnosis or drug administration. As mentioned in the preceding section, the general finding is that better memory performance results when a person's internal state at the time of recall matches the internal state that prevailed at the time of learning. A similar finding has been obtained when a person's external rather than internal environment is manipulated. For example, Godden and Baddeley (1975) had students in a university diving club learn some lists of words on land and other lists while submerged under water. When memory was tested using a free recall procedure (the divers wrote answers on weighted boards when they were under water), it was found that performance was significantly better when the test environment matched the environment in which learning had occurred (34.6 percent of the words were recalled) rather than when the two environments differed (23.6 percent of the words were recalled). Smith, Glenberg, and Bjork (1978, experiment 4) obtained similar results using a much less drastic environmental manipulation. They had subjects study a list of words in one room of a university building and free-recall the words about 24 hours later either in the same room or in another room in the building. The two environments were made to be noticeably different. One had bare walls, a tiled floor, and much experimental equipment strewn about. The experimenter wore jeans and a t-shirt and conducted sessions just during the morning hours. The other room had posters and pictures on the walls and a carpeted floor. There were books and plants arranged in the room and a faint smell of perfume in the air. The experimenter wore a suit and tie and conducted sessions only during the afternoon. The results of the recall test showed that performance was about 50 percent better when the testing environment matched the learning environment: Subjects recalled about 12 percent of the words when the environments matched and 9 percent when the environments differed. These results again conform to the principle that retrieval is enhanced to the extent that information in the retrieval cue matches information associated with the to-be-retrieved information in memory. That is, in these two experiments, it seems as though environmental information became stored with information about the words during the study sessions. This environmental information, when present at the time of testing, became a part of the retrieval cue and helped to enhance the match between the cue and the memory trace information.

Amount of Matching Information in the Long-Term Store: The Cue Overload Principle

Another factor that affects the probability of a cue's successfully retrieving a memory is the number of different representations in the long-term store that contain information that matches the information in the cue. For example, if the long-term store contains the associated information A–B and also the associated information A–C, then the retrieval cue A will match parts of both of these sets of long-term traces. In general, the more of these different sets of traces (A–B, A–C, A–D, etc.) there are in the long-term store, the less effective a cue will be in retrieving any one of them.

As an illustration of this principle, suppose you take a psychology class in which you learn the definition of the term that refers to the forgetting of information that results from subsequently learned information. Imagine that you later encounter this definition in a quiz and are asked to supply the appropriate term. Perhaps after reading the definition, you can't immediately recall the term but you do remember certain things about it. You remember that the term consists of two words, the first beginning with the letters "ret" and the second beginning with a vowel. This information can be thought of now as a retrieval cue. According to the principle being discussed here, your chances of successfully using this cue to retrieve the proper term will be diminished if, in addition to previously having encountered the correct term (retroactive interference), you have also encountered a term that is inappropriate for the question being asked, but that matches the retrieval cue (e.g., retrograde amnesia).

A great many experiments have obtained data that conforms to this principle. Many of these experiments have utilized paired-associate lists. In an experiment performed by Underwood (1945), for example, subjects learned a list of 10 adjective pairs, such as *strident–flabby* and *overt–rural*. Then they learned either zero, two, four, or six additional lists. These additional lists all utilized exactly the same set of stimulus words (the first word in each pair). The lists differed only in that each had new response words paired with the stimulus words. Thus, list 1 might have contained the paired associate *strident–flabby*, list 2, *strident–hasty*, list 3, *strident–futile*, and so on. Successive paired-associate lists like this in which the same set of stimulus words is paired with new responses in each list are often referred to using the letters A–B, A–C, A–D, and so forth. The object of Underwood's (1945) experiment was to determine the effect of learning lists A–C, A–D, A–E, and so forth on the ability of a subject to retrieve the originally learned responses, B, when provided with the stimulus words, A. Underwood found that when a stimulus word had been associated with seven different response words, subjects who were presented with the stimulus word were almost never able to remember immediately the first word that had been associated with it. However, when subjects did not learn any lists after the first A–B list, but instead engaged in an irrelevant task for the same period of time that would have been required to study six additional lists, they successfully recalled the responses to more than 40 percent of the stimulus words. This shows that a cue becomes less effective in retrieving a memory from the long-term store when there exists in the store a number of distinct memories each associated with information represented in the cue.

What mechanism is responsible for this retrieval failure? Watkins and Watkins (1976) have suggested that an important cause of forgetting in this sort of experiment is *cue overload*. This term, cue overload, implies that a retrieval cue has only a certain amount of energy available to activate representations in the long-term store. As the number of memory representations that match the cue increases, this energy gets increasingly more spread out. Each activated representation, then, gets less strongly aroused the more representations there are that match the cue. In our tuning fork analogy, this is equivalent to having a vibrating tuning fork (the cue) surrounded by a circle of identical tuning forks (the long-term memories) that match the vibrating tuning fork. If we stipulate that the size of the circle must increase when more tuning forks are present in the long-term store that match the vibrating tuning fork, then each tuning fork in this set will be moved further away from the vibrating tuning fork and consequently be less strongly activated by it. From now on the principle that a cue will be less effective in retrieving a memory trace when there are other similar traces in the long-term store will be referred to as the cue overload principle.

In the experiment by Underwood (1945) that was just described, the extraneous information that eventually overloaded a retrieval cue was learned *after* the to-be-recalled information had been learned. As mentioned previously, forgetting that is produced in this way is referred to as retroactive interference. It is also possible to produce cue overload from information learned *prior to* the presentation of to-be-recalled information. Forgetting that is due to previous learning is termed *proactive interference*. One experimental demonstration of proactive interference was reported by Underwood (1945). In this study, as in the one just described, all subjects learned a list of 10 adjective pairs to a criterion of 60 percent correct. (This criterion means that subjects were able to provide correct responses to at least 6 of the 10 stimulus words.) We will refer to this list of adjective pairs as list A–B. After learning list A–B, subjects were kept busy for 25 minutes with a task that was unrelated to the A–B learning task and then were tested on list A–B. As in the previous study, the test required the subjects to provide the B response words when the A words were presented. The issue this experiment addressed was how forgetting of this A–B list varied as a function of the number of previously learned lists. Subjects had learned either zero, two, four, or six lists prior to learning list A–B. These previously learned lists all contained the same stimulus words used in the A–B list. Thus, in terms of symbols, subjects who had learned six interfering lists first learned lists A–C, A–D, A–E, A–F, A–G, and A–H, and then list A–B. The results of the test on list A–B showed that forgetting of the *B* response terms increased with the number of previous lists the subject had learned. When subjects had learned no lists prior to list A–B, they recalled correct responses to about 40 percent of the stimulus words. On the other extreme, when subjects had learned six previous lists, their performance fell to slightly under 20 percent correct.

Both proactive and retroactive interference illustrate the principle that a retrieval cue becomes less effective in retrieving an individual memory when there is an increase in the number of long-term memories containing information that matches the information in the cue. It must be mentioned that although the two experimental examples that were just presented both utilized a paired-associate learning procedure, the cue overload principle is not restricted to this particular paradigm. One can also observe the effects of cue overload when a list of *individual* words is either preceded (Craik & Birtwistle, 1971) or followed (Watkins & Watkins, 1976) by another list of individual words. For example, Craik and Birtwistle (1971) presented subjects with eight lists of 15 common unrelated words, each list for immediate free-recall. Approximately 8.5 words were recalled from the first list, but only about 5.5 were recalled from the eighth list. The increased forgetting over the eight lists was probably due in large part to cue overload. In this case, the cue that became overloaded most likely contained information about the learning context, which words from all lists had in common. That is, since words from all eight lists were learned in the same experimental setting, information about the setting can be assumed to have become associated with each word. Attempts to recall words from the most recently presented list using a cue such as "words I learned today in this room" would be subject to increasingly more cue overload as the experiment progressed, for the cue would contact more matching traces after eight rather than just one list had been learned.

The Number of Memories a Cue Has Retrieved: Blocking

A third factor that influences a cue's ability to retrieve a particular memory trace is the number of other memory traces the cue has already retrieved. The more items a cue has already retrieved, the less it will be able to retrieve additional items. Because access to these additional unretrieved items seems to have been blocked by the items that have already been retrieved, we will refer to this forgetting phenomenon as *blocking*.

Most of us have experienced blocking. Perhaps in attempting to recall the name of a friend we have not seen or thought about for many years, we inadvertantly retrieve the name of some other old friend. Now, every attempt to recall the name we are searching for only brings this inappropriate name to mind. Our failure to retrieve the correct name is being blocked by the other name we have retrieved.

This phenomenon of blocking has been demonstrated experimentally. In one experiment (Karchmer & Winograd, 1971), American college students were given a list of 25 of the 50 states in the United States to study for five minutes. A second group of subjects studied names of the other 25 states. After the study period, both groups wrote down as many of the names of these states as they could recall. In the three minutes allowed, these subjects recalled most of the 25 names they had studied. Then, the subjects were asked to write down the names of states that they had *not* studied. Of the 25 states they had not studied, each group recalled an average of 17.81 names. A control group, however, that had not previously studied a set of 25 states names and was asked to write down as many state names as possible, recalled an average of 20.96 names from each of the two sets of 25. Thus, the subjects who studied and first recalled the names of certain states recalled 17 percent fewer of the remaining states as compared with the control group. It seems that the act of recalling half the names from the set of 50 states tended to block the retrieval of names of the other 25 states.

It has proven possible to produce blocking by having an experimenter provide subjects with items that match a cue instead of having the subjects actually recall these blocking items themselves. As an example of this sort of situation, if you are trying to retrieve the name of an old friend and an inappropriate name is provided to you by someone else, that inappropriate name will be capable of exerting a blocking effect. This should not be surprising since a retrieval process will be involved even if another person supplies the name; that is, you will have to retrieve this inappropriate name from your long-term store in the process of identifying the sounds that form the name. Allan Brown (1979) has provided an experimental demonstration that blocking can be produced this way. He presented subjects with a single word and then a definition. For example, he might have shown subjects the word *shorthand* and then the definition, "a system of printing and writing for blind persons making use of raised dots." Subjects had to decide whether the word suited the definition. If it did not, they were to provide the correct word. Brown found that when the single word was not correct but was related to the correct word, subjects failed to retrieve the correct word more often than when the single word was unrelated to the correct word. In the present example, the correct word subjects should have supplied was *braille.* The subjects were less successful in retrieving the word *braille* when they had been shown the related word *shorthand* rather than an unrelated word such as *cantaloupe.* For the 32 different definitions in the study, subjects retrieved the correct responses 89.37 percent of the time when an unrelated word was presented, but only 85.94 percent of the time when a related word was presented. The related word evidently blocked the ability of the retrieval cue (the definition) successfully to retrieve the appropriate response from memory. Additional evidence of blocking was obtained using a reaction time measure. Brown found that the average time to provide the correct response for a definition was 5.56 seconds when a neutral word had been presented with a definition. However, when a related word had been presented, it took subjects an average of 7.37 seconds to provide the correct word. Brown also found that there was more blocking as the number of related words presented just before the definition increased. For example, if subjects first saw the three words *elbow, wrist, knee,* then the definition "the joint between the foot and the leg," it took them longer to retrieve the correct word, *ankle,* than when just the word *wrist* had been presented. Average reaction time for the three-related-word condition was 6.89 seconds; average reaction time for the single-related-word condition was 5.16 seconds.

This blocking effect, which is also known as retrieval inhibition, has been found in numerous experiments (e.g., A. Brown, 1981; J. Brown, 1968; Watkins, 1975). An account offered by Rundus (1973) attributes blocking to an increase in the strength of a retrieved representation. Since a retrieval cue will most readily retrieve a strong representation in memory, further use of the cue will favor a re-retrieval of already retrieved representations. Rundus proposes that when a retrieval cue is no longer likely to contact new memories, further retrieval attempts will be abandoned. Other explanations of this phenomenon have been proposed by Raaijmakers and Shiffrin (1981) and Mueller and Watkins (1977).

In terms of our tuning fork analogy, we can perhaps think of blocking as occurring in the following way. A set of silent tuning forks initially surrounds a vibrating tuning fork that is acting as a retrieval cue. Should one of the tuning forks in the silent set get activated by the cue, this tuning fork may be envisioned to move closer to the vibrating tuning fork and to displace the remaining tuning forks in the silent set to positions further away from the cue. The increased distance of the silent tuning forks from the cue will now lessen the cue's ability to activate them.

Applying the Retrieval Factors to Experimental Findings

The three factors that affect retrieval underlie a number of remembering phenomena. In this section some experimental findings will be described and then analyzed in terms of these retrieval factors. We will see that a wide variety of results can be accounted for in a general way with these factors. We will begin with experimental outcomes that exemplify the principle that retrieval is most successful when information in the cue closely matches information contained in the memory trace.

The Match between Information in the Cue and in Memory

In a study by Anderson and Pichert (1978), two groups of subjects were given a story to read. One of these subject groups was instructed to read it from the perspective of a burglar. Here is part of the story:

> The two boys ran until they came to the driveway. "See, I told you today was good for skipping school," said Mark. "Mom is never home on Thursday," he added. Tall hedges hid the house from the road. The pair strolled across the finely landscaped yard. "I never knew your place was so big," said Pete. "Yeah, but it's nicer now than it used to be since Dad had the new stone siding put on and added the fireplace.". . . There were three upstairs bedrooms. Mark showed Pete his mother's closet which was filled with furs and the locked box which held her jewels. His sisters' room was uninteresting except for the color TV which Mark carried to his room. Mark bragged that the bathroom in the hall was his since one had been added to his sisters' room for their use. The big highlight in his room, though, was a leak in the ceiling where the old roof had finally rotted. (Pichert & Anderson, 1977, p. 310)

A 12-minute period of unrelated activity followed the subjects' reading of the story. Subjects were then asked to write down as much of the story as they could remember. Five minutes after this first recall period had ended, subjects were instructed to recall the whole story a second time. The critical manipulation in this study was the instruction to half of the subjects in each group to alter their perspective on this second recall attempt. Half the subjects who had originally studied and recalled the passage from the perspective of a burglar were now instructed to adopt the perspective of a potential homebuyer. As a result of adopting this new perspective, these subjects showed an increase in their recall of information relevant to the homebuyer perspective (e.g., information about the number of rooms, size of the lawn, condition of the roof). It should be noted that the other group in the experiment adopted these two perspectives in the opposite order. They began with the homebuyer perspective and just before the second recall, half of the group switched to the burglar perspective. On the average, subjects who changed perspective on the second recall exhibited up to a 10-percent increase in recall of information relevant to the new perspective, while subjects who maintained the same perspective on the second recall showed about a 3-percent decrease in information recalled that was relevant to the other (never-mentioned) perspective.

Why did shifting perspectives allow subjects to recall information that they had previously been unable to remember? The reason must be that the new perspective allowed subjects to generate retrieval cues that better matched the previously unretrieved information in memory. For example, a subject who read and first recalled the story from the perspective of a homebuyer might have originally generated retrieval cues suitable for extracting information about such things as the condition of the house, the size of the property, and the number of rooms in the house. Such cues, however, would not be well-suited to retrieve information that may have been of concern to a burglar, such as whether the house was hidden from the road and whether it was occupied when the boys arrived. When a subject adopts a burglar's perspective, questions such as this become relevant.

What information did subjects put into their retrieval cues? It is hard to determine this precisely. However, based on interviews Anderson and Pichert conducted with some of their subjects after the experiment was over, it appears that subjects often imagined themselves in the role of either a homebuyer or a burglar and then generated questions that they knew would have been of concern to a person playing that role. Here is a transcript of some of these interviews.

—You say "OK, I'm a burglar, now what do I want to get out of this house," and then you write it down . . . I knew that there were a lot of things, like furs and stuff, that had been described, but I couldn't remember them because I wasn't programmed that way the first time. I ended up putting pretty much what I put the first time. I remembered that one of the doors was kept unlocked. I hadn't remembered that the first time but when it said I was supposed to be a burglar that popped into my head. [*Q: Why do you think that popped into your head?*] Well, because a burglar would want to know that!

—Well, a funny thing happened. When he gave me the homebuyer perspective, I remembered the end of the story, you know, about the leak in the roof. The first time through I knew there was an ending, but I couldn't remember what it was. But it just popped into my mind when I thought about the story from the homebuyer perspective. (Anderson & Pichert, 1978, pp. 9–10)

The Flexibility of Encoding.   It must be emphasized again that people can be quite flexible in the way they process information. Two people who encounter the same stimuli may store different information about it. This, of course, will have an effect on the type of cues that will allow a person to retrieve the information successfully. Again, we can say that the best retrieval cue will be one that matches information a subject has stored in memory.

What determines the information a person chooses to store? In a previous discussion of Frost's experiment, it was mentioned that people will store information they judge will be useful in the future. Another more direct influence on how a subject in a memory experiment encodes information is simply the instructions the experimenter provides. For example, in the Anderson and Pichert (1978) study, instructions about the perspective that was to be taken no doubt had a strong influence on the information a subject stored. (One interesting aspect of this study is that subjects evidently stored not only information relevant to their perspective, but some other information as well. Their experiment showed that with the proper cues, this other information can also be retrieved.)

Some other studies will now be described that will illustrate people's flexibility in encoding information and the importance of there being a match between information in a retrieval cue and information in memory. Imagine that you have just read a list of words that includes the word *piano.* Which cue do you think would be more effective in allowing you to recall your having encountered the word *piano:* the phrase "something with a nice sound," or the phrase "something heavy"? A study by Barclay and co-workers (Barclay, Bransford, Franks, McCarrell, & Nitsch, 1974) showed that the effectiveness of a recall cue can be strongly influenced by the context in which a person studies a word. In the experiment, two groups of subjects read a short list of sentences. One group read sentences such as "The man lifted the piano" and "The camper escaped from the animal." The other group read different versions of these sentences. They read sentences such as "The man tuned the piano" and "The camper petted the animal." Three minutes after reading all sentences, subjects were given a list of cues to help them recall certain critical nouns from each sentence (these nouns arc the words *piano* and *animal* in our two examples). As an example, the word *piano* was cued with the phrases "something heavy" and "something with a nice sound." The word *animal* was cued with the phrases "something friendly" and "something ferocious." The two cues were not provided consecutively in the test, but instead were separated by a number of cues for other nouns; the experimenter had informed subjects before the test that each noun might be cued more than once. You'll notice that both groups of subjects in this experiment were attempting to recall exactly the same critical nouns. However, the context in which these critical nouns occurred in the experiment differed, and these differences were reflected in the two cues: One cue in each pair was appropriate to each word's context and the other was inappropriate. Barclay et al. found that appropriate cues were effective significantly more often (47 percent of the time) than inappropriate cues (16 percent of the time).

This result is interesting because it shows that the same word can be interpreted in different ways depending on the context in which it occurs. When the word piano is encountered in the context of an object to be lifted, information about its weight tends to be stored in preference to information about its musical properties. Information about a piano's sound is emphasized when the context calls attention to its musical qualities. Again, we can see that people can be flexible in the information they store in memory. Even a concrete, unambiguous concept can be thought of as consisting of a variety of attributes. The attributes that arc stored will be affected by context. The information that is stored, in turn, will determine what cues will be most effective in the retrieval process. In the Barclay et al. experiment, appropriate cues better matched the information that subjects had stored in memory. As a result, these appropriate cues were best able to retrieve the stored information.

Consider another experimental finding, one that has been described by Watkins and Tulving (1975) in the following way:

> Recent experiments on human memory have demonstrated a curious phenomenon: People can recall a word they studied earlier, but they cannot recognize it. In these experiments, a person sees a word such as *chair* among other to-be-remembered words, and later on sees the same word *chair* in a recognition test. He looks at the test word *chair,* decides that it was not in the list he had studied earlier, and proceeds to examine other items. A short while later, however, when he is asked to recall all of the words from the list he had studied, he will put down, among other words, the word *chair.* (p. 6)

This result is unusual because it is generally found that a person performs better on recognition tests than on recall tests. This is why students often prefer to take a multiple choice exam rather than an essay exam.

To understand better why subjects in Watkins and Tulving's (1975) experiment performed better on a recall than a recognition test, some details of the experimental procedure must be presented. Subjects in this experiment (experiment 5) first learned a list of 24 paired associates, such as *ground–cold, lady–queen*, and *crust–cake*. The word pairs were presented once at a three-second rate, and subjects were instructed to try to learn to associate each response word with its stimulus word. After this study session, subjects were engaged in an irrelevant task for 12 minutes and then given a recognition test. On the recognition test, subjects circled words that they recognized as being response words from the previously studied list. Of the 24 response words included on the test (the test also contained new words), approximately 60 percent were correctly recognized. However, when subjects were next supplied with all 24 stimulus words (e.g., *ground, lady, crust*) and asked to recall the proper response words, they were able to provide about 73 percent of them. Thus, they recalled more words than they recognized.

Why was recall performance here higher than recognition performance? Tulving has proposed that this, as well as some other related findings (Thomson & Tulving, 1970; Tulving, 1968; Tulving & Thomson, 1973; Watkins, 1974a), can be attributed to the relation between information in a retrieval cue and information that has been stored in memory. Tulving has stated this relation in his *encoding specificity principle:* "Specific encoding operations performed on what is perceived determine what is stored, and what is stored determines what retrieval cues are effective in providing access to what is stored" (Tulving & Thomson, 1973, p. 36). It should be realized that implicit in the encoding specificity principle is the assertion that retrieval will be most effective when the cue contains information that matches information stored in the to-be-remembered trace. How does this explain the results of the Watkins and Tulving experiment? One explanation (Reder, Anderson, & Bjork, 1974) is that the information a subject stores about the response word is considerably different when the word is encountered in the context of the stimulus word as opposed to when it is encountered in isolation. For example, different information about the word *cold* is stored when it is studied in the context of the word *ground* as opposed to when it is studied by itself. When a word has been studied in the context of another word, such as in Watkins and Tulving's (1975) experiment, a retrieval cue consisting of just the response word itself will not be maximally effective in contacting a memory of the encounter with the word. It's as if the word *cold* by itself is a different concept than the word *cold* in the context of the word *ground*. If information supplied by each retrieval cue in a recognition test is sufficiently different from the information a subject has stored during the learning process, performance on the recognition test will suffer. Performance on this recognition test can fall below the level attained with a cued recall test if the recall test provides cues that better match the to-be-remembered memories. Evidently, this is what occurred in Watkins and Tulving's (1975) experiment. Again, this conforms to the principle that retrieval is affected by the extent to which information in a cue matches information in the long-term store.

Cue Overload

The List Length Effect. Before summarizing an experiment by Murdock (1962), I will describe the serial position effect because it will aid in understanding the figure used to present Murdock's data. Many memory experiments require that a list of words be studied and then free-recalled immediately. For example, a subject may be presented with a list of 20 common English words and, as soon as the last word has been presented, attempt to free-recall them. One aspect of the free-recall process that has been of interest to psychologists is the effect of order of presentation of the words on the probability of free-recall; that is, experimenters have wanted to know how well the first word in the list is recalled, how well the second word is recalled, and so on. A great many experiments have consistently found that the words in the middle of a list are recalled the least often, while the first and last few words in a list are recalled most often. When these recall data are plotted as shown in Figure 5–4, a U-shaped function results. This variation in recall with order of presentation is known as the *serial position effect.*

In Murdock's (1962) experiment, subjects were presented with lists of varying lengths; the experiment included 20-, 30-, and 40-item lists. After hearing the words in a list, subjects free-recalled them. Murdock found that the longer a list, the lower the probability of recalling any particular word from it. This phenomenon of decreased probability of recall with increased number of items in a list is known as the *list length effect.* Murdock's data are shown in Figure 5–4 in the form of serial position curves, one for each list length. It can be seen that recall of all three list lengths exhibited the serial position effect. Of relevance to the manipulation of list length, however, is the fact that the serial position curve for the 20-item list is higher overall than that for the 30-item list, which, in turn, is higher than that for the 40-item list.

What causes the list length effect? Watkins and Watkins (1976) have suggested that it is due to cue overload. That is, they suggest that in the free-recall process a subject uses a retrieval cue such as "words I learned in

Figure 5–4
Serial position curves for lists of different lengths.

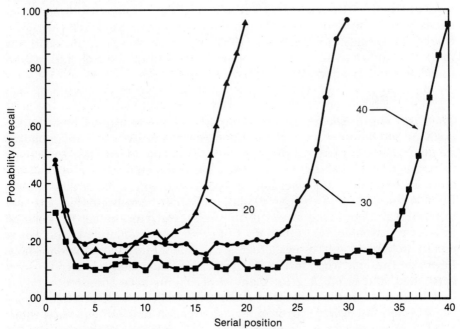

Adapted from B. B. Murdock, "The serial position effect of free recall." *Journal of Experimental Psychology,* 1962, 5, 482–488. Copyright 1966 by the Americal Psychological Association. Reprinted by permission of publisher and author.

the list I just studied." Because more words are subsumed by this cue when the list is longer, this cue, or any equivalent one the subject uses, will become overloaded and less efficient in retrieving list words.

It must be pointed out that the list length effect does not apply to words from the last few positions of a list. This can be seen in Figure 5–4, which shows that the last few words are recalled equally often from lists of 20, 30, and 40 words. The reason for this is that words from the end of a list are not typically being recalled from the long-term store. Thus, they are not influenced by the retrieval factors that we have discussed. More will be said about this in the next chapter.

Buildup and Release from Proactive Interference.   A study by Craik and Birtwistle (1971) will now be described and analyzed once again in terms of the cue overload principle. Subjects in this study were first read a list of 15 words from one conceptual category. For example, the subjects may have heard a list of 15 animal names. Immediately after hearing the list, subjects free-recalled them. Then a second list of 15 new words from the same category was read. Subjects again free-recalled these words after hearing all 15. This process was repeated for a total of four lists. Craik and Birtwistle found that recall performance was best for the first list, but declined steadily for the second, third, and fourth list. How can this decline in performance be explained? Again, we can suggest that retrieval cues were becoming overloaded as subjects learned more words from the same category. Thus, when subjects had learned only one list of animal names, the cue "animal names learned in the experiment" matched only 15 items; however, this cue matched 60 items after the fourth list had been presented.

It is interesting to note that, as with Murdock's (1962) study, the decrease in recall found by Craik and Birtwistle did not apply to the last few words in each list. That is, recall of words from the last few positions in each list was not adversely affected by subjects' having studied a number of previous lists. The reason is, again, that subjects were not recalling the last words in a list from their long-term stores. Instead, these words (which, incidentally, were always the first to be recalled) were being obtained from the short-term store.

What prediction would you make about the recall performance of subjects in Craik and Birtwistle's experiment who were read a fifth list of 15 words drawn, this time, from a new conceptual category? Craik and Birtwistle included this manipulation in their experiment. Instead of presenting a fifth list of, say, animal names, they presented half the subjects with a list of 15 fruits and vegetables, while the other subjects received more words from the category of animals. On the basis of the cue overload principle, it could be expected that the recall performance of subjects given words from the new category would be restored to the level attained on the first list learned. The reason, of course, is that the new retrieval cue (e.g., "fruits and vegetable names I just studied") would apply just to 15 items in memory. Thus, the cue would not be as overloaded as the one utilized for the recall of words from the fourth list. As the data in Figure 5–5 show, this is exactly what Craik and Birtwistle found. The solid lines in this figure represent words recalled from the long-term store. Craik and Birtwistle attributed recall of words to the long-term store if sufficient time and activity had intervened between a word's presentation and its recall so as to ensure that the word was no longer present in a person's short-term store. Since cue overload is a long-term store phenomenon, we would expect only information that is being recalled from the long-term store to be affected by the experimental manipulations used here. Indeed, Figure 5–5 shows that for all subjects, information from just the long-term store was less likely to be recalled the more similar lists a subject had learned previously. Since this steady decrease in memory performance results from an accumulation of previously learned information, it is referred to as a *buildup of proactive interference.* Figure 5–5 also clearly shows how memory performance on list 5 suddenly improved for the subjects who studied new material. This sudden improvement in memory that results from a change in the nature of material being learned is termed *release from proactive interference.*

Blocking

Output Interference. Much earlier in this text, in the section on the iconic store, a memory phenomenon was described that must at the time have seemed rather bizarre. This was the phenomenon of *output interference,*

Figure 5–5
Number of words recalled as a function of number of lists studied. Solid lines represent words recalled from the long-term store; dotted lines represent words recalled from the short-term store; triangles represent words recalled when all five lists are drawn from the same conceptual category; circles represent words recalled when the fifth list consists of words drawn from a different category than used in the four prior lists.

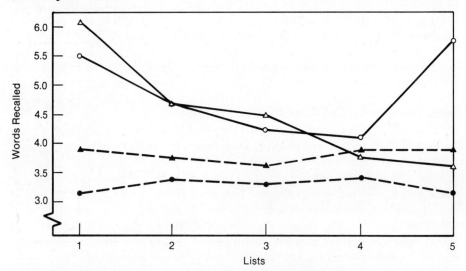

Adapted from F. I. M. Craik and J. Birtwistle, "Proactive inhibition in free recall." *Journal of Experimental Psychology,* 1971, *91,* 120–123. Copyright 1971 by the American Psychological Association. Reprinted by permission of publisher and author.

the finding that the act of recalling some items from a list will lower the chances of recalling any other items. We will now consider this form of forgetting in more detail by examining an experiment by Smith (1971). Smith's work (Smith, 1971; Smith, D'Agistino, & Reid, 1970) has been influential in calling the attention of psychologists to output interference for information in the long-term store.

In Smith's (1971) experiment, subjects were first told that words from seven different categories were going to be presented. The categories named were animals, trees, sports, vegetables, insects, occupations, and vehicles. Subjects were then shown a list of words made up of groups of seven words from each of these categories. Thus, a subject may have seen a list consisting of seven animal names, then seven tree names, then seven sports, and so on. After seeing all 49 of these words, subjects were presented with the seven category names, one at a time. Each category name served as a cue for the subject to recall words from that category. Smith found that the order in which the cues were presented made a significant difference in a subject's performance. As can be seen in Figure 5–6, the later in the recall sequence a cue was presented, the fewer words from the cued category a subject could recall.

Figure 5–6
The number of words recalled per category as a function of the position of the category in the testing sequence.

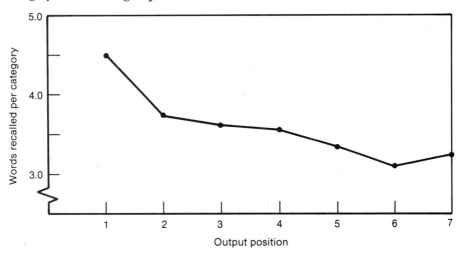

Adapted from A. D. Smith, "Output interference and organized recall from long-term memory. *Journal of Verbal Learning and Verbal Behavior,* 1971, *10,* 400–408.

It should be noted that Smith had been very careful to control for the order in which categories had been learned. To achieve this control, he had varied the order in which different subjects had learned the seven categories. Thus, for some subjects, the seven words in the animal category had been learned first; for other subjects, these words had been the second set of seven that were learned; for other subjects, they were the third set learned, and so on. Smith had also been careful to control for the order in which categories of words were tested. Again, he achieved this control by testing some subjects with the category "animals" first, while some subjects were tested on this category second, and so on. Thus, what Smith's data show are that, no matter what order a subject learned information, and what category of words they had learned, the later in the output sequence any of the categories was tested, the more poorly the subjects would recall information from the category. It seems then that the act of recalling information learned in the study interfered with the ability to recall additional information that was learned. This is what is called *output interference.*

The precise mechanism responsible for output interference has not yet been determined. However, some psychologists (e.g., Brown 1981; Roediger & Schmidt, 1980) have suggested or implied that the same mechanisms responsible for retrieval inhibition of the sort that were described in our discussion of blocking also may underlie output interference. This will be the view taken here. Output interference will be considered another manifestation of retrieval blocking. In this case, the act of recalling some words from a list in response to the experimenter-provided retrieval cue blocks a subject's ability to recall additional list words. In terms of our tuning fork analogy, we can think of this as occurring in the following way. As a result of learning a list of words, a set of labeled tuning forks is established in the long-term store, with each label representing the name of a word in the list (e.g., *lion*) and also information about the learning context. When the experimenter provides a category retrieval cue, we can think of this cue as a tuning fork established by the subject in the center of a circle of these labeled tuning forks. The category cue will contain general information such as "animal names learned in this experiment." It will contact tuning forks in the circle that contain matching information. As a result of being retrieved, though, activated labeled tuning forks will tend to block the further action of any other cue containing information relevant to words presented during the experiment. We can think of this as involving a physical rearrangement in the positions of the labeled tuning forks—the activated tuning forks will approach the center of the circle and the less activated tuning forks will be displaced to positions further away from the center. If the next category cue is tree names, the cue "tree names learned in this experiment" will not be as effective a cue as if it had been presented first, for it will take more energy to reach the appropriate labeled tuning forks in the circle.

Where might a person expect to encounter output interference outside the laboratory? Perhaps in taking tests. If a test requires a person to supply the appropriate terms that go with definitions learned in class, the person is performing a paired-associate recall task. That is, the person has previously learned to associate each term with a definition, and on the test the definition is supposed to serve as a cue for the recall of the associated term. Roediger and Schmidt (1980) have shown that one can observe output interference in cued recall tests. In their experiment (experiment 4), 20 pairs of words were presented 1 at a time to subjects for study. After the last pair had been presented, subjects were given stimulus terms one at a time for 10 seconds each and asked to supply the correct response word. Performance declined for all response words the later in the test the stimulus term was presented. For the first four stimulus words presented in the test, subjects supplied correct responses an average of 85 percent of the time; for the next four stimulus words presented, correct performance was down to 83 percent. Performance continued to decline for the third, fourth, and fifth sets of four stimulus words, falling from 80 percent to 76 percent to 73 percent correct.

The Retrieval Factors in Perspective

Of the three retrieval factors discussed, the first, the extent to which cue information matches information stored in memory, is the most fundamental and the least controversial. Without some match between cue and long-term memory information, retrieval of the memory will not occur. The second retrieval factor discussed, one that we have referred to as the cue overload principle, is more controversial, partly because it was introduced quite recently (by Watkins and Watkins in 1975) and partly because it has not been described very precisely or formally (Watkins & Watkins, 1976). However, the view taken here is that cue overload is an important and powerful concept. It should have great appeal to those interested in integrating a number of discrete memory phenomena into a more general framework. The last retrieval factor introduced, the number of items a cue has retrieved, is the least studied and the least understood. The impaired retrieval resulting from the operation of this factor has been referred to here as blocking. It must be pointed out, however, that blocking is not a term that is widely used to refer to this phenomenon. Instead, psychologists generally use terms such as retrieval inhibition (Brown, 1981), output interference (Smith, 1971), or the part-list cueing effect (Slamecka, 1968) to refer to what we have called blocking. Future research is required better to determine whether the concept of blocking is appropriate for describing these forgetting phenomena.

An important point that must be made about these three factors is that more than one of them may operate at once. For example, in the list length effect, both cue overload and blocking may underlie the finding that there is a lower probability of recalling any particular list word as the list length increases. That is, in the recall of a long list, a retrieval cue such as "the list of words I just learned" will apply to many words and so will be overloaded. Additionally, words that are retrieved by this cue may exert a blocking effect. Because there are many words to be recalled from a long list, there will be increased opportunity for blocking when long rather than short lists are being recalled. Another important point that must be made is that retrieval failure is not the only explanation for forgetting. As will be described in future sections, encoding operations also play an important role in determining whether information will be remembered.

Chapter 6
The short-term store

The Relation between the Short- and Long-Term Store

There's something wrong with our basic model of the human information processing system. (See Figure 1–2.) According to the model, information coming from the environment is detected by the sense organs and first held very briefly in a sensory store. From there the information proceeds to the short-term store. We have not yet described the short-term store in any detail except to say that it is equivalent to consciousness; more will be said about it soon. Our model shows that information finally proceeds from the short-term store to the long-term store.

What's wrong with the model? The flow of information that is shown in the model, from sensory, to short-term, to long-term storage is impossible. It is impossible because information in the sensory stores is unidentified. That is, as demonstrated in chapter 2 when the iconic store was described, the information represented at this stage of processing lacks semantic content. Thus, it is impossible to tell, just on the basis of what is held in a store such as iconic memory, what the information represents; it could be a letter, a geometric form, or a face. If, as our model indicates, this unidentified information is passed next to the short-term store, it means that we become conscious of information that we have not yet identified! This certainly does not correspond to the experiences reported by most people.

How might our model be changed to represent better the flow of information among the memory stores? To answer this, we must first examine the relation between the short-term store and the long-term store. This relation is seen here to be quite simple. The short-term store consists of information from the long-term store that has been activated sufficiently to bring it to consciousness. Activation, in turn, is the product of retrieval. In terms of our tuning fork analogy, this activation is represented by a labeled tuning fork beginning to vibrate as a result of its matching some other vibrating tuning fork. The possibility that the short-term store is just a temporary arousal of information in the long-term store has been raised by a number of psychologists (e.g., Shiffrin & Atkinson, 1969; Crowder, 1976, p. 40; Hintzman, 1978, p. 316). The following quote by Wickelgren (1979a) is representative of this view.

> Retrieval is the transition of a memory trace from the passive stored state to the activated state. When attention shifts, this activation decays. However, so long as activation remains, retrieval of that association ought to be facilitated, since the trace is already partially activated. . . . Such partially activated thoughts are still on one's mind to some extent, and the entire set of such (fully or partially) activated thoughts constitute the *span of consciousness.* . . . To the extent that short-term memory is anything other than rapidly decaying long-term memory, it may be identical to . . . the persistence of activation. (p. 278)

If the short-term store consists of activated representations from the long-term store, then information must first be aroused in the long-term store before becoming the contents of the short-term store. The following revised information processing model is suggested. Information from the sensory stores that is attended to automatically makes contact with matching information in the long-term store. Representations in the long-term store that are sufficiently activated as a result of this retrieval enter (that is, become the contents of) the short-term store. This is shown diagrammatically in Figure 6–1.

Figure 6–1
A revised model of the information-processing system.

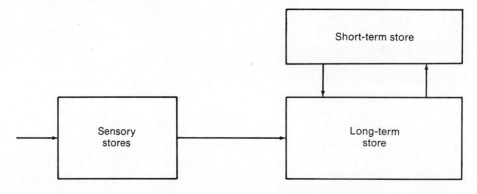

In Figure 6–1 there are double arrows between the short-term store and the long-term store. These double arrows indicate that there's a complex interplay between the two stores. Material presented in the last chapter is relevant to one form that this interaction can take. In the discussion of retrieval, it was mentioned that information in the short-term store will act as a retrieval cue and arouse information in the long-term store. Because activation energy will spread from a retrieved representation to associated representations, a person may be aware of not only information that is contained in the cue, but also information associated with it. Thus, if a person becomes aware that a friend of his is approaching, this information will be capable of retrieving other information in this person's long-term store that is associated with the representation of his friend. For example, the person might become aware that he had an argument with his friend yesterday. This information, in turn, might retrieve some other information, perhaps that arguments do not last long. Here, there is a continual process of generating information in consciousness, having that information activate related information in the long-term store, which, in turn, acts as a retrieval cue for additional information from the long-term store.

The main revision being made to the information processing model, then, is the removal of the pathway connecting the sensory stores directly to the short-term store. It should be mentioned that some other memory models (e.g., Norman & Bobrow, 1975, Figure 6.1; Reitman, 1970) that have dealt with the impossibility of there being a direct connection between these stores have made a modification equivalent to that suggested here. They have specified that a recognition process occurs along the path between the sensory stores and the short-term store. The recognition process allows the information in the sensory stores to be identified by finding matching information in the long-term store. However, by removing the path between the sensory and short-term stores, the model being proposed here makes it more explicit that this process utilizes long-term store information prior to any involvement of the short-term store.

Encoding and Retrieval in the Short-Term Store

In preceding chapters the encoding, storage, and retrieval properties of the iconic store and the long-term store were discussed. The short-term store will now be examined in terms of these same three properties. The encoding and retrieval properties of the short-term store can be described quickly. Since we can be conscious of semantic information as well as information that corresponds to all of our senses, we will conclude that all forms of information can be represented in the short-term store. As for the retrieval properties of this store, we can state that no additional retrieval is possible, for information in consciousness is as available as it possibly can be.

Storage Properties of the Short-Term Store

Capacity

The question of short-term store capacity is not as easy to answer. The difficulty is due to the close relation between the short- and the long-term store. One aspect of this close relation that is particularly troublesome for the issue of storage capacity is the ability of memory traces in the long-term store to form rapidly from information that is being held in the short-term store. It has been estimated that long-term memories begin to be established within seconds or even milliseconds (Wickelgren, 1979a) after information has entered the short-term store. This means that if you are presented with some information and if you think about the information for just a second or two, you will have begun to establish a representation of that information in your long-term store. As a result, you may later be able to retrieve that information from your long-term store. To better understand why this raises difficulties, imagine that we decide to determine how much a person can store in the short-term store by reading aloud a series of words and then asking the person to try to repeat the words back immediately. If the person performs perfectly on a list that contains just two items, we increase the length of the list and next read a list that consists of three different words. We continue to increase the list in this way until the person begins to make errors. Let us say that we find that a person can no longer perform this task perfectly when the list is more than seven items long. Is it appropriate to say that this person's short-term store capacity is seven words? It is not, because we do not know whether these words are being held just in the short-term store or whether the person has stored some of them in the long-term store and is basing recall partly on these long-term traces.

One method that has been used to estimate the short-term store capacity relies on the serial position effect (Waugh & Norman, 1965). The serial position effect, as explained previously, is the finding that memory performance is best for words presented at the beginning and end of a list. Psychologists often refer to the good memory performance for words from the early serial positions as the *primacy effect*. The term *recency effect* is used to describe the good memory performance for the last few words in a list. The middle of a list, in which memory performance is relatively poor, is referred to as the *asymptote* of the serial position curve. (See Figure 6–2.)

Figure 6–2
The primacy, asymptote, and recency portion of an idealized serial position curve.

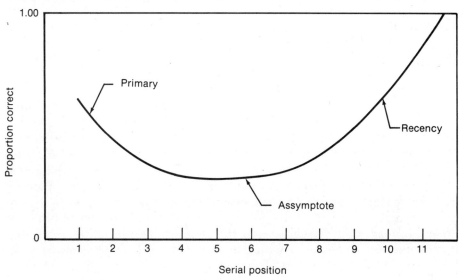

One common assumption made about the serial position effect in free-recall studies is that recall performance for words from the asymptote is based on information that has been stored just in the long-term store. On the other hand, it is assumed that the recency effect is usually based not only on information that has been stored in the long-term store, but also on information still present in consciousness. It is reasonable to assume that consciousness plays a role in the recency effect and not in memory for words from earlier serial positions, because the most recently presented words will have just been aroused to consciousness and therefore be the most likely still to show the continued effects of this arousal. According to these assumptions, we can estimate the capacity of the short-term store simply by calculating how much more information is recalled from the recency portion of the serial position curve than from the asymptote. Calculations have indicated that the short-term store can hold up to two to three words or, in more general terms, two to three familiar units (Glanzer & Razel, 1974; Watkins, 1974b).

Age and Capacity of the Short-Term Store.   As children grow up they generally show an improved ability to recall the stimuli they encounter. In old age, however, when a person is about 65 years old, there is a tendency for recall performance to worsen (Schonfield & Stones, 1979). Are these variations in memory performance with age due to changes in the storage capacity of the short-term store? A reasonable way to investigate this is to use serial position data to calculate the short-term storage capacities of different age groups. Thurm and Glanzer (1971) employed this method. They investigated how free-recall performance of five-year-olds differed from that of six-year-olds. Children in the study were given lists of between two and seven items to free recall. The items in each list consisted of colored drawings of objects such as a ball, an apple, a bike, and a balloon. The pictures were presented one at a time for 1.5 seconds each, and subjects were asked to call out the name of the object pictured before the next one was presented. After all pictures in a list had been shown, subjects immediately free-recalled the object names. The serial position curves for the different list lengths of these two age groups are shown in Figure 6–3. It can be seen that although older children recalled more words, there was no appreciable difference between the two age groups in the recency portion of these serial position functions. Thus, Thurm and Glanzer (1971) concluded that the short-term store capacity does not get bigger as children's recall abilities improve. It seems, instead, that the changes in this memory performance are related to changes in the efficiency with which information is stored in the long-term store. We will have more to say about the factors that affect this long-term memory component later in the text.

Craik (1968) investigated this same relation between short-term store capacity and memory abilities using subjects from the other end of the age distribution; he set out to determine if the decline in free recall performance that accompanies old age involves a diminished short-term store capacity. To make this assessment, Craik presented a young (mean age, 22.5 years) and an older (mean age, 65.2 years) group of subjects with lists of up to 20 unrelated words. Free-recall performance of the older subjects was consistently lower than that of the young subjects for all list lengths used (lists were 5–10, 15, or 20 words long). For example, older subjects free-recalled an average of 5.5 words from the 20-item lists, whereas young subjects free-recalled an average of 7.6 of these words. Craik used serial position curves to determine whether this lower recall of older subjects reflected a smaller short-term store capacity. Using three different formulas, each based on a different mathematical and theoretical analysis of serial position effects, Craik discovered that there was no evidence that short-term capacity of the two subject groups differed: One method of calculation showed that the short-term store capacity of young and older subjects was about equal; another showed that the young subjects had a larger capacity; and the third showed that the older subjects had a larger capacity. Craik concluded that there was no systematic change in short-term store capacity with age. It is interesting to note that when Craik used the same method

Figure 6–3
Serial position curves for five-year-old (broken line) and six-year-old children (solid line) for lists of different lengths.

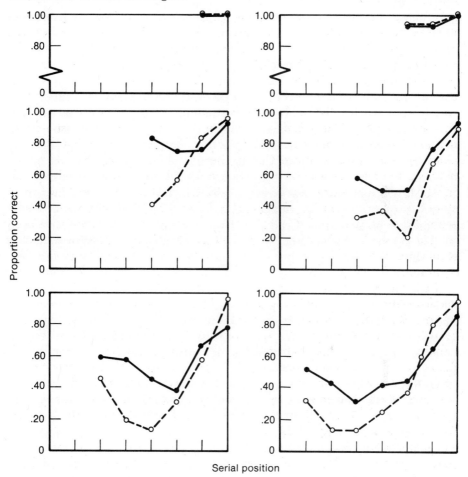

Serial position

Proportion correct

From A. T. Thurm and M. Glanzer, "Free recall in children: Long-term store vs. short-term store." *Psychonomic Science*, 1971, *23*, 175–176. Copyright 1971 by The Psychonomic Society. Reprinted by permission.

that Glanzer and Razel (1974) used to calculate short-term store capacity, he also found capacity estimates of about 2 items—1.9 for young subjects and 2.5 for older subjects.

It seems from these studies that the capacity of the short-term store does not change much with age. Thus, young children seem to be able to be conscious of as many "things" as older people are.

Negative Recency and Short-Term Store Capacity.   It must be cautioned that the process of accurately estimating short-term store capacity is quite difficult because it rests on a number of theoretical assumptions about the serial position curve, assumptions that are not shared by all researchers. For example, Glanzer and Razel and Thurm and Glanzer calculate short-term store capacity by assuming that the contribution of the long-term store can be estimated from the asymptote of the serial position curve. Thus, they assume that there is an equal contribution of long-term memory to recall of each of the last several words in a list. The phenomenon of *negative recency,* however, indicates that this assumption is incorrect. Negative recency is the finding (Craik, 1970) that when a free-recall test is delayed so that memory performance must be based entirely on information in the long-term store, words from the end of a list are the least well recalled. That is, the last few words in a list are recalled more poorly than even words from the asymptote of the serial position curve. (See Figure 6–4.) This indicates that the recency effect may be based more on the contents of the short-term store than assumed in the calculations of Glanzer and Razel and Thurm and Glanzer. When this possibility is taken into account (Watkins, 1974b), revised calculations indicate that the short-term store capacity is about three familiar units.

Units for Measuring Short-Term Store Capacity.   When we ask how much information the short-term store can hold, we are really asking how much a person can be conscious of at once. In the preceding discussions we have answered this by saying that based on the serial position effect, a person can be conscious of approximately three familiar units. What exactly is a familiar unit? That depends on a person's experiences. To understand this better, we must once again examine the way information is represented in the long-term store.

A principle of memory that dates back at least as far as Aristotle is the principle of contiguity, which asserts that events that occur close together in time or space become associated together in memory. Thus, because lightning and thunder co-occur in nature, mention of the word lightning usually brings the word thunder to mind. It is commonly assumed by psychologists today that underlying this principle of contiguity is the ability of the long-term store to form associations among information represented

Figure 6–4

Serial position curves for immediate and final free-recall. The final free-recall occurred some time after learning had ceased and exhibits the phenomenon of negative recency.

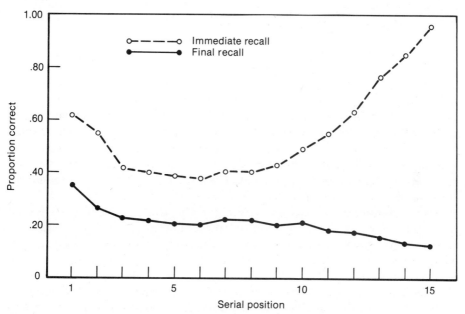

From F. I. M. Craik, "The fate of primary memory items in free recall." *Journal of Verbal Learning and Verbal Behavior*, 1970, *9*, 143–148. Copyright 1970 by Academic Press. By permission.

there. What kinds of information have become associated together in our long-term stores? Glance quickly at the symbols in Figure 6–5A and B. Which could you reproduce from memory more accurately based on your quick inspection? To a person who is not familiar with the Chinese language, the English word will be much easier to duplicate because the long-term store will contain a representation of the word that has all the component elements of the word associated together. That is, all the lines and angles that form each letter of the word will be associated together, and the letters, in turn, will be associated together to form the word. On the other hand, there will be no corresponding sets of associated elements for the Chinese character in the long-term store of a person who does not read Chinese.

According to the principle of contiguity, the lines and angles of each letter have become associated together, and the letters in the word have

Figure 6–5
An example of an unfamiliar and a familiar stimulus.

A   B

HOUSE

become associated together because we have encountered these stimuli repeatedly in close physical and temporal succession. As a result, instead of a set of separate representations, we have a single, unified representation for the word. In general, a single, unified representation such as this is often referred to as a *chunk*. The exact number and nature of the elements in a chunk will, of course, depend on a person's experiences.

One consequence of having these chunks in the long-term store is that a series of newly encountered stimuli that match a chunk in the long-term store will be treated as a single unit by the information-processing system. The following example suggested by Simon (1974) demonstrates this. Read and try immediately to recall these words from memory: *Lincoln, milky, criminal, differential, address, way, lawyer, calculus, Gettysburg.* Now read and try to recall the following words: *Lincoln's Gettysburg address, Milky Way, criminal lawyer, differential calculus.* The words are easier to remember in this new arrangement because they match already existing chunks in memory. Consequently, instead of having to retain nine individual chunks, a person has only four to remember.

Chunks in the Game of Chess.   Studies performed on chess experts have produced evidence of the importance of chunks in the long-term store and of the role of experience in developing these chunks. The relevance of chunks to chess expertise became apparent from studies performed by De-Groot (1965). DeGroot was interested in determining how chess experts differed from less skilled players. He investigated various possibilities, such as the number of moves that expert and weaker players consider and the extent to which expert and less-skilled players follow through each move by imagining what future moves could result from a currently considered action. None of the differences examined by DeGroot distinguished skilled from less-skilled players except for the performance on a memory task. The task required that a player look for five seconds at chess pieces arranged on a board and then try to reconstruct the same arrangement on another chessboard. DeGroot found that the expert players could reproduce the arrangement of the chess pieces nearly perfectly; weaker players performed this task much more poorly.

A more recent replication of this same result has been obtained by Chase and Simon (1973). They studied the performance of three chess players, a master, a class A player, and a beginner. Each was given five seconds to look at a chessboard that contained 24–26 pieces. The arrangement of the pieces corresponded to the middle of actual chess games described in various chess books and other publications. Chase and Simon found that the number of pieces correctly placed by the three players varied directly with their experience at the game. The master, class A player, and beginner correctly placed 62 percent, 34 percent, and 18 percent of the pieces, respectively. Does this indicate that chess experts have better memory abilities, in general, than weaker players? To determine this, deGroot (1965) and Chase and Simon (1973) tested players' memory performance for chess pieces arranged not in actual game configurations, but randomly on the board. In both studies it was found that the ability of skilled and less-skilled players to reproduce these positions after a five-second viewing did not differ. For example, in the Chase and Simon study, the performances of the master, class A player, and beginner were all approximately 12 percent correct.

These data indicate that chess experts do not possess a superior memory ability. Rather, the data suggest that through experience chess experts develop an ability to see patterns in the arrangements of chess pieces instead of seeing just individual pieces. This ability, no doubt, is acquired in much the same way that a person learns to recognize that the lines that form the letter *A* represent a unified pattern and not a series of individual features. Again, it is the ability of the long-term store to form associations that makes this possible. Chase and Simon described the advantage that chess experts derive from this chunking ability.

> One key to understanding chess mastery, then, seems to lie in the immediate perceptual processing, for it is here that the game is structured, and it is here in the static analysis that the good moves are generated for subsequent processing. Behind this perceptual analysis, as with all skills . . . lies an extensive cognitive apparatus amassed through years of constant practice. What was once accomplished by slow, conscious deductive reasoning is now arrived at by fast, unconscious perceptual processing. It is no mistake of language for the chess master to say that he "sees" the right move. (p. 56)

Thus, the chess expert is readily able to perceive good moves because of the ability to recognize arrangements of chess pieces that according to past experience have developed into successful offenses.

Chunks and Short-Term Store Capacity.   The concept of a memory chunk has been introduced to describe the units used to measure short-term store capacity. A chunk, as just explained, is a set of closely associated representations in the long-term store. Because the component representations that comprise a chunk are strongly connected together, the chunk behaves as if it is a single memory representation. How does the presence of chunks in the long-term store affect the short-term store? Because we are considering the short-term store to consist of information in the long-term store that has become activated, an activated chunk in the long-term store, which acts as a single unit there, will behave as if it were also a single unit in the short-term store.

One implication of this is that the capacity of the short-term store, as determined from a serial position curve, should be the same no matter how big or small the chunks are that a person recalls. That is, if an experimenter presents a person with a list of unrelated words, each word will be treated as a chunk, and it will be appropriate to measure the capacity of the short-term store in units of words. On the other hand, if an experimenter presents a subject with words that form familiar phrases, such as "to be or not to be, that is the question," then the appropriate unit of measurement will be phrases and not individual words. Both cases should produce identical short-term store capacity estimates.

An experiment by Glanzer and Razel (1974) produced results that accord with this possibility. Subjects in the experiment were read lists of 15 familiar proverbs, each of which was no more than six words long. Examples are "Every cloud has a silver lining," "Don't believe everything you hear," and "Practice makes perfect." Subjects free-recalled the proverbs immediately after the last one had been presented. Glanzer and Razel also read a list of 15 unrelated words to another group of subjects who free-recalled the words immediately after the list had been presented. Estimates of short-term store capacity for these two types of materials were comparable when the measurement unit was chunks. For the lists consisting of proverbs, the short-term store was estimated to hold 2.2 chunks. For lists consisting of unrelated words, the capacity was also estimated to hold 2.2 chunks. Glanzer and Razel based this latter estimate not only on their own data, but also on data produced from 32 other free-recall experiments in which subjects were given lists of unrelated words for immediate free-recall. It should be noted that the method used by Glanzer and Razel to calculate short-term store capacity did not take the negative recency finding into account. As explained earlier, it is likely that if this phenomenon had been taken into account, estimates of short-term store capacity for both kinds of lists would have been slightly greater, perhaps around three chunks.

Fate of Information in the Short-Term Store

What happens to information in the short-term store? Two possibilities are generally considered. One is that information decays from this store, and the other is that it can be displaced by new information entering the store. That decay from the short-term store is a reasonable possibility can be readily seen from our tuning fork analogy of memory. Let us think of the long-term store as consisting of a collection of tuning forks, each representing a memory chunk. Imagine that one of these tuning forks becomes aroused through a retrieval process and begins to hum. This humming fork now represents information in consciousness, or the short-term store. What will happen to this vibrating tuning fork as time goes by? If the tuning fork is not reactivated, it is reasonable to suggest that its activation energy will decay.

Before describing the evidence often cited to support this decay process in the short-term store, it must be mentioned that a decay hypothesis is very difficult to test. One reason for this difficulty is that a test of this hypothesis requires that once a representation has become activated it must not be reactivated during the time that the decay process is suspected to be occurring, or else the decay will be counteracted. Since reactivation can be achieved by rehearsal, a method must be devised for preventing a person from rehearsing. This is quite difficult to achieve. Try, for example, not to repeat or even think about the following five words for 15 seconds after you read them: *flag, lamb, drum, bath, mile.* One way to avoid rehearsing information is to turn your attention to some other task. Perhaps you tried to avoid rehearsing the five words by looking up from the page and thinking about something else. Although such *distractor activity* is commonly used to prevent rehearsal, it is best avoided in this situation because it may lead to some displacement of information from the short-term store. For example, if you looked up from the page after reading the five words and thought about a TV program you watched last night, information about the TV program was occupying your short-term store. This new information could possibly interfere with information about the words in the short-term store, perhaps by displacing the information, that is, by pushing the information out of storage (see below).

Reitman (1971, 1974) proposed a technique that she hoped would both prevent rehearsal and also minimize displacement. The technique required subjects to engage in a difficult task, one that necessitated a great deal of attention. This task, known as a tone detection task, involved listening for a very faint tone that was occasionally presented through earphones. Subjects were instructed to press a response key every time a tone was detected.

Reitman realized that this tone detection task would not guarantee that subjects were, in fact, doing absolutely nothing and that no new information was entering their short-term stores. However, for those periods during which no tone was actually presented, Reitman expected that subjects would approach these conditions as closely as possible.

Reitman (1974) used the following procedure to test the hypothesis that information decays in the short-term store. She presented five words simultaneously to subjects for 2 seconds and then had them engage in the tone detection task for 15 seconds. After the 15-second period, subjects attempted to free-recall the five words. Free-recall performance was found to decline by about 24 percent during this 15-second interval. Reitman interpreted this as "clear evidence for decay" (p. 376). It must be realized, however, that this conclusion rests on the assumption that the tone detection task did not introduce new information into the short-term stores of the subjects and that the 24 percent decline in memory performance was due to a loss of information from the short-term store and not to a failure to retrieve the information from newly established traces in the long-term store. Evidence from serial position effects gives some indication that this latter assumption may be correct: Watkins, Watkins, Craik, and Mazuryk (1973) found that an attention-demanding nonverbal task similar to that used by Reitman affected the free-recall of only the last few words in a list. If it is assumed that free-recall of these words is based primarily on information residing in the short-term store, this indicates that the distractor task affected the short-term rather than the long-term component of memory.

The second possible fate of information in consciousness is displacement. To understand why this possibility is considered by psychologists, refer again to our tuning fork analogy and imagine that several tuning forks in our model of the long-term store are activated successively. How will the behavior of a vibrating tuning fork be affected by having other tuning forks begin to vibrate? Since we have found that the short-term store has a capacity of about two to three chunks, it must not be possible to have more than this number of tuning forks vibrating with sufficient amplitude to bring the information represented in each to consciousness. Thus, when two or three tuning forks are already activated, any other tuning fork that is activated must trigger some dampening process (or a process that has an equivalent effect) that acts on an already vibrating tuning fork to prevent the capacity of the short-term store from being exceeded. Here, it is as if each newly aroused representation displaces an already aroused representation from consciousness.

Evidence to support this displacement hypothesis comes from serial position data. The evidence, again, rests on the assumption that the recency effect is based on recall of words held in the short-term store. If new information displaces information held in the short-term store, what will happen to the recency effect when a subject pays attention to some extraneous stimuli presented just before free-recall is begun? There should be a reduction in the recency effect that will be exhibited as a flattening of the serial position curve at terminal list positions. This is, in fact, just what occurs. An experiment that demonstrates this was performed by Glanzer and co-workers (Glanzer, Gianutsos, & Dubin, 1969). In this experiment subjects studied and free-recalled lists made up of 12 words. Just before beginning to free-recall some of these lists, however, subjects were given some distractor words to read. Glanzer and his co-workers found that the more distractor words subjects read, the less pronounced was the recency effect. This can be seen in Figure 6–6. The two solid lines represent free-recall performance of subjects who read two distractor words before free-recalling the list. The two distractor words evidently reduced the recency effect considerably. The reduction in the recency effect, however, was more sizeable when

Figure 6–6
Serial position curves for free-recall after a delay of two (solid lines) or six (broken lines) words read in two (squares) or six (circles) seconds.

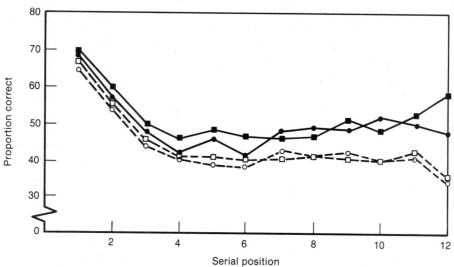

Adapted from M. Glanzer, R. Gianutsos, and S. Dubin, "The removal of items from short-term storage." *Journal of Verbal Learning and Verbal Behavior,* 1969, *8,* 435–447. Copyright 1969 by Academic Press. By permission.

subjects read six distractor words before free-recalling the list words. Free-recall performance after the reading of the six distractor words is shown by the two dotted lines in the figure.

The reason for there being two lines to represent each distractor condition in Figure 6–6 must be explained. It is generally true that the more things a person has to do, the longer it will take to do them. In the experiment we are considering, this means that it will take longer for six distractor words to be read than for two words to be read, assuming that each word is processed at the same rate. This can pose a problem. Since we know that decay is a likely fate of information in the short-term store, and since the effects of decay will accumulate over time, how can we tell whether the reduction in the recency effect is a function of the number of distractor words read or the time it takes to read them? To help separate these two factors, the experimenters had subjects read two distractor words during either a two-second period or a six-second period. It can be seen from the two heavy lines in Figure 6–6, one of which represents the six-second period and one of which represents the two-second period, that reading time made little difference. This same conclusion can be drawn from comparing the other lines in the figure that represent the reading of six words in either two or six seconds. Since the number of distractor words read, rather than the amount of time required, makes a difference in this experiment, Glanzer et al. concluded that displacement was an important mechanism in the short-term store, a more important one than decay.

Duration of Storage

The preceding discussion has shown that there are two possible means of removing information from the short-term store, decay and displacement. In discussing the duration of short-term storage it must first be noted that the displacement mechanism is not very well suited to be characterized in terms of a time interval, since this mechanism is based on the number of interfering inputs to the store and not on the time it takes to deliver them. If we had to assign some time measure to characterize short-term store duration when a person is encountering distractor stimuli, the best we could do is to say that information will be stored until the person has attended to three or more distractor items. The decay mechanism, on the other hand, is theoretically suited to being characterized in terms of a temporal interval. However, there are practical considerations that make such a determination difficult. To begin with, it is quite difficult to isolate and study the decay mechanism. As Reitman's (1971, 1974) experiments have shown, extraordinary procedures must be implemented to achieve this. Even with the methods devised by Reitman, ones that have been judged to be ingenious (Postman, 1975), the isolation of the decay from the displacement mechanism may still not be complete. Furthermore, even if these methods are considered to be successful, there is still the difficulty of separating memory performance that is based on the short-term store from that based on newly established long-term traces. For instance, in Reitman's (1974) study, in which there was a 24-percent decline in memory for five words after 15 seconds of tone detection, it is difficult to know the extent to which the percent correct performance is being based on information still remaining in consciousness and the extent to which performance is being based on information being retrieved from newly established long-term traces. Although it is likely that much of the forgetting in this study was due to information decaying from the short-term store, someone could still claim that Reitman provided no firm evidence to reject the possibility that information was being lost entirely due to retrieval failure from the long-term store and that no decay of information for the approximately three words being held in the short-term store had occurred.

Because it is so difficult to investigate the decay process in isolation, no estimate of short-term storage duration will be made here. From a practical point of view, this may not be a serious omission, since studies such as that of Glanzer et al. (1969) indicate that displacement may be a more potent factor than decay for the removal of information from this store.

Schizophrenia and Displacement from the Short-Term Store

Under everyday, nonlaboratory conditions, we are subject to a continual barrage of information from our environment. This information is all potentially able to displace information currently residing in our short-term stores. Were this flow of information to go unchecked from our environment to our short-term stores, we would be unable to hold on to a thought for very long, because new information would constantly be displacing the information currently in consciousness. This does, of course, happen occasionally. We have all experienced having our attention be diverted by something around us, and have found ourselves asking, "Now where was I before I got distracted?" Normally, however, we can exercise some control over irrelevant, distracting stimuli using our powers of attention. By being selective in where we direct attention, we filter out distractions. As a result, we can do things such as carry on a conversation in a crowded room where other conversations are simultaneously taking place.

What would happen if we could not use our powers of attention to properly filter out stimulation that was tangential to our present focus of concern? It should be obvious that this sort of deficit would leave the contents of our short-term stores vulnerable to displacement by any stimulus from our environment. We would continually be distracted, moving from one thought to another, unable to hold on to any idea for very long. Does this ever occur? Some psychologists (e.g., McGhie & Chapman, 1961) have suggested that this condition is a primary characteristic of the mental disorder known as schizophrenia.

The term *schizophrenia* was introduced by Swiss psychiatrist Eugen Bleuler in 1911. He believed that thought disorders were the primary feature of this condition, saying that the state of mind of the schizophrenic resembles what most of us experience "in dreams and lack of attention, and in so called mind wanderings" (Bleuler, 1950, p. 205). More recent observations have conformed to this view:

> One of the defining characteristics of schizophrenia is an impairment in the area of perceptual functioning. Specifically, schizophrenics have been noted to have difficulty in focusing on relevant stimuli and ignoring irrelevant stimuli. Examples of this are numerous in daily interactions with people. The schizophrenic has trouble following conversation or watching television for he/she is easily distracted by his/her own thoughts as well as by extraneous noise in the environment. It is as if he/she cannot block out the irrelevant information but attends to all, whether pertinent or not. (Place & Gilmore, 1980, p. 409)

Additional insight into the schizophrenic condition comes from interviews conducted with schizophrenic patients. Published reports of some of these interviews give support to the view that schizophrenics experience attentional deficits. One such series of interviews was conducted by Andrew McGhie and James Chapman (1961). These researchers talked with 26 schizophrenic patients who were at early stages of their illness (as confirmed by later observation). The patients were encouraged to talk about recent changes in their experiences and about their present difficulties. Here are excerpts from some of the patients' responses.

> Patient 23: Everything seems to grip my attention although I am not particularly interested in anything. I am speaking to you just now but I can hear noises going on next door and in the corridor. I find it difficult to shut these out and it makes it more difficult for me to concentrate on what I am saying to you. Often the silliest little things that are going on seem to interest me. That's not even true; they don't interest me but I find myself attending to them and wasting a lot of time this way. I know that sounds like laziness but it's not really.

> Patient 13: My concentration is very poor. I jump from one thing to another. If I am talking to someone they only need to cross their legs or scratch their heads and I am distracted and forget what I was saying. I think I could concentrate better with my eyes shut.

> Patient 22: When people are talking I just get scraps of it. If it is just one person who is speaking that's not bad, but if others join in, then I can't pick it up

at all. I just can't get into tune with that conversation. It makes me feel open—as if things are closing in on me and I have lost control. (pp. 104–106)[1]

Barbara Freedman and Loren Chapman (1973) have criticized McGhie and Chapman's study for being too informal in that no structured set of questions was asked, no control subjects were interviewed, and no objective data analysis was performed. To remedy this, Freedman and Chapman (1973) interviewed 20 schizophrenic and 20 nonschizophrenic patients, asking them a series of approximately 50 questions. Included were questions such as "What about your concentration? How has that been?" and "Have you noticed that so much seems to be going on all the time now that you cannot focus your attention on just one thing?" The results of this study confirmed the view of schizophrenia held by McGhie and Chapman. It was found that many more of the schizophrenic than nonschizophrenic patients (90 percent versus 60 percent) reported recent changes in their ability to concentrate. Furthermore, significantly more schizophrenic than nonschizophrenic patients (55 percent versus 15 percent) attributed problems in concentration to difficulties in focusing attention on relevant stimuli and thoughts. Freedman and Chapman supplemented their data with some subjective observations of the schizophrenic experience.

> Some described this experiment as an increased distractibility by external stimuli . . . and others as a distractibility by irrelevant thoughts. . . . For example, Schizophrenic 14 reported spontaneously that when he sat down and tried to read, "I get easily distracted." Schizophrenic 1 said that he could now be distracted by "any noise or anything else." Before any of the inquiries about attention were made, Schizophrenic 4 spontaneously explained that with books he had
>> a hard time concentrating, getting into the actual reading of them (because) probably an external stimulus would take my attention off the book . . . a sound or just perhaps a lack of interest at one moment while something like of piece of sunlight is going on over here and that would probably start me thinking. (p. 50)

Experimental evidence to support this attentional deficit view of schizophrenia has been obtained by Oltmanns (1978). Oltmanns presented schizophrenic and normal subjects with short lists of five common words for immediate free-recall. The lists were presented auditorally by a female either with or without some extraneous, irrelevant speech that subjects were instructed to ignore. The extraneous speech consisted of another set of five

[1] From A. McGhie and J. Chapman, "Disorders of attention and perception in early schizophrenia." *British Journal of Medical Psychology*, 1961, *34*, 103–116. Copyright 1961 by The British Psychological Society. Reprinted by permission.

common words read alternately with the list words in a male voice. For some of the recall tests, subjects were instructed to free-recall the critical words (those read by the female) by first reporting the last two words read by the female, and then by reporting the other three words in any order they wished. This instruction was given to help assure that all subjects were using a similar recall strategy and thus to help make interpretation of the data less ambiguous. Let us consider what results we could expect if schizophrenic subjects are more distractible than normal subjects. If the irrelevant words attract the attention of the schizophrenic patients, then these words should tend to displace the other, critical list words from these persons' short-term stores. This will shorten the length of time that these critical words are processed. As a result, there will be less opportunity for long-term traces of these words to be formed. Serial position curves for free-recall performance of the schizophrenic patients should reflect this by showing depressed performance at pre-recency portions of the curve, since these positions primarily index long-term store performance. The last word or two from the critical lists should not be strongly affected by the extraneous speech, since these words are subject to so few displacing stimuli. That is, unlike the experiments of Glanzer et al. (1969), in which the to-be-recalled list is followed by a series of two or more distractor words, the extraneous words in the Oltmanns experiment alternate with the critical list words. Thus, the last to-be-recalled word is followed by no more than one distracting word. In fact, since half of the trials in the Oltmanns experiment began with the male reading a distractor word first, half of the time the last critical list word was followed by no distractor word. Thus, most of the effect of the distraction should be reflected in the pre-recency portions of the serial position curves.

Figure 6–7 shows the results. The serial position curves for the normal subjects who recalled the word lists with and without extraneous speech are shown in Figure 6–7A. The corresponding data for the schizophrenic patients are shown in Figure 6–7B. It can be seen that the schizophrenic patients were more affected by the irrelevant speech than were the normal subjects. Similar curtailment of processing in the short-term stores of schizophrenic patients as a consequence of the presence of extraneous speech has been demonstrated by Pogue–Geile and Oltmanns (1980).

It must be mentioned that the finding of increased distractibility of schizophrenics does not mean that this distractibility is necessarily the cause of the psychosis. Rather, distractibility should be regarded as a symptom of the condition. It must also be mentioned that this attentional deficit analysis of schizophrenia is somewhat controversial partly because not all experimental measures of distractibility show schizophrenic patients to be more vulner-

Figure 6–7
Number of words recalled as a function of serial position for normal (A) and schizophrenic (B) subjects under neutral (solid lines) or distractor (broken lines) conditions.

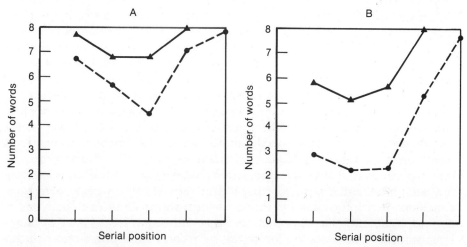

Adapted from T. F. Oltmanns, "Selective attention in schizophrenic and manic psychoses: The effect of distraction on information processing. *Journal of Abnormal Psychology,* 1978, *87,* 212–225. Copyright 1978 by the American Psychological Association. Reprinted by permission of publisher and author.

able than normal persons (Straube & Germer, 1979) and partly because there is some question as to how specific this deficit is to just schizophrenic patients (Oltmanns, 1978; Hemsley & Zawada, 1976). In any case, whatever the role of attentional deficits in schizophrenia, it is clear that the inability to use attention to filter out stimuli leaves information in the short-term store highly susceptible to displacement.

Summary

It was proposed here that a person can become conscious of information that has been sufficiently activated in the long-term store. Such information can be described as being in a person's short-term store. In describing the encoding, storage, and retrieval properties of this short-term store, the emphasis was on the storage properties. It was mentioned that no discussion of retrieval from the short-term store was necessary because information in the short-term store is as available as it can be. As for the encoding properties of this store, it was briefly mentioned that, just as in the long-term store, all forms of encoding are possible; this should not be surprising given the proposal that the short-term store consists of aroused information from the long-term store.

Description of the short-term store's storage characteristics began with a discussion of the issue of capacity. Based on serial position data, it was suggested that the store can hold between two and three chunks. This capacity estimate rests on several assumptions about serial position effects, the most critical being that the recency effect reflects information being output principally from the short-term store. In discussing the fate of information in short-term storage, evidence for two forgetting mechanisms—decay and displacement—was described. Reitman's (1974) finding that subjects forget information during a 15-second tone detection task has been interpreted as evidence for decay. The finding of Glanzer et al. (1969) that the recency effect is attenuated by distractor activity occurring just before free-recall has been interpreted as supporting a displacement mechanism. It may be concluded that information in the short-term store is subject to both decay and displacement. Nothing conclusive was said about the duration of short-term storage. The close relation of the short- and long-term stores and the difficulty in isolating the short-term store from the effects of displacing stimuli have made study of the duration of short-term storage difficult.

Part 2
Strategies

Chapter 7
Short-term memory

Introduction

Few tools are available to aid the psychologist in studying human memory. Although there is some use made of sophisticated technology, such as the magnetoencephalogram, which measures weak magnetic fields generated by brain activity, and computerized transaxial scanning for positron emission to measure regional blood flow in active parts of the brain (LeDoux, Barclay, & Premack, 1978), much of the time the study of memory is conducted using simpler devices. The reason is that no technology yet exists to allow psychologists to peer unobtrusively into the human brain and sensitively detect the critical changes occurring there during learning. Instead, psychologists must resort to manipulating and observing what goes in and what comes out of the information processing system. Lachman, Lachman, and Butterfield (1979) describe the current approach to studying human cognition in the following way:

> We see an appropriate parallel between our science and that of the cell endocrinologist who likened his work to that of an industrial spy. Sitting on a hillside above a factory with field glasses, he watches railroad cars arrive with raw materials. They are taken into one end of the factory, while at the other end trucks pick up completed products. The spy's job is to figure out what transpires in the factory. Every once in a while he can send in a car of materials he has selected, and later he can see what comes out; but he cannot take a trip through the factory. We are in a similar position with respect to human mentation. We cannot observe it directly. We must infer what happens inside by watching what goes in and what comes out. (p. 123)

This approach is not without its risks and difficulties. One difficulty in using this approach is in selecting the contents of the "car of materials." It is possible that an unwise selection of materials can lead to conclusions about activities in the "factory" that do not represent what is most typical of it. This seems to have occurred in the study of short-term memory.

What is short-term memory? This term has not previously been mentioned. We have, however, discussed the short-term store in detail. It will be important to distinguish between these two terms. Whereas the short-term store refers to a memory *store* with properties that distinguish it from other memory stores, the term short-term memory refers to a *strategy* that makes use of both the short-term store and the long-term store.

A person uses short-term memory when attempting to keep as much information as possible temporarily in a highly available state. For example, a person is using short-term memory when trying to briefly remember a phone number that has just been obtained from a directory. This short-term memory strategy is characterized by such things as the use of rehearsal, a preference for auditory encoding, and a capacity limit in excess of three chunks. It must be emphasized, however, that short-term memory is not a memory store, but rather a flexible strategy that makes use of both the short-term store and the long-term store. In this chapter the characteristics of short-term memory will be described. Some of the misconceptions about short-term memory brought about by an unwise selection of experimental input conditions will also be mentioned.

Some Characteristics of Short-Term Memory

There is a great deal of inconsistency in the use of the term short-term memory in the psychological literature. Some use it to refer to a separate memory structure. For example, Klatzky (1980) states that the human information-processing system consists of three principle storage structures: sensory register, short-term memory, and long-term memory. Similarly, Wingfield and Byrnes (1981) refer to sensory memory, short-term memory, and long-term memory as "three structurally distinct memory stores" (p. 11). The view adopted here, however, is one expressed by Craik and Lockhart (1972).

> It is now widely accepted that memory can be classified into three levels of storage: sensory stores, short-term memory (STM) and long-term memory (LTM). Since there has been some ambiguity in the usage of the terms in this area, we shall follow the convention of using STM and LTM to refer to experimental situations, and the terms "short-term store" (STS) and "long-term store" (LTS) to refer to the two relevant storage systems. (p. 672).

According to this convention, short-term memory (STM) is a strategy used when the experimental situation calls for information to be retained for just a short time.

One experimental paradigm that is often used to investigate short-term memory is the Brown–Peterson task, so called because it was devised independently in England by Brown (1958) and in the United States by Peterson and Peterson (1959). A trial in a Brown–Peterson task usually begins with the experimenter reading three stimuli to a subject who immediately repeats the three items. The subject then engages in a distractor task that lasts anywhere from 0 to 18 seconds. The experimenter often initiates the distractor task by presenting a three-digit number to the subject. The subject will have been instructed beforehand to count backwards from the number, usually by three or fours at a one-second rate. This backward counting task, which is quite difficult, is intended to prevent the subject from rehearsing the three stimuli. What the experimenter wishes to determine from all of this is how rapidly the subject forgets the three stimuli once the subject's attention has been turned to the distractor task. To make this determination, the experimenter will interrupt the subject's backward counting after a variable period of time (usually within 0–18 seconds) and ask that the three items be recalled. Then another trial will begin with three new stimuli and another three-digit number. Typically, it is found that over approximately 18 seconds of backward counting, recall of the three stimuli falls steadily to a stable level. (See Figure 7–1.) As will be demonstrated in the next section, performance in this STM task reflects a contribution of both the short- and the long-term stores.

The Short- and Long-Term Stores in STM

The Brown–Peterson task is typical of STM tasks in that it presents a subject with information that is to be retained for just a short period of time. As shown in Figure 7–1, performance in this task is generally quite accurate after 0–3 seconds of distractor activity, but falls steadily to a stable asymptotic level within 18 seconds. The usual account of the poorer memory after 18 seconds of distractor activity is that performance initially reflects output from both the short-term and the long-term stores; however, due to the effects of distractor activity, recall after 18 seconds primarily reflects just long-term storage.

How do we know that information is being recalled primarily from the long-term store after 18 seconds in this task? Based on what we know about displacement in the short-term store, it is reasonable to assume that the 18 seconds of distractor activity will remove the to-be-recalled information from the short-term store. This will require that performance then depends

Figure 7–1
Results of a typical Brown–Peterson task. The data show recall of a stimulus in terms of percent correct as a function of duration of distractor activity performed during the retention interval.

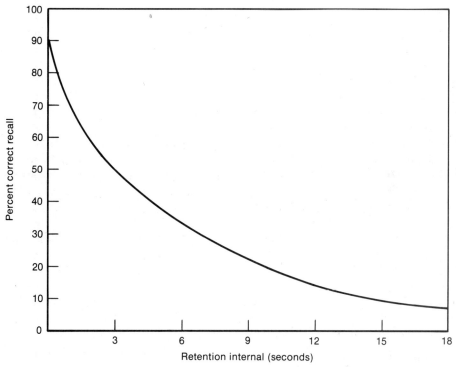

Adapted from L. R. Peterson and M. J. Peterson, "Short-term retention of individual verbal items." *Journal of Experimental Psychology,* 1959, *58,* 193–198. Copyright 1959 by the American Psychological Association. Reprinted by permission of publisher and author.

just on information available in the long-term store. Another reason we can draw this conclusion is that recall behavior after 18 seconds of distractor activity exhibits phenomena typical of retrieval from the long-term store. One of these retrieval phenomena is the buildup of proactive interference.

It has been mentioned in previous discussions that forgetting of information from the long-term store can result from previous learning. This is the phenomenon of proactive interference. It has also been mentioned that proactive interference can be accounted for with the cue overload principle. That is, the inability of a cue successfully to retrieve a memory from the long-term store can be due to the cue's making contact with a number of previously formed memories; this is thought to place an extra load on the cue, which depletes the cue's ability to arouse the information being sought in memory. The point to be made here is that this same forgetting process has been found to influence memory performance after 18 seconds of distractor activity in the Brown–Peterson task. Since proactive interference is a long-term store phenomenon, its presense signals involvement of this store. In the following discussion relevant evidence will be presented.

Buildup of Proactive Interference.   If proactive interference contributes to forgetting in the Brown–Peterson task, recall should worsen as a subject receives more learning trials. The poorer performance can be expected because with more learning trials, a retrieval cue will match increasingly more stimuli in memory and thus become progressively more overloaded. A well-known experiment by Keppel and Underwood (1962) demonstrated this. In their study, Keppel and Underwood first showed subjects a letter trigram (e.g., *KQF*) for two seconds and then had subjects count backwards by threes from a three-digit number. Recall of the trigram was attempted after 3, 9, or 18 seconds of backwards counting. This process was repeated twice more using different trigrams each time. The recall data are shown in Figure 7–2. From the line labeled T–1, which represents recall of the first trigram presented, it can be seen that performance was perfect even after 18 seconds of the distractor activity. However, for the second and third trigram, labeled T–2 and T–3, respectively in the figure, it is obvious that there was increasingly more forgetting over the 18-second retention interval. Evidently, retrieval cues (e.g., "the three letters I just studied") were becoming more overloaded with each additional learning trial.

There are two interesting conclusions that can be drawn from this experiment. One is relevant to forgetting in general and the other to our discussion of STM. Of relevance to forgetting in general is the conclusion that forgetting after several seconds of distractor activity is due not only to the absence of information in memory but also to difficulties in retrieving information that is potentially available. Keppel and Underwood's study showed that when the retrieval difficulties are circumvented by testing memory after just one learning trial, recall performance is close to perfect. The other conclusion that can be drawn from this experiment, one that is relevant to STM, is that subjects in this task are basing recall after several seconds of distractor activity principally on information in the long-term store. This is shown by the susceptibility of information recalled after 18 seconds to proactive interference, a phenomenon characteristic of the long-term store. Evidence from another experiment reported by Keppel and Underwood (1962, experiment 3) strengthens this conclusion. They showed that recall after three seconds of distractor activity showed no evidence of a buildup

Figure 7–2
The performance of subjects on the first three trials of Keppel and Underwood's (1962) study. The figure shows percent correct recall as a function of retention interval for each of the first three trials in a Brown–Peterson task.

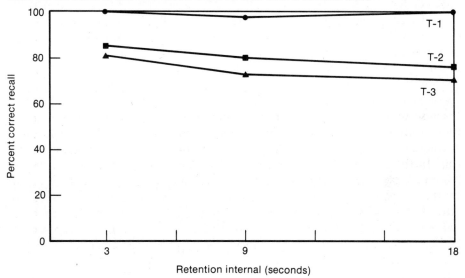

Retention internal (seconds)

Adapted from G. Keppel and B. J. Underwood, "Proactive inhibition in short-term retention of single items." *Journal of Verbal Learning and Verbal Behavior*, 1962, *1*, 153–161. Copyright 1962 by Academic Press. Reprinted by permission.

of proactive interference; instead, recall after three seconds was as good on later trials as it was on the first trial. (See Figure 7–3.) This indicates that proactive interference was affecting recall only at the longer delays, those beyond which short-term storage could be involved.

The Hebb Task. Other evidence that STM involves the long-term store comes from a task devised by Hebb (1961). Subjects in Hebb's experiment were presented with a list of nine digits read at a rate of one every second. 24 of these lists were read to subjects, whose task was to immediately repeat back in the correct order the nine digits from the list just presented. Although subjects were expecting a different list of numbers on each of the 24 trials, Hebb repeatedly presented one list on trials 3, 6, 9, 12, 15, 18, 21, and 24. Hebb was interested in knowing whether the repetition would lead to improved performance on this list, even when subjects were unaware that the list was being repeated. Hebb found that performance on this repeated list improved. The first time it was presented, only about 15 per-

Figure 7–3
Proportion correct recall as a function of number of trigrams learned and tested.
The tests were conducted after either a 3- or 18-second retention interval.

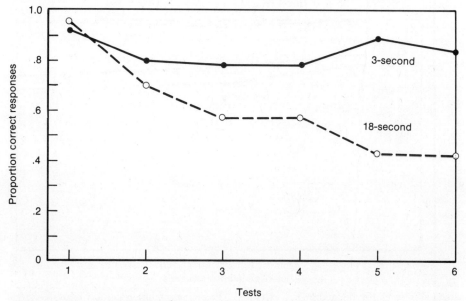

From G. Keppel and B. J. Underwood, "Proactive inhibition in short-term retention of single
items." *Journal of Verbal Learning and Verbal Behavior*, 1962, *1*, 153–161. Copyright 1962
by Academic Press. Reprinted by permission.

cent of the subjects recalled it perfectly. However, by the eighth repetition,
60 percent of the subjects were recalling it correctly. Performance on nonre-
peated lists, however, was consistently around 20 percent correct. These
data show that in a typical STM task in which subjects are trying to store
as much information as they can briefly, the long-term store is utilized.
This is evidenced in Hebb's task by the steady improvement in performance
on the repeated list. We can be sure the improving performance is based
on information in the long-term store, since a great deal of information is
presented and recalled between repetitions of each list, too much information (two new lists) to allow the repeated information still to be in consciousness. An experiment by Melton (1963) showed that a similar effect of repetition occurs in this task when as many as eight different lists intervene
between repetitions. Thus, we can conclude that the long-term store plays
a role in STM tasks.

Acoustic Codes in STM

Conrad's Experiment. An experiment performed by Conrad (1964) was influential in convincing psychologists of the important role that acoustic encodings play in STM. Conrad showed that even though a short sequence of letters had been presented visually, errors subjects made in immediately recalling these letters were primarily based on the sounds and not on the visual properties of the letters. Subjects in Conrad's experiment were shown a series of six letters at a rate of .75 seconds each. After each list of six letters had been presented, subjects immediately attempted to write them down in the correct order. To make the data analysis easier, Conrad looked only at the lists on which subjects had made a single error. Conrad found that this single error in the recall of each list was not random. Instead, there was a significant tendency to recall a letter that sounded like the correct letter. As an example, if a subject made a mistake in recalling the letter *B*, the incorrect substitution was most likely to be the letter *P*. As other examples, subjects most often incorrectly substituted the letter *F* for the letter *S*, *T*, for *C*, and *B* for *V*. Conrad strengthened his conclusion that subjects were making errors based on the sounds of letters by showing that there was a strong correlation between the errors his subjects made in this memory experiment and the errors subjects made in a listening task. This listening task required another group of subjects simply to listen to and try to identify single letters recorded in noisy surroundings. The errors subjects made, for example calling the letter *B*, *P*, were similar in both tasks. (See Table 7–1.)

Further Work on Acoustic Codes. The data from Conrad's experiment show that subjects were recoding visual stimuli into an acoustic form. In effect, the subjects seemed to speak each letter to themselves and store the sounds rather than the visual properties of each letter. While Conrad left open the possibility that other forms of information could be encoded in an STM task, some psychologists (e.g., Baddeley, 1966; Neisser, 1967) subsequently found reason to believe that acoustic encoding was a characteristic property of STM. Many of the experiments that helped convince psychologists of the acoustic nature of STM coding were based on similarity effects. An experiment by Baddeley (1966) exemplifies this approach. Subjects were shown 24 lists of five words, each word being displayed for one second. Immediately after seeing each list, subjects attempted to recall the words in the order they had been presented. In one experiment, two kinds of lists were used—accoustically similar lists that consisted of words such as *map, cab, mad, man,* and *cap,* and accoustically dissimilar lists that consisted of words such as *cow, pit, day, rig,* and *bun.* Baddeley found that

Table 7–1
Confusion data for the listening and memory recall tasks used by Conrad (1964).

Listening confusions

		Stimulus letter								
		B	C	P	T	V	F	M	N	S	X
Response letter	B.	.	171	75	84	168	2	11	10	2	2
	C	32	.	35	42	20	4	4	5	2	5
	P	162	350	.	505	91	11	31	23	5	5
	T	143	232	281	.	50	14	12	11	8	5
	V	122	61	34	22	.	1	8	11	1	0
	F	6	4	2	4	3	.	13	8	336	238
	M	10	14	2	3	4	22	.	334	21	9
	N	13	21	6	9	20	32	512	.	38	14
	S	2	18	2	7	3	488	23	11	.	391
	X	1	6	2	2	1	245	2	1	184	.

Recall confusions

		Stimulus letter								
		B	C	P	T	V	F	M	N	S	X
Response letter	B	.	18	62	5	83	12	9	3	2	0
	C	13	.	27	18	55	15	3	12	35	7
	P	102	18	.	24	40	15	8	8	7	7
	T	30	46	79	.	38	18	14	14	8	10
	V	56	32	30	14	.	21	15	11	11	5
	F	6	8	14	5	31	.	12	13	131	16
	M	12	6	8	5	20	16	.	146	15	5
	N	11	7	5	1	19	28	167	.	24	5
	S	7	21	11	2	9	37	4	12	.	16
	X	3	7	2	2	11	30	10	11	59	.

From R. Conrad, "Acoustic confusions in immediate memory." *British Journal of Psychology*, 1964, *55*, 75–84. Copyright 1964 by Cambridge University Press. Reprinted by permission.

subjects' recall performance for the accoustically similar lists was only 1.7 percent correct, while performance for the accoustically dissimilar lists was 58.3 percent correct. Baddeley also compared ordered recall of lists of semantically similar words (e.g., *big, long, large, wide,* and *broad*) with that of lists of semantically dissimilar words (e.g., *old, foul, late, hot,* and *strong*). There was very little difference in performance for these two types of lists. Recall of semantically similar lists was 64.7 percent correct, while that of semantically dissimilar lists was 71.0 percent correct.

What conclusion can be drawn from the detrimental effect on ordered recall produced by acoustic similarity but not semantic similarity? Baddeley concluded that "subjects show remarkable consistency and uniformity in using an almost exclusively acoustic coding system for the short-term remembering of disconnected words" (p. 364). To understand better the logic that relates similarity effects to memory encoding, imagine that you are in the following situation. You are watching a horse race in which the first three finishers happen to look exactly alike to you and are identifiable only by the numbers they carry. A friend of yours who misses the end of the race asks you to point out the first three finishers in order. If, in the excitement of the race, you fail to store information about the numbers that identify each horse, and instead store information only about the physical features of each animal, you will be unable to distinguish correctly among the first three finishers. Consequently, you might resort to guessing and so be prone to making errors. Thus, if your performance was poor in this task, one could conclude that you stored information about the physical appearance of the horses but not about their identifying numbers. In general, when a series of items has a similar encoding in memory, ordered recall of that series will be poor. Thus, to test for the presence of a particular encoding dimension in memory, one assesses whether a list containing items that are highly similar along that dimension leads to poorer ordered recall compared with a list of items that differ along that dimension. Referring back to our discussion of STM, since Baddeley found that acoustic similarity and not semantic similarity had a detrimental effect on ordered recall, he could infer that subjects had stored acoustic information rather than semantic information in memory.

Is STM Limited to Just Acoustic Codes? This chapter began with the suggestion that memory research is analogous to the activities of a spy who, to understand the work performed in a factory, unobtrusively observes the nature of the raw materials entering the factory and the finished products that are manufactured. Correspondingly, in the case of STM encoding, a psychologist determines the nature of the memory code not by peering directly into a person's brain but instead by observing the responses of subjects who are presented with certain stimuli.

A problem with this approach lies in the selection of the input conditions. If someone consistently observes the same "raw materials" entering the system and observes the same products exiting from it, the conclusion might be reached that only one manufacturing process can occur. However, this may not be correct. If different materials were presented or if the materials were presented in a different way, perhaps different output would result. This would indicate that the system was capable of other kinds of processing. Shulman (1970) made a suggestion very much like this concerning STM coding. He proposed that experiments that found evidence for acoustic but not semantic STM codes did not impose learning conditions on subjects that were conducive to semantic encoding. According to Shulman, acoustic codes are generally easily and rapidly formed. The abundant experimental evidence for acoustic STM coding, in Shulman's view, was the result of demands typically imposed on subjects in STM experiments to rapidly encode and store as much information as possible. Shulman hypothesized that if the rate of stimulus presentation was slow and if the learning task placed more of an emphasis on the retention of semantic information, then evidence for semantic encodings could be obtained.

Shulman tested this by presenting subjects with 10-word lists. Words were shown at one of three rates, .35 seconds, .70 seconds, or 1.4 seconds. After a list had been presented, the experimenter briefly displayed an instructional signal and then a probe word. The instructional signal indicated to subjects what kind of decision had to be made about the relation between the probe word and words in the list just presented. Three types of decisions were possible: (1) Was the probe word identical to any of the list words? (2) Was the meaning of the probe word similar to the meaning of any of the list words? and (3) Did the probe word sound like any of the list words, even though the two words differed in how they were spelled? As examples of these situations, if the probe word *bawl* was preceded by the instructional signal I, subjects knew they were to judge whether the probe word was identical to any of the 10 list words they had just studied. Thus, if they remembered seeing the word *bawl* in the list, they pressed a "yes" key as fast as they could; otherwise, they pressed a "no" key. On the other hand, if the probe word *bawl* was preceded by a letter signalling that a judgment should be made based on sound, then a subject who had been shown the word *ball* in the previous list would have correctly pressed the "yes" key. Finally, if the instructional signal called for a semantic judgment to the probe word *speak*, then the subject would have pressed the "yes" key if the word *talk* had been included in the list.

Assuming information in STM is coded acoustically, what predictions would you make about performance in this task for judgments based on the sound of a probe word? You already know that STM consists of a memory contribution from both the short- and long-term store. Since the last few words from each 10-word list will be the most likely to still be in the short-term store, and thus be highly available when the probe is introduced, performance for the last few list words should be best. That is, if the probe word is *bawl*, then it should be easier for a subject correctly to signal "yes" in the task when the similar-sounding word *ball* occurred at the end rather than at the beginning of the list. As can be seen from Figure 7–4, this result was obtained. Let us now turn to the experimental condition that required subjects to make decisions based on a probe word's semantic properties. If a subject could not store semantic information in STM, then we should find a pattern of results very different from the one just described. One difference would be that performance would not be at a better-than-guessing level. Another difference would be that performance for words presented early and late in each 10-item list would be equally poor. Neither of these possibilities was observed. As Figure 7–4 shows, performance in the semantic judgment condition was quite high. For all serial positions combined, subjects correctly recognized synonyms of the probe word 72.4 percent of the time. Furthermore, performance varied as a function of serial position, with words at the end of a list being judged the most accurately. Thus, subjects must have had semantic information available in this STM task.

Why was there evidence of semantic coding in this STM task but not in those devised by other experimenters? Shulman suggests that because acous-

Figure 7–4
Proportion correct as a function of serial position of the probed word and type of decision demanded by the probe. The decisions called for a judgment of whether or not the list word was identical to the probe word (O–O), whether it sounded the same as the probe word (□–□), or whether it had the same meaning as the probe word (△–△).

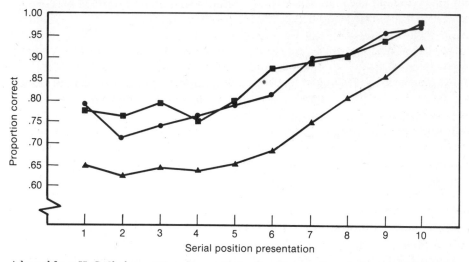

Adapted from H. G. Shulman, "Encoding and retention of semantic and phonemic information in short-term memory." *Journal of Verbal Learning and Verbal Behavior,* 1970, *9,* 499–508. Copyright 1970 by Academic Press. Reprinted by permission.

tic codes are easier to form than semantic codes, subjects will prefer to code information acoustically. However, if the memory task requires that semantic decisions be made about information presented in the STM task, subjects will store information about the stimulus' meaning. According to Shulman, because his task often required that semantic decisions be made, his subjects included meaningful information in STM. To support the claim that semantic codes are not as easily formed as are acoustic codes, Shulman showed that performance requiring semantic decisions was worse when the rate of presentation of list words was faster. That is, on the average, subjects performed the semantic recognition task best when the list words were presented at a rate of 1.4 seconds. Their performance was progressively lower for words presented at the .70- and .35-second rate. This indicated to Shulman that the formation of semantic codes takes time. On the other hand, performance on the task requiring acoustic decisions did not improve when the rate of presentation of lists was slower. Shulman took this to mean that acoustic codes were so readily formed that they were fully developed within .35 seconds. In sum, Shulman's evidence indicates that subjects are capable of storing other kinds of information in STM situations in addition to acoustic information.

The Flexibility of STM Coding.   The conclusion that people can store other forms of information in STM besides acoustic information may not seem very surprising. What might have been more surprising was that psychologists could even consider the possibility that coding in STM was exclusively acoustic. After all, if this were true, it would mean that people could not really be aware of the meaning of the stimuli they were maintaining their STM's, only of the sounds of the stimuli. In fact, a number of psychologists in addition to Shulman did challenge this claim. Conrad (1972), for example, rejected the possibility that encoding in STM was exclusively acoustic, stating that it is "inconceivable that subjects totally ignore all the other identification cues presented in verbal material visually presented or not" (p. 176). A study using deaf schoolchildren provided evidence for this assertion. Conrad presented short lists of letters to deaf and normal-hearing subjects. Two types of lists were utilized. One contained just acoustically similar letters, such as *C,T,P,V,D*, while the other contained just visually similar letters, such as *Z,N,K,Y,X*. All letters in each kind of list were displayed simultaneously for one second. After seeing each list—every subject was shown 18 different instances of each kind of list, alternately—subjects attempted to write down the sequence of letters in their correct order. Conrad found that STM performance for the two types of lists was very different for the deaf and normal-hearing subjects. The normal-hearing subjects were adversely affected much more by acoustic similarity than by visual similarity, while the opposite was true for the deaf subjects. For example, on lists that were five letters long, normal-hearing subjects made 20.3 percent errors when letters were acoustically similar and only 8.8 percent errors when letters were visually similar. The opposite pattern of errors was produced by a group of subjects recruited from a school for deaf children. They made 9.8 percent errors on acoustically similar lists and 20.0 percent errors on visually similar lists. These data indicate that the two groups of subjects were using very different STM encodings. Normal-hearing subjects tended to utilize acoustic codes while deaf subjects utilized some other code. Conrad (1972) was cautious about concluding that the code used by his deaf subjects was necessarily visual. Because many of the deaf children tested in the experiment finger-spelled the letters when lists were displayed, Conrad suggested that the STM code might have consisted in part of finger-spelling information. There is evidence to support this possibility. Shand (1982) used a procedure similar to that previously described to have been used by Baddeley (1966). The procedure entailed visually presenting five-word lists to subjects at a one-second rate. The subjects in Shand's study were all college students who had been deaf since birth but had become proficient in using sign language. Subjects were shown two types of lists. One included words that were signed in a similar way—all required a wrist rotation by a hand located near the signer's face. The other type of list consisted of words that were not signed in a similar way but were acoustically similar. Shand found that the ordered recall of lists based on sign similarity was significantly lower than that of lists based on acoustic similarity. An average of 59 percent of the acoustically similar lists were recalled perfectly, while an average of only 44 percent of the similar-sign lists were recalled perfectly. This shows that the deaf subjects included information about the signs of list words in STM.

These experiments by Shulman (1970), Conrad (1972), and Shand (1982) show that coding in STM is not exclusively acoustic. Rather, the type of information that is stored in an STM experiment can change according to the demands made by the experiment and the experiences and preferences of the subject. Other experiments have shown that subjects can also encode visual information in STM when the task demands it (den Heyer & Barrett, 1971; Tversky, 1969). Thus, STM coding, although often acoustic, is by no means limited exclusively to this form of information. Postman (1975) has reviewed the issue of coding in STM. After describing the mounting evidence that codes other than acoustic may be included in STM, he commented that "the idea that people would mouth the sounds of words for several seconds at a stretch without knowing what they were saying was always a bit unsettling" (p. 300).

Rehearsal

The view being taken here is that STM is a strategy people use when they are attempting to keep as much information as possible available for a short time. In discussing the code used in STM, I have explained that subjects in STM experiments frequently choose to store information about the sounds of stimuli. It has been emphasized, however, that the use of an acoustic code is not imposed by the structure of the memory system. Rather, the use of acoustic codes seems to be part of a strategy adopted by subjects.

Why would someone choose to encode information in an acoustic form rather than in some other form? For example, in Conrad's (1964) experiment, why did subjects recode visually presented letters into their corresponding sounds? One previously mentioned reason is that acoustic codes seem to be easily and rapidly formed. Another reason, one that will be elaborated on here, is that acoustic codes can be conveniently rehearsed.

Rehearsal as a Form of Speech.   An experiment by Locke and Fehr (1970a) shows how closely rehearsal resembles the process of speaking. When we speak certain sounds, such as *b*, *v*, or *f*, we must make distinct movements of our lower lip. These sounds that require this lip movement are known as labial phonemes. Locke and Fehr reasoned that if rehearsal is like silent speech, a person who is rehearsing words that contain these labial phonemes will make very small movements of the lower lip. This may seem like a reasonable but not very likely possibility. Try, for example, to repeat the letter *b* silently to yourself a few times. Did you detect movements of your lower lip? Locke and Fehr did not rely on subjects' reports or on visual observation to test their hypothesis. Instead, they used very sensitive electrodes that they taped to each subject's lower lip and chin. These electrodes were capable of detecting electrical activity in the muscles when they made very slight, even imperceptible movements. Subjects in the experiment were asked to perform the following simple task: Observe a series of five words presented one at a time at a rate of 1.5 seconds, wait 10 seconds, then recall the five words in order. Two kinds of lists were used. One was composed of words containing labial phonemes whose pronunciation therefore required movements of the lower lip. Examples of these words are *bomber, favor,* and *baffle.* The other kind of list was comprised of words that did not contain labial phonemes. Locke and Fehr expected that during the 10-second waiting period that preceded recall of each five-word list, subjects would rehearse the words. Thus, to the extent that rehearsal resembles silent speech, lip muscle activity should have been detected on lists that contained labial phonemes. In fact, this is just what occurred. Significantly more lip muscle activity was evidenced during the rehearsal period for words that contained a labial phoneme. The data of one subject whose results conformed especially clearly to this pattern are shown in Figure 7–5.

Rehearsal is a Strategy. Rehearsal appears to be a process that people learn to use rather than something that is automatic. Locke and Fehr (1970b) have demonstrated this by showing that even though young children between four and five years of age know how to name objects, they do not

Figure 7–5
Electromyographic tracings of one subject during the presentation and rehearsal of a labial (top panel) and nonlabial (bottom panel) stimulus.

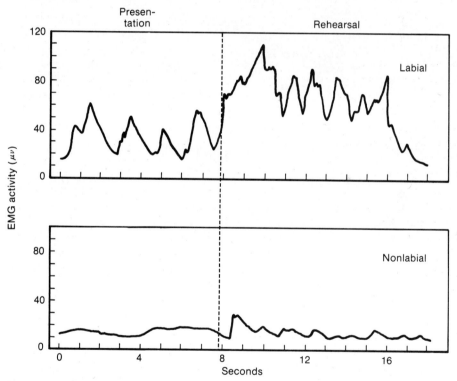

From J. L. Locke and F. S. Fehr, "Subvocal rehearsal as a form of speech." *Journal of Verbal Learning and Verbal Behavior*, 1970, 9, 495–498. Copyright 1970 by Academic Press. Reprinted by permission.

spontaneously use rehearsal to help temporarily maintain the names in memory. The experiment again required detection of electrical activity in muscles of the lower lip. Children between four and five years of age were shown lists consisting of three pictures. The pictures were of objects that could be easily named by the children. Two kinds of picture lists were used. One showed objects whose names contained a labial phoneme (e.g., *oven*) and the other showed objects whose names did not contain a labial phoneme. Children in the study were asked to look at each picture in a list during the 4 seconds it was displayed, then, after a 12-second wait, to recall the names of the three objects. Recordings of electrical activity of the children's lower lip muscles taken during the 12-second rehearsal period showed no difference in activity for labial and nonlabial object names. This indicates that the children were not speaking the object names silently to themselves during the 12-second delay. However, there was significantly more lip muscle activity during the actual viewing of just those objects whose names included labial phonemes. Taken together, these findings indicate that the children were naming the objects to themselves when the pictures were shown, but were not rehearsing these names during the 12-second delay. The data on one subject are shown in Figure 7–6.

Evidence from other studies (e.g., Allik & Siegel, 1976) indicates that by the age of eight years, children use rehearsal spontaneously in memorizing information.

Maintenance Rehearsal.   Rehearsal is generally suggested to have two functions in memory: (1) It maintains information in a highly available state, and (2) it builds up information in the long-term store. At one time it was thought that these two functions always occurred simultaneously. That is, it was suggested (Atkinson & Shiffrin, 1968) that rehearsal both maintained information in consciousness and transferred information into long-term storage. However, experimentation has since revealed that rehearsal may, under certain conditions, maintain information in a highly available state without necessarily improving the probability that the information can later be recalled.

Rehearsal that just maintains information in a highly available state but does not improve its long-term recall is termed *maintenance rehearsal.* A person is using maintenance rehearsal if information is being repeated over and over in a rote fashion, without much thought being given to the meaning of the information. Experimenters that have investigated the effect of maintenance rehearsal on long-term memory have often varied the duration of the rehearsal period and then determined whether there was any corresponding effect on the probability of remembering the information. The

Figure 7–6

Electromyographic tracings of the lip muscle activity of one child during the presentation, rehearsal, and recall of a labial (top panel) and nonlabial (bottom panel) stimulus.

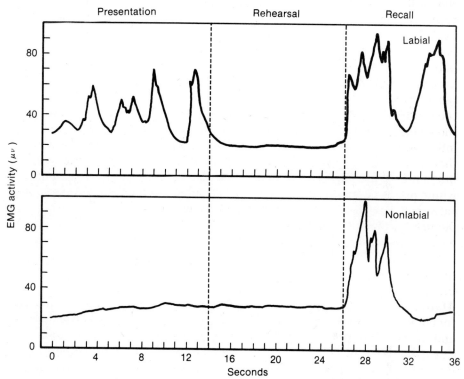

From J. L. Locke and F. S. Fehr, "Young children's use of the speech code in a recall task." *Journal of Experimental Child Psychology*, 1970, *10*, 367–373. Copyright 1970 by Academic Press. Reprinted by permission.

usual, but perhaps somewhat surprising, finding has been that long-term recall does not improve the longer a person engages in maintenance rehearsal.

Before describing some of this evidence, I must make a few general comments about experimental research. In designing an experiment, a psychologist has to make sure that the task assigned to a subject will induce the intended behavior. An experiment that investigates maintenance rehearsal, for example, must utilize a task that causes a subject to repeat information in a rote fashion; the subject must be attempting just to maintain information for varying periods of time and must not be aware or even suspect that the information being rehearsed will eventually have to be recalled or recognized. Any such suspicion could cause the subject to depart from the maintenance rehearsal strategy. Such a departure would be difficult to detect and would, of course, invalidate any conclusion that might be drawn from the data.

For investigating maintenance rehearsal, what kind of task would satisfy these requirements? Consider the following ingenious task devised by Craik and Watkins (1973). Subjects were told that they would hear lists of 21 words. They were informed that after each entire list had been read, they were to write down the last word from that list that had begun with the letter G. To see how this task can induce varying periods of maintenance rehearsal, consider the following abbreviated list: *daughter, oil, rifle, garden, grain, table, football, anchor, giraffe.* Consider just the words *garden* and *grain.* Upon hearing the word *garden,* a subject would begin maintaining the word in consciousness, since this word might be the last word in the list to begin with the critical letter *G,* and thus might have to be reported. However, the very next word in the list is *grain,* which also begins with the letter *G.* Thus, the subject will stop maintaining the word *garden* and instead maintain the word *grain. Grain* will now be maintained during presentation of the next three words, until another word beginning with *G,* the word *giraffe,* is presented. This task, then, induces subjects to utilize maintenance rehearsal, and allows the experimenter to control the duration of the rehearsal period by constructing lists having varying numbers of words intervening between words beginning with some critical letter.

Subjects in Craik and Watkins' experiment were presented with 27 different lists. The lists were constructed so that words beginning with a critical letter were separated randomly by 0, 1, 2, 3, 4, 5, 6, 8, or 12 words. The important finding in the study came from a surprise free recall test given one minute after the last list had been presented. Subjects were asked in this surprise test to write down all words they remembered hearing in the 27 lists. It was found that recall of the words beginning with critical letters was not affected by the duration of the maintenance rehearsal. As many critical words were recalled when short maintenance durations followed presentation of a critical word as when longer maintenance durations followed. The data are shown in Table 7–2.

Elaborative Rehearsal. Another form of rehearsal, known as *elaborative rehearsal,* is much more beneficial to free-recall from the long-term store. Whereas maintenance rehearsal entails rote repetition of some information,

Table 7–2
Percent of critical words recalled as a function of duration of the rehearsal period as indexed by the number of list words intervening between the presentation of critical items.

Rehearsal Interval:	0–2	3–5	6–12
Percent Recalled:	17.33	20.5	18

From F. I. M. Craik and M. J. Watkins, "The role of rehearsal in short-term memory." *Journal of Verbal Learning and Verbal Behavior*, 1973, *12*, 599–607. Copyright 1973 by Academic Press. Reprinted by permission.

elaborative rehearsal is a more active process in which information about an item's meaning is attended to and elaborated on. To better understand the difference between these two rehearsal strategies, imagine that two people, person A and person B, have just been introduced to someone named Arnold Brown. Contrast the strategies that A and B might adopt in an attempt to remember the name:

Person A: Arnold Brown; Arnold Brown; Arnold Brown . . .

Person B: Arnold Brown; let's see, Arnold can be a person's first or last name, as in the name Benedict Arnold; Brown can also be a color name; Arnold Brown; this person's initials are the first two letters of the alphabet and they are in alphabetical order . . .

In these imaginary thought processes, person A is using maintenance rehearsal, while person B is using elaborative rehearsal.

An experiment by Bjork and Jongeward (1975) demonstrates the different effects that these two forms of rehearsal have on long-term recall. The experimental task was somewhat like a Brown–Peterson task without any distractor activity. Subjects were shown six four-letter nouns simultaneously for 4 seconds; after a 20-second period they were required to report back the six nouns. The experimenters instructed subjects to engage in one of two rehearsal activities during the 20-second period; (1) The six words were to be repeated over and over in a rote fashion; or (2) associations were to be formed among the words or, if the subject preferred, an image could be generated for the words. These two rehearsal activities, of course, correspond to what we are calling maintenance and elaborative rehearsal, respectively. Thus, in each trial of the experiment, subjects first saw a list of six nouns for 4 seconds, then received a signal indicating which rehearsal strategy to use for the next 20 seconds. After the rehearsal period, subjects recalled the list of six words. At the end of the experiment, Bjork and Jongeward gave subjects a surprise free-recall test for all words they had encountered in the experiment. Of interest to the experimenters was whether there would be a difference in recall of words that had been given maintenance versus elaborative rehearsal. It was found that elaborative rehearsal led to the long-term recall of about twice as many words as did maintenance rehearsal.

Rehearsal Strategies and Age. It appears that just as rehearsal in general is a strategy that must be learned, so too is the more specific tactic of using elaborative rehearsal. To investigate the kind of rehearsal strategies children use on words they are memorizing for a free-recall test, Ornstein and his co-workers (Ornstein, Naus, & Liberty, 1975) asked some third-, sixth-, and eighth-grade students (their approximate average ages were 8.5, 11.5, and 13.5 years, respectively) to rehearse aloud instead of silently to themselves. The children were shown a list of 18 unrelated words at a five-second rate. Children were instructed to say aloud whatever went through their minds when they saw each word. There were five alternating study-recall trials for the list. That is, each child saw the list once, attempted to free-recall all the words, then saw the list a second time and attempted to free-recall the words again, and so on. The experimenters analyzed not only the probability of a subject free-recalling each word, but also the number of times each word was rehearsed. These data are shown in Figure 7–7A and B.

Some general comments about the serial position functions shown in Figure 7–7A will first be made. It can be seen that there is little difference in the recency effects for the three age groups. This corresponds to what has previously been discussed concerning short-term store capacity. There are differences, however, in the recall performances of the three age groups for the prerecency list words. Since performance on the prerecency words reflects information recalled from the long-term store, it is evident that younger children are less proficient than older children in storing information in the long-term store. Of relevance to our discussion of rehearsal strategies now is the finding that for the youngest subjects, frequency of rehearsal (as shown in Figure 7–7B) did not correlate with free-recall performance in prerecency serial positions. That is, even though third graders rehearsed the first few list words most often, there was no recall advantage for these words. Furthermore, even though the youngest subjects rehearsed words from the middle of the list more often than all older subjects, the recall of these words by the youngest subjects was the poorest.

How can this be explained? Ornstein and his co-workers hoped to find

Figure 7-7
Panel A shows the mean proportion of words recalled as a function of serial position for the third-, sixth-, and eighth-grade subjects. Panel B shows the mean number of rehearsals given by each age group to words from the various serial positions.

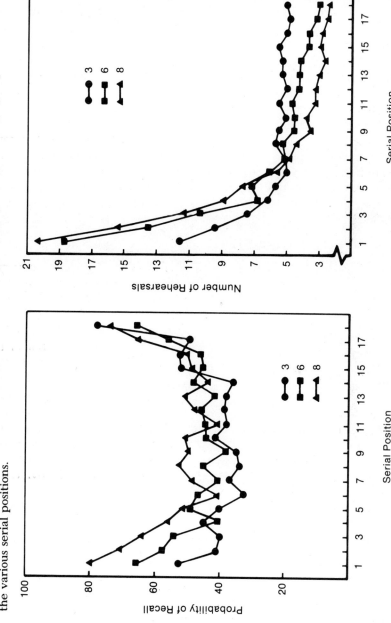

From P. A. Ornstein, M. J. Naus and C. Liberty, "Rehearsal and organizational processes in children's memory." *Child Development,* 1975, *46,* 818–830. Copyright 1975 by the Society for Research in Child Development. Reprinted by permission.

an answer in the specific rehearsal strategies adopted by the youngest and the older children. Table 7–3 shows a transcript of the rehearsals made by a typical third- and eighth-grade subject for the first four words in a list. Here's how these investigators described these rehearsal protocols:

> Note that when the first item is presented, this eighth-grade subject repeats the word three times. When the second item is presented, both words are rehearsed. When the third and fourth items are presented, all previous items are rehearsed together in each rehearsal set. Although this pattern cannot be maintained over all of the items on the list, this is an active pattern of rehearsal in which there is a considerable effort being made to incorporate several items into each rehearsal environment. . . . In contrast . . . the typical third-grade subject tends to rehearse the item currently being presented either alone or in combination with only one other item. In comparison with the rehearsal technique of the eighth grader, this is a very inactive or passive strategy. (pp. 822–823)

It appears, then, that the third graders were relying more on maintenance rehearsal than were the older subjects. The older subjects were adopting a much more active rehearsal strategy, one that apparently allowed them to form associations among different words in the list. Such a strategy, of course, is what we have been calling elaborative rehearsal.

It is interesting to note that subsequent research (Naus, Ornstein, & Aivano, 1977) has shown that the free-recall performance of third graders is generally improved when they are instructed to adopt the more active, elaborative rehearsal strategy. The instructions given to subjects in this more recent study were simply to "practice aloud the presented word with any two other words from the list" (p. 240). It was found that these instructions significantly improved the third grader's free-recall of prerecency words.

Table 7–3
Typical rehearsal protocols of a third- and eighth-grade subject.

	Rehearsal Sets	
Word Presented	Eighth-Grade Subject	Third-Grade Subject
1. Yard	Yard, yard, yard	Yard, yard, yard, yard, yard
2. Cat	Cat, yard, yard, cat	Cat, cat, cat, cat, yard
3. Man	Man, cat, yard, man, yard, cat	Man, man, man, man, man
4. Desk	Desk, man, yard, cat, man, desk, cat, yard	Desk, desk, desk, desk

From P. A. Ornstein, M. J. Naus and C. Liberty, "Rehearsal and organizaitonal processes in children's memory." *Child Development*, 1975, *46*, 818–830. Copyright 1975 by the Society for Research in Child Development. Reprinted by permission of publisher and author.

Actually, this statement needs to be qualified. The experimenters had used two rates of presentation in this study—some lists had been shown at a 5-second rate and some at a 10-second rate. It was found that the instructions to adopt an elaborate rehearsal strategy improved the recall performance of third-grade boys for words presented at both these rates. Performance went from 41 percent (this was the level of recall on the list they studied before receiving elaborative rehearsal instructions) to 50 percent for lists shown at the 5-second rate, and from 43 percent to 51 percent for words shown at the 10-second rate. For the third-grade girls, the elaborate rehearsal instructions improved free-recall performance only for lists presented at the 5-second rate. These instructions raised recall from 40 percent to 49 percent correct. Elaborative rehearsal instructions did not improve the free-recall performance of the third-grade girls for the list presented at the 10-second rate. Why not? It is known that girls at elementary school ages are generally better at dealing with verbal materials than are boys. This greater verbal facility evidently allowed these third-grade girls spontaneously to adopt the elaborative rehearsal strategy on the more slowly presented list. Evidence of this can be seen in Figure 7–8, which shows the average number of items the third graders rehearsed together during presentation of words from the different lists. It can be seen here how the rehearsal of the third-grade girls for the words presented at the 10-second rate stands out. On this list, the girls were rehearsing an average of 3.5 different words together, a number much greater than that rehearsed during their study of the list presented at the five-second rate, and a number much greater than that rehearsed by boys on both these lists. Thus, we can say that elaborative rehearsal instructions did not improve free-recall performance of third-grade girls on the list presented at a 10-second rate because the girls were using elaborative rehearsal on these lists to begin with! In accord with this conclusion is the finding that the recall performance of the third-grade girls on the list presented at a 10-second rate was high— they recalled 54 percent of the prerecency words. All of this indicates that rehearsal is not something that is innate or built into the information processing system; instead, it is a flexible strategy that people apparently learn to use to improve their memory performance.

The Capacity of STM

It is difficult to assign a capacity to STM. One reason is because STM is a strategy and, consequently, is sensitive to factors such as age and practice. An often-cited STM capacity estimate has been proposed by Miller (1956), who claimed that STM can hold seven plus or minus two chunks of information. This estimate, however, is not appropriate for all age groups. For exam-

Figure 7–8
Number of words in a rehearsal set as a function of serial position, rate of word presentation, and sex of the third-grade subject.

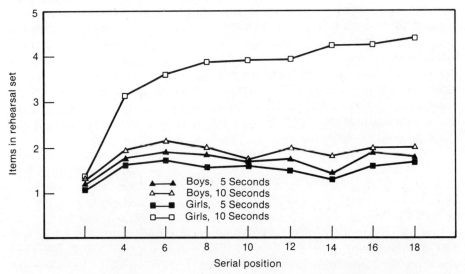

From M. H. Naus, P. A. Ornstein and S. Aivano, "Developmental changes in memory: The effects of processing time and rehearsal instructions." *Journal of Experimental Child Psychology*, 1977, *23*, 237–251. Copyright 1977 by Academic Press. Reprinted by permission.

ple, the typical digit span of children aged 3, 4.5, 7, and 10 years is three, four, five, and six, respectively (Woodworth & Schlosberg, 1954).

STM capacity estimates are also strongly affected by the type of test that is used. If the usual procedure is followed (Watkins, 1977) and a person's memory span is measured as the maximum number of digits that can be correctly recalled in order on half the recall attempts on lists of that length, then the estimate of seven plus or minus two items is a reasonable one. For example, Parkinson (1982) measured the digit spans of college students and other college-aged persons in this way and found a mean span of 6.4 items. However, if a running performance measure is used, a much lower estimate of STM capacity is obtained. In this procedure, a subject is presented with a series of unrelated stimuli at a rate of about one item per second. The subject is not told how long the list will be, only that when the list ends, as many of the last few list items as possible should be recalled in order. An experiment conducted by Pollack, Johnson, and Knaff (1959) obtained running digit span estimates of 4.2 items using college students as subjects.

This variation in STM capacity accords with the view that STM is a strategy that makes use of the short-term store and the long-term store. As mentioned previously, of these two memory stores, only the short-term store appears to have a definable capacity, one that has been estimated to be about three units. In reviewing some studies of STM capacity, Broadbent (1975) has concluded that if a limit in processing capacity exists, it appears to be three and not seven items. He suggests that "the traditional seven arises from the particular opportunity provided in the memory span task for the retrieval of information from different forms of processing" (p. 35). This is very much like the claim being made here, that it is the contribution from the long-term store that boosts performance in a STM task beyond the three-item capacity of the short-term store.

The Function of the Long-Term Store in STM

Recoding

It has already been mentioned that the long-term store plays a role in storing information in STM tasks. There is another function that this store has in STM tasks; it allows stimulus information to be recoded. One example of a recoding operation that occurs under these circumstances is the conversion of a visually presented letter into its acoustic form. It was previously mentioned that this visual to acoustic recoding has often been detected in tasks such as the one devised by Conrad (1964). It is important to realize now that the ability to translate a visually presented letter into its acoustic form depends on information in the long-term store; that is, it depends on there being associations between a letter's visual and acoustic representations. If a person does not have this information available, for example, if a person does not have information about the visual form of the letter *A* connected with the sound "ay," this recoding could not occur.

There are other ways a person can recode stimuli besides transforming its visual representation into an acoustic representation. One useful technique takes advantage of chunks that have been developed in the long-term store. In this procedure, a person studying information in an STM task attempts to find a single chunk in the long-term store that matches a number of the individual stimuli that have been presented. If such a match is found, the collection of individual stimuli are recoded into a single chunk. This lightens the storage load in STM, for in place of several stimuli, one now has only a single chunk to maintain.

An experiment by Bower and Springston (1970) illustrates this procedure. The task required of subjects was simple. They were to listen to a series of 12 letters that were read to them in a period of 10 seconds and to repeat the letters back in order. The 12 letters were not read at a uniform rate, but instead in small groups that had a short pause between each sequence of three letters. Try to perform this recall task yourself on the following string of letters. (The space between each group of three letters represents a pause.) *MFB IPH DTW AIB.* Try this again on the letter string *ECI AFD RCB SXK.* On strings such as these, subjects in the experiment were able to report back correctly an average of 7.4 letters in their proper order. Consider now performance on some slightly different letter strings: *FBI PHD TWA IBM* and *CIA FDR CBS XKE.* As you can probably tell from your own reactions to these letter strings, it was much easier for subjects to report them back in their correct order. Average performance on these strings was 9.7 correct, an improvement of about 30 percent. The reason for the improvement, of course, was that letter triads in the second arrangement corresponded to familiar units (i.e., chunks) in the long-term store. As a result, instead of having to maintain and report back 12 individual letters, a subject had only four familiar units to deal with.

In this experiment, recoding was facilitated when letters were arranged to match larger familiar units in the long-term store. An interesting experiment by Ericsson, Chase, and Faloon (1980) shows how a person can develop systems for recoding stimuli even when no obvious match at first occurs between information presented in an STM task and information that has been associated together in the long-term store. In the study, a single college student was tested over a period of approximately one and one half years. The student, S. F., had average intelligence and did not initially possess any unusual memory abilities. The experimental task given to S. F. was a memory span task. S. F. was read digits in a random order at a rate of one per second and asked to report them back immediately in their correct order. The experimenter started with short sequences of numbers. If S. F. got the sequence correct, the experimenter then read a list that was one digit longer. On trials in which S. F. made one or more errors, the experimenter decreased the subsequent digit list by one item. This procedure was followed for three to five sessions a week, each lasting an hour. On the first session, S. F. could correctly report back seven digits in order. But after approximately 190 hours of practice that took place over a 20-month period, S. F. had increased his digit span to 79 items. Here's how the authors of the study accounted for this dramatic improvement:

> The most essential part of S. F.'s skill is his mnemonic associations, which he described in great detail in his verbal reports. The principle of a mnemonic is to associate unknown material with something familiar: the advantage is that it relieves the burden on short-term memory because recall can be achieved through

a single association with an already-existing code in long-term memory. What S. F. did was to categorize three- and four-digit groups as running times for various races. For example, 3492 was recoded as "3 minutes and 49 point 2 seconds, near world-record mile time." During the first four months, S. F. gradually constructed an elaborate set of mnemonic associations based initially on running times and then supplemented with ages (893 was 89 point 3, very old man) and dates (1944 was "near the end of World War II") for those sequences that could not be categorized as times. Running times (62 percent) and ages (25 percent) account for almost 90 percent of S. F.'s mnemonic associations. (p. 1181)

Not all the improvement in S. F.'s digit span can be attributed to this recoding method. Some of the improvement was due to retrieval procedures that he developed. Nevertheless, this is an impressive demonstration of the effectiveness of the recoding operation in helping improve performance in an STM task.

It must be pointed out that the reason S. F. chose to recode digits into running times was because, being a long-distance runner himself, he had a large collection of numbers associated together in his long-term store, each corresponding to a particular running event. The experimenters report that S. F.'s running experiences enabled him to classify running times into more than 11 major catagories that ranged from times for the half mile up to the marathon. This again illustrates how the composition of chunks in the long-term store depends on individual experience. Apparently the key to successful recoding is to recognize that some newly encountered stimuli correspond to past experiences that form a chunk in the long-term store.

Rehearsal and Associative Processes in the Long-Term Store

When a person becomes conscious of some information, a representation of the information begins to form in the long-term store. As mentioned previously, this allows the long-term store to participate in the storage of information that is encountered in an STM task. In this section, the nature of the information that becomes represented in the long-term store will be considered.

Maintenance Rehearsal.   One important kind of change that results from rehearsal in an STM task is the establishment of new associations in the long-term store. Two forms of association will be distinguished here. One will be referred to as *contextual associations.* These are connections that link the representation of a familiar concept with information that identifies the specific conditions in which the concept was encountered. For example, if you were to hear your name being called out while you were sitting in a restaurant, a memory of that event would probably include a representation of your name (the familiar concept), to which was attached some context information. The context information might specify the physical surroundings in which your name was called out—the smell of the food, your mood, the lighting conditions—and the manner in which your name was presented—the sex and tone of the voice calling out your name. According to this analysis, we are considering the concept as being derived from existing, general information in the long-term store, while the contextual information is that part of the memory that represents all the details unique to the specific occurrence of the concept.

We previously made a distinction between maintenance and elaborative rehearsal. This distinction is relevant here because it appears (Woodward, Bjork, & Jongeward, 1973) that maintenance rehearsal leads principally to the formation of contextual associations. Geiselman and Bjork (1980) set out to demonstrate this using the following reasoning process: If maintenance rehearsal leads to the association of context information to concept information, then the longer information is rehearsed in this way, the more complete the association should be. Geiselman and Bjork then applied one of the three principles of retrieval described earlier in this text, the principle that retrieval will be increasingly more successful when the information in the cue more closely matches the information that was stored in the to-be-retrieved memory trace. They suggested that any memory enhancement produced by having the context information in the retrieval cue match the context that prevailed during learning would indicate that context was indeed associated with the concept as a result of rehearsal.

To see this in more concrete terms, imagine that four people are seated in a restaurant where a waiter announces the evening's specials. For some reason all four people repeat the waiter's words in exactly the way he spoke them, over and over to themselves in a mindless, rote fashion. Two of these four people rehearse the information for 5 seconds and two rehearse it for 10 seconds. Imagine now that all four are later given a test to see if they can recognize what the restaurant's specials were. In the test, one person who rehearsed the words for 5 seconds and one who rehearsed for 10 seconds is read these and other distractor menu items in the same restaurant by the same waiter. The other two people are read these same test words in another restaurant by another waiter. If the maintenance rehearsal serves to associate context and concept information, then two trends should be evident in the memory performance. First, the two people tested in the same context as the learning occurred should better recognize the specials than the two people tested in a different context. Second, the advantage of being tested in the same versus the different context should be greater for the 10-second rehearsers than for the 5-second rehearsers. The reason this second outcome can be expected is the longer rehearsal time will have allowed the learning context to be more effectively associated with the stored concept; this, in turn, will permit the 10-second rehearser to benefit more from the match between the context information represented in the retrieval cue and that encoded during learning of the menu items.

In Geiselman and Bjork's study, subjects heard a series of word triads (e.g., *kite, boot, pear*) spoken by either a male or a female. After each triad there was a silent interval that lasted for either 5, 10, or 15 seconds. Subjects were instructed to use the time to imagine that the speaker was saying the words over and over again. The experimenters did not mention that there was to be a recognition test for the words but instead led subjects to believe that the purpose of the experiment was to see how well they could repeat the words to themselves in the speaker's voice. The surprise recognition test that was given later included individual words that either had or had not been included in word triads the subjects had rehearsed. (We will refer to the words that subjects had previously rehearsed as "old" words, and the words they had not been presented with as "new" words.) The experimenters designed the test so that half of the old words were read in the same voice that subjects had earlier rehearsed and half were read in a different voice. Figure 7–9 shows that the test results conformed to the hypothesis that maintenance rehearsal associates context information with concept information. Not only was the probability of recognizing old words better when the voice reading test words matched the voice that had read them earlier, but also the difference between these two test conditions increased with longer periods of maintenance rehearsal.

Elaborative Rehearsal. There is evidence that context information becomes associated with concept information during elaborative rehearsal as well as during maintenance rehearsal (Geiselman & Bjork, 1980). However, elaborative rehearsal is distinguishable from maintenance rehearsal in that only elaborative rehearsal also leads to the formation of associations among the concepts that are being rehearsed. These association among concepts are often termed *interitem associations.*

The formation of interim associations through elaborative rehearsal helps explain the following observation. In memory-span experiments, when people are presented with a series of about 10 unrelated items for immediate ordered recall, they tend to segment successive items into small groups. For example, if presented with the numbers 1 7 6 8 3 9 4 5 2, a subject might form them into groups of three numbers by putting pauses between each successive triad. Thus, as the numbers just listed were being presented, a subject might form the sets 1 7 6 8 3 9 4 5 2. One reason people employ this strategy is that it allows for the effective use of elaborative

Figure 7–9
Probability of word recognition as a function of the match between the voice presenting the words and the voice testing the words. The solid line represents performance
when the two voices matched and the dotted line represents performance when
voices were different.

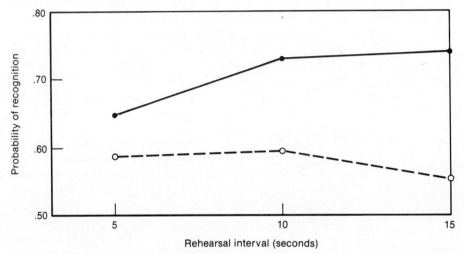

Adapted from R. E. Geiselman and R. A. Bjork, "Primary versus secondary rehearsal in imagined
voices: Differential effects on recognition." *Cognitive Psychology,* 1980, *12,* 188–205. Copyright
1980 by Academic Press. Reprinted by permission.

rehearsal, which, in turn, causes the rehearsed information to become linked
or chunked together in the long-term store. An experiment by Wickelgren
(1964) has shown that for lists of unrelated digits, rehearsal in sets of about
three items is most effective for immediate ordered recall. In this study,
sequences of 6–10 unrelated digits were read at a rate of one digit per
second. Different subjects were given different instructions about rehearsing
the digits as they were being presented. Some subjects were told just to
rehearse the most recently presented digit by itself. Other subjects were
instructed to rehearse numbers in groups of two, three, four, or five items.
Table 7–4 presents the approximate percent of lists in which ordered recall
was perfect.

How do we know that the strategy of grouping information together
during rehearsal really does lead to the formation of interitem associations?
One strong indication that these associations are formed comes from an
analysis of recall errors subjects make. If it is true that rehearsing items

Table 7–4
Percent of lists for which there was perfect ordered recall as a function of the size of the rehearsal set.

Size of Rehearsal Group				
1	2	3	4	5
57	54	65	64	59

From W. Wickelgren, "Size of rehearsal group and short-term memory." *Journal of Experimental Psychology,* 1964, *68,* 413–419. Copyright 1964 by the American Psychological Association. Reprinted by permission of publisher and author.

in groups of three's leads to associations among the three items in the rehearsal set, then these three items should behave as a single unit. Thus, one should observe that all three either tend to be forgotten or all three tend to be remembered. Data obtained by Bower and Springston (1970) confirm this. The experimenters induced subjects to rehearse items in small groups by putting one-second pauses after every third letter in 12-letter lists. In their analysis of subjects' ordered recall of these lists, Bower and Springston calculated how often a subject correctly recalled a letter when the immediately preceding letter from the list had been correctly recalled. Here's what this analysis can be expected to show if subjects do form three-item chunks: When the subject recalls the first letter of a three-item group correctly, the second and third items should also be correctly recalled. However, when an error occurs, it should occur most often on the first letter of a three-item chunk, for it is at this point that the subject either finds the chunk in memory or does not. This analysis, known as a *transition error probability* measure, is shown in Figure 7–10. Two types of letter strings were analyzed in this figure, pronounceable triads, such as *DAT BEC JAV PEL,* and strings consisting of these same letters arranged into nonpronounceable triads, such as *LDA TBR CJA VPE.* It can be seen that both cases conform to the hypothesis that subjects were chunking letters in groups of threes.

What exactly are people saying to themselves when rehearsing these sets of stimuli elaboratively? It is quite difficult to know this precisely; no doubt, there are individual differences in the specific strategies that subjects adopt. Whatever their specific strategy, though, it appears that people develop it through experience. Evidence of this comes from the findings (Harris & Burke, 1972) that temporal pauses between groups of three digits does

Figure 7–10
Transition error probability as a function of serial position for pronounceable and shifted triads.

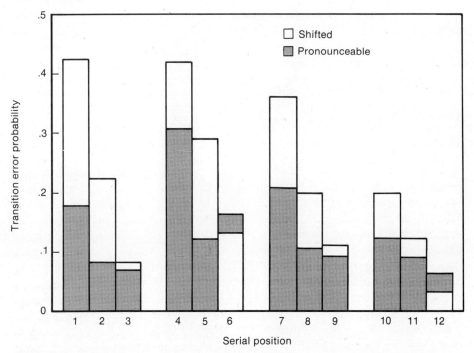

Adapted from G. H. Bower and F. Springston, "Pauses as recoding points in letter series." *Journal of Experimental Psychology,* 1970, *83,* 421–430. Copyright 1970 by the American Psychological Association. Reprinted by permission of publisher and author.

not improve the immediate ordered recall performance of second graders (mean age, 7½ years) for nine-item lists, but does improve the performance of fourth graders (mean age, 9½ years). This accords with a finding that was discussed earlier, that elaborative rehearsal is generally not a spontaneously employed strategy in children at or below the third-grade level (Ornstein, Naus, & Liberty, 1975).

Mental Associations in Perspective

The two associative processes we have distinguished, context associations and interitem associations, are important not just because they underlie performance in STM tasks; they are important principally because they make possible much of the memorization that goes on in everyday situations. One way to get an appreciation of the role that these two associative processes play in remembering is to observe what happens when they are impaired. Reference has been made at several points in this text to persons with amnesia. It has been mentioned that psychologists are in general agreement that amnesics have an impaired ability to form new long-term memory traces. A number of psychologists (e.g., Huppert & Piercy, 1976; Stern, 1981; Wickelgren, 1979b) have suggested that the amnesic deficit can more specifically be attributed to an impaired ability to form new context associations in the long-term store. To understand better the significance of this suggestion, consider what would happen if you were unable to associate context information with information about familiar concepts. Under these circumstances, if you encountered a familiar stimulus, perhaps a friend or a family member, you would not be able to associate events surrounding this particular encounter with the familiar stimulus. Thus, at a later time you would have no recollection of the meeting.

Ordinarily, contextual associations appear to form automatically. We consequently don't repeatedly tell the same joke to someone, because we remember such things as where we last told the joke and who was present at this time. Furthermore, when we change residence, we don't drive to the home we used to live in five years ago, because we will have formed new associations between the concept of home and our more recent living environment. Such behavior, however, may not be avoidable if the ability to form context associations has been impaired. Here is an incident related by Milner (1968) about the amnesic patient H. M. The incident occurred 14 years after the operation that severely impaired H. M.'s ability to form such associations.

> He attempted to guide us to his house . . . when we were driving him back from Boston. After leaving the main highway, we asked him for help in locating his house. He promptly and courteously indicated to us several turns, until we arrived at a street which he said was quite familiar to him. At the same time, he admitted that we were not at the right address. A phone call to his mother revealed that we were on the street where he used to live before his operation. With her directions, we made our way to the residential area where H. M. now lives. He did not get his bearings until we were within two short blocks of the house, which he could just glimpse through the trees. (p. 217)

How Different Are Context and Interitem Associations?   It is often difficult clearly to distinguish context associations from interitem associations. Consider a study investigating the abilities of amnesic patients to learn lists of 12 paired associates (Winocur & Weiskrantz, 1976). In this experiment patients were shown 12 unrelated word pairs (e.g., *chair–bake)* for two seconds each and were told to try to learn to associate the words together. A test given after the fourth learning trial required subjects to supply the correct response term when presented with a stimulus word. Whereas control subjects gave correct responses on the test to about 10 of the 12 words, amnesics gave an average of about 1 correct response. It is not perfectly clear here if this poor performance by the amnesic patients should be interpreted as the result of an impaired ability to form interitem associations or context associations. Although one can view this task as involving the formation of associations between two familiar concepts, the stimulus and the response words, one can also view it as involving the formation of associations between response word and its presentation context, where the presentation context includes the stimulus word. According to the latter interpretation, the paired associate learning deficit again indicates there's an impairment in the formation of contextual associations.

It must be pointed out that psychologists do not know whether context associations are substantially different from interitem associations. They both appear to be formed rapidly and their formation does not necessarily require that any conscious effort be expended. Perhaps one can view these associations as resulting from the same fundamental mechanism, one that causes any information that is simultaneously present in the short-term store to become associated together. According to this analysis, maintenance rehearsal leads principally to contextual associations because it involves the repetition of a single item while the person has some awareness of the general context or situation in which the item is being encountered. On the other hand, elaborative rehearsal, being a much more active process, usually involves the simultaneous arousal of several concepts in consciousness as well as some awareness of the situational context. This tends to establish interitem links among the rehearsed information as well as context associations.

Associations in Evolutionary Perspective.   Some psychologists who have viewed memory from an evolutionary standpoint (e.g., Razran, 1971; Rozin, 1976) have suggested that as the nervous system of vertebrates has evolved, more sophisticated associative abilities have supplemented the primitive associative mechanisms. An example of a primitive associative process is that which underlies classical conditioning. In this process, after repeatedly experiencing the pairing together of some neutral stimulus (e.g., the sound of a bell) and a reflex-triggering stimulus (e.g., food, which stimulates the reflex of salivation), an organism will begin to emit the reflexive response when the neutral stimulus alone is presented. Here, an association appears to have been formed in the organism's mind between representations of the neutral stimulus and those of the reflex-triggering stimulus. This kind of associative learning is primitive in the sense that it occurs in simple organisms such as worms, fish, and insects. Other, more complex associative abilities are manifested in higher vertebrates, such as birds and mammals (see Hintzman, 1978, pp. 188–193). The most sophisticated associative abilities are those that have been described here to occur when humans rehearse information. These context and interitem associations are sophisticated in that they are flexible (they act on any information that enters the short-term store, not just on particular stimuli that evolution has prepared us to associate) and also in that they are rapidly formed.

It is important to realize that normally, these sophisticated, high-level associative abilities coexist with the more primitive associative capabilities. Many forms of amnesia, however, appear to impair these sophisticated, higher-level associative mechanisms differentially, leaving the amnesic patient still capable of lower forms of learning. An interesting demonstration of this has been reported by Weiskrantz and Warrington (1979). In this study, two amnesic patients were classically conditioned to blink an eye upon perceiving an audiovisual stimulus (a tone and a light that came on together). The conditioning was achieved by pairing the audiovisual stimulus repeatedly with a brief puff of air that caused the subjects to reflexively blink an eye. Both subjects showed strong evidence of conditioning after the procedure had been carried out for 50 or more trials. Conditioning was evidenced by a subject blinking an eye when the audiovisual stimulus was presented alone. The following conversations are excerpts from two interviews conducted by the experimenter with one subject, A. S. The first interview occurred a day after A. S. had received 200 conditioning trials; the second interview occurred just 16 minutes after A. S. had received 80 more conditioning trials during the second day of the experiment. (The letter E below stands for experimenter).

Interview 1

E: Mr. S., can you remember what you were doing the last time you were here?

A. S.: Well—I listened to stories and I had to give certain answers about them after they had been played to me or shown to me.

E: But can you remember what happened here with this gadget?

A. S.: Now—er—it had to do with working of my brain, hadn't it?

E: Well, maybe, but can you say any more than that about it?

A. S.: . . . and my eye.

E: Oh yes?

A. S.: You were dealing with my right eye and seeing if it was responding properly to stimuli.

E: Yes. What sort of stimuli; can you remember?

A.S.: Well, you had patterns. They were on the picture that was shown to me, and these patterns had a certain effect on me. And if the eye responded correctly then you knew that the eye was all right.

E: Just patterns? You can't remember anything else? You remember what happened with this part of the gadget here? [*pointing to the nozzle of the air puffer*].

A. S.: Well, it got a bit overheated, I think, and you had to treat it, like a doctor treats his patient. [*No apparatus failure, in fact, had occurred.*]

Interview 2

E: Can you remember what was happening with this equipment here—what were you doing?

A. S.: Now (pause). I've just forgotten for the moment; it's at the back of my mind.

E: Yes, well just have a guess.

A. S.: I was telling where the position of certain things were in relation to others?

E: I see. And where was your head?

A. S.: My head was on this ledge.

E: Yes, and what happened when your head was on that ledge? Can you remember?

A. S.: Well, I looked—I kept my attention on that point there and then I answered several questions. Then, no, no; I kept my attention on there and watched the picture, as it were, and this flashed and I gave an answer.

E: I see.

A. S.: Which was a form of, I think, some Eastern language.

E: Some what?

A. S.: Some Eastern language, I think. [A. S. was fluent in several languages.] (pp. 190–191)[1]

This conversation shows that A. S. had practically no memory for any of the details of the conditioning procedure. What details he did supply apparently were fabrications based on other past or imagined experiences. In spite of this memory dificit, however, A. S. still had the necessary mental associative capacity to acquire a conditioned response.

Summary

Short-term memory was described as being a strategy that people use to temporarily maintain as much information as possible in memory. The

---

[1] From L. Weiskrantz and E. K. Warrington, "Conditioning in amnesic patients." *Neuropsychologia*, 1979, *17*, 187–194. Copyright 1979 by Pergamon Press, Inc. Reprinted by permission.

strategy has several characteristics. First, it utilizes both the short- and long-term stores. The role of the long-term store is evidenced by the influence of proactive interference on information being maintained in an STM task. Keppel and Underwood's (1962) study has demonstrated that forgetting in a Brown–Peterson task is due to the buildup of proactive interference, a forgetting mechanism that acts on information in the long-term store. The Hebb task also points to an involvement of the long-term store in STM. A second characteristic of STM is that it commonly involves an acoustic code. Although Conrad's (1964) study showed that people tend to transform visual stimuli into an acoustic representation in a STM task, other studies, most notably one by Shulman (1970), have shown that when the situation demands it, other kinds of information, including semantic information, may be stored. A third characteristic of the strategy of STM is that it utilizes the rehearsal process. Rehearsal is a skill that must be developed. It can serve not only to maintain information in a highly accessible state, but to encode information into a format that will allow it to be subsequently retrieved from the long-term store. These two functions of rehearsal involve somewhat different rehearsal strategies known respectively as maintenance and elaborative rehearsal. Maintenance rehearsal is a much easier form of processing than elaborative rehearsal and as such tends to be developed at a younger age. It was mentioned that STM is a rather flexible strategy. As a result, it is difficult to assign a fixed capacity to STM that is invariant with age and type of testing method. The often-mentioned capacity of seven items is most applicable to adults tested using the standard memory span technique.

The role of the long-term store in STM was examined in more detail. Evidence was presented that information in the long-term store can be used to recode information being processed in an STM task. This recoding can greatly increase the number of stimuli maintained in STM. The associative processes underlying the long-term store's role in an STM task were also discussed. It was suggested that when using maintenance rehearsal, a person primarily establishes long-term associations between an item and its presentation context. Elaborative rehearsal produces not only context associations, but also interitem associations. It was suggested that both forms of association are the result of cognitive abilities that have been recently developed in an evolutionary sense.

Chapter 8
Encoding for retrieval

What should go through the mind of a person who is trying to remember something? This question is important because, as suggested at the end of the chapter on STM, traces will be formed in the long-term store to represent whatever a person thinks about. But the establishment of long-term traces will be of no use unless they can later be retrieved. Thus, to determine what a person should think about and therefore what should be stored, we must again consider the factors that affect retrieval. In the upcoming discussions, encoding strategies will be described that, in accord with these factors, will enhance the probability of a memory's retrieval.

Overlap between Information in the Cue and the Memory Trace

One important factor previously described to affect a memory's chance of being retrieved is the extent to which information in the cue matches information in the memory trace. The more complete the overlap of cue and trace information, the better the chance of retrieval. In our previous discussions of this retrieval factor, situations were described in which the probability of retrieval was affected by manipulations made at the time of retrieval, and thus after encoding had occurred. The Anderson and Pichert (1978) study exemplifies this approach. Here, the story of the two boys exploring a house was encoded from the perspective of either a burglar or a homebuyer. After the first recall attempt, retrieval of additional story information occurred for subjects who adopted the alternate perspective (i.e., the perspective they had not adopted when reading the story). It is important to note here that the increased remembering was produced by an alteration in the retrieval environment. That is, the increased overlap between cue and previously unrecalled trace information was brought about by manipulating the information in the cue. In contrast to this approach, the emphasis now will be on increasing the match between cue and trace information by manipulating information that is stored in the trace. If one likens a memory trace to money in the bank, the former approach is analogous to finding ways to withdraw money from a bank account once the money has already been deposited. The current approach, however, is like finding ways to facilitate withdrawals by choosing particular bank accounts suited to the conditions under which retrieval of the money is expected to occur. Here, one is facilitating retrieval at the time the money is deposited rather than at the time it is withdrawn.

Paired-Associate Learning

In order to adopt an encoding strategy that allows optimal overlap of cue and trace information, one must have some knowledge of the retrieval cues that will later be available. It is often possible to know this. For example, in paired-associate learning paradigms, a subject is presented with pairs of stimuli to study and later asked to provide the response term when given the stimulus term. Here, one knows in advance what the cue will be. In order to have the cue maximally overlap the to-be-retrieved memory trace, the learner should attempt to associate the members of each pair of items together into a unified chunk. This will allow one of them to be retrieved when the other is presented.

What should a person think about in order to facilitate the association between two items? Thinking about (i.e., rehearsing) the items simultaneously should have some effect. However, studies have shown that other, more effective strategies are available. Bower and Winzenz (1970) investigated the effect of four different strategies on paired-associate learning. Subjects in the study were shown three lists, each made up of 30 different pairs of unrelated concrete nouns (e.g., *book–cat*). Four groups of subjects were given different instructions about how to learn to associate stimulus and response words. A repetition group was told simply to rehearse each pair of words together silently for the five seconds it was displayed. A sentence-reading group was presented with a sentence that contained the two words (e.g., The *book* fell on the *cat*.) and instructed to use the sentence to associate the words together. A sentence generation group was asked to make up a meaningful phrase or sentence to relate the words in each pair. Finally, an imagery group was instructed to form a mental image in which the two objects named in each pair were interacting in some way (e.g., an image of a cat screeching as a book lands on its tail). Memory was tested in two ways immediately after each list had been shown. On a cued recall test, half the stimulus words from the list were presented one at a time and subjects were asked to provide the appropriate response word; and on a recognition test, subjects were presented with a stimulus word and five response words from the list, and asked to select the response word that had previously been paired with the stimulus word. The average percent correct responses for the three lists according to study condition are shown in Table 8–1. From the table it can be seen that the repetition condition, although producing some association between the stimulus and response words, was inferior to the other three methods. In the recall test, which was more sensitive to differences among the four study conditions, imagery led to the highest performance, followed by sentence generation and sentence reading.

Why were the memory performances of the sentence-reading, sentence-generation, and imagery groups better than that of the repetition group? There may be a number of reasons for this that are specific to each of the three procedures. Some of these reasons will soon be presented. However, before doing so, I will suggest one reasonable, general account of the effectiveness of these three learning strategies as a whole. To understand the suggestion that will be proposed, consider first how the three methods differ as a whole from rote repetition. One way they differ is that all three make use of previous memories in which associations between the two concepts already exist. The suggestion to be made here is that these previously formed associations can be "updated" and used to tie together the specific items being presented. The important thing to be noted here is that since the basic association process has already occurred, much of the work will have already been done. The updating will consequently involve such things

Table 8–1
Average percent correct responses in each study condition according to type of test.

Test	Study Condition			
	Repetition	Sentence-Reading	Sentence-Generation	Imagery
Recall	37.1	54.5	76.7	87.3
Recognition	80.2	87.3	98.7	97.8

Adapted from G. H. Bower and D. Winzenz, "Comparison of associative learning strategies." *Psychonomic Science,* 1970, *20,* 119–120. Copyright 1970 by the Psychonomic Society. Reprinted by permission.

as the addition of context information to the previously formed association and the addition of specific details about the identity of the objects that have been perceived. As an example, consider how the sentence "The book fell on the cat" may help associate the words book and cat. According to the hypothesis just presented, this sentence corresponds to experiences we have stored in memory. Even though we may not have actually seen a book falling on a cat or even though we may not remember a specific incident like this, we all have stored in memory the concept of books or, more generally, heavy objects, falling on living things, ourselves as well as cats. We can use this general knowledge in associating the concepts book and cat. To do this we have to update this concept. In this example our updating may require us not only to attach context information to the concept, information indicating that this concept was encountered under these circumstances, but also to associate some specific information about the nature of the heavy object (a book) and the living thing (a cat). What is important here is that the familiar concept already has the heavy object linked to the living thing; consequently, we will be saved the effort of reforming this association.

This kind of account is often envoked to explain the beneficial effect of relevant prior knowledge on new learning. In a study by Bransford and Johnson (1972), for example (see chapter 1), it was found that a story title such as "Washing Clothes," when presented prior to the reading of a paragraph that described a clothes-washing process without the aid of concrete referents, facilitated comprehension and memory of the paragraph. It has been proposed (Alba, Alexander, Hasher, & Caniglia, 1981) that the title allowed subjects to use general, integrated knowledge in the long-term store to help tie the story's sentences together.

It is interesting to note that the three encoding strategies in the Bower and Winzenz experiment that utilized a subject's general knowledge were not equally effective for cued recall. Although relative to the repetition condition subjects benefited from having the experimenter provide a meaningful sentence linking the two words together, when subjects generated sentences on their own, cued recall performance was even better. Bower and Winzenz account for this by suggesting that subjects who generate their own sentences comprehend the relationship between the two nouns more fully than subjects who have the experimenter provide a sentence. Bower and Winzenz's data also show that for cued recall, the imagery strategy was significantly better than even the sentence-generation strategy. That interacting imagery is an effective strategy for associating stimuli together is a pervasive finding in the psychological literature. Because of its importance, this topic will be discussed in more detail in the next section.

The Interacting Imagery Strategy.   There appear to be two components that contribute to the effectiveness of the interacting imagery strategy. One component is the presence of visual encodings and the other is the presence of interaction. The value of visual encodings to memory has often been demonstrated. For example, Epstein, Rock, and Zuckerman (1960, experiment 4) compared the cued recall abilities of subjects who had studied pairs of concrete nouns with those shown pairs of pictures of the objects named by the nouns. Thus, one group of subjects studied pairs of nouns such as *pipe–clock,* whereas the other group studies pairs of pictures in which these two objects were shown separated by some distance. Subjects were told to try to associate the word or picture on the left with the one on the right. A test given 30 seconds after the last pair in a list had been presented showed that subjects who had studied the pictures were able to provide significantly more correct responses (65 percent) than those studying the words (50 percent).

Of course, in Bower and Winzenz's experiment, subjects in the imagery condition were not shown pictures of objects; they were given nouns and asked to form images of the concepts named by the nouns. If there is any relevance here of the finding that memory for a picture of a concept is superior to memory for its name, it must be shown that imagery leads to the same kind of encodings that result from presentation of a visual stimulus. An experiment by Bower (1972) helps demonstrate this by giving evidence that imagery instructions lead to an involvement of the same mental apparatus used in visual perception. The experiment was based on the premise that two tasks that utilize the same mechanism will compete for that limited resource and therefore tend to interfere with each other. Bower had subjects learn paired associates using either an imagery or a rote repetition strategy. At the same time that subjects were learning the word pairs, they performed one of two distractor tasks. A visual distractor task required subjects to use a finger to track a rapidly moving wavy line. A tactile distractor task required subjects to shut their eyes and attempt to keep a raised string that moved from side to side centered between two fingers. It was found that the visual distractor task interfered with paired-associate learning done under imagery instructions. Cued recall performance under imagery instructions fell from 66 percent to 55 percent when the nature of the distractor task went from tactile to visual. However, cued recall performance under the rote repetition instructions was no different when learning occurred simultaneously with the tactile or the visual distractor task. Both led to 28 percent correct recall. Thus, it appears that imagery indeed makes use of some of the same mechanisms involved in visual information processing.

The effectiveness of interacting imagery as an encoding strategy in paired-associate learning is due not only to the involvement of the visual system, but also to the presence of an interaction between the imaged components. Numerous studies have shown the value of interaction to the imagery operation in paired-associate learning (e.g., Bower, 1970; Wollen, Weber, & Lowry, 1972). For instance, Bower, (1970) asked subjects to study three lists of 30 pairs of unrelated concrete nouns. Subjects were instructed to attempt to associate the noun pairs together using either a rote rehearsal, a separation imagery, or an interacting imagery strategy. The separation imagery group was instructed "to vividly image the A and B referents but to keep them noninteracting, well-separated in imaginal space, as though they were separate still photographs on different walls of a room" (p. 530). The interecting imagery group was instructed to image the two objects named by the words, interacting in some manner so as to form a coherent, integrated scene. An example of an interacting image corresponding to the word pair *dog–bicycle* is an image of a dog riding a bicycle. In a cued recall test given immediately after each list had been presented, interacting imagery proved to lead to significantly superior association between stimulus and response words. Percent correct performance for the interacting imagery, separation imagery, and rote repetition strategies were 53 percent, 27 percent, and 30 percent, respectively. Thus, imagining two objects interacting rather than separated in space nearly doubled the number of response words correctly provided for the stimulus words.

It must be noted that even though forming a mental image has been found to be of benefit in paired-associate learning (e.g., Epstein et al., 1960), one can also facilitate paired-associate learning by forming verbal descriptions of an interaction between objects named by noun pairs. For example, Suzuki and Rohwer (1968) have shown that paired associate learning of noun pairs such as *rock* and *bottle* is significantly better when a sentence such as "The *rock* hit the *bottle*" rather than the sentence "The *rock* and the *bottle*" is presented. This finding indicates the importance of interaction to the paired-associate learning process over and above that of imagery.

Bizarreness in Interacting Imagery. One tactic that is sometimes suggested to facilitate paired-associate learning is bizarreness. For example, in their nationwide bestseller, *The Memory Book*, Lorayne and Lucas (1974) suggest that to associate two items "you need a ridiculous—impossible, crazy, illogical, absurd—picture or image" (p. 25). Studies, however, have shown that bizarreness is not generally important in the associative process. A well-known study by Wollen, Weber, and Lowry (1972) demonstrated this. The stimuli used were pairs of concrete unrelated nouns, such as *piano–cigar*. To control subjects' learning strategies, the experimenters presented the nouns together with pictures of the objects named by the nouns. The pictures showed the objects either separated in space or interacting in some way, and the objects or their interactions were pictured either in a nonbizarre or a bizarre fashion. (See Figure 8–1.) Four groups of subjects studied a list of nine pairs of items in which all pairs were shown in a noninteracting–nonbizarre, noninteracting–bizarre, interacting–nonbizarre, or interacting–bizarre configuration. The results of a cued recall test showed that bizarreness did not affect performance. For both interacting and noninteracting configurations combined, bizarre pictures led to 54 percent correct recall compared with 56 percent correct recall for nonbizarre pictures. As expected on the basis of other studies, however, the presence of interaction

Figure 8–1
Examples of bizarre and nonbizarre pictures of two items in either interacting or noninteracting configurations.

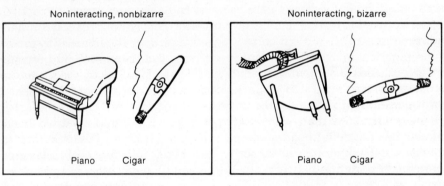

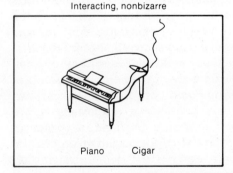
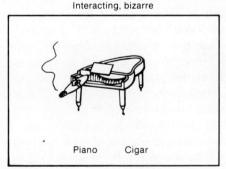

From K. A. Wollen, A. Weber and D. H. Lowry, "Bizarreness versus interaction of mental images as determinants of learning." *Cognitive Psychology,* 1972, *3,* 518–523. Copyright 1972 by Academic Press. Reprinted by permission.

was important. For bizarre and nonbizarre pictures combined, interaction led to 74 percent correct cued recall, while that for separation was 36 percent.

Interaction and Associations. We have been assuming that interacting imagery instructions improve paired-associate learning by facilitating the encoding of associations between mental representations of the interacting objects. That is, we have assumed that if one pictures a dog riding a bicycle, then connections between the concept of dog and that of bicycle will be promoted. Such an assumption certainly seems to be a reasonable interpretation of the improved cued recall that results when interacting imagery instructions are used. However, no independent evidence has yet been given that interaction promotes the encoding of associations. Evidence of this nature will now be presented.

On a general level, it is reasonable to presume that if the mental representation of concept A is linked to that of concept B, then the activation and retrieval of concept A should allow some activation energy to spread through the associative bond to concept B. This is the presumed basis of the phenomenon of priming that was discussed in chapter 3. In this previous discussion of priming it was noted that the time required to recognize that a letter string (e.g., *bread*) spelled an English word was lowered when a semantically associated word (e.g., *butter*) rather than an unrelated word (e.g., *shoe*) was presented just prior to the letter string. Thus, we can assume that when priming occurs the presence of associations between the primed stimulus and the priming stimulus can be inferred. McKoon (1981) performed an experiment to determine whether this sort of evidence of association could be obtained for objects that had previously been observed to be interacting. McKoon reasoned that if interaction promotes the formation of associations, then activation of the mental representation of one member of a pair of interacting items should prime the mental representation of the other member. Specifically, McKoon showed subjects simple line drawings taken from children's coloring books. All pictures showed two cartoon characters either interacting or not interacting with each other. Examples of these two conditions are shown in Figure 8–2. Interactions consisted of behaviors such as conversing or exchanging an object. Subjects studied lists made up of 30 such pictures shown at a four-second rate. Memory was then tested with a series of slides, each showing an individual character. Some of these characters were exactly as they had been pictured in the previously studied slides and some were new characters. When viewing each test slide it was subjects' task to signal as quickly as possible whether or not they recognized having seen the character before. McKoon was concerned primarily with responses subjects made to slides of previously presented characters. The single character shown on these test slides had been seen earlier in either an interacting or a noninteracting relation with a second character. McKoon found that when one character from each previously studied pair was shown on a test slide that immediately preceded presentation of the other member of the pair, reaction time to the second pair member was speeded. For example, if, as in Figure 8–2, a subject

Figure 8–2
An example of two stimuli used by McKoon (1981). The left-hand panel of the top row shows an example of an interaction between two characters. The left-hand panel of the bottom row shows two characters in a noninteracting relation. The other panels represent test stimuli in which individual characters are presented for recognition.

From G. McKoon, "The representation of pictures in memory." *Journal of Experimental Psychology: Human Learning and Memory*, 1981, 7, 216–221. Copyright 1981 by the American Psychological Association. Reprinted by permission of publisher and author.

had studied a picture of a policewoman talking to a pig, then, on the test, a subject would react faster to the slide showing just the pig if the preceding test slide had shown the policewoman rather than some other character. Priming was also observed in the responses made to pairs of characters that had been studied in noninteracting relations. Of most importance, however, was the finding that significantly more priming occurred for pair members that had been interacting (120 milliseconds) rather than not interacting (45 milliseconds). McKoon concluded that in the mental representations of the pictures that subjects had studied, "interacting characters are more closely (or strongly or probably) connected than noninteracting characters" (p. 219).

Some Practical Applications

A great deal of the memorization that occurs outside the psychological laboratory can involve paired-associate learning. For example, when learning a foreign language, a person must associate a foreign word with an English word. Similarly, when introduced to a stranger, a person is presented with the task of associating a name and a face together. A simple task such as remembering what grocery items to buy can also be thought of as a paired-associative learning task; here one attempts to associate the concept of buying (or some equivalent concept) with individual grocery items.

The Keyword Method. A procedure to aid the learning of a foreign language vocabulary was devised by Atkinson and Raugh (1975). Their *keyword method* makes use of interacting imagery to help associate each foreign word with its English translation. The method, which requires two simple steps, will be demonstrated with the Spanish word *caballo*, which means horse. The first step requires that a person pronounce the foreign word and come up with a keyword—any English word or short phrase that sounds like the foreign word or part of the foreign word. The Spanish word *caballo*, for example, is pronounced something like *cob-eye-yo*. The English word *eye* sounds like part of this word and thus should make a suitable keyword. The second step is to form an image of the keyword interacting with the English translation of the foreign word. An image of a giant eye resting on a horse's back would be suitable. Now, to remember what *caballo* means, a person pronounces the word; this should allow the keyword (*eye*) to be retrieved from memory, which, in turn, should trigger retrieval of the associated concept encoded in the interacting image (i.e., the word *horse*).

To test the effectiveness of this method, Atkinson and Raugh (1975) presented two groups of subjects with 40 Russian words. The words were delivered through headphones at a 10-second rate. For one group of subjects, the keyword group, the Russian words were always accompanied by the visual display of a keyword that the experimenters had prepared. For example, the reading of the Russian word *zvonok* (pronounced like *zvahn-oak*) might have been accompanied by the display of the keyword *oak*. This keyword appeared in brackets on the left side of a small screen. The English translation of the Russian word appeared simultaneously on the right side of the screen. In our example, this translation is the English word *bell*. Subjects were instructed to generate an interacting image that incorporated the keyword and the English translation of the Russian word. Subjects were also told that if no suitable image came to mind, they could form a meaningful sentence or phrase to join the two words. For the other group of subjects, the control group, only the English translation of the foreign word was displayed on the screen. These control subjects were asked to learn the meaning of each Russian word using whatever method they wished (they were not instructed in the use of the keyword method). For three consecutive days, all subjects, who were Stanford undergraduates with no prior knowledge of the Russian language, were presented with a new list of 40 Russian words. (See Table 8–2.) On the fourth day, subjects were tested on all 120 Russian words. The test required that they provide the English translation for each Russian word that was read to them. The test showed that the keyword subjects got 72 percent of the words correct, while the control group got only 46 percent of the words correct. The advantage of the keyword method was still evident after one to two months when subjects were given a surprise retest on all of the words. On this delayed test, keyword subjects correctly provided English translations to 43 percent of the words, while control subjects correctly translated only 28 percent of the words.

Other experiments have verified the effectiveness of this method in aiding the acquisition of foreign language vocabulary (e.g., Griffith, 1981; Pressley, Levin, Hall, Miller, & Berry, 1980). Try it yourself with the Russian words shown in Table 8–2. It has been found (Atkinson, 1975) that the keyword method can be effective not only in facilitating the retrieval of English translations of foreign words, but also in aiding retrieval of the foreign word in response to the English word. In Atkinson's (1975) experiment, a keyword group and a control group first learned a list of Spanish words to the same criterion; that is, after several learning trials, both groups could provide English translations to the same number of Spanish words. Both subject groups were then given English translations of the Spanish words and asked to provide the Spanish words. On this backward association test, the keyword group's score was 19 percent above that of the control group.

In spite of this success, this method does have its limitations. One is that the formation of backward associations (i.e., from the English word to the foreign word) is not always facilitated. Pressley et al. (1980) found that al-

Table 8–2

Sample items from a list of Russian vocabulary words together with keywords and English translations.

Russian	Keyword	Translation
Vnimánie	pneumonia	Attention
Délo	jello	Affair
Západ	zap it	West
Straná	strawman	Country
Tolpá	tell pa	Crowd
Linkór	Lincoln	Battleship
Rot	rut	Mouth
Gorá	garage	Mountain
Durák	two rocks	Fool
Ósen'	ocean	Autumn
Séver	saviour	North
Dym	dim	Smoke
Seló	seal law	Village
Golová	Gulliver	Head
Uslóvie	Yugoslavia	Condition
Dévushka	dear vooshka	Girl
Tjótja	Churchill	Aunt
Póezd	poised	Train
Krovát'	cravat	Bed
Chelovék	chilly back	Person

From R. C. Atkinson and M. R. Raugh, "An application of the mnemonic keyword method to the acquisition of a Russian vocabulary." *Journal of Experimental Psychology: Human Learning and Memory*, 1975, *1*, 126–133. Copyright 1975 by the American Psychological Association. Reprinted by permission of publisher and author.

though subjects using the keyword method for a single-study trial were often able to retrieve the appropriate keyword when given an English word, they had difficulty in generating the entire foreign word from the keyword. For example, a subject who had studied the Spanish word *caballo*, when later given the English word *horse* and asked to provide its Spanish equivalent, might have been able to retrieve the keyword *eye* but not the rest of the sounds that formed the word *caballo*. It appears that to facilitate these backward associations, a keyword should be chosen that sounds as much like the whole foreign word as possible. Alternately, a subject must be given enough practice with the foreign word so that it is treated like a chunk; under these conditions, the keyword will be better able to retrieve the foreign word in its entirety. Evidence in support of this claim comes from an experiment of Pressley et al. (1980) that showed that it required four learning trials for subjects using the keyword method to surpass control subjects in providing foreign word translations of English words. Another limitation of the keyword method is that untrained subjects often have difficulty generating their own keywords. In a study by Raugh and Atkinson (1975), subjects who were attempting to use the keyword method to learn Spanish words were asked to generate their own keywords. If they were unable to generate suitable keywords, however, they were given the option of requesting that one be provided. It was found that subjects requested keywords for 89 percent of the words. A further limitation is that some words appear to be less suitable for learning by the keyword method than others. For example, Atkinson (1975) reports that second-year Russian language students who had used the method in a 10-week course judged it to be less useful for adjectives than for nouns. It should be noted that all these limitations to the use of the keyword method are limitations only in the sense that the keyword method leads to no better learning than do control conditions. In general it appears that the keyword method never interferes with the vocabulary learning process in any way; it only facilitates it.

A Face–Name Mnemonic.   A memory method that is very much like the keyword method has been used to help link names and faces together. The method, which has been recommended by practitioners of memory aids (Lorayne & Lucas, 1974; Roth, 1957) requires the following steps. First, upon hearing a person's name, one generates a concrete word or series of words that sound like the name. For example, for the name Conrad, one may generate the words *con* (as in the word *convict*) and *rat*. The next step is to pick a prominent feature of the person's face. For example, if Conrad has bushy eyebrows, that feature could be selected. Finally, one forms an image based on the words derived from the name and the prominent facial feature. In this image, concepts identified by the "name words" should interact with the facial feature. In the present example, one may visualize a small convict in a striped suit being chased by a rat through Conrad's bushy eyebrows. To recall the person's name, one inspects the face and picks out the prominent facial feature. This retrieves the visual image, which in turn allows the name words to retrieve the person's name.

Experimental investigations have shown that the method does improve one's ability to recall correctly a name when one is later cued with the person's face. For example, Morris, Jones, and Hampson (1978) showed two groups of subjects 13 photographs of faces, each with a name written on the bottom. All subjects initially used whatever method they wished to associate the face and name during the 10 seconds each photograph was displayed. Memory was tested by presenting the photograph of each face without the name beneath it and asking subjects to recall the name. After this first test, the experimenters gave subjects in one group practice with the face–name learning method. Subjects in this group, the experimental group, practiced the method on 10 face–name pairs. Both groups of subjects next attempted to learn a new set of 13 faces and names, with the experimental group utilizing the method they had just been taught. An immediate test on these 13 items revealed that the learning method significantly improved performance. Performance of the subjects using this learning method rose 77 percent, while that of the other subjects did not change significantly.

McCarty (1980) has noted that people just learning to use this method may initially find it difficult quickly to generate English words that sound like a person's name. Lorayne and Lucas (1974) suggest that practice will help make a person proficient in generating these words. Here are some examples of the words these professional mnemonists generated to remind them of people's last names: *Alexander = lick sand; Anderson = hand and son; Bennett = bend net; Chisholm = chisel; Farber = far bear; Hopkins = hop kin; Travers = travels.*

The "Peg-Word Method" and the "Method of Loci."   In the two memory methods just presented, the learner is presumed to know in advance what cues will be available to trigger retrieval. Both methods derive their effectiveness from interacting imagery that effectively ties each retrieval cue to to-be-recalled information. The memory methods to be described here also use interacting imagery to associate a retrieval cue with to-be-recalled information. The difference is that these methods repeatedly use a highly structured set of retrieval cues that have previously been stored in memory.

In the peg-word method, the set of retrieval cues that must first be committed to memory consist of the following number-rhyme pairs: 1 is *bun;* 2 is *shoe;* 3 is *tree;* 4 is *door;* 5 is *hive;* 6 is *sticks;* 7 is *heaven;* 8 is *gate;* 9 is *wine;* 10 is *hen.* This list can be used to help remember up to 10 items in order. The method requires that each concrete noun in the number-rhyme list, that is, each peg word, be imagined interacting with one of the items one wishes to remember. For example, assume that a person wanted to remember to buy these items: milk, tomatoes, shoe laces, envelopes, lightbulbs, oranges, eggs, bread, batteries, and toothpaste. To use the peg-word method to recall these items, one would begin by forming an association between the first peg-word, *bun,* and the first item that is to be remembered, *milk.* An image of milk pouring out of a carton onto a soggy bun would be suitable. The word tomato would then be imagined interacting with the second peg-word, *shoe.* This would be repeated for each item in the list. To recall the list, one would simply think of the number one, which would retrieve the rhyming peg-word *bun,* which, in turn, would retrieve the word *milk* from the previously formed image that incorporated the bun and the milk. A benefit of using this method is that it allows information to be recalled in order.

An experiment by Bugelski, Kidd, and Segmen (1968) has demonstrated the effectiveness of this method. Briefly, subjects in this experiment who were instructed in the use of the peg-word method showed a significant improvement in their ability to recall words from a 10-item list, whereas control subjects who didn't use the method showed no improvement. It must be pointed out that the method used to test subjects' memories in this experiment was a bit unusual in that it was designed to be very sensitive to knowledge of a stimulus' position in a list. For the test, the experimenter called out numbers from 1 to 10 in a random order at a four-second rate and subjects had to supply the word from the list position corresponding to each number. In scoring the recall performance, the experimenters gave subjects two points for recalling the correct word; if the subject recalled a word that had been presented in the list but not at the position corresponding to the number called out by the experimenter, the subjects was given just one point. In terms of this point system, the scores of subjects who used the peg-word method on a second list of words improved from 11.07 to 14.73, whereas the scores for control subjects who used their own learning methods were 11.27 and 11.25 for a first and second list, respectively.

In the peg-word method, the same series of peg-words is used for every set of items that is being memorized. One question that can be asked is whether the repeated use of these peg-words seriously hurts memory performance. On the basis of the cue overload principle, this is a likely possibility, since the same cue (e.g., the word *bun*) will begin to match a growing number of traces in the long-term store. To investigate this, Bugelski (1968) asked two groups of subjects to study six lists of 10 concrete nouns. One group was instructed to use the peg-word method and the other attempted to learn the words in serial order by whatever method they desired. A comprehensive recall test was given after all six lists had been presented. For the test, the experimenter called out the numbers 1 through 10 in ascending order and subjects attempted to write down words from all six lists that had been presented in that serial position. There was a dramatic difference in performance for the two groups. The group using the peg-word system correctly recalled 63.4 percent of the words, while the control group correctly recalled about 32 percent of the words. It appears, then, that whatever detrimental effects there are to the repeated use of the same peg-words, the method is sufficiently effective as a memory aid to offset them and give the learner an advantage. In considering the impact of reusing peg-words as retrieval cues, it is important to realize that just because the same peg-words are reused does not mean that they will be pictured in exactly the same way each time. In fact, from Bugelski's (1968) data, it seems that subjects generally image the peg-words in different ways on each use. Interviews conducted after the recall test had been completed attempted to determine, among other things, whether subjects were "using the *same* shoe or wine throughout the six lists or varying them" (p. 331). It was found that subjects apparently generated identical images of a peg-word less than 10 percent of the time. Variations in the encoding of each peg-word could help reduce cue overload. For example, if one generates an image of a different shoe on six separate occasions, then the regeneration of an image of any one of these six shoes at a later time will best match only one of these stored images rather than all six equally. To best recall all six images under these circumstances, it would be necessary to generate a variety of shoe images until matches to all those encoded using the peg-word method had been found.

The *method of loci* resembles the peg-word method in a number of ways. It utilizes as retrieval cues a sequence of already-memorized items that the learner must associate, through interacting imagery, with items that are to be retained. The difference between the two methods lies in the nature of the set of memorized items that function as retrieval cues. In the method of loci these are familiar features of one's environment. For example, a person may use locations in a house for this purpose. No matter what familiar locations are employed, to use the method one simply takes a mental walk through the familiar territory, picturing various landmarks encountered along the way. Each of these locations one associates with a to-be-recalled item through interacting imagery. Thus, if a house is chosen as the set of retrieval cues, one might imagine walking in the front door and seeing a staircase. To remember the word *ashtray,* one might picture a giant ashtray rolling down the stairs. Continuing with the imaginary walk through the house, one might next visualize encountering a sliding door that leads to a living room. To remember the word *ruler,* one could picture a ruler being squeezed by the sliding door. This process would be repeated for each item that is to be remembered. To recall the items, one would imagine reentering the house and encountering the set of locations in their usual order. These locations should trigger retrieval of each item from the interacting image. As with the peg-word method, the method of loci allows information to be recalled in serial order.

The method of loci was known by the ancient Greeks, who recommended it be used for remembering speeches. Memory was more essential in those days since instruments of the sort we currently use to record our thoughts were not commonly available. The unknown author of an ancient text, *Ad*

Herennium, written between 86 and 82 B.C. suggested that this memory method could be used in a court of law. To remember that a defendant was to be charged with killing a man by poison in order to gain an inheritance, the author of the text recommended that images be formed, each representing a key aspect of the sequence. Thus, the first image might incorporate a familiar location together with a man lying ill, the second, an adjacent location and the defendant holding poison, and so on. Whereas a present-day lawyer would be able to retain these facts in a file folder, his counterpart in ancient times would be forced to rely more on memory to preserve these details (Yates, 1966).

Limitations of the Peg-Word Method and Method of Loci.   Both memory aids just described have limitations to their usefulness. One is that it takes time to apply them. For example, in the previously described study by Bugelski et al. (1968), it was found that although the subjects using the peg-word method performed significantly better than control subjects, this difference was only evident when the rate of presentation was slower than one word every two seconds. Another limitation is that these methods are most appropriate for remembering individual concrete nouns rather than abstract concepts or sentences on a word-by-word basis. It is possible, however, to use these methods to remember information that is not already concrete and picturable if ways can be found to transform the information into a concrete image. As an example of this, consider the task of remembering the first few presidents of the United States in order. To apply the peg-word method to this task, one should first transform each president's name into a similar-sounding picturable object and then imagine the object interacting with a peg-word. Thus, to remember the sequence of names beginning with Washington, Adams, and Jefferson, one could imagine a *washing* machine in which a *bun* was being spun around, *Adam* wearing a fig leaf and lacing a *shoe,* a person named *Jeff* and his *son* (I hope you know someone named Jeff) sawing down a *tree,* and so on.

Objections to the use of memory aids such as the method of loci have been voiced since ancient times (Yates, 1966). A common attitude toward mnemonics is revealed in the following passage by Miller (1956)

> When I was a boy I had a teacher who told us that memory crutches were only one grade better than cheating, and that we would never understand anything properly if we resorted to such underhanded tricks. She didn't stop us, of course, but she did make us conceal our methods of learning. Our teacher, if her conscience had permitted it, no doubt could have shown us far more efficient systems than we were able to devise for ourselves. Another teacher who told me that the ordinate was vertical because my mouth went that way when I said it and that the abscissa was horizontal for the same reason saved me endless

confusion, as did one who taught me to remember the number of days in each month by counting on my knuckles. (pp. 44–45)

The objections people have to the use of memory methods might lessen if the reason for mnemonics' effectiveness were better understood. In general, when we learn something we form new associations. For example, when we learn that the abscissa is the name of the horizontal axis, we form an association between the term abscissa and this property of being horizontal. What a memory aid does is help ensure that this connection is formed and that the cue used to access the memory chunk will be effective. Experimenters often note that when subjects are asked to memorize information in any way they desire, the subjects tend to improvise various learning strategies that are usually inferior to the techniques described here (Morris & Reid, 1970). The advantage of using techniques such as the method of loci is that they have been proven to be highly efficient.

The Cue Overload Principle

In the preceding discussions, encoding strategies were described that enhanced memory performance by ensuring that cues available at retrieval maximally matched the to-be-retrieved memory traces. Matching in these cases was achieved by encoding techniques such as interacting imagery, which promoted the association or chunking of target information with information in the prospective retrieval cue. In this section, encoding strategies will be described that also allow the learner to enhance an item's retrievability. These techniques, however, affect retrieval by manipulating the extent to which retrieval cues will be overloaded. It will be shown that encoding operations that store distinctive information about an item will best allow a cue to retrieve the item.

Distinctiveness and Memory: Background Information

The von Restorff Effect. The importance of distinctiveness to remembering must seem obvious to the nonpsychologist. As the following passage shows, the unknown author of the ancient Roman text *Ad Herennium* was well aware of the role that distinctiveness could play in remembering.

When we see in every day life things that are petty, ordinary, and banal, we generally fail to remember them, because the mind is not being stirred by anything novel or marvellous. But if we see or hear something exceptionally base, dishonorable, unusual, great, unbelievable, or ridiculous, that we are likely to remember for a long time. Accordingly, things immediate to our eye or ear we commonly forget; incidents of our childhood we often remember best. Nor could this be so for any other reason than that ordinary things easily slip from the memory while the striking and the novel stay longer in the mind. (Yates, 1966, p. 9)

Modern-day scientific investigation of memory for distinctive information was stimulated by experiments of the German psychologist Hedwig von Restorff in 1933. The so-called von Restorff effect refers to the finding that recall of an item from a list is heightened if the item is made distinctive. One manipulation that has been used to make a list item distinctive is printing it in a color that differs from that of other items in the list. Other manipulations that have been successful at producing von Restorff effects include varying the size of the print used on a list of visually presented words (Kroll, 1972) and changing the sex of the voice reading a list of words (Titus & Robinson, 1973).

Many factors are likely to contribute to the heightened remembering of distinctive stimuli. One of these involves retrievability. That is, it has been suggested (Bruce & Gaines, 1976) that a distinctive item in a list will be encoded distinctively in memory. Thus, included in the encoding of the distinctive item will be information specific to just that item. During retrieval, cues containing the distinctive information will consequently make contact with the trace of just the distinctive item. On the other hand, cues containing information common to all other list items will match many traces in memory. In accord with the cue overload principle, the less overloaded cue—that for the distinctive item—will be the most likely to effect retrieval. As an example of this, suppose that a subject in a memory experiment is shown 15 common one-syllable words 1 at a time and is asked to study the words for a free-recall test. Except for the eighth word in the list, all words are animal names; the eighth word, however, is a clothing item. An experiment like this was performed by Gumenik and Slak (1970). They found that the clothing word was recalled significantly more often when it was embedded in a series of animal names rather than in a list of clothing names. According to a retrieval explanation, the cue "article of clothing I studied in the experiment" is a less-overloaded and therefore a more effective cue for the clothing word when the other words in the list are animal names rather than clothing words.

The point of mentioning the von Restorff effect is to acquaint the reader with experimental evidence supporting the common assumption that distinctiveness can facilitate remembering. This discussion is not intended to illustrate how a person can select encoding strategies that produce distinctive memories (although we are building up to this). In the experiment just described, for example, the subjects were not necessarily intentionally encoding the clothing word distinctively so that it would later be easily retrieved. Rather, the distinctive encodings were most likely produced incidentally as the subjects attended to the meanings of each word. The role of intentional strategies aimed at heightening the distinctiveness of an item's encoded representation may be greater in other experimental demonstrations of the von Restorff effect, those in which subjects are given explicit instructions to pay special attention to a certain word in the list (e.g., Bruce & Gaines, 1976, experiment 1; Waugh, 1969). Under these circumstances it is likely that subjects attempt to incorporate unique information in the trace of the to-be-remembered item.

Release from Proactive Interference. The effect of distinctiveness on memory is also evident in the phenomenon known as release from proactive interference. As explained previously, this phenomenon refers to the improvement in memory performance for recently presented material that differs in some way from the previously presented material. Release from proactive interference is easily demonstrated using the Brown–Peterson task. For instance, a subject might first be shown three words for 2 seconds, perform a distractor task for 20 seconds, and then attempt to recall the words. This procedure, if repeated for two more trials using different sets of three words each time, will lead to successively poorer recall performance. The decline in performance can be attributed to the buildup of proactive interference, a phenomenon we previously analyzed in terms of cue overload. Continuing with the imaginary experiment again, if on the next trial, which is called the *release trial,* three *numbers* (rather than three words) are presented and then tested after 20 seconds of distractor activity, performance will be found to recover substantially, approaching the level attained on the first trial. An experiment like this has been performed by Reutener (1969, 1972). Reutener's data have been summarized graphically by Wickens (1972) and are shown in Figure 8–3. The figure combines two experimental conditions, one in which a group of subjects was given three Brown–Peterson trials with words and then a fourth trial with numbers, and another in which a group was given three trials with numbers and then shifted to a trial with words. The control data combine two other subject groups, one receiving all four learning trials with words and the other receiving all four learning trials with numbers. The distractor task performed by each group during the 20-second retention interval was a color-naming task. It can be seen that the shift between these two classes of materials caused performance to recover to the level attained on the first learning trial. Other demonstrations of release from proactive interference, ones that generally involve a less dramatic increase in recall performance than that reported by Reutener, have been obtained by shifting other stimulus attributes (see Wickens, 1972 for a review).

What role does distinctiveness play in the release from proactive interfer-

Figure 8–3
The release from proactive interference obtained by Reutener (1969, 1972) when the material on the fourth trial of a Brown–Peterson task was switched between words and spelled-out numbers (e.g., thirty-three).

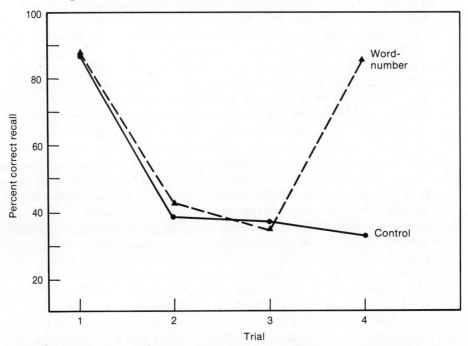

The figure is from D. D. Wickens, "Characteristics of word encoding." In A. W. Melton and E. Martin (Eds.), *Coding Processes in Human Memory*, Washington, D.C.: Winston, 1972.

ence? The reason performance declined over the first three learning trials in Reutener's experiment is because, by trial three, a retrieval cue tended to match information in memory encoded not only on the immediately preceding trial, but on the two previous trials as well. That is, by trial three, a cue such as "words I just learned in the experiment" matched the stimuli from trials one and two, as well as the stimuli the subject was attempting to recall from trial three. Since a cue like this becomes progressively more overloaded and therefore less effective as the experiment continues, performance declines. However, a switch in the class of the material allows unique cues to be generated, cues that are less overloaded because they match just the most recently presented information.

Another explanation of the phenomenon of release from proactive interference may have occurred to you. It may seem possible that repeated trials with the same type of material cause subjects to become bored and to not pay attention to the stimuli; with a change in material, the subjects' attention is again aroused. According to this account, memory performance declines over trials 1–3 because a subject stores progressively less information or lower quality information for the stimuli, and performance rebounds on trial four because the encoding process is revitalized. This explanation differs from the cue overload account in that it ties variations in performance not to the distinctiveness of information in memory (and therefore to the degree to which a cue will be overloaded), but to the presence or absence of stimulus information in memory. An experiment by Gardiner, Craik, and Birtwistle (1972) shows that this attention-based account is not appropriate. Using a Brown–Peterson paradigm, these experimenters demonstrated that release from proactive interference can occur even when a subject is not aware at the time of study that there has been a shift in the nature of the material. Subjects in this experiment were unaware that a shift in the material had occurred because the shift was so subtle. For one group of subjects the shift was between names of garden flowers and wild flowers; for another group it was between indoor and outdoor sports. Because the change in the nature of the stimuli was not obvious, subjects who were not informed at any time during the experiment that a shift had occurred on trial four showed no release from proactive interference. The key finding in the experiment, however, was that subjects who were informed of the shift just before they attempted to recall the stimuli from the fourth learning trial did show a release from proactive interference. (See Figure 8–4.) It is important to realize that the only difference between the subjects who did and did not show release from proactive interference was whether or not they were informed about the shift. Since this information was given *after* the material had been studied, the release from proactive interference cannot be attributed to differences in the quality or quantity of information subjects had stored. Rather, the improved performance on trial four appears to have involved distinctiveness in both the encoding and the retrieval stages of processing. It seems that all subjects in the experiment automatically encoded features of the stimuli presented on trial four that distinguished the stimuli from those presented on the three preceding trials. This, in turn, allowed subjects who were informed about the shift just before the test to generate recall cues that most closely matched just the trial-four stimuli.

This discussion of the experiment by Gardiner et al. indicates that release from proactive interference can occur even without a subject's attention being drawn to the special nature of the material introduced on the release

Figure 8–4
The release from proactive interference obtained by Gardiner et al. (1972) from a subtle shift in the attributes of the to-be-recalled stimuli. The dotted line shows the performance of subjects who were informed just before recall of the trial-4 stimuli of the nature of the shift. The solid line shows performance of control subjects who were not informed about the shift.

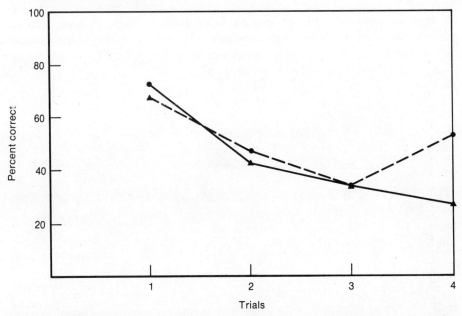

Adapted from J. M. Gardiner, F. I. M. Craik and J. Birtwistle, "Retrieval cues and release from proactive inhibition." *Journal of Verbal Learning and Verbal Behavior*, 1972, *11*, 778–783. Copyright 1972 by Academic Press. Reprinted by permission.

trial. Would a more sizeable release from proactive interference occur when attention arousal is added to the factors that were just described to produce release from proactive interference? Gardiner et al. included a condition in their experiment that showed that no significant enhancement in recall was produced by calling a subject's attention to the alteration in the release trial material. It was found that a group of subjects who was informed about the shift (e.g., from garden flowers to wild flowers) just *before* receiving the trial-four stimuli showed about the same degree of release from proactive interference as the group informed about the shift during the recall stage. Although attention arousal has been suggested to play a role in remembering under certain circumstances (e.g., Brown & Kulik, 1977), it does not seem to be a critical factor in this experimental paradigm.

Encoding Strategies and Distinctiveness: Levels of Processing

You would have no trouble answering yes or no to any of the three questions written below. Yet, depending on which question was answered, dramatic differences could result in your memory for the words you judged.

1. Is the word on the right written in capital letters?   *HOUSE*
2. Does the word on the right rhyme with *fish?*   *dish*
3. Is the word on the right a type of animal?   *tiger*

These questions are relevant to an approach to memory presented in 1972 by Craik and Lockhart that they called the levels-of-processing view. According to this view, a person's memory performance will be determined by the level at which a stimulus is processed: shallow-level processing, in which attention is paid to the physical attributes of a stimulus, leads to poor performance for that stimulus; deep-level processing, in which attention is paid to the semantic properties of the stimulus, produces accurate performance. The first question listed above examplifies a task involving shallow processing, while the third question examplifies one that involves deep processing. It should be understood that shallow and deep tasks are just the extreme ends of a continuum of processing levels. Craik and Lockhart suggested that processing at levels between these extremes would produce intermediate memory performance. Question 2 listed above is an example of a task that involves an intermediate level of processing.

Craik and Lockhart's (1972) article was purely theoretical. They presented no new experimental evidence to support their view. However, a subsequent investigation by Craik and Tulving (1975) succeeded in obtaining much new experimental evidence to support the levels-of-processing view. In one experiment (experiment 2), subjects were asked three types of questions to induce them to process words from a list at different levels. As in question 1 above, one type of question concerned the typescript of the word, that is, whether it was written in upper- or lower-case letters; a second concerned the sound of the word, whether or not it rhymed with another word; and a third concerned the semantic properties of the word. Subjects were shown 60 words 1 at a time, each preceded by one of the three types of questions. For example, just before seeing the word *market*, a subject might have received the question "Does the word rhyme with *weight?*" For each type of question the correct answer was "yes" half the time and "no" the other half. When answering the 60 questions, subjects were not aware that their memory for the words they were judging would later be tested. Thus, the subjects were not intentionally memorizing the words as they answered each question; rather, any memory resulting from the task was incidental.

Figure 8–5
Percent of words recognized as a function of processing level. The data combine performance for words responded to with yes and no answers.

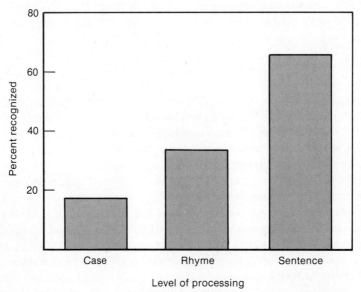

Adapted from F. I. M. Craik and E. Tulving, "Depth of processing and the retention of words in Episodic memory." *Journal of Experimental Psychology: General*, 1975, *104*, 268–294. Copyright 1975 by the American Psychological Association. Reprinted by permission of publisher and author.

On the surprise recognition test given shortly after the 60 words had been processed, it was found that in accord with the level-of-processing view, memory was strongly influenced by the level at which subjects had processed the words. As shown in Figure 8–5, recognition was best for words processed at a deep level and worst for words processed at a shallow level.

Craik and Tulving (1975) performed a series of additional experiments aimed at determining whether other factors besides the level at which a stimulus was processed could account for their results. For example, since subjects in the study that was just described required more time to make semantic judgments than rhyme judgments and more time to make rhyme judgments than typecase judgments, it is possible that processing time rather than the kind of processing task was responsible for the variation in memory performance. This possibility was not confirmed. Craik and Tulving found that even when subjects were given a very difficult, time-consuming, shallow-level task, one that required twice as much processing time as a deep-level task, recognition performance on a surprise test was still much lower for words processed at a shallow level (54 percent correct) than at a deep level (76 percent correct). In this experiment, the difficult surface-level task basically required that subjects identify each letter in a word as either a consonant or a vowel, using the letter *C* and *V*, respectively. According to this system, the word *brain* corresponds to the letters *CCVVC.* Specifically, in the experiment, subjects were first shown a series of *C*s and *V*s on a card (e.g., *VCCCV*), then a word (e.g., *uncle*). If the pattern of *C*s and *V*s matched the arrangement of consonants and vowels in the word, the subject answered "yes"; otherwise, the subject answered "no." The deep-level task required that subjects decide if a word would make sense if inserted into the blank space of a sentence. As an example, a subject might have seen the sentence, "Near the bed she kept a _____," and then the word *clock*. As just mentioned, the difficult shallow-level task led to more inferior memory performance than the deep task.

The last experiment reported by Craik and Tulving in their 1975 article offered the most stringent test of the effectiveness of processing level on memory. As in the first levels-of-processing experiment described here, subjects were shown 60 words 1 at a time, each preceded by a question about the word's typecase, pronunciation, or semantic properties. Unlike the previous experiment, however, subjects were told before seeing the words that their memory for the words would later be tested with a recognition procedure. In addition, to determine whether subjects could be induced with a monetary reward to improve their memory performance for words processed at shallow levels, Craik and Tulving offered to pay one group of subjects 6 cents for each "typecase question" word they later correctly recognized, but only 3 cents for each "rhyme question" word and 1 cent for each "category question" word. The monetary incentive proved to be ineffective in overcoming the advantage of deep over shallow processing. The recognition performance of this subject group for the typecase, rhyme, and semantic processing conditions was 53 percent, 62 percent, and 82 percent, respectively. The recognition performance of other subjects in the experiment who were offered different monetary incentives than this group showed that payments had absolutely no influence on performance. For example, other subjects who were paid 6 cents for recognizing each word processed at a semantic level still got 82 percent correct on the test, and subjects who were paid only 1 cent for the "typecase question" words got about 51 percent correct. Craik and Tulving summarized their findings in the following way:

> It is abundantly clear that what determines the level of recall or recognition of a word event is not intention to learn, the amount of effort involved, the difficulty of the orienting task, the amount of time spent making judgments about

the items, or even the amount of rehearsal the items receive; rather it is the qualitative nature of the task, the kind of operations carried out on the items, that determines retention. (p. 209)

Depth and Distinctiveness.   A number of factors contribute to making deep-level processing tasks beneficial to remembering. The factor that will be emphasized first is distinctiveness. The point to be made in ensuing discussions is that shallow processing tends to produce encodings that incorporate information common to many other memory traces. Deep processing, on the other hand, leads to the formation of distinctive encodings. As a result, the stimuli that have been processed at a deep rather than a shallow level will be less subject to cue overload at retrieval and consequently be more retrievable.

If it is distinctiveness that is a factor in the enhanced memorability of deeply processed stimuli, then deeply processed stimuli that are made less distinctive through some experimental manipulation should be less well remembered. In fact, if distinctiveness is the key factor in making deeply processed information well-remembered, all or most of the benefit of deep processing should be removed by some manipulation that substantially decreases the distinctiveness of each deeply encoded memory trace. Moscovitch and Craik (1976) investigated this possibility. Before describing the procedure they employed, however, a brief comment about distinctiveness must be made. Distinctiveness is a relative term; when we say something is distinct or different, we are comparing it with other objects or events. In the case of memory encodings, a memory trace can be distinctive in two senses. It can differ from other encodings formed in a particular situation (e.g., during a single psychology experiment) or it can differ from every other encoding in memory. To make this more concrete, imagine that in a psychology experiment you studied a list of common nouns, only one of which was printed in capital letters. Here, the capitalized word is distinctive only with respect to the other words in the list. Since in the past you have encountered and encoded many words written in capital letters, this encoding is not unique with respect to other encodings in memory as a whole. On the other hand, if you encounter the word *xylophone* in a list of common words, this word will be distinctive not only with respect to the other words in the list, but also with respect to the encodings of all words in your memory. That is, since *xylophone* is such an uncommon word, there will not be many other traces of the word in memory.

Let us return now to Moscovitch and Craik's experiment. Subjects in one of the two groups in the experiment, the control subjects, processed 60 words on one of two levels: for each word, subjects answered either a rhyme question or a question dealing with the word's semantic properties. Thus, the following sequence of events may have occurred as part of this control condition in the experiment.

1. Rhyme: Does the word rhyme with *boat?*   *coat*
2. Category: Is the word in the category "fruits"?   *peach*
3. Category: Is the word in the category "animals"?   *frog*
4. Rhyme: Does the word rhyme with *house?*   *foot*

It can be seen here that a different question was asked for each word and that some words required a "yes" response and some a "no" response. As expected, the procedure led to much better memory for the deeply processed words. It should be mentioned that this was an incidental learning task; that is, subjects were not aware at the time they were answering questions about the words that their memory for the words would later be tested. In the surprise test that was administered after all 60 words had been processed, the experimenters cued subjects with each question that had been asked, and subjects were supposed to provide the word that had accompanied the question. Thus, according to the example questions given above, when the experimenters provided the question "Is the word in the category 'animals'?", the subject was supposed to provide the word *frog.* As just mentioned, this testing procedure revealed that the semantically encoded words were more frequently recalled. For words given a "yes" response on the judgment task (see p. 227 for a discussion of the different effect on memory of answering "yes" and "no" to a question), it was found that approximately 83 percent of the semantically encoded words were correctly recalled, while only about 34 percent of the rhyme-encoded words were correctly recalled.

To determine whether it was distinctiveness that enhanced the recall of semantically processed words, Moscovitch and Craik made the following manipulation for another group of subjects: instead of using a different question for each semantically encoded word, they reused the same question a number of times. Thus, whereas the control group had received 10 different category questions for 10 words in the list, this second group received the same category question for 10 words (e.g., for all 10 words it may have been asked "Is the word in the category 'fruits'?"). This resulted in a substantial decrease in performance on the surprise cued recall test. Instead of the 83 percent correct performance that control subjects achieved on semantically processed words, this group of subjects correctly recalled only 50 percent of the semantically processed words. Again, this applies just to words answered "yes" in the judgment task.

Why didn't performance for the semantically processed words in this second group of subjects fall all the way down to the 34 percent correct level of the rhyme-encoded words? Part of the reason may be that the manipulation made by Moscovitch and Craik decreased the distinctiveness of these words principally with respect to other words in the list, and not with respect to all other memory traces in general. That is, even if 10 words are encoded semantically in response to the same question, semantic processing allows so much varied and detailed information to be encoded that extensive overlap with previously formed encodings is unlikely. For example, a word such as *piano* that is encoded semantically on one occasion will very likely not overlap completely with all other encodings of the same word or of other words (cf., Barclay et al., 1974). The situation is very different for words encoded on more shallow levels. Since there is not such a varied range of distinctive sounds as there are meanings, the potential overlap of newly encoded auditory information with previously encoded information of this sort will be high. Moscovitch and Craik expressed this point in their article:

> Words encoded primarily in terms of their physical or phonemic features will not be particularly unique since many other encoded word episodes share the same features. For words encoded physically or phonemically, there are relatively small alphabets of features, used in various combinations, to encode the events. For semantically encoded words, on the other hand, the forms of encoding are virtually limitless and, speculatively, these semantic encodings are less overlapping in their content than are physical and phonemic encodings. (p. 452)

Since the extent to which a cue is overloaded in a memory experiment should be determined by the amount of matching information the cue contacts in memory—matching information encoded not only during the experiment but before the experiment as well—one could not reasonably expect a distinctiveness manipulation of the sort Moscovitch and Craik used to produce equivalent cue overload in the nondistinctive semantic condition, as in the rhyme-encoding condition.

Other Evidence for the Role of Distinctiveness in the Levels-of-Processing Effect.   If the property of distinctiveness is principally responsible for the variation in memory performance with changes in the level at which a stimulus is processed, two predictions can be made. One is that memory for deeply processed stimuli whose encodings have been made less distinctive should fall to near the performance attained with shallow processing. The experiment of Moscovitch and Craik that was just described provided evidence that confirms this. A second prediction is that memory for stimuli processed at shallow levels whose encodings are made distinctive through some experimental manipulation should be remembered almost as well as deeply processed information. Evidence of this sort will now be presented.

Consider a shallow-level processing task that requires processing a word in terms of its sound. What kind of manipulation would make the pronunciation of a word more distinctive? Eysenck (1979) adopted the following procedure: He compiled a list of words whose pronunciations did not fully correspond to their spellings. For example, from the way the word *comb* is spelled, one might think it should be pronounced something like the word *bomb;* and from the way the word *glove* is spelled, it may seem as if it should be pronounced like the word *cove.* To achieve distinctiveness, Eysenck had subjects pronounce words that had this irregular grapheme–phoneme correspondence the way they should be pronounced if they sounded the way they were spelled. Eyesnck expected this manipulation to establish a unique representation of these words in memory, one in which the acoustic properties associated with each word differed from the acoustic properties typically associated with each word. In the first phase of his experiment, Eysenck presented subjects with 96 words; 24 of these words were pronounced the way they typically are and 24 were pronounced in the distinctive way. The remaining 48 words were processed at a semantic level. A surprise recognition test for the words confirmed the distinctiveness interpretation of the levels-of-processing effect. Performance in the typical pronunciation task condition was approximately 34 percent correct, while that in the distinctive pronunciation task condition was approximately 42 percent correct. The level of memory performance resulting from the distinctive pronunciation task was very close to that produced by the semantic task, which led to a mean performance of about 43 percent correct. Thus, this study indicates that distinctiveness improves memory for stimuli processed at shallow levels.

Practical Applications.   The extraordinary memory abilities of the Russian mnenonist, S., apparently were due in large part to distinctive encodings. When S. encountered a stimulus that most people would not judge to be in any way distinctive, he seemed to react automatically to the stimulus in such a way as to make it distinctive and thus discriminable from other stimuli. Here is a report of his reactions to several tones that were played to him during some laboratory experiments:

> Presented with a tone pitched at 500 cycles per second and having an amplitude of 100 decibels, he saw a streak of lightning splitting the heavens in two. When the intensity of the sound was lowered to 74 decibels, he saw a dense orange color which made him feel as though a needle had been thrust into his spine. Gradually this sensation diminished.
>
> Presented with a tone pitched at 2,000 cycles per second and having an amplitude of 113 decibels, S. said: "It looks something like fireworks tinged with a

pink–red hue. The strip of color feels rough and unpleasant, and it has an ugly taste—rather like that of a briny pickle. . . . You could hurt your hand on this."

Presented with a tone pitched at 3,000 cycles per second and having an amplitude of 128 decibels, he saw a whisk broom that was of a fiery color, while the rod attached to the whisks seemed to be scattering off into fiery points. (Luria, 1968, p. 23–4)[1]

According to Luria (1968), the psychologist who studied S. extensively, S. invariably reacted in the same way to a tone each time it was presented. We can presume that this sort of reaction helped S. to remember an encounter with a stimulus because the representation would elicit cues that exactly matched a previous encounter. There will be minimal cue overload and thus excellent recognition performance under these circumstances.

Of course, most people are not capable of reacting in this way to the stimuli they encounter. However, the level-of-processing view suggests an alternative. According to this view, memory will be facilitated if a person thinks about some meaningful aspects of the stimuli that are encountered. One interesting application of this strategy concerns memory for faces. Studies have shown that when semantic judgments are made about each face that is encountered, memory of the faces will be better than if either a nonsemantic judgment or no judgment in particular is explicitly made. In an experiment by Smith and Winograd (1978), for example, subjects were shown photographs of 50 faces at an eight-second rate. One group of subjects was instructed simply to try to remember the faces. Another group was not informed that their memory for the pictures would later be tested; instead, they were asked to judge whether or not each face looked friendly. This can be considered to be a deep-level task because a subject will have to think about the meaning of the stimulus. Finally, a third group was given a shallow-level processing task; they were asked to judge whether or not each face had a big nose. On a recognition test given immediately after all 50 faces had been processed, subjects who had judged the friendliness of faces were best able to discriminate between pictures they had and had not previously seen. If one calculates performance on the test by subtracting false-alarm rate (i.e., occasions on which a subject signals he recognizes a stimulus that actually was not shown) from hit rate (i.e., occasions on which a subject correctly recognizes a previously shown stimulus), then performance was about 54 percent for both the intentional-learning subjects and the nose-rating subjects, while the performance was about 68 percent for the subjects who had engaged in the deep-level task of rating the friendliness

---

[1] From A. R. Luria, *The Mind of a Mnemonist.* New York: Basic Books, 1969. Copyright 1968 by Basic Books, Inc. Reprinted by permission.

of each face. Winograd (1978) has summarized the effects of level of process-ing on face recognition in the following way:

> From a practical point of view, it can be said that research on memory for faces has identified a useful mnemonic aid. If you want to increase your power to remember the appearance of faces, simple mental effort or intent to remember is not as effective as implicitly asking yourself some form of the following question at the time you meet someone you wish to remember: Would I buy a used car from this person? (p. 257)

Other research by Winograd (1981) has confirmed that distinctive encodings play an important role in producing this heightened memory for faces pro-cessed at a semantic level (see also Daw & Parkin, 1981).

The effect of processing level on memory can also be seen in advertising campaigns. Consider a campaign undertaken by the British Broadcasting Corporation (BBC) to alert its listeners of some changes in the broadcast frequencies of several radio stations. The new station frequencies were an-nounced over radio and TV in the form of jingles as well as more formal presentations. These announcements were aired at least 10 times per hour and were supplemented by newspaper advertisements and direct mailings of informative stickers designed to adhere to radio dials. This saturation advertising campaign lasted for about three months. Bekerian and Baddeley (1980), two English psychologists, were interested in determining how effec-tive the advertising campaign would be. It was their suspicion that the campaign might not succeed. In their words, "since BBC listeners were not required to process the information in the announcements or jingles at an identifiably semantic level, one might expect on this basis that relatively little would be retained" (p. 18). Their suspicion proved to be correct. After the advertising campaign had been underway for two months, subjects were interviewed to determine how well they could identify the new station locations. Although each subject had been exposed to an average of about 1,000 presentations of the information, and although 84 percent of them knew the exact date that the stations would change their frequency, only about 17 percent of the subjects could accurately indicate the new station locations. The researchers concluded that "a campaign involving well over 1,000 presentations per subject, costing nearly half a million pounds, and prosecuted very vigorously over a wide range of communication media, has had spectacularly little effect" (p. 23).

Consider now an advertisement that induces a listener to participate more actively in the information exchange. Thompson and Barnett (1981) have suggested that two kinds of approaches invite this sort of listener involve-ment:

The first is the catchy jingle that is repeated a couple of times and then ends abruptly just before the last repetition of the product name. The urge to complete the jingle and, thus, to generate the product name, is almost irresistible. The second is the ad with the friendly but bumbling salesman (or woman) who, at the end of the ad, urges us to be sure to "buy Heever Clooners—uh, I mean Hoover Cleaners. . . ." Once again, the urge to immediately correct the spoonerism, and, hence, to generate the product name, is extremely strong. (p. 241)

To test the effectiveness of this strategy experimentally, Thompson and Barnett presented subjects with 16 simulated radio advertisements for fictitious products. In one condition, subjects heard the product name mentioned at both the beginning and the end of each 25-second announcement. In a second condition, other subjects heard the same advertisements with mention of the product name omitted at the end of each. A third group was treated identically to this second group except that they were instructed to write down the missing product name immediately after hearing each advertisement. Fifteen minutes after all 16 advertisements had been presented, a surprise recall test for product names was administered. It was found that for groups one, two, and three, free recall was 16 percent, 29 percent, and 46 percent correct, respectively. Thus, it appears that inducing subjects to generate information facilitates memory for the generated information. It has been suggested (Graf, 1980) that this so-called generation effect may be analyzed in a levels-of-processing framework. That is, the generation of missing material may require that a subject analyze a stimulus more deeply than one that is provided. Thus, in the case of an advertisement, the generation of a product name that is missing or obviously misrepresented requires that a person think about and understand the kind of information that has been given and the kind of information that may suitably be inserted.

Other Factors That Account for the Levels-of-Processing Effect

In chapter 5 three factors that affect retrieval were presented. They were (1) the extent to which a cue matches a to-be-retrieved trace; (2) the number of traces in memory that match a cue; and (3) the number of traces a cue has already retrieved. (Retrieval failure that results from this third factor we previously termed blocking.) In the present chapter, encoding strategies have been described that facilitate remembering through operation of either the first or the second factor mentioned above. No mention has been or will be made of encoding operations that affect memory through operation of the third retrieval factor. The reason is that encoding operations that diminish cue overload by making traces distinct will also decrease the number of memories that a cue will retrieve. Thus, encoding strategies that produce an effect on memory via the second retrieval factor will have a similar effect through the third factor. This should not be too surprising, since both cue overload and blocking can be thought of as resulting from too much information in memory that matches a retrieval cue.

It is important to realize that a particular encoding strategy may affect memory through the simultaneous operation of both the first and second retrieval factors mentioned above. That is, an encoding strategy may be effective not only because it allows for an extensive overlap between cue and trace information, but also because this overlap is restricted to just the to-be-retrieved trace itself. This appears to be true for the levels-of-processing effect. Although the previous discussions emphasized distinctiveness and hence cue overload as the underlying mechanism for the levels-of-processing effect, it also seems that deep processing facilitates retrieval by allowing cues to match to-be-retrieved information better. The role of this cue-trace matching factor will be evident in the discussions that follow.

Yes versus No. Many experiments that manipulate the level at which a subject processes a stimulus require that the subject judge the stimulus on some basis and respond with a "yes" or "no" answer. It has not previously been mentioned that a person's answer can have a sizeable effect on memory for the stimulus. For example, Craik and Tulving (1975, experiment 1) found that "yes" answers in a rhyme judgment task led to 78 percent correct recognition of the judged words, while "no" answers led to only 30 percent correct recognition. A similar pattern of recognition performance resulted from a semantic level task. When asked if a word belonged to some category, words that were judged to belong to the category were later recognized 93 percent of the time, while words judged not to belong to the category were recognized only 63 percent of the time.

How can this difference be explained? One possibility that has received some support (Craik & Tulving, 1975) is that questions that are answered affirmatively allow information in the question to be integrated with the encoded word. For example, suppose you were provided with the sentence frame, "The boy met a _____ on the street," and asked whether or not the word *friend* fitted the sentence. Your answer would be affirmative because you have experienced many incidents in which such an event occurred. The important thing to realize here is that as a result of these previous experiences you will have formed traces in memory that incorporate the information about friends, meetings, and streets; that is, this information will already be associated together in memory. This associated information can consequently be updated to fit the present encounter with the sentence frame and the word. Contrast this with the combination of the sentence "The girl placed the _____ on the table," and the word *cloud.*

Here, there is little chance that corresponding information has been associated together previously in memory.

What is the effect of there being these previously formed associations between a word and the encoding question? One important consequence is that information in the encoding question will be able to function as an effective retrieval cue for the word. That is, since the encoding question (let us represent this with the letter A) is linked to the to-be-retrieved word (B), the presence of information A at the time of retrieval will be capable of contacting the information B.

It seems likely that semantic processing can be so effective because of the vast and varied number of associations that go into attributing meaning to a stimulus. One can think of each of these associations as a potential retrieval cue for the stimulus. What a semantic-orienting task does is arouse a subset of these retrieval cues and, in effect, store them together with the to-be-retrieved stimulus. In a sense, then, the semantic task puts potential retrieval cues to work.

According to these claims, what should be of most importance to memory is not whether a person answers "yes" or "no" to a question, but the extent to which the processing task arouses information that has already been associated with the to-be-retrieved stimulus. Thus, memory for a stimulus should be no different in a levels-of-processing experiment if a person's answer to an orienting question is "yes" or "no," as long as both the "yes" and the "no" responses entail equivalent arousal of preexisting associations to the stimulus. Evidence of this can be seen in an experiment performed by Craik and Tulving (1975, experiment 6). Subjects were given questions such as "Taller than a man?" followed by a word such as *elephant* or *mouse*, or "More valuable than $10?" followed by a word such as *button* or *jewel*. On a surprise cued recall test, subjects were presented with the questions and asked to provide the word they had previously judged. No difference was found in the recall of words answered "yes" or "no." For the 16 words answered "yes," 36 percent were recalled, and for the words answered "no," 39 percent were recalled. Although Craik and Tulving did not design their experiment to examine the exact hypothesis being proposed here, it seems reasonable to speculate that the equivalent recall of words answered "yes" or "no" in this study resulted because there was no difference in the extent to which the two types of questions aroused existing memory associations. For example, it seems unlikely that there is any difference in the degree of preexperimental association between the size of a man versus elephant and a man versus mouse.

As a further illustration of how important it is that the processing task arouse information in memory that is already associated with the to-be-remembered stimulus, consider the following two passages constructed by Anderson and Reder (1979). Both present equally detailed information about the word pair *dog–chair*. However, the first arouses general information that the reader will have already stored in memory, while the second presents information that will probably not correspond as readily to previously stored experiences.

> A. The dog loved his masters. He also loved to sit on the chairs. His masters had a beautiful black velvet chair. One day he climbed on it. He left his white hairs all over the chair. His masters were upset by this. They scolded him.
>
> B. The word *dog* is in the book. The word *dog* is also known to be above the word *chair*. The book has the word *chair* printed in large red letters. On one page, the word *dog* is larger than the word *chair*. The word *dog* has its green letters printed beside the word *chair*. The book tells about this. The book illustrates the word *dog*.

Although no experiments have been performed to contrast the effect on memory of these two types of passages, the advantage of the first seems obvious; so obvious, in fact, that, in the words of Anderson and Reder "we have not been motivated to perform the experiment" (p. 390). According to the view presented here, the first passage will lead to superior memory for the word pair because it allows much detailed information to be associated with this encounter. This, in turn, can affect memory in two ways. First, it allows a person to use a number of cues to contact the words. Second, the detailed information associated with the word makes each distinct and thus easily discrimable from other memories.

Processing Levels in Perspective

The levels-of-processing view as originally presented by Craik and Lockhart (1972) proposed that memory of an event improves as the event is processed at deeper levels. Processing at the semantic level was proposed to produce the best memory performance and processing at the level of a stimulus' physical features was proposed to lead to the poorest memory performance. Subsequent experimentation, however, showed that the simple designation of a task as "semantic processing" did not always allow an accurate prediction of the level of memory performance. For example, it was found (Craik & Tulving, experiment 7) that memory for the word *apple* would be better recalled if judged as being suitable for the sentence "The small lady angrily picked up the red _____" as opposed to the sentence "She cooked the _____." Thus, the feasibility of using just processing level to predict memory performance was called into question. To account for this finding, Craik and Tulving suggested that the *elaborateness* of processing within any level was also an important determinant of memory performance. Thus, elaborate shallow-level processing was proposed to lead to better memory than nonelaborate shallow processing, and elaborate semantic processing was supposed to lead to better memory than nonelaborate semantic processing. In terms of the two sentence frames just mentioned, this encoding elaboration view proposes that the first sentence frame led to better recall of the word *apple* because the sentence was much more detailed than the second sentence, and thus caused richer, more elaborate information to be stored with the word.

Other investigations have further restricted the generality of the original levels-of-processing view. It has been found, for example, that better memory performance can result from a shallow rather than a deep processing task when cues in the memory test are more suitable to the shallow encodings rather than the deep encodings (Morris, Bransford, & Franks, 1977). In addition, as mentioned earlier in this chapter, processing that leads to more distinctive encodings, regardless of the processing level, enhances memory performance.

What is the effect of these findings on the levels-of-processing view of memory? The suggestion made throughout this chapter is that an encoding strategy improves memory performance to the extent that it (1) enhances the degree to which a retrieval cue matches the encoded memory and (2) allows the cue to match the encoded memory uniquely. Much of the time, semantic processing is effective in heightening retrieval in both these ways. However, to say that memory for a stimulus is good because the rememberer has processed the stimulus semantically is not really appropriate. The good memory performance is more accurately attributed to the factors that increase retrievability of the traces. Thus, processing level is seen here to be a convenient descriptive term rather than an explanatory principle. The experimental findings that have not accorded well with the original levels-of-processing view underscore the importance of treating processing level as a descriptive term rather than a theoretical principle. According to the view presented here, these experimental findings can be accounted for with one or more of the retrieval factors.

Summary

In this chapter it was shown that encoding strategies that facilitate remembering put information into memory in a form that allows it to be readily retrieved. What makes retrieval succeed? According to previous discussions, two important factors are the extent to which cue information matches information in the to-be-remembered trace and the extent to which a cue is overloaded.

The first part of the chapter discussed encoding techniques that bring about maximal overlap of cue and trace information. These techniques all involved systems for enhancing the associations of information in a potential retrieval cue with to-be-remembered information. Symbolically, this approach may be described as follows: If event B is to be remembered, and if event A will be present in the retrieval environment, retrieval of B will be made more likely if A becomes associated in memory with B. Interacting imagery was shown to be highly effective in this regard. This technique is incorporated in a number of mnemonic aids, such as the keyword method for learning foreign language vocabulary, the peg-word method, the method of loci, and a mnemonic for associating names and faces. Other techniques, such as generating sentences that incorporate the items that are to be remembered, are also effective. It was suggested that the effectiveness of these methods may be due to their making use of preexisting associations in the rememberer's long-term store.

The second part of this chapter discussed encoding strategies that facilitate retrieval by minimizing the extent to which a future retrieval cue will be overloaded. Diminished cue overload was suggested to result from distinctive encodings. Memory phenomena such as the von Restorff effect and release from proactive interference were offered as illustrations of this. The levels-of-processing view of memory was then discussed in some detail. It was shown that an important reason that deep processing facilitates remembering is because this form of processing establishes distinctive memory traces. Experiments by Moscovitch and Craik (1976) and Eysenck (1979) were described. These studies showed that the effects on memory of both semantic- and feature-level processing could be made to vary through manipulations designed to affect the distinctiveness of a subject's encodings. It was shown that at both of these processing levels, increased trace distinctiveness led to enhanced memory. Other discussions pointed out that deep processing can facilitate remembering through the arousal of the rich and elaborate semantic network that each of us has built up in our long-term store. This elaborate information that is already associated with the to-be-remembered item can aid remembering both by later serving as an effective retrieval cue (in accord with the discussions made in the first part of this chapter), and also by making the encoding of the item distinctive.

Chapter 9
Concepts

Introduction

One night in 1973 William Schrager was arrested. Two New York City policemen had seen him driving slowly down a street after he had idled the engine of his recently stalled car for a short time. The suspicious behavior attracted the policemen's attention, and when they noticed that the driver matched the description of a person being sought in connection with some sexual assaults, Schrager was stopped and arrested. Schrager claimed that he was a newly appointed assistant district attorney, but he had no papers to substantiate this claim. Throughout that night and into the morning hours Schrager was questioned and put in lineups. Four women picked him out of these lineups, identifying him as the person who had molested them. Schrager, it turned out, was who he claimed to be, a newly appointed assistant district attorney, innocent of the charges of sexual assault. Also innocent of the crimes was a Sanitation Department chauffeur named John Priolo, who had been previously arrested and, like Schrager, identified by several victims of sexual attacks.

What Schrager and Priolo had in common was a physical resemblance to the actual attacker. They both were 5 foot 4 inches tall with dark receding hair. The crimes, however, were apparently committed by a third person who was arrested for stabbing a girl and who later admitted to some of the crimes of which Schrager and Priolo had been accused. This third person, too, was 5 foot 4 inches tall with dark receding hair. Police, embarrassed by the mistakes, talked in amazement of the close resemblance between each mistakenly identified person and the confessed perpetrator, describing the matches as "twins," "doubles," and "dead ringers" ("Oh say can you see," 1973).

Although this incident may be taken as an illustration of the unreliability of eyewitness identification, this is not its intended purpose here. Rather, of present interest is the ability that underlies these errors. This is the ability to detect similarity, the capacity to judge that events or objects "go together" in some sense. As will be described in this chapter, this ability allows us to do more than recognize faces; it enables us to form concepts. We will see that concept formation is a vital process, one that allows us to take many shortcuts in processing information from our environment. We will also see that our ability to detect similarity, which underlies our acquisition and utilization of concepts, can, as in the case of eyewitness identification, cause us to make costly errors in interpreting our environment.

Similarity, Retrieval, and Concepts

Medin and Schaffer (1978) make these comments about concepts:

> One of the major components of cognitive behavior concerns abstracting rules and forming concepts. Our entire system of naming objects and events, talking about them, and interacting with them presupposes the ability to group experiences into appropriate classes. Young children learn to tell the difference between dogs and cats, between clocks and fans, and between stars and street lights. Since few concepts are formally taught, the evolution of concepts from experience with examplars must be a fundamental learning phenomenon. (p. 207)

What is a concept? In general terms it is an abstract mental representation formed from a collection of stimuli that have properties in common. For example, the concept of "cat" stands for or represents many instances of this kind of animal, all of which share certain characteristics, such as a particular body shape and size (see Rosch & Mervis, 1975). One important indication that a concept has been formed is that the learner treats or reacts to instances of the concept in much the same way. For example, once a child has acquired the concept of "cat," all instances of this concept will be called cats. Here, the same language label is being assigned to a variety of instances.

How are concepts formed? The point to be made here is that concepts are formed from a basic property of the retrieval system, the tendency of newly encountered information to contact and arouse from memory information that matches it.

The Role of Similarity in Concept Acquisition

We have all learned that objects that support seated individuals are usually called chairs. How was the concept of "chair" acquired? It is likely that

in our encounters with chairs that we experienced early in life, the word
chair was spoken to us. As we subsequently came upon objects that physically or functionally resembled these chairs, these previous experiences with
chairs were retrieved from our long-term store. Since these previous experiences included the spoken word *chair,* the word *chair* would tend to be
activated by these encounters. Consequently, we might speak the word,
aided by feedback from adults as to its appropriateness, whenever an object
in our environment activated the representation of "chair" in memory.
What is important to note is that, according to this proposal, the tendency
to react to a variety of objects in much the same way (they are all called
chairs) occurs because stimuli from the environment arouse matching information in memory.

An Experimental Demonstration of the Importance of Similarity.   What
prediction would you make about the following situation? The parents of
child A wish to teach their child the concept of "chair" and the concept
of "bed." The parents point to a chair in the living room that child A is
sitting on and say the word *chair.* They later point to the bed the child is
lying on and say the word *bed.* The parents of child B also wish to teach
these same concepts to their child. Again, they point to the bed that child
B is lying on and say the word *bed.* However, when teaching child B the
concept chair they point to a chair that the child has, on previous occasions,
seen fold out into a bed. Which child do you think will best be able correctly
to identify newly encountered objects as either chairs or beds? Obviously,
child A. The reason underlying this prediction again involves the tendency
of the retrieval system to find matching information in memory. That is,
since child B has the word *chair* associated in memory with both bed-like
and chair-like objects, future encounters with a bed-like object might cause
either or both representations to be retrieved. Thus, B will be more likely
than A to make mistakes in identifying beds and chairs in the near future.

A study by Mervis and Pani (1980), using five-year-old kindergarten students as subjects, produced results very much in accord with this prediction.
Mervis and Pani did not attempt to teach the children how to differentiate
beds from chairs; the children had already learned these sorts of concepts.
Instead, the experimenters attempted to teach the children some new concepts using stimuli created specially for experimental investigations of concept acquisition. The experimenters prepared their stimuli with three requirements in mind. First, they realized that in the real world a person
generally encounters a variety of different instances of a concept. With
regard to the concept "chair," for example, a person may encounter instances such as armchairs, office chairs, and barber's chairs. To reflect this
diversity in their experimental stimuli, Mervis and Pani built some variation

into their stimuli; thus, all instances of a concept did not look exactly alike. A second requirement that affected the makeup of the experimental stimuli came from the notion that the kinds of concepts that people usually distinguish among often share more abstract properties with other concepts. For example, a person will generally distinguish beds from chairs (Rosch & Mervis, 1975), yet both are more generally regarded as being articles of furniture. Thus, even though concepts appear to be distinguishable from one another at some basic level, they also share certain properties with one another on some higher, more abstract level. To represent this in their stimuli, Mervis and Pani prepared two different sets of stimuli that, although distinguishable, also shared certain common features. Mervis and Pani called these pairs of stimulus sets *contrast sets*. A last requirement that affected the makeup of the experimental stimuli came from the observation that in the real world, objects may have properties in common with a number of concepts and so not be easily categorized as to which concept they represent. For example, chairs may fold out into beds, beds may be used for sitting, and chairs may be used for sleeping. In this case, an object may be classified on a general level as being an article of furniture, yet not be clearly identified as a member of a more specific concept. To have their stimuli reflect this, the experimenters had certain stimuli possess properties that were common to both contrast sets.

To get a better understanding of the kind of stimuli used in the experiment, look at Figure 9–1A. The set of four stimuli on the left represent instances of one concept (these are analogous to instances of the concept "chair"). You will notice that the four instances are not identical, but that they do have a lot in common. On the right of Figure 9–1A is a single instance of a concept from the contrast set. You will notice that this single instance has some general physical resemblance to instances of the other concept, but at the same time has a number of different specific features (the two concepts are analogous to sets of beds and chairs, both of which are articles of furniture). Finally, notice that in the concept depicted on the left of Figure 9–1A, not all instances are equally good representatives of the concept. Note, in particular, that the fourth instance looks very much like it belongs in the contrast set. This fourth instance, then, is not a good representative of the concept on the left in the sense that it has many properties in common with members of another concept (this is analogous to a chair that converts into a bed and so is not a very good example of a chair). In addition to these two sets of stimuli, Mervis and Pani prepared two other pairs of contrast sets according to these same criteria. A good instance of each pair of all these sets is shown in Figure 9–1B.

Mervis and Pani's experiment was quite straightforward. Two groups of

Figure 9–1
Part A shows four instances of one concept and a single "good" instance of a member
of the contrast set. Part B shows a "good" instance of each of the three pairs of
contrast sets. In Mervis and Pani's (1980) study, each of these six sets represented
in part B included three other instances.

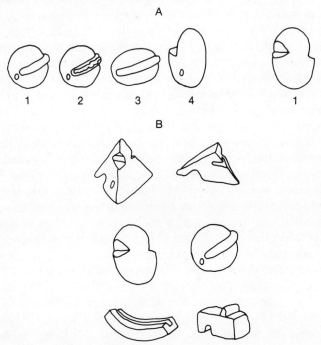

From C. Mervis and J. Pani, "Acquisition of basic object categories." *Cognitive Psychology*,
1980, *12*, 496–522. Copyright 1980 by Academic Press. Reprinted by permission.

five-year-olds participated in the study. One group was shown a good instance of each of the six sets of stimuli. As each instance was presented
the experimenter called it by a different nonsense name (e.g., *naete*). Once
subjects in this group had been presented with all six objects and their
names, they were drilled until they could recognize each object by name
and also recall each name when an object was presented. The experimenters
then began to present these subjects with all 24 stimulus objects one at a
time. Subjects were told that these objects, most of which had not already
been studied by the children, were really the same kinds of things as they
had just seen and that they should name them using one of the names
they had just learned. In general, subjects found this to be an easy task.

They made almost no errors in naming the three best instances of each concept (they were correct about 99 percent of the time). However, they tended to make many more errors in supplying the correct name for the poor instance of each concept. For these poor instances, subjects either failed to supply any name or supplied an incorrect name about 28 percent of the time. In every case in which an incorrect name was assigned, the name of the object from the contrast set was given. This outcome is analogous to a child being quick to identify new instances of the concept "chair" if the concept was originally learned from encounters with a chair that was highly representative of the concept. The errors made by subjects in this group are analogous to errors made in identifying a poor example of a chair, one that resembles a bed.

As mentioned previously, these results are just what would be expected if it is assumed that underlying the acquisition of concepts is the tendency of newly encoded information to retrieve matching information from the long-term store. Results that further supported this assumption came from a second group of young subjects. The five-year-olds in this second group were treated exactly like subjects in the other group except that they were shown poor instances of each of the six concepts. Thus, subjects in this second group learned the concept names when shown instances such as object 4 in Figure 9–1A. If we assume that subsequently encountered objects will tend most effectively to retrieve representations in memory that contain the most matching features, one would expect this subject group to make many errors in naming the remaining objects. This is just what occurred. When shown all 24 stimuli, these subjects correctly identified only about 59 percent of the better instances of each concept (e.g., objects 1–3 in Figure 9–1A). Evidently, because the poor instances of each concept resembled the instances of the contrast set, the better instances of each contrast set tended to retrieve inappropriate names from memory. This, of course, is analogous to a child mistakenly calling a bed a chair after having learned the concept "chair" from a chair that converts into a bed.

Hull's Experiment.   A more subtle demonstration of the role of retrieval in concept acquisition comes from an experiment by Hull (1920). Hull's experiment shows that concepts can be acquired without a great deal of conscious effort being expended. Subjects in this study were first shown 12 different Chinese characters, one at a time. Shortly after each character was presented, the experimenter identified it with a different nonsense name, such as *oo, yer, deg,* or *ling.* The set of 12 characters and their names were presented over and over again until subjects were able to supply each name correctly before the experimenter provided it. The experimenter next showed subjects a new set of 12 Chinese characters. The subjects were told that their task was to try to learn the names of each of these new characters. Subjects were also told that to make the task easier, the same set of 12 nonsense names used with the first set would be reused. An important additional instruction was that on the first presentation of each character, subjects should attempt to guess its name. Subjects were then shown the 12 new characters one at a time; they attempted to guess the name of each character in the two and one-half seconds before the name was supplied by the experimenter. The procedure was repeated until subjects had learned the names of all 12 characters. The same learning process was then repeated with four additional sets of 12 new characters.

The most interesting data produced by the subjects was their guesses of the character names the first time each character was shown. The data clearly showed that subjects steadily improved in their ability to guess these names correctly. It should be understood that these guesses were made before the experimenter ever told subjects what each correct name was. As an example of this improvement in guessing performance, subjects shown the second set of 12 characters correctly guessed the names of only about three of them. However, for the sixth set of characters, subjects correctly guessed the names of about seven of them.

What accounted for this improvement in performance? Unknown to the subjects, Hull had embedded a particular feature in a number of different Chinese characters. This is shown in Figure 9–2. It can be seen that each set of 12 characters consists of exactly the same set of 12 basic features; the only difference among the sets is that the repeated features are embedded in somewhat different surrounding markings each time. The arrangement of the characters shown in Figure 9–2 emphasizes the presence of the repeated, common features. It should be understood that in the experiment, the characters in each set were presented in a random order and that no drawings of previously presented characters were available for subjects to inspect.

The steady improvement in subjects' abilities to guess the name of each newly presented character indicates that subjects were recognizing, either consciously or unconsciously, that there were similarities between a newly presented character and a series of previously presented characters. This may be considered to have resulted from the tendency of newly encoded information to arouse matching information in memory automatically. That is, even though subjects might not have consciously been trying to search for similar events in memory, there would be a tendency for characters containing a particular feature most strongly to arouse memories that also contained this same feature. This, in turn, would have tended to arouse the name that had been previously associated with this visual information.

Figure 9–2
An example of some of the characters used by Hull (1920). It can be seen that the same concept appears in every row in somewhat different contexts.

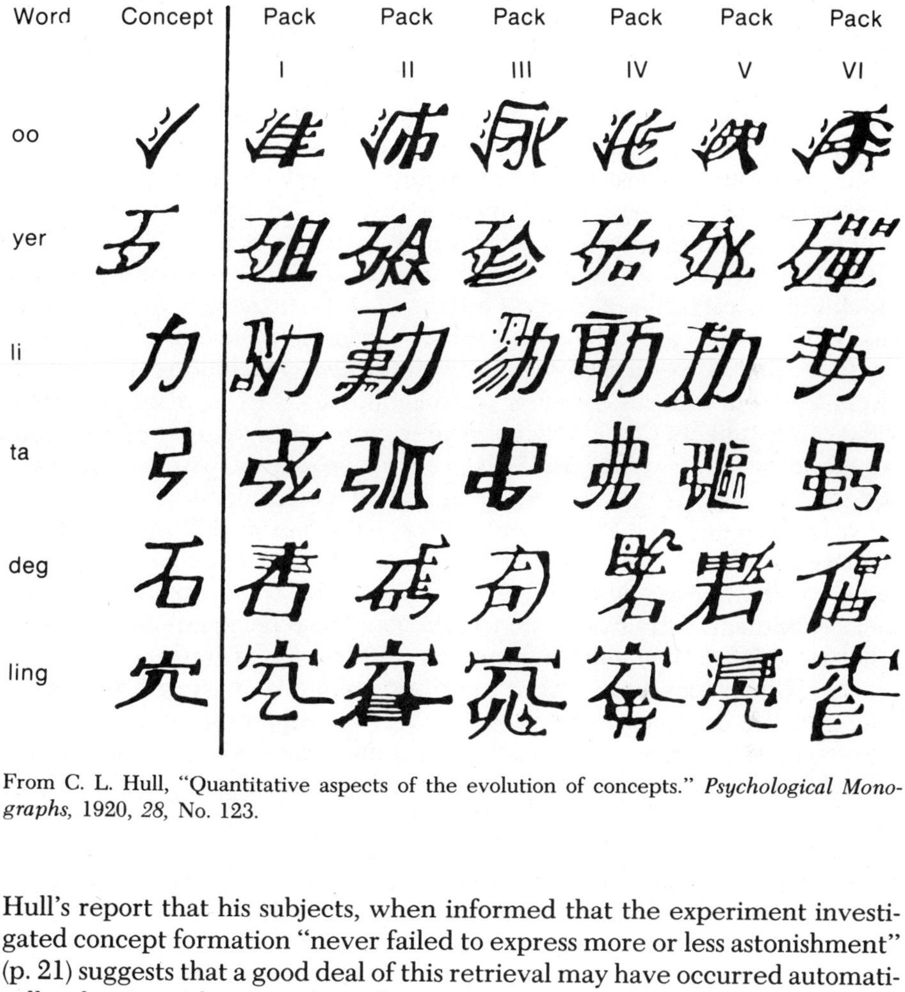

Word	Concept	Pack I	Pack II	Pack III	Pack IV	Pack V	Pack VI
oo							
yer							
li							
ta							
deg							
ling							

From C. L. Hull, "Quantitative aspects of the evolution of concepts." *Psychological Monographs*, 1920, *28*, No. 123.

Hull's report that his subjects, when informed that the experiment investigated concept formation "never failed to express more or less astonishment" (p. 21) suggests that a good deal of this retrieval may have occurred automatically, that is, without a subject having consciously attempted to search for matching information in memory.

Retrieval of Imperfectly Matching Information

S. had a rather startling deficit. He had trouble recognizing people, a problem due, he claimed, to people's inconstant facial expressions. Each time S. encountered someone, the person's expression could be slightly different. On one occasion the person might look happy; on another, annoyed, tired, or anxious. Why would someone with an extrordinarily good memory have this problem? One explanation involves distinctive encodings. Previously, the beneficial aspects of distinctive encodings were stressed. It was pointed out that if a stimulus is encoded distinctively, a retrieval cue that matches the encoded trace will not be overloaded and therefore be most capable of successfully retrieving it. Distinctive encodings can hinder successful retrieval, however, when retrieval occurs with cues containing distinctive information that does not match the distinctive information in the to-be-remembered trace. Consider, for example, S.'s reactions to tones. When a 30-cycle-per-second tone was played to him, S. encoded some very distinctive information about it, information that included color—that of old, tarnished silver—and shape—a strip 12–15 centimeters wide that narrowed in the distance. To a tone of 50 cycles per second, on the other hand, S. reacted by envisioning the colors brown and red and the taste of sweet and sour borscht. Because his reactions to these two tones were so different, it is likely that a new encounter with a 50-cycles-per-second tone would not have reminded S. of his previous encounter with the 30-cycle-per-second tone. This same reasoning can also be applied to S.'s memory for faces. Imagine that upon meeting a person, S. encoded much detailed information about the person's face, information that went far beyond just visual information and included taste, tactile, and other sensory impressions. On a subsequent encounter with this person, if the person's expression was different so that very different sensory impressions were aroused in S.'s mind, it is likely that these sensory impressions would fail to retrieve information encoded from the earlier encounter with the person. Here, retrieval will have failed because of an insufficient match between the distinctive information in the cue and that in the memory trace.

What does this deficit have to do with concept acquisition? In order to acquire and use concepts normally, it seems to be necessary for retrieval to occur even when newly encoded information does not exactly match information stored in memory. Consider an experiment by Posner and Keele (1968). Subjects in this study were first trained to recognize instances of several concepts. In one study (though not the study we shall be most concerned with), the concept that was learned was a triangle made of nine dots. In learning to recognize the concept, subjects were not shown patterns of dots that depicted a perfectly formed triangle (or prototype triangle, as we shall refer to it) but instead were shown distorted instances of the triangle formed by randomly moving each of the nine dots that made up the prototype pattern. Figure 9–3A shows a prototype triangle and one distorted instance of the concept.

Figure 9–3
Part A shows a prototype triangle and a distorted instance of the prototype. Part B shows a prototype of a random pattern.

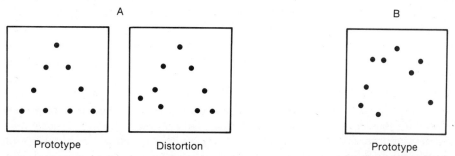

From M. I. Posner, R. Goldsmith and K. E. Welton, "Perceived distance and the classification of distorted patterns." *Journal of Experimental Psychology*, 1967, *73*, 28–38. Copyright 1267 by the American Psychological Association. Reprinted by permission of publisher and author.

While the concept of triangle was learned in two of the experiments reported by Posner and Keele in their 1968 article, some more abstract concepts were learned in the study that will be of interest to us here (experiment 3). These abstract concepts were just random patterns of nine dots. The prototype of one such concept is shown in Figure 9–3B. As in the case of the triangle, Posner and Keele prepared different instances of each random dot concept by randomly moving each of the nine dots of the prototype pattern.

The experiment began with a presentation of four distorted instances of each of three different prototype patterns. The instances were presented one at a time in a random order, and subjects had to learn to categorize each into one of three different groups. (The ability of subjects in this experiment to respond in the same way to a variety of stimuli indicates that they had learned the three concepts.) After subjects had acquired the concepts, they were presented with a series of dot patterns to categorize. These included not only old instances that subjects had just learned to categorize, but also prototype patterns from which these distorted instances had been derived. Subjects were instructed to categorize these test patterns by responding as quickly as possible with the name of one of the three concepts they had just learned. Predictably, it was found that subjects were most accurate in correctly identifying old instances, that is, ones they had learned to categorize. These old patterns were correctly identified 87 percent of the time. Of more interest, however, was the finding that when shown the prototypes of each concept, subjects were able to make correct identifications 85 percent of the time. You must realize that subjects had never seen the prototype of each concept previously, just the distorted instances of each. In spite of this, however, they had learned something about the prototype. We could not expect such behavior from an individual who, after encoding a stimulus, only retrieved it when encountering identical stimuli in the environment. In this experiment, such a person would fail to recognize the prototype since it had not, in fact, been previously encountered.

It is interesting that S., whose distinctive encoding practices hindered his retrieval of nonidentical information from memory, appeared to have difficulty dealing with abstract concepts. He is reported to have not clearly understood such concepts as nothing and infinity and also to have had trouble understanding poetry.

Summary

The view of concept acquisition presented so far is quite simple. Underlying the development of concepts is the retrieval system, which finds information in memory that matches the information being attended to. The arousal of closely matching information in memory allows the currently attended stimulus to be treated in much the same way as the similar stimuli were treated in the past. Thus, if chair-like objects in the past were sat upon, a newly encountered chair-like object may also be used for this form of support. The similar treatment of a variety of objects or events indicates that a concept has been acquired.

This simple view of concepts is not the only one possible. In the upcoming discussions some alternative views of concepts and the concept-acquisition process will be presented. The position to be taken here is that these alternate approaches are just extensions and complications of the simple position just presented.

Complications

Schemas

Not all psychologists would interpret the data of Posner and Keele's (1968) experiment as indicating that prototype test patterns were retrieving a collection of stimuli from memory that matched each prototype imperfectly. To understand the alternative interpretation of the data, we must investigate another way concepts may possibly be represented in memory. This alternative view is that as a result of having encountered a variety of instances of a concept, a person derives a representation of the central tendency of the instances; that is, the learner derives a single representation that best summarizes the many instances that have been encountered. This *schema,* as it is often termed (Bartlett, 1932), is thought to be stored in memory in addition to representations of the various instances that have been encountered (Posner & Keele, 1968).

Evidence that has been interpreted to support this claim comes from a study Posner and Keele (1970) performed as a follow-up to their 1968 study. This second experiment was nearly identical to the previous one. Subjects were first shown four highly distorted instances of each of three different prototype patterns. Again, the prototypes were composed of nine randomly arranged dots. In the first phase of the experiment, subjects learned to classify each pattern correctly into one of three categories. In the second phase of the experiment, subjects were divided into two groups. One group was dismissed and asked to return one week later. The other group continued with the experiment immediately. The task in the second phase, just as in the earlier experiment, was to attempt to classify a series of dot patterns. The series consisted of two instances of each prototype pattern that subjects had learned to classify in the first phase of the experiment and the three prototype patterns. The series also contained some new distortions of the prototype patterns that subjects had not previously been shown—two new small distortions and two new large distortions of each prototype. The data of interest were not only the differences in speed and accuracy with which subjects could classify the different types of test patterns, but also the changes in these measures over time. Of most relevance to the issue of schema formation was the finding that during the one-week delay between concept learning and the test, subjects showed more forgetting of the old distortions than of the prototypes. Specifically, recognition of old distortions fell from 82 percent correct to 69 percent correct, whereas recognition of the prototypes fell from 65 percent to 60 percent correct. Posner and Keele reasoned that if classification of prototype patterns was based on memory of just individual instances, the ability to classify these prototypes should have declined as rapidly as the ability to classify previously studied instances. Of relevance to the claim that in addition to this schema, subjects had stored information about the individual instances was the finding that old distortions were classified more accurately and faster than all the new stimuli. The difference in performance was most pronounced between old and new highly distorted patterns: Whereas subjects correctly classified 82 percent of the old highly distorted instances of each prototype, the new highly distorted instances were correctly classified only 51 percent of the time.

This indicates that subjects could not have been basing performance just on a schema, since this would have led to equivalent performance for both new and old highly distorted instances.

Feature Frequency Versus Feature Averaging Schemas.   Although not everyone agrees that a concept is represented as a schema in the mind, those who do have contrasted two bases on which a schema may be formed (Franks & Bransford, 1971; Goldman & Homa, 1977). One basis presumes that a schema consists of the feature values that occur most frequently in the instances of the concept. For example, if three of four faces that make up a concept have long noses and the fourth has a short nose, the schema that represents these faces will contain a long nose, since that is the more frequently occurring nose length. The same frequency considerations will determine the mouth, eyes, and other facial features included in the schema. Another proposed basis for schema formation is an averaging of the feature values that make up each instance. If three faces have long noses and one has a short nose, this model predicts that the schema will contain a fairly long nose, one whose length is the mean of the four nose lengths.

A number of studies (e.g., Goldman & Homa, 1977; Reed, 1972; Strauss, 1979) have attempted to determine which of these models is more appropriate. An experiment by Strauss (1979) illustrates a typical approach to the problem and the kind of conclusions often drawn. Strauss (experiment 1) had subjects study two series of 14 faces that were shown at a five-second rate. The faces in one series had rather extreme feature values in the sense that their dimensions were either quite large or small. For example, the lengths of faces and noses tended to be either great or small. So, too, was the separation between eyes and the width of the nose. Thus, one face in this series might have had eyes widely separated, a narrow, short nose, and a long face. In this set of faces, which shall be termed the extreme set, feature values were varied so that the shortest or narrowest instance of each was represented six times, the longest or widest of each six times, and a middle value of each only twice. Thus, for the feature face length, six faces were extremely short, six were extremely long, and two were of intermediate length. This same variation applied to eye separation, nose width, and nose length. After subjects had seen the 14 faces in this extreme set, the experimenter showed them a pair of test faces that had not been included in the set of 14. Subjects were instructed to select the test face that appeared to be more familiar. These test faces had been prepared so that it could be determined whether subjects had formed a schema based on average or most frequent feature values. To allow this determination, one test face consisted entirely of features having average dimensions. The other was composed just of features having extreme dimensions. This latter test face, of course, represented feature values that had occurred most frequently in the set of 14 faces that subjects had just observed. It should be noted that because each feature had two extreme values in the set of 14 faces (e.g., face length was either very long or very short), the experimenter prepared two versions of the test face containing extreme values. For half of the subjects the test pair consisted of one of these extreme faces and the average face; for the other subjects, the test pair consisted of the other extreme face and the average face. These two pairs are shown in Figure 9–4A. Which face seemed more familiar to subjects? The results were quite clear. Most of the subjects, 71 percent of them, chose the test face composed

Figure 9–4
Part A shows the pairs of test faces judged by the two groups of subjects in Strauss' (1979) experiment who had seen the set of extreme faces. Part B shows the test pairs judged by subjects who had seen the moderate set.

A   B

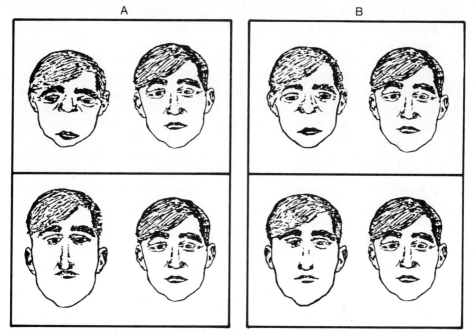

From M. S. Strauss, "Abstraction of prototypical information by adults and 10-month-old infants." *Journal of Experimental Psychology: Human Learning and Memory,* 1979, 5, 618–632. Copyright 1979 by the American Psychological Association. Reprinted by permission of publisher and author.

of the extreme feature values, that is, the face that consisted of the most frequently occurring values.

Although the subjects' behavior in this task clearly seems to favor the view that a schema consists of the most frequently occurring feature values represented in instances of the concept, a very different conclusion seems appropriate from another learning condition that Strauss included in his experiment. Strauss had subjects learn another set of 14 faces that were constructed in much the same way as the faces in the extreme set. The only difference was that the dimensions of the facial features in this second set were less extreme than those in the first set. Thus, in this second set of faces, which shall be referred to as the moderate set, there were six faces with slightly short noses, six with slightly long noses, and two with noses of average length. The same distribution of dimensions applied to nose width, eye separation, and face length. Subjects were again presented with a pair of test faces after they had viewed all 14 faces in the moderate set and asked which seemed more familiar. The pairs of test faces used for this set were constructed in a manner analogous to that of the extreme set. The two test pairs for this set are shown in Figure 9–4B. Subjects' preference in this task was again clear. This time, however, most subjects, 76 percent, said that the average face seemed more familiar.

The conclusion Strauss drew from these data was that people form a schema that is based on average feature values when there is not much variation among the values of the features represented by instances of the concept, that is, when all instances are quite similar. However, when the instances of the concept contain a feature whose value differs noticeably from instance to instance, people tend to form a schema based on the most frequently experienced value.

Are Schemas Necessary? Some psychologists have questioned whether a person really does form a schema to represent a concept. Those who have questioned the existence of schemas (e.g., Hintzman & Ludlam, 1980; Medin & Schaffer, 1978; Neumann, 1977) have argued that the behavior of subjects in concept acquisition studies can be adequately accounted for with memory models that assume storage of only concept instances and not schemas in addition to these instances.

A study by Hintzman and Ludlam (1980) exemplifies this view. As mentioned earlier, one of the strongest pieces of evidence favoring the view that subjects form a schema is the finding that the ability to classify a prototype pattern declines more slowly over time than the ability to recognize old instances of the concept (Posner & Keele, 1970). Hintzman and Ludlam wished to show that it is not necessary to assume that subjects form a schema in order to obtain this result. They suggested that these same behaviors can be expected from a model that makes a number of assumptions about the storage, retrieval, and forgetting of individual instances of a concept. According to this model, once a subject has learned a concept, all that is stored in memory is the individual instances of the concept. When a stimulus is then presented and the subject is asked to identify the pattern, the identification behavior is determined by the instances of the concept that the stimulus retrieves from memory. This, in turn, is determined by the extent to which the stimulus resembles traces stored in memory. Traces containing information that best matches information in the stimulus will be most likely to be retrieved. The category information associated with the retrieved instances will then determine how the stimulus is categorized.

To demonstrate the validity of their model, Hintzman and Ludlam programmed a computer to behave in accord with the constraints of their model. Information about six instances of each of two concepts was entered into the computer's memory to simulate the learning of the two concepts. Then, to simulate the concept-identification phase of a typical experiment, old instances, new instances, and a new prototype of each concept were entered, one at a time, into the computer. The computer calculated the degree to which each of these stimuli matched the instances of the two concepts already stored in memory and arrived at a decision, based on mathematical criteria, about how the stimulus should be classified. Hintzman and Ludlam found that by manipulating the decision criteria and by making certain assumptions about the way forgetting of stored instances occurs, the computer could simulate the concept-identification behavior of human subjects. More importantly, it was shown that when forgetting of learned instances of a concept was simulated, the classification of old instances of each concept could decline faster than that of prototype patterns.

Encoding Strategies and Schemas. It seems, then, that the notion of schema may not be necessary to account for the different forgetting rates of prototypes and old instances of a concept. Are schemas necessary to account for findings such as those of Strauss (1979), who showed that subjects base categorization of new stimuli on either average or most frequent feature values occurring in learned instances of a concept? Neumann (1977) has pointed out that subjects who are learning to form a concept may not encode each feature value of every instance of a concept in a very precise way, but instead may encode a range of values in a similar way. Thus, when a subject briefly studies a face with a fairly long nose and then one with a fairly short nose, the subject may encode each nose in about the same way. That is, the subject may casually observe that each face has an average-size nose and so store just this information in memory. When later presented with a prototype face having an average-size nose, the subject may find this facial feature to be quite familiar because it matches the encodings of noses encountered on these two prior occasions. In this case, what may appear to be evidence for an average-based schema may actually involve no schema at all, but a decision based on a match between a feature in the newly presented stimulus and a feature encoded a number of times in memory.

Evidence that the difference between a schema based on the most frequent versus the average feature value is dependent on how precisely a feature value is encoded comes from a study by Neumann (1977). Subjects in this experiment were shown a series of eight drawings of faces at a 10-second rate. Although the faces had a number of features in common, they varied along certain dimensions: age, face length, and nose length. Five different values of each of these dimensions were possible. For example, the dimension of age could vary from 20 to 60 years in 10-year increments, a variation accomplished by drawing in different numbers of lines on a face. Even though five different values were possible for each of these three dimensions, the set of eight faces that subjects initially viewed contained only the most extreme values on these dimensions. For example, one drawing may have depicted a person about 60 years old with a very short nose and a very long face. Ten minutes after viewing the faces, subjects were shown a series of test faces and asked to rate on a six-point scale how confident they were of having seen the face before. Included in the test series were five faces composed entirely of one of the same five values of each of the three dimensions. If we use the numbers one to five to represent the values that age, face length, and nose length could assume, respectively, one test face can be described as consisting of the values 1,1,1, another 2,2,2, another 3,3,3, and so on. It is with these five test faces that we shall be most concerned. Before describing how confident subjects indicated they were of seeing each of these test faces, I must mention that Neumann had given different information to subjects before they studied the series of eight faces. One group of subjects, the informed group, was told which facial features would change; that is, they were told that faces would vary in terms of their age, nose length, and face length. Another group of subjects, the uninformed group, was not given this information. The reason Neumann alerted subjects in the informed group about the facial features that were going to vary was to call their attention to these features. Neumann expected that this increased attention would lead to a more careful and precise encoding of these facial features. Thus, the instruction was expected to cause subjects in the informed group to encode the variable facial features more accurately than subjects in the uninformed group. The subjects' confidence ratings in the recognition task confirmed these expectations. Subjects in the informed group were most confident of having seen the test faces composed just of the extreme valued dimensions, the 1,1,1 face and the 5,5,5 face. However, subjects in the uninformed group were most confident of having seen the 3,3,3 face. The confidence ratings that each of these groups gave to the five test faces are shown in Figure 9–5. These results indicate that the difference between what appears to be a schema based on frequency and one based on averages may involve just a difference in encoding strategy and not a fundamental difference in the process by which feature values are abstracted from instances stored in memory.

An experiment by Strauss (1979, experiment 2), which used 10-month-old infants as subjects, obtained evidence that also conforms to this view. Strauss performed the experiment as a follow-up to the study described earlier in this chapter. The purpose of the experiment was to determine

Figure 9–5
The distributions of mean confidence ratings for the five different test faces that were judged by groups of subjects who were either informed or not informed about the facial dimensions that would vary.

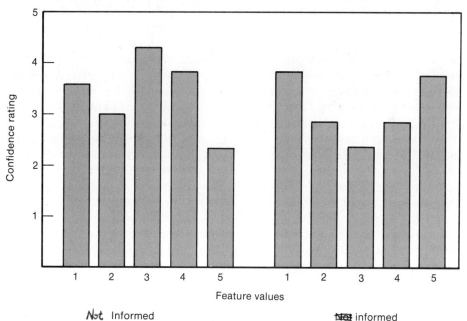

Adapted from P. G. Neumann, "Visual prototype formation with discontinuous representation of dimensions of variability." *Memory & Cognition*, 1977, 5, 187–197. Copyright 1977 by the Psychonomic Society. Reprinted by permission.

whether infants would form a schema based on average or most frequent feature values. It will be recalled that in Strauss's previously described study, adults had been shown two series of 14 faces, one made up of faces having mostly extreme-valued features (e.g., very long noses, very short faces), and the other made up of faces having less-extreme-valued features. After seeing each series of faces, the adult subjects were shown a new face made up entirely of average-valued features and one made up entirely of the feature values occurring most frequently in the series of 14 faces. Strauss had found that these adult subjects had thought that the average-value test face best resembled faces in the moderate set and that the high-frequency-value test face best resembled faces in the extreme set.

Of course, one cannot perform a study exactly like this on 10-month-old infants. Instead Strauss modified the procedure to take advantage of the finding that infants tend to pay attention to novel stimuli. Strauss expected that if infants formed a concept from observing the series of 14 faces, then, when shown a pair of test faces, they would look for a longer time at the test face that seemed less familiar to them. The procedure, again, first entailed presenting a series of 14 faces to the subjects. One group of infants was shown the extreme set, and another group was shown the moderate set. Then, a pair of test faces was displayed. The results indicated that both groups of infants preferred to look longer at the test face made up of the most frequently occurring feature values rather than the average values. This indicated to Strauss that the schema developed by both groups of infants was based on average values of the features.

Why did infants who observed faces in the extreme set find the average-values test face to be the more familiar? Accuracy of encoding might have contributed to this outcome. In general, it has been found that people make use of past experiences when encoding newly presented stimuli. It has been found, for example, that a person is much better at recognizing faces that are members of his own race rather than members of some other race. Malpass and Kravitz (1969) showed black and white university students photographs of 10 black and 10 white faces. In a recognition test, these subjects exhibited significantly better recognition of own-race rather than other-race faces. The explanation that has been offered for this finding is that a person will generally have experienced own-race faces most often and thus will best be able to use this past experience to encode new own-race faces accurately. The relevance of this for Strauss's study is that infants will have had much less experience with faces than will adults. This lack of experience can be expected to hinder accurate and detailed encoding of facial features. Thus, faces that would be encoded by an adult in a distinctive way might tend to be encoded in much the same way by an infant.

Assuming that the infants in Strauss's experiment encoded the features of the 14 faces from the extreme set in much the same way, the average-valued test face would have better matched and retrieved stored instances from memory than would the extreme-valued test face.

In addition to helping illustrate how encoding processes might affect the kind of schema that a subject appears to form, this study also indicates the automatic nature of concept acquisition. Although it is difficult to be certain, it seems likely that the infants in Strauss's study were not consciously attempting to form a concept from the series of faces they observed. Consequently, it seems that, as in Hull's (1920) experiment, the acquisition of a concept was due in large part to the tendency of newly encoded information to retrieve similar information in memory automatically. Clear evidence that the infants had, in fact, acquired a concept from their exposure to each set of 14 faces came from the finding that when shown a pair of test stimuli in which 1 test face was completely different from any face previously displayed and the other test face was an average-valued face, the infants looked at the different face significantly longer than they looked at the average-valued face. Thus, the infants could determine that a face that resembled previously encountered instances "belonged with" those faces.

Schemas and the Retrieval View.   Do people form and store schemas in addition to representations of individual instances of a concept? The view that schemas exist would most strongly be supported by evidence that showed that there are schemas that are based on average- rather than most frequent-feature values. The reason that average-feature value schemas provide better support for the concept of schema is that an average-value schema will contain information not contained in individual instances of a concept. For example, if a person encounters a series of faces that have either long or short noses, an average-value schema will store information about a medium-length nose, a value that never will have occurred in the previously encountered instances. A schema such as this will clearly not be attributable to storage of just the individual instances of the concept. Our preceding discussions, however, have shown that unequivocal evidence to support the existence of average value schemas is lacking. It appears, instead, that the averaging process may be occurring during encoding of the individual instances of the concept.

Even though the existence of schemas cannot be unequivocally established, the concept of schema is a useful one and shall continue to be used in this text. The reader must realize, however, that when a subject is described as having retrieved a schema, the person might actually have retrieved just representations of individual instances of the concept from memory.

Hypotheses

In our discussions of concept acquisition, an underlying mechanism based on memory retrieval has been stressed. The point to be made now is that concept acquisition may be facilitated by supplementing this retrieval mechanism with consciously applied strategies. An experiment by Heidbreder (1946a, 1946b) illustrates a situation in which a subject might resort to using strategies. Heidbreder presented subjects with a series of nine different drawings. As in Hull's (1920) experiment, Heidbreder named each drawing using a nonsense syllable the first time the drawing was presented. After subjects had learned to name these drawings, they were shown a second series of nine drawings. The subjects were asked to guess the names of these new drawings and were prompted by the experimenter if they guessed incorrectly. Subjects again learned to name the nine drawings; after they had done so, they were presented with a new series to learn. The process was repeated with 16 series of drawings. To get a better sense of the experimental task, look at Figure 9–6, which shows three series of drawings used in the study. See how easily you can supply the names to the drawings shown in the third series.

Table 9–1 shows the correct identification of each concept. It also lists the average number of drawing series needed by subjects to learn to name each concept correctly. In general, Heidbreder found that concrete concepts such as buildings and trees were discovered first, followed by spatial concepts and then concepts based on numbers.

How did subjects perform this task? Heidbreder did not design the study to investigate this question. However, you can probably tell from your own behavior with the drawings shown in Figure 9–6 that a speedy solution to the task can be accomplished by generating hypotheses about the dimensions of each drawing that might be critical to each concept. For example, in looking at the first drawing in series one of Figure 9–6, you may have thought that the critical aspect of objects named *ling* was that they are clothing items. This hypothesis, of course, would have been disconfirmed in series two when the two hexagons were identified as *ling*.

Continuity versus Noncontinuity Theory.   How can it be demonstrated that people do, in fact, acquire concepts by generating hypotheses? This question has in the past been considered quite important because it was part of a wider debate that contrasted a conditioning model of behavior with a cognitive model. According to a conditioning view, an organism acquires a concept by forming and strengthening associations between attributes of a stimulus and some explicit or implicit response. For example, if a person hears a particular word every time a triangle is presented but

Figure 9–6
Some of the stimuli and the names used in Heidbreder's (1946) study.

From E. Heidbreder, "The attainment of concepts: I. Terminology and methodology." *Journal of General Psychology*, 1946, 35, 173–189.

never when any other geometric form (e.g., a circle or a square) is presented, the conditioning model suggests that an association between the attribute, triangle, and the word will be established and strengthened in memory. According to this model, the response of producing this word will generalize to other triangles to the extent that the new instance resembles the previously encountered instances.

This view of concept acquisition has been termed *continuity theory* (Krechevsky, 1938) because it suggests that the associations which underlie development of a concept will build up continuously as more instances of the concept are experienced. In contrast to this view, the *noncontinuity theory* supposes that an organism forms hypotheses in the concept-learning situation. The hypotheses specify the specific attributes of the stimulus that might be critical in discriminating positive instances of the concept from negative instances. For example, to discover why an experimenter says a particular

Table 9–1
The mean number of series needed by subjects in Heidbreder's (1946) study to learn each concept. Column one indicates the concept underlying each name that was assigned.

Concept	Number of Trials
Relk (face)	3.35
Leth (building)	3.48
Mulp (tree)	3.94
Fard (0)	4.46
Pran (≠)	5.05
Stod (∝)	5.19
Ling (2)	6.14
Mank (6)	8.76
Dilt (5)	10.22

From E. Heidbreder, "The attainment of concepts: II. The problem" *Journal of General Psychology*, 1946, *35*, 191–223. Copyright 1946 by the Journal of General Psychology. Reprinted by permission.

word when certain stimuli are presented, a subject in a concept-learning study may hypothesize that the word is emitted only when red objects are present in the stimulus. Here, the subject has selected a particular attribute of the stimulus and will actively test whether or not the attribute accurately predicts the experimenter's future utterances of the word.

These two views were at one time extensively investigated using laboratory rats as subjects. The experimenters often presented rats with pairs of complex stimuli, only one of which marked a path or door that led to a reward. The animal had to learn to recognize the critical attribute(s) that distinguished the reward-producing, or positive instances of the concept, from the negative instances. How did experimenters determine whether or not rats form hypotheses? One method involved changing the critical attribute that distinguished positive from negative instances of the concept. This change was made before the animal subjects showed evidence of having fully acquired the concept. For example, if pathways in a maze that were marked with triangles always led to a reward and pathways marked with circles never led to a reward, this method entailed switching the designation of these symbols after an animal had experienced these instances a number of times, but before the meaning of these symbols had been fully learned by the animals. The two models of concept learning make different predictions about the effects of this reversal. According to a continuity model, this change should retard learning of the new concept because the associations between stimuli and responses relevant to the new, changed concept will conflict with the previously learned associations. On the other hand, a noncontinuity model, which presumes that organisms form hypotheses, predicts that learning should be sudden, that is, should occur only when the organism discovers the correct hypothesis. Thus, if the meaning of a critical attribute is changed before the relevance of the attribute is discovered, no retardation in learning should occur.

Which theory did the experiments support? Some experiments (e.g., McCulloch & Pratt, 1934) seemed to support the continuity model and others (e.g., Krechevsky, 1938) seemed to support the noncontinuity model. Levine (1975), in reviewing the controversy, comments that "many researchers contributed to this controversy with one or more reversal experiments. For each experiment performed by researchers of one theoretical persuasion, flaws were claimed by proponents of the other" (p. 19). However, a particularly compelling experiment performed by Spence in 1945 temporarily decided the controversy in favor of the continuity view. The reign of the continuity theory lasted until the 1960s, when, as part of the trend towards a cognitive approach to behavior, the view began to predominate that concept learning could involve hypothesis formation. This hypothesis model is now dominant (Levine, 1975), at least with regard to human concept learning.

Human Concept-Learning Paradigms.   Experiments that have supported the view that human subjects form and test hypotheses in laboratory concept-learning studies have usually employed either *concept formation* or *concept identification* procedures. In a concept-identification study, the experimenter presents subjects with complex stimuli composed of a variety of dimensions. For example, the stimuli in general may consist of the dimension's shape, size, and color. Each of these dimensions may assume one of a fixed number of values (also referred to as attributes). For instance, shape may have the values "triangle" or "circle," size may have the values "large" or "small," and color may have the values "red," "green," or "blue." A particular stimulus that subjects are shown will be composed of a value of each dimension. Thus, subjects may be shown a drawing of a large red triangle or a small blue circle.

What must subjects do when shown each of these stimuli? In experiments modeled after animal studies, subjects were required to make a verbal response when presented with a stimulus. The verbal response indicated whether the subject believed the stimulus was a positive or a negative instance of the concept. A positive instance was analogous to a choice in a maze-running situation of a path that led to a reward. In the human concept-identification studies, the reward subjects obtained by making a correct choice was hearing the experimenter say "right"; an incorrect choice, of course, caused the experimenter to say "wrong." The experimenter concluded that the subject had learned the concept correctly when the subject made a long string of correct responses to a series of stimuli.

The distinction between a concept-identification paradigm and a concept-formation paradigm is that in a concept-identification study the subject is made aware of the dimension of the stimulus that could be important in allowing the concept to be learned. For example, at the beginning of a concept-identification study, the experimenter could inform a subject that color, shape, and size are important and that the subject must identify the correct combination of values of these dimensions in order to learn the concept correctly. In a *concept-formation* study, on the other hand, subjects must learn on their own which dimensions of the stimulus are relevant. Heidbreder's (1946a, 1946b) experiment is an example of a concept-formation study since no mention was made to subjects about what the relevant dimensions of the stimuli might be. As described earlier, subjects had to discover on their own that number was relevant in some cases and shape relevant in others. The concept-formation paradigm is more analogous to concept learning that takes place outside the laboratory because rarely is one informed about what dimensions may be important in defining concept membership. On the other hand, the concept identification procedure can be advantageous for experimental purposes since it helps to ensure less variable performance by subjects by allowing them all to consider the same set of dimensions from the outset of the learning process.

Experimental Evidence for Hypothesis Behavior in Humans.   A study that was influential in convincing psychologists of the importance of hypothesis formation in human concept learning was performed by Bower and Trabasso (1963). The study assessed whether changing the rule that defined a concept had any effect on the rate at which the concept was learned. As with previously mentioned animal studies, it was reasoned that if subjects form hypotheses about the rule underlying classification of concept instances, the rate of concept learning should not be slowed when the rule change comes before the subject has correctly discovered the concept. However, if the subject gradually strengthens associations between mental representations of the attributes of each instance of the concept (e.g., "red," "triangle") and the response category of the instance (e.g., right, wrong), this associative process should conflict with new associations that underlie learning of the changed concept.

Bower and Trabasso's study conformed to a concept-identification paradigm. Subjects were shown a series of cards, each containing colored geometric forms. Six dimensions were represented, including color (red or blue), size (large or small), shape (square or hexagon), and number (three or four figures). As each stimulus was presented, subjects classified it by naming it with the numbers one or two. The experimenter informed subjects whether each response was correct or incorrect. For one group of subjects, the control group, there was no change in the rule that determined how instances of the concept were classified. Specifically, the control subjects were always told "correct" if they said "one" to red stimuli and "two" to blue stimuli. For the subjects in the reversal group, however, this rule was not kept the same throughout the experiment. For the first five trials of the experiment, the experimenter said "correct" when subjects called blue stimuli one and red stimuli two. After five trials, the experimenter reversed this rule and began to say "correct" if the subjects called red stimuli one and blue stimuli two. What effect did switching the rule have on the speed at which the concept was identified? Bower and Trabasso's data indicate the rule change had no effect. On the average, it took subjects in the reversal group no longer than subjects in the control group to identify the concept. Bower and Trabasso determined this by noting how long it took each subject to begin to respond consistently correctly to each stimulus. It was decided that if subjects made 16 consecutive correct responses, the subject had correctly identified the concept. Bower and Trabasso found that for the control subjects, this string of 16 consecutive responses began after an average of 28.6 trials. That is, on the average, the last error the control subjects made occurred on the 28.6th learning trial. For subjects in the reversal group, the last error occurred on trial 29.0, a number not significantly different than the value obtained by the control subjects.

The conclusion Bower and Trabasso drew from these data was that the subjects in this experiment formed hypotheses about what rule determined how each instance was classified. For example, if the first stimulus shown was three small blue hexagons, a subject might have hypothesized that hexagons should be called one and have proceeded to test this possibility by saying "one" to all stimuli containing hexagons. When this hypothesis was found to be incorrect, another would have been formulated and tested. According to this view, as long as a subject has not yet discovered the correct hypothesis, it makes no difference whether the experimenter has said "correct" or "incorrect" to previously presented instances; these previous stimuli and responses are essentially forgotten (or never were adequately encoded). It must be pointed out that it was possible for a subject in Bower and Trabasso's study to discover the correct hypothesis before the rule was changed on trial 5. In fact, a few subjects in the experiment showed evidence of having done this. The data of these subjects were not included in the analysis.

Retrieval and Hypotheses. The retrieval view of concept acquisition being advocated in this text is that the memory-retrieval system is fundamental to the acquisition of concepts. According to this view, when an individual encounters a stimulus, matching information from memory will automatically be aroused. This retrieval operation will arouse not only the matching information but also those events that had been associated with the previous encounters with the stimulus. This will allow the individual both to realize that the newly encountered stimulus is familiar and to be reminded of events surrounding these previous interactions with the stimulus. Thus, if a child sees a small four-legged animal, the child may be reminded not only that other small four-legged animals have been encountered previously, but also that in many of these previous encounters, the word *dog* was spoken. The child may consequently be tempted to call the new stimulus a dog.

How does this retrieval view compare with the continuity and noncontinuity views? It can be seen that the retrieval view is quite similar to the continuity position. Both assume that associations underlie the acquisition of concepts and that these associations are aroused by newly encountered stimuli that match information in these encodings. The retrieval view, however, unlike the continuity view, does not imply that concept acquisition need be gradual. Rather, memory retrieval can fail under certain circumstances; then, when different, more appropriate cues are generated retrieval can occur successfully, thus producing the kind of sudden concept-acquisition behavior characteristic of the noncontinuity view.

Encoding Processes and Retrieval Failure. When will retrieval fail? In a concept acquisition situation, a newly encountered instance of a concept may fail to retrieve a previously encoded instance of the concept when both are not encoded in the same way. To better understand this point, consider Heidbreder's (1946) study again. Look back at Figure 9–6 and find the drawing in column 1 that is labelled *mank*. What do you see pictured? It would not be surprising if you said birds. Look now at the drawing in the third column that is supposed to be labelled *mank*. It is the second drawing from the top. What do you see pictured there? Triangles? Recall now a point that has been made repeatedly in this text, the assertion that people do not necessarily encode just the physical attributes of a stimulus, but their own interpretations of and reactions to the stimulus as well. Thus, as was demonstrated in a study by Carmichael, Hogan, and Walter (1932) if a person is presented with a picture of two circles joined by a straight line, the person may store the information that a picture of a barbell was presented. Similarly, when looking at the drawings shown by Heidbreder, a subject will store not only information about the physical attributes of the stimulus, but information about what the stimulus means as well. The relevance of this to the role of the automatic retrieval mechanism in concept acquisition should be apparent. Since retrieval requires that a newly encountered stimulus match a previously encoded stimulus, and since the information encoded about a stimulus goes much beyond the physical attributes of the stimulus, retrieval will be most likely to occur when a person interprets a currently presented stimulus in the same way that a previously encountered concept instance was interpreted. In the case of Heidbreder's concept named *mank,* it is not surprising that learning was so slow. If the first instance was interpreted as birds, another instance encoded as triangles would be a poor retrieval cue for this previously encoded instance.

What do subjects do when a newly presented stimulus fails automatically to retrieve any similar instances of some concept from memory? This is a difficult question to answer. Perhaps a person will try to take a different view of the stimulus in an attempt to generate new retrieval cues that will better match old instances; perhaps a person will attempt to guess the identification of the stimulus. In both of these cases, a solution to the concept learning problem could be sudden. For example, in the case of Heidbreder's experiment, if a person decided to generate retrieval cues based on the number of objects pictured in a stimulus rather than on the identity of objects, this new retrieval cue could suddenly trigger arousal of previously observed stimuli and their associated name (providing that this information had been stored from these previous encounters). But no matter what a person does under these circumstances, it seems that, in general, when the acquisition of a concept is not readily mediated by the retrieval system, concept learning will be difficult, and the subject may resort to developing and using strategies. The strategies will likely lead to sudden learning, thus producing evidence that appears to accord with the noncontinuity view.

Experimental Procedures That Can Lead to Retrieval Failure.   Procedures that are most likely to discourage reliance on the retrieval mechanism are those which, like Bower and Trabasso's (1963) study, are modeled after animal conditioning experiments. In studies based on this "classical" approach, subjects are shown stimuli (e.g., green triangle, blue squares) and are expected to discover how to classify them correctly into positive and negative instances of the concept. The point to be made here is that certain of these rule-based concepts force a subject to resort to strategies to acquire the concepts because the concept instances have little physical similarity to one another and thus hinder operation of the retrieval system. As a result, behavior more in accord with the noncontinuity view will be produced.

Consider, for example, the stimuli shown in Figure 9–7. These stimuli represent combinations of three dimensions, each with four levels. The dimensions (and their values) are color (red, yellow, green, and blue), shape (circle, cross, triangle, and star), and number (one, two, three, and four). Experimenters who have adhered to this classical approach to concept learning have generally constructed concepts on the basis of one of four rules. These four rules will now be illustrated with concepts in which red and cross are the particular values relevant for the dimensions of color and shape.

In a *biconditional concept,* positive instances will have either both of these values or neither of them. That is, in our example, positive instances will be those that show red crosses and those that show neither crosses nor red objects. Thus, in Figure 9–7, the positive instances are the fifth to eighth stimuli in row one and all stimuli in rows two to four except those that show crosses. Consider these positive instances as a whole. What properties do they have in common? They certainly do not all look alike. All colors, shapes, and numbers are represented. Similarly, in the negative instances as a whole, all colors, shapes, and numbers are represented. It would

Figure 9–7
Stimuli formed by combining three dimensions, each of which has four values.

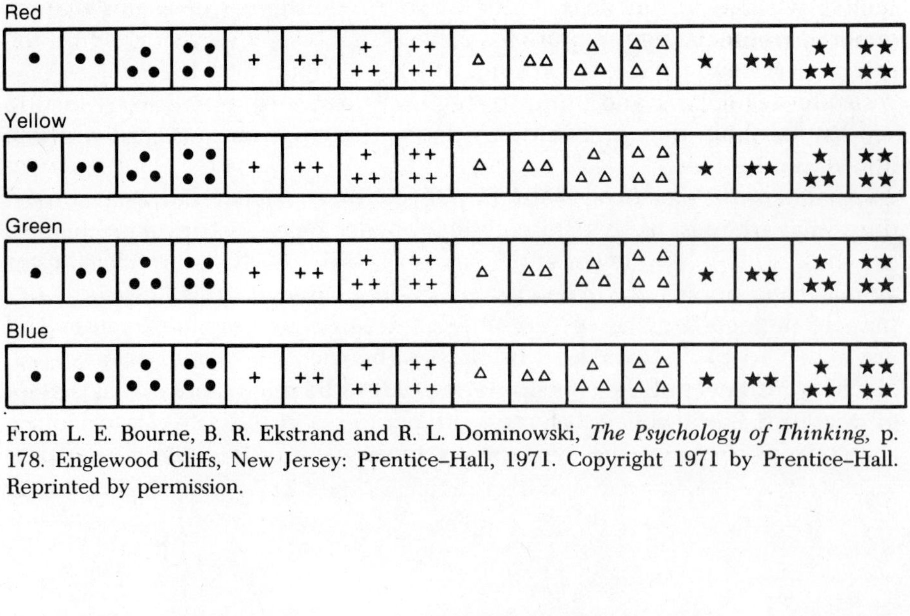

From L. E. Bourne, B. R. Ekstrand and R. L. Dominowski, *The Psychology of Thinking,* p. 178. Englewood Cliffs, New Jersey: Prentice–Hall, 1971. Copyright 1971 by Prentice–Hall. Reprinted by permission.

be unlikely, therefore, for a person to acquire this concept readily on the basis of a retrieval mechanism since there would be no strong tendency for a stimulus presented during the course of an experiment to retrieve one of these stimulus sets differentially. Another form of concept that also will be difficult to acquire on the basis of a retrieval mechanism is a *conditional concept*. Such concepts are formed using an "if . . . then" rule. For the values being considered relevant here, the rule would be: If a pattern shows a cross, then it must be red to be an example of the concept. Thus, positive instances of this concept are the fifth to eighth stimuli in row one and all stimuli in rows two to four. Again, considering the sets of positive and negative instances as a whole, there will be little similarity among members of the sets, especially members of the positive set. Consider next concepts formed according to an *inclusive disjunctive* rule. In our example, this rule would state that all stimuli that are crosses or red or both are positive instances of the concept. This would include all stimuli in row one and the crosses in rows two to four. Again, there is some variety in the stimuli that comprise the positive and negative sets, but less so than in the two preceding concepts. That is, in this type of concept, although all shapes, numbers, and colors are represented in the positive instances, most of these positive instances are red. Similarly, among the negative instances, although all numbers are represented, not all shapes and colors are. Finally, consider *conjunctive concepts*. Positive instances of this type of concept contain both relevant values. Thus, in our example, the positive instance must depict red crosses. In Figure 9–7, only patterns five to eight in row one are positive instances; all the other patterns are negative instances. Although there is very little similarity among members of the negative set, members of the positive set have much in common—they are all red crosses.

If retrieval is an important, fundamental mechanism in concept acquisition, we would expect that any interference with the retrieval process would retard the rate of concept acquisition. Bourne and his co-workers (1976) have found evidence that conforms with this view. They began by considering some previous work with concept learning that had shown that subjects generally find biconditional concepts to be the most difficult to acquire, followed by conditional, disjunctive, and conjunctive concepts, in that order. Bourne et al. wished to determine why concept difficulty was ordered in this way. They proposed that a memory mechanism was responsible. According to their hypothesis, a subject in a concept-acquisition study acquires information about the feature values of stimuli that occur among positive and negative instances of the concept. In arriving at a decision about how to classify new instances, a subject consults memory to determine which values, in the past, occurred most consistently among positive or negative instances. Thus, if a subject has previously observed three positive instances of a concept in which the color red always occurred and in which the shape of triangle, square, and circle each occurred once, the subject will treat color as a key dimension that determines how an instance is categorized and will treat shape as being unimportant because no particular value of this dimension occurred consistently. In Bourne et al.'s words:

> Frequency theory stipulates that subjects will keep some record of the differing frequencies of the various stimulus values within positive and/or negative instances of the concept. It is the case that, for all conceptual rules, the relevant values are distinguishable from the irrelevant ones simply on the basis of differential frequency. By merely "keeping track" of the frequencies of all the values in positive or negative instances, the subject can discover the relevant ones. (pp. 295–296)

To determine whether this memory mechanism could account for the acquisition difficulty of the various concepts, Bourne et al. analyzed data from previous experiments. They found that in general the concepts that have been the most difficult to acquire are those in which the relevant feature values of a concept did not occur much more frequently than irrelevant values among instances presented to a subject. Bourne et al. also conducted several experiments of their own. These experiments showed that variations in the differential frequency with which relevant versus irrelevant values occur among concept instances causes the difficulty of concept acquisition to vary correspondingly. Bourne and his co-workers conclude that:

> The results of these experiments support the following conclusions. Differences in the frequency of occurrence represent a potent source of information which subjects use to identify the relevant values of an unknown concept. While there are a variety of frequency differentials available, the most effective cue is provided when the relevant concept value occurs within a particular category with a substantially different frequency than other values on the same stimulus dimension. . . . For the present experiments the theory would suggest that the subject sets up within-category frequency counters for each value on each stimulus dimension. The subject scans these counters periodically in search of significant differentials. Once a differential is detected, the subject attends to and responds primarily on the basis of the dimension within which that differential exists. (p. 308)

This accords with the view presented here in that memory is proposed to underlie the acquisition of concepts and in that feature values that commonly occur among instances of a concept will be the natural basis for determining how a new instance is categorized, that is, whether it is called a positive or a negative instance of the concept.

Other Factors that Encourage Hypothesis Formation.   It seems, then, that retrieval can be regarded as the fundamental basis for concept acquisition, with hypothesis formation an additional strategy that builds on the operation of the retrieval system. What factors in addition to those already discussed will favor the use of hypotheses to supplement the natural and automatic operation of the retrieval system? One factor is the time pressure that a subject may feel. In an experiment like Bower and Trabasso's, for example, a subject is asked to make a response each time a stimulus is presented—the subject has to signal whether or not the stimulus is a positive or negative instance of the concept. In effect, the subject is being tested each time a stimulus is presented to determine if the concept has been acquired. Under these circumstances, a speedy solution will likely be attempted. This will encourage the formation of hypotheses rather than reliance on a gradual process of discovery based principally on the retrieval system. The complex nature of the stimuli may also discourage reliance on just the retrieval system. For example, in an experiment like Bower and Trabasso's, a subject is shown complex stimuli made up of a variety of attributes. The stimuli are in view for about six seconds, during which time the subject must make some response and then listen to the reply of the experimenter. It is unreasonable to expect a subject to attempt accurately to encode each attribute of the stimulus, associate his response to each attribute, and perhaps attempt to modify these associations when the experimenter gives corrective feedback. Instead, it will be much easier for a subject to adopt the strategy of focusing on a subset of the attributes in the stimulus and trying to test whether these are important in determining how stimuli are classified. Such behavior, of course, leads to sudden rather than gradual acquisition of a concept.

Concepts in Nature: The Work of Eleanor Rosch

In the so-called classical concept-learning approach, exemplified by the experiments of Bourne and his co-workers (e.g., Bourne, 1970; Bourne & Guy, 1968; Bourne et al., 1976), a subject is presented with a variety of stimuli composed of combinations of discrete attributes and is expected to learn how to classify stimuli correctly into positive and negative instances of a concept. This approach began to be seriously questioned in the early 1970s, principally as a result of studies performed by Eleanor Rosch and her co-workers (e.g., Rosch, 1977; Rosch & Mervis, 1975; Rosch et al., 1976).

Before listing Rosch's major objections to this classical approach, I will refer once again to the analogy between the psychologist studying the human mind and the spy sitting on a hilltop attempting to analyze the manufacturing process occurring in a factory: The method used in both cases involves observing and, whenever possible, altering the nature of the materials entering the system and noting the effects of the input on the nature of the system's output. It was noted previously that this method can lead an observer to make erroneous conclusions about the system's fundamental processing capabilities if the observations are based on unusual or unrepresentative input conditions. Rosch (1977) has made a point very much like this with regard to concept-learning studies. Her objections to the classical approach center on the nature of the stimuli that constitute positive and negative categories of the experimental concepts. In the following quote, three objections to these artificial concept categories are presented.

> Any study of category learning and use . . . will be conceived and carried out by methods which depend upon the investigator's prior concept of what a category is. The overwhelming preponderance of American studies, in attempting to treat categories scientifically, have defined and treated them as though they were digital—that is, as though they were composed of discrete units which are either–or in nature. Thus, most studies carry the unexamined assumption that categories are *arbitrary logical conjunctions of criterial attributes* which have *clearcut boundaries* and within which all instances possessing the criterial attributes have a *full and equal degree of membership*. . . . While the limited and controlled nature of the stimuli in concept formation tasks has made possible the collection of a large body of precise information about learning and problem solving, such tasks may not be representative of the majority of natural concepts. (Italics mine. pp. 18–19)[1]

The point Rosch is making, of course, is that since the input conditions in the classical approach are not representative of what occurs outside the laboratory, the subjects' responses in these experimental paradigms will not be representative of their normal behavior.

What exactly is wrong with the stimuli used in the classical approach? As specified in the preceding quote, Rosch objects first to the idea that concepts may be formed from any arbitrary combination of attributes. According to the classical approach, if two dimensions have been specified, each with two values—for example, color (red, green) and shape (square, triangle)—then four combinations of these values are possible—red square, green square, red triangle, green triangle. Rosch argues that in the real world, attributes somehow "go together." For example, Rosch and Mervis (1975) point out that we find that animals that fly usually have feathers and a beak, while animals that walk about usually have fur and mouths. Here, the point is that we do not find arbitrary combinations of values of dimensions such as mode of locomotion (flying, on foot), coat (fur, feathers),

---

[1] From E. Rosch, "Human categorization." In N. Warren (Ed.), *Studies in Cross-cultural Psychology*, London: Academic Press, 1977. Copyright 1977 by Academic Press. Reprinted by permission.

and oral opening (mouth, beak). (The reader may wish to think of this as the "chickens don't have lips" objection.)

A second objection Rosch makes is that concept categories in nature are usually not clearly delineated. In the classical approach, however, each stimulus either clearly is or is not a positive instance of a concept. Rosch and others have pointed out that rather than being *well-defined,* the boundaries of natural concepts are *ill-defined* or *fuzzy.* The following passage from Brownell and Caramazza (1978) illustrates this.

> Category boundaries are vague rather than precise. The property of vagueness can be illustrated with the following example. A man who is 4 ft. 10 in. tall is clearly not a tall man, at least relative to American males today. If ⅟₁₆ in. is added to his height, he will still not be tall. If a second ⅟₁₆ in. is added, he will still be less than tall. Yet, if this incrementing is continued, the man will eventually become tall. Given this end result, the problem of specifying the meaning of the concept tall—the boundary for the category "tall men" in this context— reduces to identifying the single increment of ⅟₁₆ in. that will make the difference between membership and nonmembership in the category "tall." Unfortunately, identifying the single, criterial increment is not possible. Category boundaries are not precise; instead, there is a range of values on the height dimension, from roughly 5 ft. 8 in. to 6 ft. 0 in., for which there is not a clear and discrete distinction between membership and nonmembership. (p. 489)

A third objection Rosch has to the stimuli used in the classical approach has to do with how representative each instance is of a concept. In the classical approach, one instance is no more or less representative of a concept than another. For example, if the concept is blue, then a small blue triangle and a large blue circle are both equally good instances. Rosch points out, however, that in nature all instances of a concept are not equally prototypical—some are more representative than others. As an example, people judge robins and sparrows to be more typical instances of the concept bird than are chickens or ducks (Smith, Shoben, & Rips, 1974).

Basic-Level Concepts.   What does Rosch propose in place of the assumptions underlying the classical approach? A fundamental proposal put forward by Rosch and her co-workers (e.g., Rosch et al., 1976), is that rather than concept categories encompassing arbitrary groupings of items, concepts are developed around natural clusters of similar events and objects.

Which objects in our environment are similar? Rosch et al. do not maintain that everything given the same concept name will be identical or even highly similar. Consider a hierarchical arrangement of concepts in which more abstract concepts subsume increasingly more specific concepts. Figure 9–8 shows how the abstract concept "furniture" can be broken down into more specific concepts. Rosch et al. maintain that even though there may be little similarity among instances of a concept at a highly abstract, *superor-*

Figure 9–8
The heirarchical partitioning of the abstract concept "furniture" into more specific concepts.

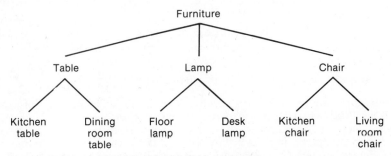

From the taxonomy described by Rosch et al. (1976).

dinate level, there is a particular level of abstraction at which concept instances have a very high degree of similarity. This level of abstraction Rosch et al. term the *basic* level. Consider the category "furniture." Do objects that are termed *furniture* have much in common? Is a chair similar to a table or a lamp? Not really. When Rosch et al. asked subjects to list all the attributes of the category "furniture," the subjects could not think of any appropriate attributes common to all instances of this concept. However, when subjects were asked to list the attributes of concepts at a lower, less abstract level—concepts such as "chair"—subjects were suddenly able to reliably produce a substantial number of attributes common to concept instances. For example, subjects tended to agree about the kinds of properties possessed by chairs—they listed attributes such as legs, seat, and back. Similarly, for the concept "table," subjects were able to list a number of attributes shared by all instances. The level of abstraction at which this high degree of similarity among instances suddenly developed, Rosch et al. termed the basic level. The term *basic-level concept* can more formally be described as the highest level of abstraction in a hierarchical arrangement of concepts at which instances of a concept show a high degree of similarity. It must be pointed out that Rosch et al. found that concepts at the next lower level of abstraction, the *subordinate* level, were also judged by subjects to have many common attributes. For example, in the case of the subordinate-level concept, "kitchen chair," subjects listed many attributes common to all instances. As can be seen in Table 9–2, however, the most dramatic increase in number of common attributes among concept instances occurred in the transition from superordinate to basic level concepts rather than in the transition from basic to subordinate level concepts.

Table 9–2
The number of common attributes listed by subjects for instances of categories at three levels of abstraction.

	Level of abstraction		
Category	Superordinate	Basic	Subordinate
Musical instrument	1	6.0	8.5
Fruit	7	12.3	14.7
Tool	3	8.3	9.7
Clothing	3	10.0	12.0
Furniture	3	9.0	10.3
Vehicle	4	8.7	11.2

From E. Rosch, C. Mervis, W. Gray, D. Johnson, and P. Boyes–Braem, "Basic objects in natural categories." *Cognitive Psychology*, 1976, *8*, 382–439. Copyright 1976 by Academic Press. Reprinted by permission.

In the study just described, similarity among concept instances was determined by the number of attributes subjects judged concept instances had in common. Rosch et al. investigated some other bases on which concept instances may resemble one another. In one study (experiment 2) subjects were asked to imagine and write down the kinds of body movements they made when interacting with instances of a particular concept. Again, it was found that few common body movements were displayed in interactions with different instances of each superordinate concept (e.g., "furniture" and "musical instruments"). However, there was a sudden increase in the number of similar body movements made in interactions with instances of each basic-level concept (e.g., "chair" and "piano"). Finally, Rosch et al. demonstrated (experiment 3 and 4) that similarity in terms of an object's shape showed the greatest increase when the level of abstraction of a concept decreased from the superordinate to the basic level rather than from the basic to a subordinate level. That is, while instances of a superordinate concept, such as "furniture," do not all look very much alike, instances of basic-level concepts, such as "chair," do.

What does all this mean? Consider the following conversation between persons A and B.

> **A:** Let me see if I have this straight. There are certain concepts with instances that don't resemble one another very much.
>
> **B:** Right. These concepts are at highly abstract, superordinate levels.
>
> **A:** And there are certain concepts at more concrete levels that have instances that are quite similar.

B: Right. Basic-level concepts.

A: So what has been shown here? Has it been shown that similarity is important in concept formation or has it been shown that similarity is not important in concept formation?

B: Well, similarity is very important for basic-level concepts.

A: Yes, but it's not important for higher-level concepts. What does all this say about the role of similarity in concept formation?

From a number of additional experiments performed by Rosch et al., it can be concluded that similarity among concept instances is very important to concept acquisition. The findings that point to this conclusion show that basic-level concepts (in which similarity among concept instances is very apparent) are psychologically the most important concepts. In one experimental demonstration of this (experiment 7) subjects were read a concept name, such as "chair." Half a second later a picture of an object was shown. Subjects had to press one of two response keys to indicate whether the pictured object and the concept name matched. It was found that subjects were fastest to detect matches and mismatches when the concept name was at the basic level rather than at the superordinate or subordinate level. Thus, when a subject was shown a picture of a living room chair, the fastest reaction time was obtained if the word *chair* rather than *furniture* or *living room chair* had previously been presented. This indicated to Rosch et al. that objects are identified first at the basic level and that "superordinates are derived by inference from the class membership of the basic object and that superordinates are derived from observation of attributes—additional to those needed to perceive the basic object—which are relevant to subordinate distinctions" (p. 414).

Another demonstration of the psychological importance of basic-level categories came from an experiment performed on children aged three and four years old (experiment 8). Rosch et al. wished to determine if these children would be better able to group objects together at the basic or the superordinate level. The experiment entailed presenting children with pictures of three objects and instructing the subjects to point to the two that were "the same kind of thing." Some children received sets of three pictures in which two pictures showed instances of the same superordinate concept. For example, the three pictures may have shown a car, a train, and a cat. Here, the car and the train are instances of the superordinate category vehicle. Other subjects received sets of pictures in which two pictured objects came from the same basic-level concept. For example, the three pictures may have shown a grey cat, a black cat, and a car. It was found that the children were able to match objects at the basic level virtually perfectly: The three-year-olds were correct 99 percent of the time and the four-year-olds, 100 percent of the time. However, for the superordinate-level concepts, the three-year-olds were correct only 55 percent of the time and the four-year-olds, 96 percent of the time. Thus, the similarity among basic-level objects is apparent to children as young as three years old. Children at this age, however, are less able to see similarities among instances of a superordinate-level concept. Rosch et al. argue that this difference in behavior towards basic and superordinate level objects is not due to children having learned to group items according to their basic-level names. That is, they claim that a child is not good at detecting that two cars are the same kind of thing just because the child knows they both are called cars. Rosch et al. base this claim on the finding that, when questioned, the children very often could not correctly name objects that they correctly sorted at the basic level. This experiment, then, indicates that objects at the basic level are judged by children to be more similar than objects at the superordinate level, and it supports the idea that the first concepts children develop are based on these obvious similarities that they detect.

The Internal Structure of Concepts.   Do the findings of Rosch indicate that similarity plays no role in concepts that are more abstract than basic-level concepts? The answer appears to be that similarity is also important in higher-level concepts, but its role is less obvious. For a better understanding of this, Rosch's view of a concept's internal structure must be considered.

Rosch and Mervis (1975) have pointed out that not all instances of a concept are equally good instances; that is, some instances are more typical of a concept than others. For example, when Rosch (1975) had subjects rate instances of superordinate level concepts according to how well each instance fit their idea of the concept, she found that for the category "furniture," a chair was rated as a better instance than a bed, which, in turn, was judged to be better than a piano. Table 9–3 shows how subjects ordered 20 instances of each of six concepts in terms of how representative each instance was of the concept.

What makes one instance of a concept a better representation of the concept than another? Rosch and Mervis (1975) have argued that the most prototypical concept instances are those that have the most attributes in common with other instances of the concept and the fewest attributes in common with instances of other concepts. As an example, a car is a good representative of the concept "vehicle," because a car has properties in common with many other vehicles—it has wheels, it is driven, it transports people, and so forth. Similarly, a chair is a good example of furniture because a chair has so many attributes in common with other articles of furniture.

Table 9–3
The rankings given by subjects to instances of six categories. From Rosch and Mervis (1975).

Rank	Furniture	Vehicle	Fruit	Weapon	Vegetable	Clothing
	Category					
1	Chair	Car	Orange	Gun	Peas	Pants
2	Sofa	Truck	Apple	Knife	Carrots	Shirt
3	Table	Bus	Banana	Sword	String beans	Dress
4	Dresser	Motor-cycle	Peach	Bomb	Spinach	Skirt
5	Desk	Train	Pear	Hand grenade	Broccoli	Jacket
6	Bed	Trolley car	Apricot	Spear	Aspara-gus	Coat
7	Book-case	Bicycle	Plum	Cannon	Corn	Sweater
8	Foot-stool	Airplane	Grapes	Bow and arrow	Cauli-flower	Underpants
9	Lamp	Boat	Straw-berry	Club	Brussel sprouts	Socks
10	Piano	Tractor	Grapefruit	Tank	Lettuce	Pajamas
11	Cushion	Cart	Pineapple	Teargas	Beets	Bathing suit
12	Mirror	Wheel-chair	Blueberry	Whip	Tomato	Shoes
13	Rug	Tank	Lemon	Icepick	Lima beans	Vest
14	Radio	Raft	Water-melon	Fists	Eggplant	Tie
15	Stove	Sled	Honey-dew	Rocket	Onion	Mittens
16	Clock	Horse	Pome-granate	Poison	Potato	Hat
17	Picture	Blimp	Date	Scissors	Yams	Apron
18	Closet	Skates	Coconut	Words	Mush-room	Purse
19	Vase	Wheel-barrow	Tomato	Foot	Pumpkin	Wristwatch
20	Tele-phone	Elevator	Olive	Screw-driver	Rice	Necklace

From E. Rosch, and C. Mervis, "Family resemblances; Studies in the internal structure of categories." *Cognitive Psychology*, 1975, 7, 573–605. Copyright 1975 by Academic Press. Reprinted by permission.

Rosch and Mervis demonstrated this by having subjects list the properties of the various instances of the six concepts listed in Table 9–3. A strong correlation was found between the number of attributes an instance had in common with other instances of the concept and the rating of the instance's prototypicality of the concept. Furthermore, Rosch and Mervis found evidence to support their claim that the most prototypical instances of these concepts had the least in common with other concepts. They found this by asking subjects to list three categories to which each instance was thought to belong. From these responses, a measure of "category dominance" was derived which, Rosch and Mervis claim, indexed the degree to which the most frequently named superordinate concept dominated other, less frequently named concepts. Rosch and Mervis found that for each concept category listed in Table 9–3, there was a strong correlation between category dominance and the rated prototypicality of each instance. Thus, an instance such as chair, which was rated to be highly representative of the concept "furniture," was found to have a high dominance in the category "furniture," and an instance such as telephone, which was rated to be poorly representative of the concept "furniture," was found to have a low dominance in the category "furniture."

One thing these findings show is that even with an abstract concept such as "furniture," in which instances are not all alike, the instances that are psychologically the most important are the ones that are the most similar to other instances. Thus, similarity, once again, has been shown to play a key role in structuring concepts.

Similarity and Retrieval in Natural Concepts. Rosch's work underscores the central role that similarity plays in concept behavior. The role of similarity is most evident at a certain level of concreteness, the level that Rosch et al. (1976) call the basic level. Consistent with critical role similarity is proposed to play in concept behavior are the findings that concepts at this basic level are the first to be acquired in a developmental sense and are the most rapidly identified.

Why do we form concepts that are less clear-cut than basic-level concepts? As will be discussed in the next chapter, we save time and effort by treating a variety of different items in much the same way. At the same time, however, this effort to achieve economy entails our paying a price. We treat things as being equivalent even though they may really be quite different. In spite of the error, or noise, this introduces, however, the role of similarity is still apparent. The instances of our more noisy concepts that are most representative of the concept are the ones that are most similar to the entire collection of instances and least similar to instances of other concepts. Once again, similarity plays a key role in structuring concepts.

Why is similarity so pervasive in concept behavior? At a general level, the answer is simple: retrieval is based on similarity. Information that is attended to tends to retrieve similar information from memory. It is the retrieval system that allows concepts to be acquired because it essentially treats a variety of discrete instances in much the same way.

Summary and Conclusion

It takes time to acquire a concept, especially if instances of the concept are noisy, that is, if each is quite distorted from some central tendency or prototype. In time, however, an observer will begin to recognize what is stable and constant among instances and will not be distracted by the noise.

Psychological theories are much like concepts. They are attempts to derive what is constant from a series of noisy instances. Unlike what occurs in a concept-learning experiment, however, the theories we propose do not receive reliable feedback as to their appropriateness; no authority is available to unequivocally say correct or incorrect. This makes the task more difficult. The difficulty seems especially apparent in the case of theories of concept acquisition. The view presented in this chapter is that the constant, underlying element in concept acquisition is the retrieval system. This retrieval system allows concepts to be acquired because it is able to find information in memory that matches the information currently being attended to. The purpose of this chapter has been to illustrate this important role that retrieval plays in concept acquisition and to show that much of the work in the area of concept acquisition is compatible with this retrieval view.

The chapter began with illustrations, through the experiments of Mervis and Pani (1980) and Hull (1920), of how stimuli tend to retrieve similar events from memory and thus elicit reactions identical to those previously associated with these similar stimuli. This, it was claimed, was the basis for concept acquisition, for an organism is led in this way to respond to a variety of discrete objects or events in much the same way. Some complications of this basic view of concept acquisition were then presented. The first dealt with whether or not, through experience, some single, unified representation was developed in memory to stand for each concept. Evidence for the existence of these schemas was described. It was concluded that although the notion of schema was a useful one, there does not yet appear to be firm evidence that schemas exist; instead, it seems that concepts may be represented in memory just by traces formed from individual encounters with concept instances. The next issue dealt with was whether or not concepts were formed by some automatic, passive mechanism or whether a more active strategy was required, one that entailed forming hypotheses. The point developed here was that an automatic mechanism—the retrieval system—was basically responsible for concept acquisition, but that more active strategies could build on and supplement the actions of the retrieval system and allow concept acquisition to be facilitated. Concepts in nature were then discussed. It was shown that although the role of similarity (and, thus, retrieval) was not apparent at all levels of abstraction, wherever similarity among concept instances was apparent, the concepts were psychologically the most important.

Chapter 10
Concepts and their functions

Concepts (i.e., schemas) are important in our everyday interactions with the world because they contribute to our perception, identification, comprehension and memory of stimuli. In this chapter these roles of concepts will be examined. It will be shown that although concepts can be of great benefit to us, their use is not without its drawbacks.

Concepts and Perception

Concepts allow us to know a great deal about things we have never previously encountered. To understand this point better, imagine having entered someone's house for the first time. Even though you have never seen the inside of the house before, you may still know quite a lot about it. This information can be derived from general knowledge about how houses are designed. Thus, because you are likely to have learned that kitchens are generally on the first floor of a house and often toward the back, you will not go upstairs in search of this room.

Concepts affect our interactions with the world not only in high-level cognitive tasks, such as finding our way in a novel environment, but also in more fundamental tasks, such as perceiving and identifying objects. For a demonstration of this, look at the object shown in Figure 10–1. Can you tell what it is? One reason you may have trouble identifying the object is because it is drawn in a sketchy, abbreviated form. Yet, if you were given information that allowed you to use conceptual knowledge in the perception process, its identity may seem quite apparent. Thus, if you are told that

Figure 10–1
An incomplete figure that can be identified with the aid of top-down processing.

From R. Leeper, "A study of a neglected portion of the field of learning—the development of sensory organization." *Journal of Genetic Psychology*, 1935, *46*, 41–75. Copyright 1935 by the Journal of Genetic Psychology. Reprinted by permission.

the figure shows a large animal, one that might be encountered in the jungles of Africa or India, you may suddenly see an elephant's trunk, legs, and tail quite clearly. The point is that conceptual knowledge can supplement information in the environment and allow a person to identify a stimulus after just a sketchy or partial analysis of it.

An experiment by Friedman (1979) has made this same point in a more carefully controlled manner. Briefly, subjects in this study were shown drawings of various scenes, including a city, an office, and a kitchen. Each drawing showed objects typical of each scene. For example, the picture of the kitchen included a stove, a sink, and a refrigerator. However, in addition to these typical objects, each scene also included a few atypical items. For instance, a picture of a kitchen may have included a fireplace. Before each drawing was shown, the experimenter announced its general subject matter (e.g., a kitchen). Eye movement monitors then recorded the movements of each subjects' eyes for the 30 seconds a drawing was displayed. Friedman found that subjects looked approximately twice as long at objects when they were unexpected in a scene as opposed to when they were expected. The conclusion Friedman drew from this was that

> when a person knows in advance the general context of what he or she is going to see, this information allows global memory structures such as [schemas] to be used to detect objects expected to be in that context, resulting in relatively short first fixations to them. . . . Identification of low probability objects appears to require a more complete and presumably more data-driven analysis of their visual details. (p. 336)

Top-Down Processing

The use of conceptual information in the long-term store to facilitate processing of environmental stimuli is known as *top-down processing*. The reason the process is given this name is best understood by referring to the basic model of the information-processing system shown earlier in Figure 1–2. In this simple model, the flow of information, as indicated by the arrows, is principally in a left-to-right direction, that is, from the sensory stores to the short-term store to the long-term store. The one arrow pointing in the other direction goes from the long-term store to the short-term store and is meant to represent the arousal and "transfer" of information from the long-term store into conscious awareness. To incorporate top-down processing into this basic model, that is, to allow conceptual information in the long-term store to influence the perception process, psychologists (e.g., Norman & Bobrow, 1975) have found it necessary to extend the flow of information in this right-to-left direction from the long-term store to some stage prior to short-term storage. Figure 10–2 illustrates this modification. The new arrow represents a top-down flow in the sense that information

Figure 10–2
A portion of the revised human information-processing model proposed by Norman and Bobrow (1976). This model incorporates top-down processing whereby information in the long-term store (LTM) is used to supplement information that has not yet become the contents of the short-term store (STM).

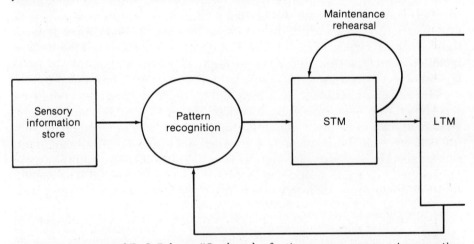

From D. A. Norman and D. G. Bobrow, "On the role of active memory processes in perception and cognition," Figure 6.1, p. 117, in C. N. Cofer (Ed.), *The Structure of Human Memory,* San Francisco: Freeman, 1975. Copyright 1976 by W. H. Freeman and Company. Reprinted by permission.

in the long-term store is regarded as being at the highest level (since it contains the most extensively processed information), while information in the sensory stores is regarded as being at a fairly low, unrefined level.

The Identification of Speech.   One important identification process that is facilitated by top-down processing occurs as part of our everyday comprehension of speech. A good demonstration of this comes from an experiment performed by Miller and Isard (1963). These experimenters read subjects three types of sentences. Normal sentences, such as "Romantic poetry describes eternal love" and "Spilled ink leaves ugly spots," were constructed according to standard rules of grammar and were intended to be perfectly understandable. Anomolous sentences, such as "A jeweler exposed the annual fire-breathing document" and "Colorless yellow ideas sleep furiously" were grammatically correct but made no sense. Finally, random strings of words, such as "Attended liquid the audience chocolate holy a" and "Sleep roses dangerously young colorless" were ungrammatical and made no sense. Subjects in the study were asked to shadow the sentences, that is, to listen to the sentences and repeat each word aloud as they heard it. As might be expected, subjects were best able to shadow the normal sentences. Subjects correctly shadowed 88.6 percent of the normal sentences but only 79.3 percent of the anomolous sentences and 56.1 percent of the random strings.

These differences in performance can be interpreted as reflecting differences in the extent to which top-down processing could be utilized. In processing the normal sentences, subjects could make use of the rules or grammar and their general knowledge of the world; that is, like most of us, these subjects had learned through years of experience with the English language how sentences are formed. They knew such things as the parts of speech that generally precede and follow other parts of speech. In addition, they had developed general knowledge of the things people are likely to say based on the meanings of various words in a sentence. All of this long-term knowledge was most useful in aiding subjects to shadow the normal sentences rather than the anomolous sentences and random strings.

The effects of top-down processing are highlighted by situations that prevent it from occurring. For example, it is likely that a person's initial difficulty in comprehending a recently learned foreign language stems from an inability to rely on top-down processing. When a language is new to a person, the person will not yet have built up a store of experiences in memory to allow the anticipation of the kinds of words that precede and follow other words. Thus, even though a person may understand the meaning of each individual word in a foreign language, when encountering a series of words in a sentence it may be necessary for the person to attend closely to each word individually and then attempt to integrate them into a meaningful whole. For a native speaker, much of this work will have been performed many times in the past; the knowledge gained from these experiences will be stored in memory and available for top-down processing.

The Automaticity and Effectiveness of Top-Down Processing. It should not be concluded from the preceding discussion that a person will necessarily be aware of using top-down processing. Rather, top-down processing can be so automatic and effective that a person will not be aware that it has occurred. An experiment by Warren (1970) illustrates this. Warren recorded the sentence "The state governors met with their respective legislatures convening in the capital city." He then removed the first "s" sound in the word *legislatures* and replaced it with the sound of a person coughing. When 20 subjects heard this recording of the sentence together with the cough, 19 of them reported that they had not noticed that any speech sounds were missing. They reported this even though the experimenter had told them before the recording was played that a cough may completely replace part of the sentence they were about to hear. The one subject who reported having detected a missing sound incorrectly identified its location in the sentence. It seems, then, that top-down processing was so effective in filling in the missing speech sound and was used so automatically by the subjects, that they were not aware of the gap in the sentence.

Distorting Perception with Top-Down Processing

From these discussions it can be concluded that our conceptual knowledge facilitates the perception of environmental stimuli by allowing us to function with less-than-complete stimulus information. While we generally benefit from top-down processing in terms of time and effort saved, our use of this form of processing can be detrimental. The adverse effects come from using inappropriate concepts to analyze environmental information. Under these circumstances, perceptual distortions are possible.

An incident related by Skinner (1979) provides anecdotal evidence of this. In the 1930s, Skinner constructed a device that emitted a series of vowel sounds such as "uh-uh-i-e-uh." When these sounds were played against a background of noise, they sounded like speech through a wall. Skinner reports that people who heard this machine "talking" would think they heard certain meaningful phrases. For example, someone who was concerned that he was deceiving another person said he heard the machine say "I am a traitor." What the machine actually said was "i-uh-uh-a-uh." Someone with inferiority feelings once heard the machine say "You're a failure." This person, who had also studied for the priesthood, heard the machine say on another occasion "Father O'Conner." It seems that the concerns and prior experiences of these individuals were being used to supplement the nonsense sounds being produced by the machine.

Another illustration of how top-down processing may have distorted perception comes from the field of astronomy. In the late 1800s, a number of astronomers observed a network of fine lines covering the planet Mars. These were observed by an Italian astronomer, Schiaparelli, in 1877, and some years later by the noted American astronomer Percival Lowell. Lowell and his assistants are reported to have sighted up to 700 of these fine lines as well as about 51 double lines, that is, pairs of parallel lines (Hoyt, 1976). Based on these observations, Lowell developed and published a theory that these lines were canals, constructed by intelligent forms of life to divert water from the planet's polar icecaps to the dry interior regions. The network of canals, Lowell believed, was visible on earth only because of the vegetation that grew on the borders of the canals, which he estimated to be 30 miles wide. Not all astronomers were able to observe these canals. The issue of the canals' existence and of the possibility of life on Mars was therefore a controversial matter. To bolster his position, Lowell had photographs made of the planet, which to him and his assistants clearly showed the presence of the canals. Again, not all of those who observed the photographs could clearly discern these canals. The controversy over the Martian canals' existence raged until Lowell's death in 1916; it was conclusively settled by the series of Mariner space probes in the late 1960s and early 1970s, which showed no evidence of canals or of life on Mars.

Why did Lowell and others so clearly see canals on Mars' surface? Ray Hyman, a psychologist at the University of Oregon, has suggested (personal communication) that top-down processing may have played an important role. According to this account, Lowell had preconceived notions of what existed on Mars. That is, before beginning his extensive observations of Mars, Lowell had heard of other astronomers' claims that canals may be present on the planet. From these claims Lowell had formed the hypothesis that intelligent life existed on Mars. It may be that when he observed the features on Mars, a task made difficult by the relatively primitive technology available at that time, Lowell used these preconceived notions to fill in and supplement the indistinct features and markings on the planet's surface, forming what looked to him to be a network of straight lines.

Experimental Evidence. An experimental demonstration of the distorting influence that top-down processing can exert on perception comes from a study by Palmer (1975). Subjects in this experiment were instructed to name each object shown to them in a briefly exposed (20–120 milliseconds) picture. Examples of the stimuli shown to subjects include a line drawing of a mailbox and a line drawing of a drum. One of Palmer's findings was that even though all pictures were displayed in exactly the same way, under certain experimental conditions, subjects were quite likely to incorrectly give an object the name of something it physically resembled. For example, a picture of a mailbox may have been incorrectly identified as a picture of a loaf of bread. However, under other conditions, subjects were quite accurate in correctly identifying the pictured objects.

What caused the accuracy of identification to vary? Subjects' expectancies appear to be the cause. To manipulate what subjects expected to see in a briefly exposed picture, Palmer preceded presentation of each picture with a two-second display of either a contextual scene or a blank scene. An example of a contextual scene is shown in Figure 10–3A. Palmer found that the tendency of subjects to mistake an object for a physically similar object was most likely to occur if the contextual scene was appropriate to that incorrectly named object. For example, if a contextual scene showed a kitchen setting, the subsequent brief display of a drawing of a mailbox often (about 50 percent of the time) caused subjects mistakenly to identify the object as a loaf of bread. However, if the contextual scene was appropriate

Figure 10–3
Part A shows an example of a contextual scene. Part B shows some drawings of target objects that were briefly displayed to subjects shortly after a contextual scene or a blank scene had been presented.

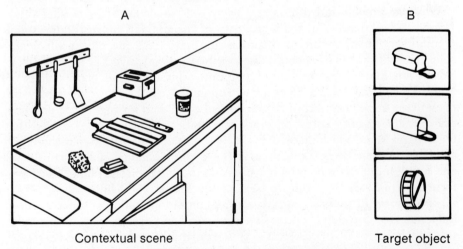

A

B

Contextual scene   Target object

From S. E. Palmer, "The effects of contextual scenes on the identification of objects." *Memory & Cognition*, 1975, *3*, 519–526. Copyright 1975 by the Psychonomic Society. Reprinted by permission.

to the briefly displayed object, for example, a drawing of the front yard of a house in the case of the picture of a mailbox, then subjects very rarely (less than 10 percent of the time) made this identification error. Similarly, if a blank scene preceded the briefly displayed object, this identification error was also infrequent. (It occurred less than 20 percent of the time.) It seems, then, that people's perceptions can be biased by what they expect to encounter in their environment.

Concepts and Comprehension

Concepts are important not only in the process of perceiving and identifying stimuli, but also in the process of combining stimuli into larger, more meaningful units. The effect of concepts on comprehension has been demonstrated experimentally a number of times. For example, when Bransford and Johnson (1972) presented subjects with the "Washing Clothes" passage (see page 5), subjects who heard the passage without knowing the title reported that it was difficult to comprehend. On a seven-point scale, on which 1 indicated that the passage was very difficult to comprehend and 7 indicated that it was very easy to comprehend, the average rating of these subjects was 2.29. However, the average rating of subjects who were given the title before hearing the passage was 4.50. It is generally assumed that the provision of the title before presentation of the passage facilitated the subjects' comprehension of the passage by allowing subjects to supply additional, relevant information from memory. This general, conceptual knowledge is suggested to have allowed subjects to supplement the given information with suitable information from the long-term store. For example, a sentence such as "First you arrange things into different groups" could, with the aid of conceptual knowledge, be interpreted as an instruction to arrange clothes into separate piles based perhaps on color or on the kind of washing process required. It has also been suggested (Alba, Alexander, Hasher, & Caniglia, 1981) that the use of concepts facilitated comprehension in this experiment by allowing subjects to use already-integrated information to tie together the individual sentences in the passage. The integration function of concepts will be elaborated on in the following discussions.

Integration, Comprehension, and Memory

When an observer uses concepts to comprehend stimuli, the ability to recall the stimuli is enhanced. An experiment by Bower, Karlin, and Dueck (1975) illustrates this. In the experiment, two groups of subjects were shown a series of 28 drawings at a 10-second rate. The drawings were "droodles," nonsense pictures that could be given amusing interpretations. Figure 10–4 shows two droodles that were used in the study. Drawing A can be interpreted as a midget playing a trombone in a phone booth, and drawing B can be interpreted as an early bird who caught a strong worm. In the experiment, only subjects in one group, the label group, were given an interpretation for each drawing; subjects in the control group received just the drawings alone. After they had studied all of the pictures, subjects in both groups were asked to sketch the drawings from memory as best they could. The label group performed significantly better on this task than the control group. Subjects in the label group correctly reproduced 70 percent of the pictures, while subjects in the control group correctly reproduced only 51 percent of the pictures.

Similar results have been obtained with verbal stimuli. For example, Bransford and his co-workers (Bransford & Johnson, 1973; Bransford & McCarrell, 1974) have reported an experiment in which subjects encountered sentences that were either easy or difficult to comprehend. Easy-to-understand sentences, such as "The account was low because Sally went to the bank" and "The car was moved because he had no change," were subsequently remembered much better than difficult-to-understand sen-

Figure 10–4
Examples of two "droodles" shown to subjects by Bower, Karlin, and Dueck (1975, experiment 1).

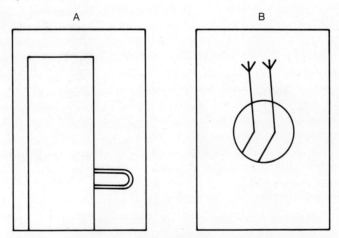

From G. H. Bower, M. B. Karlin and A. Dueck, "Comprehension and memory for pictures." *Memory & Cognition*, 1975, *3*, 216–220. Copyright 1975 by the Psychonomic Society. Reprinted by permission.

tences. Examples of difficult sentences are "The notes were sour because the seam was split" and "The haystack was important because the cloth ripped." It was found, however, that when subjects were given context cues at the time the sentences were presented and recalled, cues that made the difficult sentences as understandable as the easy sentences, differences in recall of the two sentence types were significantly reduced. The cues used for the two difficult sentences were *bagpipes* and *parachute,* respectively.

Bransford and Johnson (1972) and Dooling and Lachman (1971) have found this same effect of comprehension on memory with longer passages. In the "Washing Clothes" passage of Bransford and Johnson, for example, subjects who were informed of the title before hearing the sentences later recalled 32 percent of the "idea units" in the passage. Subjects who either heard no title or were informed about the title just before recall was attempted remembered only 16 percent and 15 percent of the idea units, respectively.

The Integrating Effect of Concepts. How do concepts enhance the recall of newly encountered information? One important mechanism seems to be the integrating power of concepts. That is, new stimuli that are identified with the components of a concept will tend to become integrated. For instance, the concept or schema of "washing clothes" consists of a number of components, including dirty clothes, detergent, and water. These component elements, of course, have become strongly linked or associated together to form a chunk in memory. To the extent that newly encountered stimuli can be identified with this schema, they will also be associated together.

Experimental evidence to support this view comes from a second experiment reported by Bower, Karlin and Dueck (1975). The purpose of this study was to determine whether an interpretation given to drawings facilitates recall by causing "unification or knitting together of the disparate parts of the picture into a coherent whole or schema" (p. 218). Subjects were shown 30 pairs of nonsense pictures at a 12-second rate. Three examples of picture pairs are shown in Figure 10–5. Although Figure 10–5 doesn't indicate it, one picture in each pair in the experiment was drawn on white paper and the other was drawn on pink paper. Before the study began, subjects were informed that after seeing all 30 pairs of pictures, they would be shown each drawing that had appeared on the white background and would have to sketch from memory the paired drawing that had appeared on the pink background. As in the previously described study by these researchers, when the drawings were being presented, half of the subjects were given an interpretation that the experimenters expected would help tie the pair members together into a meaningful unit. For example, pair

Figure 10–5
Three stimulus pairs shown to subjects in Bower, Karlin, and Dueck's (1975) second experiment.

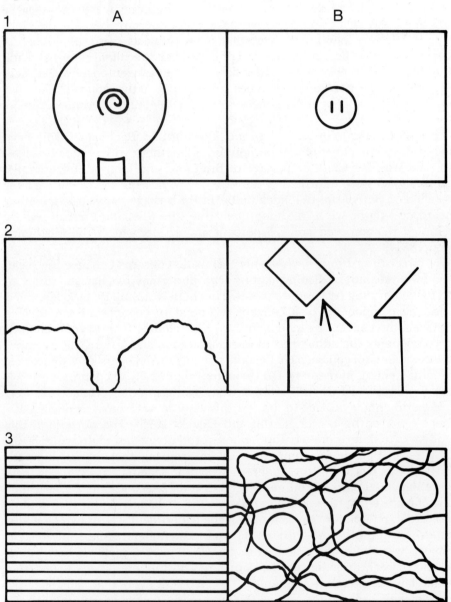

From G. H. Bower, M. B. Karlin and A. Dueck, "Comprehension and memory for pictures." *Memory & Cognition*, 1975, *3*, 216–220. Copyright 1975 by the Psychonomic Society. Reprinted by permission.

A in Figure 10–5 was interpreted as the rear end of a pig disappearing into a fog bank with his nose appearing on the other side of the fog bank; pair B was suggested to be two piles of dirty clothes and the act of pouring detergent into a washing machine; pair C was suggested to represent uncooked spaghetti and cooked spaghetti with meatballs. In the memory test, subjects who had heard these interpretations recalled 73 percent of the paired drawings, while subjects who had heard no interpretation recalled only 44 percent of the drawings. Similar results were obtained from a recognition test that was administered subsequently. In this test, subjects were given a deck of cards containing, in a random order, all 30 drawings that had been presented on the white background and all 30 drawings that had been presented on the pink background. The subjects were asked to pair these drawings together again. Once more, subjects who had received the meaningful interpretation during the study period performed significantly better than the control subjects. Those given the label correctly paired 91.7 percent of the drawings, while those not given the label paired only 55.4 percent of the drawings. It appears, then, that general knowledge can help link newly encountered stimuli.

A similar point has been made by Alba and his co-workers (1981). They were interested in better understanding the effect of schemas on comprehension and memory. Specifically, they wished to know what caused subjects in Bransford and Johnson's (1972) study to remember a passage better when a suitable title (e.g., "Washing Clothes") is provided before the story is presented. Alba et al. performed a simple experiment whose outcome was surprising. Subjects in the study read the "Washing Clothes" passage from Bransford and Johnson's study either with or without first receiving the title. Subjects' memory for the passage was then tested with either a free-recall test (experiment 1) or a recognition test (experiment 3). The recall test produced the expected result; subjects who had received the title before reading the passage recalled it significantly better than subjects not receiving the title. The results of the recognition test, however, were surprising. On this test, subjects were presented with sentences that either had or had not been included in the passage (e.g., "Soon, however, it will become just another facet of life" and "Mistakes can damage the material"). It was found that subjects were equally good at recognizing old and new sentences on the test. Thus, according to the recognition measure, the title had no effect on subjects' memory for the passage.

From these results, Alba and his co-workers concluded that the title allowed subjects to integrate individual sentences into a more cohesive unit. That is, presentation of the title affected only the associations among the various sentences, not the encoding of each individual sentence itself. Thus, subjects remembered individual sentences from the passage equally well when they read the passage either with or without first hearing the title. This allowed both subject groups to perform equally well on the recognition test. However, because subjects who heard the title before reading the passage tended to integrate the sentences together in memory, they did better on the recall test. The reason there was a difference on this test is that recall depends more strongly than recognition on associations among to-be-remembered items, since the recall process involves using one sentence or idea to retrieve another, which, in turn, retrieves another.

A suggestion very much like this one of Alba et al. was put forward earlier in this text when the effect of interacting imagery on cued recall was discussed. In this discussion it was proposed that interacting imagery derives its effectiveness from already-associated information in the long-term store tying newly encountered stimuli together. The resulting association between the two newly encountered stimuli later enables one of them to retrieve the other from memory. In both the interacting imagery situation and the passage-plus-appropriate-title situation, improved memory performance results from encoding processes that allow the retrieval process to operate effectively.

Concepts and Inferences

The filling-in-gaps function and the integration function of concepts are not unrelated. The connection between the two and their role in comprehension is illustrated in the process of forming inferences. Consider the following sentences (taken from Kintsch, 1976, p. 100): "A burning cigarette was carelessly discarded. The fire destroyed many acres of virgin forest." To comprehend this message a person must use general knowledge about cigarettes, combustion, and forest fires to infer something that was not explicitly stated: that the carelessly discarded cigarette started the forest fire.

This process of drawing inferences, which involves both filling in missing information and connecting segments of a stimulus, is vital to the comprehension of written and spoken messages. Numerous studies have indicated the important role of inferences in comprehension (e.g., Bartlett, 1932; Bransford & Johnson, 1972, 1973; Kintsch, 1976). One such indication is that when inferences are difficult to make, perhaps because the message does not arouse an appropriate schema in a subject's long-term store, the message is found to be difficult to comprehend (Bransford & Johnson, 1972) and difficult to remember (Dooling & Lachman, 1971). Another indication is that when different sentences in a passage contain repeated references to the same concept, thus giving the passage a property known as *referential cohesion*, the passage is more rapidly read and understood than one lacking such cohesion. For example, it has been found (Haviland & Clark, 1974) that subjects read and understand the second sentence in passages such as the first one below significantly faster than the identical sentence in passages such as the second one below:

1. Ed was given an alligator for his birthday. The alligator was his favorite present.
2. Ed was given lots of things for his birthday. The alligator was his favorite present.

Haviland and Clark found that average comprehension time for the second sentences in referentially cohesive pairs (as examplified by passage 1) was 835 milliseconds, while that for the second sentence in the less cohesive pairs was 1,016 milliseconds. It seems reasonable to assume that a portion of the extra processing time devoted to passages that lack referential cohesion is spent making inferences. Miller and Kintsch (1980) have made a similar point:

> If a segment of text is read that is not related to the current contents of working memory, long-term memory must be searched to locate a part of the text that can interrelate what has been read previously with the current input segment. . . . This search will not always be successful: A segment of text may be encountered that bears no explicit connection with what has already been said. This could be due to a major topic shift in the text, the author's carelessness, or the improper segmentation of the text by the reader. When coherence fails in this way, the reader must generate a connecting or bridging inference that will connect this segment with the preceding text. (p. 336)

Memory for Inferences. It should not be surprising that a person who makes inferences when processing a stimulus will store information about these inferences in memory. In this sense, inferences made during the processing of some stimulus should be no different than any thoughts triggered by a stimulus; both should result in some relevant information being stored. The question to be addressed now is whether people are able accurately to distinguish memory of internally generated information from memory of information encountered in their external environment. Put another way, the question is: How well can we separate fact from fantasy?

An experiment by Johnson and her co-workers (Johnson, Raye, Wang, & Taylor, 1979) was based on the following premise: If people are able to differentiate clearly between memories of imagined and actual experiences, then a person who encounters an item, let us say, twice during a day and does not subsequently think anymore about the item, should, at the end of the day, be just as accurate at estimating how often the item was encountered as a person who supplements two encounters with the item by frequently visualizing or thinking about it. To examine this possibility, the experimenters gave subjects two tasks that alternated throughout the experiment. One task was to observe a short series of pictures of common objects, and the other was to form a mental picture of some of these objects when shown the word that named the object. Thus, during the experiment, a subject might have been shown a picture of a mailbox and later have encountered the word *mailbox* and have attempted to generate a mental image of the mailbox. To be able to determine whether subjects would later be able to differentiate between their memories of having seen a picture of an object and their having imagined a picture of the object, the experimenters arranged their picture and word stimuli so that some pictures occurred twice during the experiment, some five times, and others eight times; words naming these pictures (and thus subjects' imagining of the objects) also occurred two, five, or eight times. Johnson et al. found that when subjects were later and unexpectedly asked to estimate the number of times each object had been shown to them in picture form, their judgments were influenced not only by the number of times the picture had actually been presented, but also by the number of times the object had been imagined. For example, when a picture of an object had been shown twice and also imagined twice, subjects judged that the picture had been presented about 2.5 times; however, when an object had been shown twice and imagined 8 times, subjects estimated that the picture of the object had been presented about 3.8 times. The frequency with which objects had been imagined also affected the judgments made for objects shown five or eight times. In each case, the more often a picture had been imagined, the higher the subjects' estimates of the number of previous encounters with the picture. From these data it seems that people can confuse actual and imagined events.

Similar confusions have been found between information subjects encounter in written passages and information they infer or fill in from schemas. Sulin and Dooling (1974) demonstrated this in a study that entailed the presentation of the following passage to one group of subjects:

> Helen Keller's need for professional help. Helen Keller was a problem child from birth. She was wild, stubborn, and violent. By the time Helen turned eight, she was still unmanageable. Her parents were very concerned about her mental health. There was no good institution for her problem in her state. Her parents finally decided to take some action. They hired a private teacher for Helen. (p. 256)

Sulin and Dooling had another group of subjects read a similar passage, one that differed from the passage shown above only in that the name Carol Harris was substituted for Helen Keller. In a subsequent memory test, the group that had read the Helen Keller version falsely recognized having seen the sentence "She was deaf, dumb, and blind" significantly more often than the group that had read the Carol Harris version. Sulin and Dooling suggest that subjects who read the Helen Keller version tended to supplement information presented in the passage with their general knowledge of Helen Keller. They suggest that the false recognition resulted from memory of this activated general knowledge.

Other studies have obtained similar results (e.g., Brewer & Treyens, 1981; Johnson, Bransford, & Soloman, 1973; Owens, Bower, & Black, 1979; Spiro, 1980). For example, Owens, Bower, and Black (1979) gave college students a sketch to read that described a series of mundane behaviors performed by a character. One sketch described a sequence of five activities performed by a person named Nancy. The sketch began with Nancy making coffee, then described her visiting a doctor, going to a store, attending a lecture, and, finally, going to a party. Below is the portion of the sketch that dealt with the doctor's office.

> Nancy went to the doctor. She arrived at the office and checked in with the receptionist. She went to see the nurse who went through the usual procedures. Then Nancy stepped on the scale and the nurse recorded her weight. The doctor entered the room and examined the results. He smiled at Nancy and said, "Well, it seems my expectations have been confirmed." When the examination was finished, Nancy left the office. (p. 186)

Before reading the sketch, half of the subjects, those in the informed group, were given some background information about the main character. They were told that "Nancy woke up feeling sick again and she wondered if she really were pregnant. How would she tell the professor she had been seeing? And the money was another problem" (p. 185). The other subjects read the sketch without being informed of Nancy's problems. Either 30 minutes or 24 hours after reading the sketch, subjects were unexpectedly asked to write down as much of the story as they could, as accurately as they could. Subjects who had been informed about the main character's problem recalled significantly more—between two and four times as much—extraneous information than control subjects. Much of this extraneous information consisted of details that could be inferred from the background information given about the main character. For example, the "usual procedures" undertaken by the nurse were recalled by some subjects in the informed group as "pregnancy tests," and the doctor's statement, "Well, it seems my expectations have been confirmed," was sometimes recalled as "Your fears have been confirmed." Similar errors were exhibited on a recognition test. That is, new test sentences expressing inferences that could reasonably be drawn from knowledge of the main character's problem were falsely recognized more often by the informed than the control subjects.

Distortions at Encoding versus Retrieval. In the preceding discussion, it was implied that when people incorrectly remember some event that may plausibly have occurred but actually did not, the distorted memory is purely a result of inferences encoded at the time a relevant, inference triggering event occurred. According to this account, in Sulin and Dooling's (1974) study, subjects' false recognition of the phrase "she was deaf, dumb, and blind" resulted from their retrieving and storing general knowledge about Helen Keller at the time the passage was read. There is another possibility, however. Perhaps people encode stimuli faithfully without incorporating inferences into the mental representation of the event; however, at the time of retrieval, they arouse inappropriate, extraneous information from memories encoded at other times and use this to supplement gaps in their recollections of the to-be-remembered event. According to this account, the reason subjects in Sulin and Dooling's study falsely recognized the phrase "she was deaf, dumb, and blind" was not because they had thought this at the time they read the passage, but because, at the time they tried to recall the passage, they retrieved general information from their long-term stores about Helen Keller.

How can one determine which of these two accounts is correct? One method entails preventing a person from making misleading inferences during the encoding of a critical event and instead restricting such inferences to the retrieval phase. For example, suppose you observe a traffic accident in which car A drives into car B. Later, during a questioning session, you learn that the driver of car A had been drinking. In response to questioning, you then falsely recall that you saw car A weave from side to side before striking car B. In this case, you did not store the incorrect information about car A weaving at the time you observed the event. Rather, you obtained this information at the time of retrieval from general knowledge you possess about the driving behavior of intoxicated persons. Thus, the occurrence of memory distortions under these circumstances would have to involve a retrieval rather than an encoding mechanism. To generalize from this example, it can be said that an experimenter will be able to assess the appropriateness of an encoding versus a retrieval account of schema-based memory intrusions by manipulating the time at which the schema containing the biasing information is made available.

This approach has been employed by Dooling and Christiaansen (1977). They presented groups of subjects with the passages from Sulin and Dooling's (1974) study that described behaviors that the experimenters had attributed either to a famous individual (e.g., Helen Keller) or to a fictional character (e.g., Carol Harris). The crucial manipulation made by Dooling and Christiaansen involved the time at which subjects were informed whose behaviors a paragraph described. One group of subjects was informed before reading the passage that it was about Helen Keller. Another group was told before reading the passage that it was about a fictional character, Carol Harris; however, before the memory test, these subjects were informed that the passage was not about this fictional character, but actually about a famous individual, Helen Keller. The experimenters wished to determine which of these groups would show memory distortions by falsely recognizing typical statements about Helen Keller. Their findings were that when the memory test was given two days after the passage had been presented, only the group that had been given the name Helen Keller *before* reading the passage showed evidence of memory distortion. This distortion was evidenced by these subjects falsely recognizing highly typical (but never-presented) Helen Keller statements (e.g., she was deaf, dumb, and blind) about 22 percent of the time; this can be compared with a false recognition rate of only about 8 percent for subjects who were led to believe at both study and test that the passage described Carol Harris. This finding, of course, supports the view that information encoded during learning produces memory distortions. However, in a test given one week after the passage had been presented, the experimenters found that both experimental groups showed memory distortions. The group that had been given the name Helen Keller before reading the passage falsely recognized about 23 percent of the never-presented but highly typical statements about Helen Keller, and the group given the name Helen Keller just before this test falsely recognized about 30 percent of these items. These data can be compared with a false-recognition rate for these test items of about 3 percent made by subjects who believed at both study and test that the passage was about Carol Harris. From these results, it seems that memory intrusions can be based both on inferences made and encoded during exposure to a to-be-remembered event and on general knowledge mistakenly contacted at the time retrieval of the event is attempted.

Avoiding Memory Distortions. Bartlett (1932) is often credited with having first called the attention of psychologists to the importance of schemas in both the comprehension and the remembering process. Although his usage of the terms *construction* and *reconstruction* was not entirely consistent, it seems reasonable to make the following distinction: While both terms refer to the supplementation of environmental information by information stored in schemas, *construction* refers to supplementations that occur when an event is being perceived and comprehended, while *reconstruction* refers to supplementations that occur when an event is being remembered. In Bartlett's terminology, then, we have found that memory distortions can result from both constructive and reconstructive processes.

Can anything be done to prevent these kinds of memory distortions from occurring? Spiro (1980) has pointed out that a person's encoding strategies can be effective in this respect. He has obtained evidence that if a subject in an experiment is told prior to stimulus presentation that correct memory of the stimulus is important, the subject will exhibit reduced schema-based memory distortion. Spiro obtained this evidence in the following way. He presented two groups of subjects with a story about an engaged couple. The story contained a discussion, initiated by the man, about having children. The man did not want to have children and was concerned that if his fiancée's feelings differed, their marriage plans might be jeopardized. As it turned out (in one version of the story), the woman very much wanted children and this conflict resulted in an argument and a discussion. Below is the portion of the passage that dealt with this episode:

> Marge was horrified. She had always wanted to be a mother and had her heart set on having many children. They argued bitterly over what had become a very serious problem for them. A long discussion of the status of their relationship followed. (p. 89)

Biasing information was given to both groups of subjects eight minutes after they had read the story. Subjects were informed that the couple eventually got married. In a recall test given either three or six weeks later, about 60 percent of the subjects who heard this story and the biasing information but were not warned before reading the story that their memory would later be tested made recall errors that distorted the details of the story to fit the ending. Examples of information that was mistakenly recalled are "They underwent counseling to correct the major discrepancy," and "They discussed it and decided they should agree on a compromise: adoption" (p. 91). However, of the subjects in the group that had been told the experiment would involve a memory test, only about 15 percent made such errors.

What can be done to help prevent reconstructive memory errors? Hasher and Griffin (1978) have suggested that additional retrieval cues and extra effort on the part of the rememberer may be helpful in this regard. This advice is based on the outcome of an experiment in which two groups of subjects read a passage such as the one below. The title of this passage is "Colombus Discovers the New World."

> The voyage was long and the crew was full of anticipation. No one really knew what lay beyond the new land that they were heading for. There were, of course, speculations concerning the nature of the new place, but this small group of men would be the only ones who would know the real truth. These men were participating in an event that would change the shape of history. (p. 322)

Subjects reading the passage knew at the time that a memory test would follow. Either five minutes, two days, or one week after reading the passage, subjects were asked to write it down as accurately as possible. For one group, the control group, the results were as expected. These subjects recalled less of the actual content of the story the longer the test was delayed, and at the same time falsely recalled an average of about three to four schema-related ideas on each test. The results were very different for another group of subjects, who were treated differently at the time of testing. Just before testing each subject, the experimenter "consulted her records, appeared surprised, then shocked, and apologized for a mistake she had made. The subject was told that the title of the passage he had been given was a mistake" (p. 322). Subjects were informed that the passage really should have been entitled "First Trip to the Moon." On the test, subjects given this changed title not only recalled more information that was actually presented in the passage, but also made significantly fewer recall intrusions appropriate to the original title than did control subjects. On each test, these subjects produced an average of less than one extraneous idea related to Columbus' discovery of the New World. As for their memory of the passage itself, these subjects in the changed title condition recalled nearly 30 percent of the idea units of the passage, while control subjects recalled only about 20 percent of these idea units.

Hasher and Griffin suggest that the changed title at recall resulted in more accurate performance because it led to the generation of retrieval cues that were both appropriate to the previously read passage and inappropriate to a Columbus-discovering-the-New-World schema. Why wasn't this potentially available information also retrieved by subjects in the control (unchanged title) group? Hasher and Griffin propose that people are a bit lazy. When recall is attempted, people just retrieve the most available information, even though additional information has been stored and is potentially available. Thus, if a person believes that a passage describing Columbus' discovery of the New World has been read, retrieval cues generated at the time of recall will readily contact general knowledge of this topic (which will include information never actually presented). Hasher and Griffin suggest that "under these circumstances, no special effort is expended in an attempt to retrieve the weaker detailed attributes" (p. 320). However, with additional retrieval cues and extra effort (which may entail repeated probing of memory with different cues), the extra information can be retrieved. Thus, to reduce intrusions and to heighten accuracy of recall, the rememberer is well-advised to try to change his perspective if possible (see Anderson & Pichert, 1978) and approach the task from a different point of view.

Detrimental Social Effects of Schema-Induced Distortions

Constructive Distortions.   Concepts help us to perceive and interpret our environment by allowing the environmental message to be supplemented with organized information from memory. This enables us to function adequately with incomplete environmental information. While this constructive process can be of great benefit to us by helping to reduce the barrage of environmental stimuli to manageable proportions, it can also be costly. Detrimental effects of constructive processing can arise when inappropriate concepts are used to supplement the environmental stimulus. This can lead to misidentification and misinterpretation of the stimulus. Cantor and Mischel (1979) describe how this trade-off can manifest itself in the judgments we form about people.

> The redneck bigot, the bleeding-heart liberal, the zealous revolutionary. The use of a few such simple cognitive categories about people in general reduces and simplifies what one needs to know and look for in particular people. Applying our categories about other people often allows us to feel an almost instant general understanding of someone we hardly know. After five minutes of Archie Bunker's televised tirades on the decay of the neighborhood, one may feel competent to predict simply on the basis of the belief that he is a "bigot," not only his other political views but even his taste in food, movies, and friends. . . . Categorizations simplify what would otherwise be overwhelming data and give us more economical and coherent knowledge of people. However, a reliance on preconceived typologies to structure one's perceptions of people has its costs as well as its value, potentially encouraging attributions of the characteristics associated with a category to each member even when those characteristics may not fit the individual. (p. 6)

A study by Duncan (1976) illustrates how a particular kind of concept, a stereotype, can affect the perception and interpretation of a behavior. Traditionally, social psychologists have described stereotypes not in terms of schemas or concepts, but in psychoanalytic or sociocultural terms. According to a psychoanalytic approach, stereotyping occurs because it fulfills drives and unconscious needs, such as anxiety reduction; according to a sociocultural approach, stereotyping is the product of experience (Hamilton, 1979). A more recent, cognitive approach (e.g., Allport, 1954; Tajfel & Wilkes, 1963; Taylor, Fiske, Etcoff & Ruderman, 1978), however, has stressed the similarities between stereotypes and concepts (e.g., Cantor & Mischel, 1979). According to this view, stereotypes are categories that represent a number

---

From N. Cantor and W. Mischel, "Prototypes in person perception." In L. Berkowitz (Ed.), *Advances in Experimental Social Psychology.* New York: Academic Press, 1979. Copyright 1979 by Academic Press. Reprinted by permission.

of instances that have some common characteristics. Stereotypes are seen as serving the same general purpose as other concepts—they "are inevitable consequences of our needs as perceivers to make sense of the world" (Scheider, Hastorf, & Ellsworth, 1979, p. 172). Psychologists who adhere to the cognitive view of stereotypes study the cognitive mechanisms that lead to the formation of distorted or biased stereotypes and the consequences of forming these concepts.

Duncan (1976) was interested in the effects of racial stereotypes on the perception of an ambiguous behavior: a shove given by one person to another. Subjects in the study were undergraduate college students. They were led to believe that they were watching a live debate between two other students via closed-circuit TV. The scenario shown on the TV had actually been carefully prepared and videotaped in advance. In one version that was shown to some of the subjects, what started out to be a debate between a black and a white student grew increasingly more heated and ended with the white student being shoved by the black student. Other versions of the staged debate ended with a white student shoving a black student, a white student shoving a white student, or a black student shoving a black student. After viewing the incident, the subjects, all of whom were white, filled out a rating form to describe and assess the intensity of the shove. Duncan found that the subjects' responses on this rating form were strongly influenced by the race of the assailant and victim. When it was a black student shoving a white student, 75 percent of the observers chose the "violent" category on their rating sheet to describe the behavior. However, when the shove was directed from a white student to a black student, only 17 percent of the subjects labeled it as "violent" and instead preferred to describe it as "dramatizing" or "playing around." In addition, the severity of the behavior was rated as higher when the black student shoved the white student rather than when the white student shoved the black student.

Why did white students perceive all shoves given by blacks and directed either at whites or at other blacks to be more violent then the shoves given by whites? Duncan suggests that the perceiver does not utilize just the information made available by the stimulus itself, but also makes use of conceptual knowledge in memory to interpret and label the stimulus. In the case of the shove, the conceptual knowledge used to interpret and label the behavior evidently involved a stereotype.

> One of the stereotypes frequently applied to blacks is that they are impulsive and given to crimes and violence. If one believes that blacks are more prone to violent acts then whites, it is reasonable to assume that the concept of violence is more accessible when viewing a black than when viewing a white committing the same act. In other words, the threshold for labeling an act as violent is lower

when viewing a black actor than when viewing a white actor. (Duncan, 1976, p. 591)

The result of this kind of biased observation and interpretation outside the laboratory can have serious implications. Duncan writes that "one may be tempted to ask, in the real world where violence is a fact of life, have blacks been the victims of mislabeling errors? . . . In court testimonies this could have grave consequences" (p. 595).

Reconstructive Distortions. Distortions in social judgments may occur when attempting to remember some past episode. Under this circumstance, the biased remembering may be the result of having retrieved inappropriate conceptual or stereotypical knowledge acquired independently of the to-be-remembered episode. A well-known study by Snyder and Uranowitz (1978) is often cited as evidence of this kind of reconstructive memory error. Snyder and Uranowitz asked subjects to read a supposedly true story of the life of a woman named Betty K. The three-page story described Betty K.'s childhood, education, and profession, and included information about her relations with her parents and friends in high school and college. Either immediately after reading the story or one week later, subjects were given additional information about Betty K. Some subjects were told she was currently living a lesbian life-style, while others were told she was currently living a heterosexual life-style. When Snyder and Uranowitz tested subjects' memory for the passage using a recognition test one week after the passage had been presented, they found that subjects' recognition errors were significantly affected by this additional information. For example, when presented with questions such as

In high school, Betty

a) occasionally dated men
b) never went out with men
c) went steady
d) no information presented,

subjects given the lesbian label who answered the question incorrectly were more likely to choose either the stereotypically lesbian item (alternative "b" in the above example) or some sexually neutral item than subjects given the heterosexual label. Of the subjects given the lesbian label, 54 percent of their errors were of this sort, compared with 40 percent for subjects given the heterosexual label. Labels had a similar effect on recognition errors made to stereotypically heterosexual items. That is, subjects given the heterosexual label falsely recognized answers such as option "c" above or sexually neutral items more often than subjects given the lesbian label. The percentage of subjects making this sort of error was 29 and 19 for the heterosexual- and lesbian-label groups, respectively.

It seems reasonable to attribute this sort of error to the inadvertant retrieval of stereotypical information from memory. What can be done to help prevent this retrieval of inappropriate information? As mentioned previously, extra care given during both the learning and the remembering of an event can minimize reconstructive errors. Factors such as these may possibly have brought about some failures by Clark and Woll (1981) to confirm Snyder and Uranowitz's findings. Clark and Woll attempted to improve on the experimental design used in Snyder and Uranowitz's study by carefully controlling the nature of the recognition test items. When their first experiment failed to produce any evidence of reconstructive errors, Clark and Woll repeated Synder and Uranowitz's procedure in its original form. Again, they failed to find evidence of memory distortions. This failure to replicate Snyder and Uranowitz's findings may be due partly to an awareness by students in Clark and Woll's experiments of the importance of giving Betty K.'s story a careful reading. These students may also have been very aware of the social implications of labeling and of the inaccuracies inherent in sexual stereotypes. As a result, they may have been very reluctant to choose sexually stereotypical responses on the test unless specific supporting details from the passage could be remembered. Some evidence in support of this comes from the responses subjects gave to certain questions in Clark and Woll's first experiment. These questions all concerned information that had not actually been presented in the passage about Betty K. For example, no mention was made of Betty K.'s having attended particular kinds of parties in high school. However, one question on the test requested subjects to choose among the three alternatives (a) Betty went to boy–girl parties, (b) Betty went mostly to church parties, (c) Betty went mostly to all-girl pajama parties. Questions such as this, which offered a stereotypically heterosexual, neutral, and lesbian answer, were not answered any differently by subjects given a lesbian or a heterosexual label for Betty K. This seems to indicate a general reluctance by subjects to be swayed in their choices of answer by stereotypical labels. Thus, it seems that extra effort and an awareness of the biasing influence of labels can help a person to minimize reconstructive memory errors.

Storage Factors in Memory Distortions

The preceding discussions have emphasized retrieval factors in accounting for constructive and reconstructive processes. For example, in a study such as Sulin and Dooling's (1974), in which a person incorrectly remembers reading a statement that was never actually presented (e.g., she was deaf, dumb, and blind), memory distortion is partly attributable to the retrieval (and subsequent encoding) of general conceptual information by cues presented in the passage. A retrieval account has also been offered for the findings of Snyder and Uranowitz (1978) and Spiro (1980). These studies simulated situations that occur in everyday life, situations in which a person discovers something about an acquaintance that alters or contradicts an impression formed about this acquaintance. The view expressed here has been that any memory distortions of information encoded prior to the presentation of this impression-modifying information is attributable to retrieval errors. That is, the new information is seen to act as a retrieval cue which arouses information in memory that, while it matches information in the cue, is not appropriate to the to-be-remembered event.

Psychologists who take a retrieval view of some memory phenomenon attribute the phenomenon principally to the operation of the retrieval system, not to encoding of storage factors. In this section, another possible account of memory distortions will be examined, one that is applicable principally to the reconstructive process. The account to be examined attributes memory distortions principally to storage factors.

Evidence for Erasure

Two changes were previously suggested to occur during storage in the long-term store: A memory trace's strength decays, and the trace becomes less fragile. These changes, which appear to occur most rapidly immediately after a trace has been encoded, prevent a memory from being permanently preserved in its original form. At the same time, however, these changes do not lead to the sudden removal of information from storage. Instead, the two processes seem to counteract each other in the sense that they lead traces to become less strongly represented over time, but what does remain of them is more securely stored.

There is another change that has been stated or implied by some psychologists to occur during storage, one that is relevant to the development of concepts and their role in reconstructive processing. It has been suggested (Loftus & Loftus, 1980) that under certain circumstances information in memory can be altered or even erased if it conflicts with subsequently encoded information.

Eyewitness Testimony and Erasure.   One common finding in experiments on eyewitness testimony is that a person's memory of some episode can be affected by events that occur after the episode (Loftus, 1975, 1977; Loftus, Miller, & Burns, 1978; Loftus & Palmer, 1974). For example, Loftus, Miller, and Burns (1978) showed one group of subjects a series of 30 slides in which a red Datsun drove down a side street, stopped at a stop sign, turned right, and knocked down a pedestrian crossing at a crosswalk. Immediately after seeing the slides, subjects were given a series of 20 questions to answer about the accident. Unknown to the subjects, question 17 contained some critical information that was either consistent with or inconsistent with what they had been shown. Half of the subjects in the group were asked the consistent information question: "Did another car pass the red Datsun while it was stopped at the stop sign?" (p. 22). The other subjects received the inconsistent information question. They were asked the same question except that the words *yield sign* were used in place of the words *stop sign*. After 20 minutes of unrelated activity, all subjects were shown 15 pairs of slides, 1 of which showed a picture of the red car stopped at a stop sign together with a picture of the red car stopped at a yield sign. Subjects had to choose the picture that they remembered having been shown previously. The results of this test showed that subjects who had received questions containing consistent information scored 75 percent correct on this slide pair, whereas subjects who had received inconsistent information scored only 41 percent correct. It should be noted that these test results applied not only to the subjects mentioned here, but also to another group of subjects who had initially been shown a yield sign in the slide sequence and then had received either consistent or inconsistent information about the yield sign. Thus, these results indicate that when given information about some nonexistent object, over half of the subjects later indicated that they remembered having seen that nonexistent object.

How can this memory error be explained? Loftus, Miller, and Burns suggest that the misleading information replaced the original information in the subjects' long-term stores. In their own words:

> This position would hold that when a person sees a stop sign, for example, the sign gets into memory (i.e., is encoded). If a subsequent questionnaire reports that the sign was a yield sign, that information might, according to this view, enter the memory system and cause an alteration of the original representation. The subject can now be assumed to have a yield sign incorporated into his memorial representation of the event. (p. 27)

In a number of other studies as well, Loftus and her associates (Loftus, 1975, 1977; Loftus & Palmer, 1974) have convincingly demonstrated this susceptibility of memory to biasing information presented after some critical event has occurred. For example, Loftus (1975) showed college students a videotape depicting the disruption of a class by eight demonstrators. In a subsequently presented questionnaire, 1 of the 20 questions presented to half of the subjects was "Was the leader of the four demonstrators who entered the classroom a male?" The other subjects were asked the same question except with the number 12 substituted for the number 4. A week later, when subjects were asked to estimate the number of demonstrators they remembered seeing, the subjects who had received the "12" question reported having seen an average of 8.85 demonstrators, whereas the subjects who had received the "4" question reported having seen an average of 6.4 demonstrators.

The Independent Memory Trace Hypothesis. While the findings seem quite clear, the cognitive mechanisms underlying them are not. Loftus and Loftus (1980) have admitted that although the facts are consistent with the hypothesis that biasing information erases already-encoded information, other explanations are also possible. A reasonable alternate account, one that accords well with the retrieval view of memory, is that the biasing information does not erase or interfere with the storage of the original information. Rather, information about both the original event and the biasing event are represented in memory at the time of the test. According to this account, the original information is not remembered at the time of the test because of difficulties in retrieving it.

It has proven difficult to design experiments that can clearly distinguish between these two views. Shaughnessy and Mand (1982) have attempted to bolster the retrieval view of this phenomenon by pointing out the similarities between the memory performance of subjects who receive biasing information and the memory performance of subjects in frequency-discrimination tasks. In a frequency-discrimination task, a subject is shown a variety of stimuli a varying number of times and later, when presented with a sample of the stimuli, is asked to decide which of the alternatives previously occurred most often. For example, if subjects are shown a long series of slides of individual geometric forms in which a red triangle appears three times and a blue circle appears once, and later the subjects are given a frequency-discrimination test in which a picture of a red triangle and a picture of a blue circle are presented simultaneously, the subjects will be performing the task correctly if they select the picture of the red triangle. It is important to note for the purposes of our discussion of biasing information that subjects can perform frequency-discrimination tasks satisfactorily and that this ability can be successfully accounted for by theories that assume that each presentation of a stimulus produces its own independent trace in memory, a trace that is not interfered with during storage (Hintzman, 1976; Hintzman & Stern, 1978). Getting back to the Shaughnessy and Mand experiment, these researchers demonstrated that subjects who receive misinformation about some event they previously witnessed behave very much as if they are performing a frequency-discrimination task when later asked to choose between the original and subsequent depictions of the event.

Unfortunately, however, this study does not provide unequivocal support for the independent-trace view, just as the evidence offered by Loftus does not unequivocally support a storage-disruption view.

Evidence from Other Experimental Paradigms

Storage Disruption. How can this issue be decided? Perhaps by seeking evidence from other memory phenomena and other experimental paradigms. For example, one can ask whether there is any evidence at all that information can be removed from memory once it has been encoded. The phenomenon of retrograde amnesia indicates that this can occur under certain circumstances. On the basis of a study by Loftus and Burns (1982), it seems that intrusive stimuli, such as blows to the head or electric shocks, are not required in order to produce retrograde amnesia. In Loftus and Burns' experiment, two groups of subjects were shown one of two filmed versions of a bank robbery. Both versions were identical except for their endings. Both showed a lone individual robbing a bank teller and leaving the bank. In response to the shouts of the teller, two bank employees chase after the robber. These two pursuers run across a parking lot where two boys are playing, one of whom has the number 17 on his football jersey. At this point, the two versions of the event differ. In the nonviolent version, the viewer is returned to the inside of the bank, where the manager takes charge of the situation, asking everyone to stay calm. In the violent version, the viewer sees the robber turning towards his pursuers and firing a shot at them. The bullet hits the boy in the face and he falls down with his hands clutching his bleeding face. The effect of this violent ending on memory of an immediately preceding event was clear. When asked to recall the number on the boy's jersey, only 4.3 percent of the subjects seeing the violent version were able to provide the correct response, compared with 27.9 percent of the subjects seeing the nonviolent version. Furthermore, when tested with a recognition procedure, other subjects (experiment 2) who had seen the violent version correctly picked this number from a four-alternative test question only 28 percent of the time, compared with 55 percent for subjects who had seen the nonviolent version. Statistical analysis showed that the performance of subjects in this recognition test who had seen the violent version was not significantly different from 25 percent, which is the chance, or guessing, level. This is a good indication that little information about the number was in these subjects' long-term stores.

Although the retrograde amnesia phenomenon provides evidence for disruption during storage, the conditions under which this disruption occurs are very different from those existing in the Loftus, Miller, and Burns (1978) experiment. One difference is that the disrupting events that produce retro-grade amnesic effects are traumatic or at least emotionally salient. This certainly is not true of the biasing information in the Loftus et al. eyewitness study. Another difference is that the information that is disrupted in storage is usually the information that was encoded just prior to the disrupting event. For example, in the violent version condition of Loftus and Burns' (1982) experiment, the clearest evidence of memory loss was for information encoded within four seconds prior to the commencement of the violence. However, in the biasing-information paradigm, several minutes or even a week (Loftus, Miller, & Burns, 1978, experiment 3) can intervene between the encoding of some critical information and its "removal" by some biasing information. Thus, this phenomenon of retrograde amnesia or simulated retrograde amnesia may not, in fact, be relevant to the biasing-information paradigm.

Evidence for Independent Memory Traces.   In contrast, there is much evidence to support the view that each presentation of a stimulus leads to a separate, independent memory representation of the event. For exam-ple, Hintzman and Block (1971) presented subjects with lists of 50 words in which some words appeared twice in different serial positions (e.g., the word *cat* may have appeared as both the 5th and the 19th word in the list). After the words had been shown one at a time at a five-second rate, subjects were given a recognition test that required them to judge the approximate position in the list in which the word had occurred; specifically, subjects judged whether the word had appeared in the first 10th of the list, the second 10th, etc. Subjects were able to perform this task quite accurately. For example, for words shown twice, once in a position anywhere between 3 and 8 in the list and a second time in a position between 43 and 48, 57 percent of subjects correctly recognized that the word had ap-peared twice and judged that the first presentation had occurred in about the second 10th of the list (positions 5 to 10) and that the second presentation had occurred in about the eighth 10th of the list (positions 40 to 45). Hintz-man and Block concluded that the second presentation of a word "does not destroy information in memory regarding the first, as some theories . . . would predict. The two representations apparently coexist in memory and serve to separately identify the contributions of the two different repeti-tions as the multiple-trace hypothesis predicts" (p. 301).

Additional evidence that contradicts the disruption-of-storage view comes from the paired-associate learning paradigm. It is well-known that when a subject in a memory experiment is given a list of paired associates to learn, recall of the list is hurt when a second list of paired associates is presented that utilizes the same stimulus items as the first list, paired now with new response terms (this is referred to as A–B, A–C learning). What is important to know, for our present purposes, is whether or not the storage of the list-1 responses is disrupted by the learning of related items in list 2. It has been found that when memory for list 1 is tested using a suitable recognition procedure, all evidence of retroactive interference can be removed. For example, Anderson and Watts (1971) presented subjects with successive paired-associate lists, each made of 10 number–adjective pairs (e.g., 17–*fast*). One group of subjects learned two lists that utilized the same stimulus terms but different response terms (A–B, A–C learning), and a control group learned two unrelated lists (A–B, C–D learning). In a recognition test of responses learned in list 1, it was found that the group doing A–B, A–C learning recognized as many responses (8.7) as the group doing A–B, C–D learning (8.8), provided that the distractors on the recognition test for the A–B, A–C learners did not include the competing list-2 responses. (That is, if list 1 contained 17–*fast* and list 2 contained 17–*cold*, the recognition test question for the stimulus *17* did not contain the word *cold*, only the word *fast* and four alternative response words from list 1 and/or list 2.) Because performance was above the chance level and because it was no different in the two learning conditions, it can be concluded that the A–C information did not interfere with the storage of the previously learned A–B information.

Conclusion. Loftus and Loftus (1980) have acknowledged that there is ample evidence that multiple encodings of similar or related events can coexist in memory. This evidence comes not only from laboratory studies of frequency learning and paired-associate learning, but also from experience in everyday situations. As examples of everyday evidence, we do not forget our last summer vacation when we go on vacation again; we do not forget one episode of our favorite soap opera as a result of our seeing another episode; and, as Loftus and Loftus (1980) point out, we do not forget who Jacqueline Kennedy was when we find out she has become Jacqueline Onassis.

If, as Loftus suggests, multiple independent traces can exist, when can one expect to find a disruption of traces during storage? Loftus and Loftus (1980) provide the following answer:

> We suggest that the mechanism responsible for updating memory both seeks efficiency and takes account of real-world constraints. In a situation that permits logical (real-world) coexistence, memorial coexistence is likewise allowed. Thus, the Stimulus A may be attached to both B and C, and similarly, to illustrate, allowance is made for the fact that the former First Lady may undergo a name

change in accord with her marital status. Often, however, real-world coexistence is logically forbidden. The automobile that was involved in the accident that we recently experienced stopped either at a stop sign or at a yield sign, but it did not stop at both. The shirt worn by the thief was not simultaneously green and blue. In such instances, the most economical procedure may be to dismiss one memory in favor of the other, much as a computer programmer will irrevocable destroy an old program instruction when a new one is created. (p. 419)

This suggestion seems unreasonable for two related reasons. First, it assumes that subjects engage in some fairly sophisticated reasoning when encountering contradictory information. That is, a subject must first determine whether related information is already stored in memory and then evaluate the logical constraints imposed on the two pieces of information by the real world. If it is concluded that the states designated by the two pieces of information are mutually exclusive, the first must be disregarded. A second assumption one must make if Loftus and Loftus' suggestion is accepted is that this whole reasoning process must either be performed subconsciously or be forgotten immediately. If this were not the case, people could deduce the nature of the original episode based on their remembering that they had to disregard it and replace it with other information. All of this seems unlikely.

In an attempt to probe the storage-displacement hypothesis, Loftus (1979; Loftus & Loftus, 1980) has sought to uncover evidence of the presence of the original information in memory that endures after the biasing information has been presented. All of these attempts have failed to reveal the presence of the original information. As Loftus acknowledges, this does not prove that the information is not present in the long-term store; it is merely consistent with this hypothesis. Shaughnessy and Mand (1982), however, have questioned the ability of Loftus' experimental procedures to detect sensitively the presence of stored information. After pointing out potential problems with the procedures Loftus has employed, Shaughnessy and Mand conclude that the bulk of the evidence favors the retrieval view; that is, they suggest that eyewitnesses who receive information that contradicts a previously witnessed event may fail to remember the original event properly not because the appropriate information is not present in memory, but because the information cannot be readily retrieved. They suggest that in general, when exploring a new memory phenomenon that cannot be fully understood through experimental investigation, one must apply what is known about memory as a whole to account for it. Shaughnessy and Mand conclude that there is insufficient evidence at present to cause revision of the view that retrieval difficulty rather than storage disruption accounts for the memorial consequences of misleading information.

Summary

Concepts have been shown to affect a person's perception, identification, comprehension, and memory of stimuli. While the effects of concepts are often beneficial in that they facilitate these functions, concepts can also be detrimental to these processes. Both of these consequences were dealt with in this chapter. The chapter began with a discussion of top-down processing, a form of processing that entails supplementing environmental stimuli with conceptual knowledge from the long-term store. It was shown that top-down processing is routinely used in many everyday activities, such as the perception and identification of speech. Some anecdotal and experimental evidence was presented to illustrate the distortions that can result from the use of inappropriate concepts in top-down processing. Discussion of the effects of concepts on comprehension and memory emphasized the integrating power of concepts. Detrimental memory effects were then shown to result from the same abilities and activities that allow information to be comprehended. These detrimental effects were linked to inferences based on conceptual knowledge, made both during the comprehension process and at the time of retrieval. Evidence for these constructive and reconstructive memory errors was discussed and their relevance to social interactions was illustrated with studies by Duncan (1976) and Snyder and Uranowitz (1978). The retrieval view of memory distortions was then contrasted to a storage disruption view. It was concluded that little compelling evidence is currently available to warrant adoption of the storage disruption view.

Chapter 11
The role of memory retrieval in some thinking, decision-making, and problem solving situations

Karl Duncker (1945), in writing about problem solving, made the following observation: "A problem arises when a living creature has a goal but does not know how this goal is to be reached. Whenever one cannot go from the given situation to the desired situation simply by action, then there has to be recourse to thinking" (p. 1). In this chapter we will examine the role of memory in several problem situations, that is, in situations in which a person is prevented from immediately reaching some desired answer or goal. We will see that memory can be critical to the thinking process when the problem solver is not provided with sufficient information on which to base a satisfactory solution.

Answering Questions

A person will have to think when asked a question that cannot readily be answered. Thus, a question such as "Who was your third-grade teacher?" is more likely to require thought than is the question "What is your name?" Why do some questions require thought while others do not? One answer to this can be stated in terms of retrieval cues: Information that is difficult to retrieve with the cues provided in the question will require thought. The point to be elaborated on in this section is that thought-inducing questions can provoke people to supplement the retrieval cues provided in the question with cues generated from memory.

Retrieving Personal (Episodic) Memories

A study by Williams (1976) illustrates a thought-inducing task that required remembering information from the past in response to a less-than-adequate

306

retrieval cue. Williams asked four subjects to try to remember the names of people they had gone to school with between 4 and 19 years previously. The subjects were asked to verbalize their thoughts as they performed this task. During the first few minutes, the subjects had little difficulty retrieving names. However, they soon exhausted their pool of easily available names and generally claimed to be unable to remember any more. Williams notes, however, that "with greater effort all recalled new names for many hours" (p. 15). For example, after one hour, subjects had correctly remembered an average of about 47 names and after a total of four hours they had correctly remembered an average of about 93 names.

How were these subjects able to remember all these names? Williams found that the subjects made extensive use of context cues. That is, they often generated settings in which certain people had been routinely encountered. In the following passages these contexts can be seen to play an important role in triggering retrieval of new names.

> And now I'm trying to think of the Sunset Cliffs down on Cal Western picking and just run around and go surfing. I'm trying to think of all the people that perhaps went surfing or even tide pool picking, that were in my grade. Um . . . if I could see them lined up against—there's this one cliff down at Newport Beach they always used to line up with [their] boards and sit down and look at the waves, and then I go down the row and see if there's anybody that I haven't already named. There's John Culverson. I already named him. And Rod Hackbart, and they used to go surfing, and um there are a lot of older people too. (p. 17)

> The first thing that comes to mind is . . . I mean it's almost like images of different snapshots of my high school. You know, I can think of my general science class, and waiting in the lunch line, and halls. Umm. Sort of, Jeff Thompson! He was a friend of mine. Sort of pops into mind and I think umm, we used to stand in lunch line together, and he was in my general science class. . . . I mean I guess it's almost easier for me to think of my home town, and think of people . . . that . . . I've still run into on occasion, when I go back there. And then sort of check to see if they meet the requirements. Like were they in high school with me. And I can think of people like Buddy Collendar, and John Tremble who still both live in my . . . Ah . . . home town . . . It's clear that I have to think of some other situations. It's like I want to think of, sort of prototypical situations and then sort of examine the people that were involved in those. And things like P.E. class, where there was . . . Ah . . . Gary Booth. Umm, and Karl Brist, were sort of, we always ended up in the same P.E. classes, for some reasons. Umm, . . . I can think of things like dances. And I guess then I usually think of . . . of girls (chuckle). Like Cindy Shup, Jody Foss, and Ah . . . Sharon Ellis. (pp. 1–2)

Episodic and Semantic Memory

Questions that call for thinking do not always require retrieval of information that is specifically related to some occurrence context. Rather, questions can call for retrieval of relatively context-free information. A brief consideration of the hypothesized distinction between episodic and semantic memory will allow this point to be better comprehended.

Tulving (1972) has suggested that it is possible to differentiate between two kinds of information in the long-term store: one that deals with specific occurrences from a rememberer's past and another that deals with conceptual information. Tulving has termed these two kinds of information *episodic* and *semantic,* respectively. To elaborate on this distinction, episodic memories are proposed to consist of information about events from a person's past, information that includes a representation of the context in which the event occurred. Semantic memories, on the other hand, are suggested to consist of facts and concepts that include no reference to the context or conditions under which the information was learned. Tulving (1972) expresses the differences between these two kinds of memories in the following way.

> A person's episodic memories . . . refer to his own personal past. Most, if not all, episodic memory claims a person makes can be translated into the form: "I did such and such, in such and such a place, at such and such a time." Thus, an integral part of the representation of a remembered experience in episodic memory is its reference to the rememberer's knowledge of his personal identity. . . . Information stored in the semantic memory system represents objects—general and specific, living and dead, past and present, simple and complex—concepts, relations, quantities, events, facts, propositions, and so on, detached from autobiographical reference. (p. 389)

According to this proposal, the memory of having heard a joke last Thursday in the grocery store or of having studied the word *elephant* in a memory experiment two days ago is episodic information; the knowledge that the chemical formula for water is H_2O or that January is the first month of the year is semantic information.

Are There Separate Episodic and Semantic Stores?   Although one can distinguish between episodic and semantic information, does this mean that separate episodic and semantic memory stores exist? A number of psychologists (e.g., Atkinson, Herrmann, & Wescourt, 1974; Shoben, Wescourt, & Smith, 1978) have concluded that separate semantic and episodic stores do exist. However, to adopt a view such as this requires a demonstration that within the long-term store there are memory stores that differ in the way information is encoded, stored, or retrieved. Anderson and Ross (1980) have reviewed the evidence on this issue and have concluded that there is little firm basis for the existence of a separate semantic and episodic store. Their view, and the one adopted here, is that the terms *episodic* and *semantic memory* are just useful labels for referring to two types of information stored by the same memory system.

A study by McKoon and Ratcliff (1979) has been taken to support the view that episodic and semantic memories are really the product of the same memory store. The idea behind the study was to determine whether newly learned, episodic information (that is, information that the learner could identify with a specific time and place) is treated by the memory system in much the same way as semantic information is treated. McKoon and Ratcliff decided that the phenomenon of priming in a lexical decision task is a prototypical semantic memory phenomenon. That is, when a subject is asked to determine if a letter string (e.g., *grass*) spells an English word, the decision will be speeded when a highly associated word (e.g., *green*) precedes the letter string; this priming phenomenon can be considered to involve principally semantic memory, since knowledge about only the meanings of words and not when and where the words were learned is involved. McKoon and Ratcliff set out to discover whether words learned in an episodic memory task would also be capable of priming each other. Evidence that supported this possibility would indicate that the two kinds of memories, episodic and semantic, were similar. That is, such evidence would indicate that the same kind of interword associations had been encoded and the same kind of retrieval phenomenon (spreading activation) was occurring. Subjects in the experiment studied six pairs of words, such as *city–grass*, for three seconds each. The subjects were told to learn the pairs of words for a cued-recall test. Immediately after studying the list of word pairs, subjects were given a lexical decision task in which various words and nonwords were presented. McKoon and Ratcliff found that responses to words from the recently learned list (e.g., *grass*) were primed by the recently learned associate (e.g., *city*) and that this priming effect was as strong as that produced by a preexperimentally learned associate (e.g., *green*). McKoon and Ratcliff concluded that "in terms of a distinction between episodic and semantic memories, newly learned associates are episodic associations, and so this finding is evidence for the interaction of episodic and semantic information in a prototypical semantic memory task" (p. 467).

Retrieving Semantic Information.   Let us return now to consider another situation in which a question provides an insufficient retrieval cue and thus causes the thinker to generate more appropriate cues. The situation to be described now is one involving semantic information. Before proceeding with this discussion, however, one caution must be introduced: It is often difficult to distinguish clearly between episodic and semantic memories.

The reason is that all the conceptual knowledge a person develops, that is, all semantic memories, must be based on episodic information. For example, a concept such as "animal," which is semantic information, must be acquired from specific encounters that occur under particular circumstances. While these individual, episodic memories may eventually become difficult to retrieve, they nevertheless must be present, in some form, in memory.

With this caution in mind we can examine a study by Read and Bruce (1982). The study can probably be considered to have primarily tested subjects' abilities to retrieve semantic information. In the study, college-age subjects were requested to supply the names of entertainers active during the period from 1940 to 1965. Read and Bruce were interested in how subjects went about trying to retrieve names that were difficult to remember. To investigate this, the experimenters presented subjects with either a verbal description or a picture of an entertainer. For example, a verbal description may have been "On Broadway he created the role of Charley in *Charley's Aunt,* but is perhaps best remembered as the scarecrow in the Judy Garland movie, *The Wizard of Oz*" (p. 282). Read and Bruce were most concerned with the thought process of subjects who could not immediately retrieve the appropriate name (Ray Bolger in this example). These subjects were asked to make a record of any successful attempts to remember an entertainer's name that occurred after leaving the experiment. From these records, the experimenters determined that it was very rare that a subject overcame a memory block without some active attempt at remembering—spontaneous remembering occurred only 4 percent of the time. The remainder of the successful recalls were produced by subjects actively generating information that was associated with the target individual. As an example, one subject, in an attempt to remember the actor who had played Maxwell Smart in the TV series "Get Smart" generated an image of the actor falling down in a telephone booth and, as a result, immediately recalled the actor's name (Don Adams). Another subject "recovered the name Guy Mitchell after humming the tune 'Singing the Blues' and thinking how it would sound on the radio, and the 'name fit right in'" (p. 291). Read and Bruce describe a number of other kinds of information subjects generated.

A common description was the use of a generation strategy initiated on the basis of the sound of the name or feature related to the sound of the name. There is no shortage of interesting examples. For different subjects, Ronald Reagan led to the target name Richard Egan and Nana Mouskouri to Melina Mercouri. To cite two other particularly interesting examples, one person first referred to the "wall-eyed actor" before retrieving Eli Wallach; and another, before identifying William Frawley ([who] played Fred Mertz on the television show *I Love Lucy*), first responded with Fred Williams. (p. 292)

All of this conforms to the view that the thinking process in this task, as in Williams' (1976), involved the generation of retrieval cues. It appears that one difference between a task such as Williams' that requires retrieval of episodic information and one that requires retrieval of semantic information is the nature of the cues that are generated. Episodic memories appear to be retrievable by context cues, while semantic memories appear to be best retrieved by noncontextual information.

Making Decisions

In the preceding discussion it was demonstrated that people who are asked to retrieve information from memory, information that cannot immediately be aroused to consciousness by the cues presented in the question, tend to adopt the strategy of generating additional cues from memory. These cues consist of information the thinker considers likely to have been associated with the to-be-remembered information. We will now consider the role of memory in decision making. Again, it will be shown that memory is most critical in this thinking process when the information presented in the decision situation provides an insufficient basis for arriving at an answer. Furthermore, the important role of memory will be shown to revolve around the operation of the memory-retrieval system.

Background

Many different behaviors can be construed as involving decisions. When a person forms an opinion of someone, perhaps judging that an acquaintance is nice or boring or cruel, a decision is being made. When a person predicts the future course of events, saying perhaps that it is going to rain tomorrow or that stock prices will rise, decisions are being made. In these situations the various choices or categories available to the decision maker may not be clearly defined—the person may have to generate alternatives on his own. In other, perhaps more prototypical decision situations, a person is presented with a set of alternatives and is asked to select among them. This latter kind of situation has been traditionally studied in the laboratory. The results of these studies generally reveal that, except for introducing processing capacity limitations, memory plays no crucial role in decisions. We will begin by examining the traditional approach to decision making and then consider other, less structured situations in which memory will be shown to play a more crucial role.

Expectation Models.   Which would you prefer? A sure win of $30 or an 80 percent chance of winning $45. One approach to decision making has evolved from attempts to improve gambling performance. This approach has attempted to describe the optimal behavior that a rational decision maker should adopt. This *normative* or *prescriptive* approach, as it is called, was not originally much concerned with the psychological aspects of human decision making. However, studies comparing human decision making with optimal, prescribed behavior has led to an increasing awareness that psychological factors must be taken into account if the normative approach is to have any relevance to the understanding of human behavior.

Expectation models of decision making exemplify this normative approach. Early versions of expectation models (see Coombs, Dawes, & Tversky, 1970; and Payne, 1973 for more complete reviews) described the ideal decision maker's behavior in terms of a concept known as *expected value*. The expected value of a decision is simply a numerical, long-term estimate of what will be gained or lost by making a particular decision. The underlying assumption in this approach is that a decision maker will select the option that yields the highest expected value. Expected value is obtained using the formula

$$\text{Expected value} = \sum_{i=1}^{N} \left(\begin{matrix} \text{Probability of} \\ \text{outcome } i \end{matrix} \right) \times (\text{Value of outcome } i)$$

The meaning of this formula will be explained by way of example: If someone offers to give you $5.00 every time a fair coin results in heads but to take from you $4.00 whenever the toss results in tails, the expected value of this proposition is

$$(\tfrac{1}{2}) \times (\$5.00) + (\tfrac{1}{2}) \times (-\$4.00) = .50$$

Thus, in the long run you can expect to gain 50 cents each time the coin is tossed. This proposition has a higher expected value than the option of not doing anything (which has an expected value of zero) and so, in accord with the principle that a rational decision maker will select the option having the highest expected value, should be accepted.

How well does this approach describe actual decision behavior? It appears that people's decisions do not always conform to the principle that the option having the highest expected value will be selected. Consider the decision problem posed earlier concerning the choice between a sure win of $30 and an 80 percent chance to win $45. Which option would you choose? According to the expected value model, since the first choice has an expected value of $30 and the second has an expected value of $36, choice two should be selected. Yet, when Tversky and Kahneman (1981) presented subjects with these two choices, the majority (78 percent) of them selected the first option, the one with the lower expected value.

Many other observations have been made of people's failure to conform to the principle that decisions maximize expected value (e.g., Lichtenstein, Slovic, & Zink, 1969). These observations have led to an increased consideration of the psychological factors involved in decision making. One early modification of the notion of expected value was suggested by Bernoulli in 1738. The modification stemmed from the realization that the value of some outcome is highly subjective, even when precise monetary values are involved. That is, the value of some outcome, such as winning $100, will not be the same to everyone. It will depend on a factor such as the amount of money the person already has. Similarly, the outcome of winning $50 will not necessarily be exactly half as valuable to someone as winning $100. This has led to the replacement of the notion of value by the notion of *utility,* a term that refers to the value some outcome has to an individual (or group). However, because this modification still has not always allowed decision making under risk to be accurately described (see Allais, 1953; Kahneman & Tversky, 1979), other modifications have been suggested. One such modification involves replacing the notion of mathematical probability by subjective probability (Edwards, 1955; Kahneman & Tversky, 1979). Tversky and Kahneman (1981), who incorporate this idea in their model of decision making, suggest that people generally overweight small numerical probabilities and underweight high numerical probabilities. In their *prospect theory,* Kahneman and Tversky (1979) take the subjective probability *and* the subjective value of each outcome into account in calculating the attractiveness of a decision.

What role does memory play in expectation models? When subjects are asked to make choices between various alternatives that are specified in terms of a probability and an associated value (e.g., an 80 percent chance of winning $20), there is very little room for memory to play any critical role. It is only when the information on which a decision is to be based is less fully specified that long-term memory appears to be crucial. One such situation occurs when a person has to determine on his own what the probability of an event's occurrence is. These kinds of situations have been studied by Tversky and Kahneman. Tversky and Kahneman (1973) have proposed that under these circumstances, people use two strategies for estimating an event's probability of occurrence. One has been termed the availability strategy and the other, the representativeness strategy. The ensuing discussions will emphasize the important role that memory plays in these two strategies.

The Role of Memory in Decisions: The Availability Strategy

A person who assesses an event's probability of occurrence using the availability strategy determines how readily instances of the event can be retrieved from memory. For example, to use this strategy to assess the probability of a car's battery going dead, a person will consult memory in order to determine the approximate number of incidents of car battery failure represented in memory. The heuristic, or rule of thumb, that people then employ is to estimate the probability of an event's occurrence according to the availability of the information in memory; that is, an event will be judged more probable the more readily representations of the judged event can be retrieved from memory. Thus, if a person determines that many instances of battery failure are readily retrievable from memory, the person will assess the probability of battery failure to be high.

The availability strategy is generally a reasonably accurate method of judging an event's probability of occurrence. Events that occur often will be experienced often and thus be more strongly and frequently represented in memory. Thus, it will be appropriate to base estimates of an event's likelihood on its availability in memory. In spite of the validity of this strategy, however, there are situations in which an item's availability in memory is not a good indication of the number of times the event has been encountered. Under these circumstances, the availability strategy will lead to biased estimates of an event's probability of occurrence and thus to biased decision making. The following discussions will show that availability biases may readily be understood in terms of retrieval mechanisms. That is, it will be demonstrated that the biases come about because of the way the memory retrieval system functions.

Retrieval Mechanisms and Availability Biases. To understand one way in which a retrieval mechanism might lead to erroneous frequency estimates, consider the following abstract situation. Two events, A and B, have been represented equally often in a person's long-term store. However, when the person is called on to make a judgment about the likelihood of event A occurring versus the likelihood of event B occurring, a better retrieval cue is utilized for A than for B. The result will be a mistaken conclusion that A is more probable than B, for, in accordance with the availability strategy, the representations of event A will be more available in memory and so judged to be more probable. A study by Tversky and Kahneman (1973, experiment 3) illustrates this proposed situation. In the experiment, subjects were asked to make two simple judgments about the frequency with which words containing a certain letter occur. Five letters were provided—K, L, N, R, and V—and subjects made two judgments for each.

They first judged whether a person more often encounters words that begin with that letter rather than words that have that letter in the third position; they then estimated the ratio of these two occurrences. Try this yourself with the letter K. Do you more often encounter words that begin with K than have K as their third letter? What is the approximate ratio of these two types of words? Nearly 70 percent of the subjects in Tversky and Kahneman's study judged that words beginning with these letters occurred more often than words containing these letters in the third position, and they estimated that the ratio of the two types of words was about 2 to 1. In reality, just the opposite is true. Words occur more often with these letters in the third position than in the first position. Tversky and Kahneman state that for the letter K, a typical text contains about twice as many words with *K* in the third position than in the first position.

Why did subjects make this error? It seems reasonable to attribute it to the differential effectiveness of each letter to act as a retrieval cue for the two types of words. That is, the letter K is a much better cue for words that begin with K than for words that have K specifically in the third position. This is probably related to the psychological importance of the initial letter in a word (e.g., Merikle, Coltheart, & Lowe, 1971). It may also be due to people's probable failure to store detailed letter-position information for words. For example, a person probably does not encode the specific information that the word *like* contains K in position three. Thus, the cue, "K in position three" will be a poor retrieval cue for this word.

There are other factors that can differentially affect the retrievability of two sets of traces in the long-term store and thus influence judgments based on the availability strategy. One such factor is the distinctiveness of the items encoded in memory. That is, if items in one set are more distinctive than items in another set in the sense that they stand out more strongly from other encodings in memory, then they will be more retrievable. Slovic, Fischhoff, and Lichtenstein (1976) mention one form of distinctiveness— emotional salience—as a potential source of bias in judgments made using the availability strategy. Emotional salience may have contributed to a finding of Slovic et al. (1976; also Fischhoff, Slovic & Lichtenstein, 1977) that subjects sometimes misjudge the probability of death from various causes. When asked to identify which member of each pair of lethal events was the more frequent cause of death, 75–85 percent of subjects in one study incorrectly chose the combination of pregnancy, abortion, and childbirth over appendicitis; all accidents over stroke; and homocide over suicide. In reality, appendicitis is twice as likely to cause death as pregnancy, childbirth, and abortion combined, a stroke is twice as likely to cause death as all accidents, and suicide is 1.3 times as likely to cause death as homocide.

Fischhoff et al. (1977) suggest that the distortions in these judgments may derive from the lower probability fatal event in each pair being more dramatic than the more likely but "quieter" cause. Of course, it is likely, as Fischhoff et al. point out, that the more dramatic causes of death are also the most highly publicized. Thus, a person may, in fact, be more frequently exposed to these causes of fatality in media reports. As a result, this finding should not be taken as firm evidence for an availability bias that is necessarily attributable to distinctiveness, even though such a mechanism may have contributed to these judgment biases.

Recency is another factor that can differentially increase the retrievability of instances of one class of events (Slovic, Fischhoff, & Lichtenstein, 1976). That is, if events in one class have been encoded more recently than events in another class, the more recent events will probably be more available than the older events and thus be judged more probable. Of course, in real-world situations many factors may contribute simultaneously to the differential retrievability of one class of event. Thus, the subjective probability of an event may be inappropriately increased if the event is both emotionally salient and recent. While there are little laboratory data to support the operation of these specific mechanisms in biasing probability judgments, most people can verify the influence of these factors by considering their own experiences. Tversky and Kahneman (1973) illustrate this in the following passage.

> Many readers must have experienced the temporary rise in the subjective probability of an accident after seeing a car overturned by the side of the road. Similarly, many must have noticed an increase in the subjective probability that an accident or malfunction will start a thermonuclear war after seeing a movie in which such an occurrence was vividly portrayed. Continued preoccupation with an outcome may increase its availability, and hence its perceived likelihood. People are preoccupied with highly desirable outcomes, such as winning the sweepstakes, or with highly undesirable outcomes, such as an airplane crash. Consequently, availability provides a mechanism by which occurrences of extreme utility (or disutility) may appear more likely than they actually are. (p. 320)

Availability and the Feeling-of-Knowing.   An important point to mention in regard to the availability strategy is that information need not be aroused into consciousness for an availability assessment to be made. For example, to estimate the probability of a marriage's ending in a divorce, a person need not retrieve and count specific instances of divorced couples that have been encoded in memory and then do the same for couples who have been married for many years. Instead, it appears that such judgments can be made automatically on the basis of a subconscious arousal of stored information. Evidence of this comes from studies of the *feeling-of-knowing* experience (Hart, 1965, 1967). Studies have shown that even when some information cannot be consciously recalled, a person can quite accurately assess the likelihood of the information being in memory. Hart (1965) demonstrated this by asking subjects general information questions, such as "Which planet is the largest in our solar system?," "Who painted 'Afternoon at La Grand Jatte'?", "What sea does West Pakistan border?", and "Who developed the nonsense syllable in studies of learning?" (pp. 209–211). For questions they could not answer within 10 seconds, subjects were instructed to indicate on a scale of one to six how strongly they felt they knew the correct answer, even though they could not presently provide it. After responding to a total of 75 questions, subjects were given the 75 questions again, this time in a multiple-choice format. For example, the preceding four questions were now presented as:

Which planet is the largest in our solar system?
  a) Pluto   b) Venus   c) Earth   d) Jupiter
Who painted "Afternoon at La Grand Jatte"?
  a) Monet   b) Seurat   c) Cezanne   d) Dufy
What sea does West Pakistan border?
  a) Arabian Sea   b) Caspian Sea   c) Red Sea   d) Black Sea
Who developed the nonsense syllable in studies of learning?
  a) Ebbinghaus   b) Hull   c) Pavlov   d) Wundt

Analysis of the responses given by subjects to both tests showed that there was a general tendency for recognition accuracy to increase the more highly subjects rated their feeling of knowing the answer. This was most clearly revealed by comparing answers that subjects could not recall but were certain they knew, with answers they could not recall but were certain they did not know. The percentage of correctly recognized answers for these two categories of questions was approximately 76 and 30, respectively. Hart concluded that without their having to retrieve some information successfully, subjects are able to assess relatively accurately whether the information is present in the long-term store. This same ability to monitor the contents of memory is operative in the availability strategy.

Memory and Decisions: The Representativeness Strategy

What is the probability that your best friend's marriage will end in divorce? You cannot rely just on an availability strategy to answer such a question accurately because it is not very likely that you will have stored in memory a set of representations of your best friend's marriages that did end in divorce and a set of representations of your best friend's marriages that did not end in divorce. Instead, you will probably have stored representations of couples, in general, whose marriages have or have not ended in divorce. Kahneman and Tversky (1973) suggest that under these circumstances, the strategy that underlies a person's probability judgment is likely to involve an assessment of the degree to which the specific instance being judged represents or resembles instances of a class of events stored in memory. The heuristic, or rule of thumb, that is applied is that the more typical an instance is of items in one set, the higher the probability that the instance will share other characteristics of items in that set. Thus, to use this strategy to assess the probability of one's best friend's marriage ending in divorce, a person will compare this best friend's marriage to other marriages whose outcomes are known. The probability of this marriage ending in divorce will be higher the more typical or representative the marriage is of marriages known to have ended in divorce. Alternatively, the probability of this marriage not ending in divorce will be higher the more representative the marriage is to those known to have not ended in divorce.

Just as in the availability strategy, the mechanism underlying the representativeness strategy can be understood in terms of memory retrieval. The role of retrieval becomes more evident when the term *similarity* is used in place of the term *representativeness*. That is, we can say that when judging the probability of one's best friend's marriage ending in divorce, the probability will be assessed as being high if this marriage is similar, perhaps in terms of the personalities and the nature of the relationship, to other marriages known to have ended in a divorce. Similarity, of course, is the basis on which a retrieval cue contacts information in memory. Thus, the representativeness strategy may be regarded as a product of the natural operation of the retrieval system. As such, one can think of the situation or event being judged as serving as a retrieval cue, and the sets of information in memory on which the judgment is based as being paired associates, of sorts. In the case of the marriage example, we can think of memorized marriages as being associations between various characteristics of the marriages (e.g., personalities, nature of the relationship) and some outcome (either divorced or still married). To the extent that the marriage being judged (i.e., the cue) matches some portion of a paired associate in memory (e.g., the personalities involved), it will arouse information associated with the paired information (the outcome of the marriage). Thus, the representativeness strategy revolves around the natural functioning of the retrieval system.

Biases in the Use of the Representativeness Strategy. Kahneman and Tversky suggest that while the representativeness strategy often leads to valid probability estimates, it can lead to errors. One source of bias, Kahneman and Tversky propose, results from people's tendency to rely too extensively on representativeness without taking availability considerations adequately into account. This bias is illustrated in the following experiment (Kahneman & Tversky, 1973). Three groups of subjects were utilized in the study. Two groups provided necessary control information; the third group did the probability estimating. One control group, the base-rate group, was used to determine if people have the appropriately sized categories in memory to represent differing popularities of various academic specializations. Specifically, subjects in this group were asked to estimate the percent of first-year graduate students in nine academic areas, such as medicine, computer science, and law. The estimates made by these subjects are shown in column one of Table 11–1. From these data Kahneman and Tversky determined that people could make reasonably reliable estimations of the different popularities of these areas of specialization. This information, of course, is potentially useful in probability estimation. That is, if asked to guess whether a randomly chosen graduate student was specializing in humanities and education (the most popular category given in Table 11–1) or in library science

Table 11–1
The estimated base rates of the nine areas of graduate specialization and the rankings given by the Similarity and Prediction groups in Kahneman and Tversky's (1973) study.

Graduate Specialization Area	Mean Judged Base Rate (in percent)	Mean Similarity Rank	Mean Likelihood Rank
Business Administration	15	3.9	4.3
Computer science	7	2.1	2.5
Engineering	9	2.9	2.6
Humanities and education	20	7.2	7.6
Law	9	5.9	5.2
Library science	3	4.2	4.7
Medicine	8	5.9	5.8
Physical and life sciences	12	4.5	4.3
Social science and social work	17	8.2	8.0

From D. Kahneman and A. Tversky, "On the psychology of prediction." *Psychological Review,* 1973, *80,* 237–251. Copyright 1973 by the American Psychological Association. Reprinted by permission of publisher and author.

(the least popular category), a decision maker would be wisest to base the decision on availability and to guess humanities and education.

To another control group, the similarity group, Kahneman and Tversky gave the following description of a graduate student:

> Tom W. is of high intelligence, although lacking in true creativity. He has a need for order and clarity, and for neat and tidy systems in which every detail finds its appropriate place. His writing is rather dull and mechanical, occasionally enlivened by somewhat corny puns and by flashes of imagination of the sci-fi type. He has a strong drive for competence. He seems to have little feel and little sympathy for other people and does not enjoy interacting with others. Self-centered, he nonetheless has a deep moral sense. (p. 238)

Subjects in the similarity group were asked to rank the nine areas of specialization according to how similar they thought Tom W. was to students typical of each area. As shown in column two of Table 11–1, the subjects thought Tom W. was highly typical of a computer science graduate student and atypical of a student in the social sciences. Again, this information is potentially useful to a decision maker. If a graduate student is randomly chosen from among several *equally popular* areas of specialization, then, to the extent that the student has characteristics similar to those of students typical of one field of specialization, the student can reasonably be judged to specialize in that same area.

It should be understood that neither of these control groups actually used the availability or the representativeness strategies. The base-rate group merely provided an index of the different availabilities of information pertaining to each category of academic specialization, and the similarity group provided an index of how the description of Tom W. matched the stereotypical student in each academic area. It was with the third group of subjects, the prediction group, that Kahneman and Tversky were most concerned. Subjects in this group were asked to make probability judgments. They were not instructed to use either the representativeness or availability strategy, but were merely given the description of Tom W. that was shown above together with the following instruction.

> The preceding personality sketch of Tom W. was written during Tom's senior year in high school by a psychologist, on the basis of projective tests. Tom W. is currently a graduate student. Please rank the following nine fields of graduate specialization in order of the likelihood that Tom W. is now a graduate student in each of these fields. (p. 239)

Kahneman and Tversky were interested in knowing how the likelihood judgments of these subjects would be affected by the extent to which Tom W. was similar to students typical of each area of graduate specialization (i.e., by subjects' use of the representativeness strategy) and by the extent to which information about each type of graduate student was available (i.e., by subjects' use of the availability strategy). The mean likelihood rank given by subjects is shown in column three of Table 11–1. Calculation of correlation coefficients revealed that the judgments of these subjects were nearly perfectly correlated ($r = .97$) with the judgments of subjects in the similarity group; however, their rankings were quite different ($r = -.65$) from subjects in the base-rate group, those making judgments about the relative sizes of each category of graduate student. From these results, Kahneman and Tversky (1973) concluded that subjects "predicted by representativeness, that is, they ordered outcomes by their similarity to the specific evidence, with no regard for prior probabilities" (p. 239). Strictly speaking, this disregard for prior probability, as it is called, is irrational as long as the information in the personality sketch is an imperfect predictor of academic specialization. Because subjects in the prediction group later indicated that a personality sketch could be expected to predict a student's area of graduate study correctly only 23 percent of the time, it appears that less weight should have been given to the representativeness strategy and more to the relative sizes of the various categories of graduate students. Thus, this indicates that people can rely too extensively on the representativeness strategy and that this overreliance can produce errors in probability estimation.

Availability and Representativeness in Everyday Decisions

When a person is asked whether death is more probable by homicide or suicide, whether nuclear power entails a high or a low risk, or whether a person having certain characteristics is likely to enter a particular profession, the questioner is providing the decision maker with inadequate information. Consequently, in order to arrive at a decision, the decision maker has to supply much of the missing information. In the studies by Kahneman and Tversky that were just described, this missing information had to come from the decision maker's long-term store.

In decision-making situations that commonly arise in the real world, the kinds of concepts that decision makers use to supplement the information given in a problem may be quite variable. That is, not all people judging some event or predicting the future course of events will draw upon the same set of concepts in making their decision. The point to be made now is that the concepts that a decision maker uses to supplement and fill in the gaps in a problem situation can be subtly influenced by availability and representativeness factors. That is, concepts that are most *available* and those that are most similar to or *representative* of information presented in the problem situation will be most likely to enter into someone's decision.

Availability. In certain experimental situations, the nature of the stimuli will extensively constrain the kinds of concepts a subject can utilize to arrive at a decision. For example, if I ask you which is more probable, death by measles or death by smallpox, I am giving you the names of concepts from which you must extract relevant information. In real-world decision-making situations, this might not occur. Consider the task of evaluating another person. Have you ever changed your mind about how you feel about someone? Perhaps you originally liked someone very much and felt that everything this person did was great. At some later time, however, even though this person may not have begun to behave appreciably differently, your opinion of this person may have changed. "How could I have ever liked this person?" you may wonder. "I must have been out of my mind."

Why is it that a person who observes the same behavior at two different times may judge it differently each time or that two different individuals observing the same behavior each may form a different opinion of it? Higgins, Rholes, and Jones (1977) were interested in this problem. They hypothesized that the general impression someone forms of another person is affected by the concepts that are *most available* to the person doing the judging at the time the behavior is observed. To investigate this hypothesis, Higgins et al. found a way subtly to heighten the availability of certain concepts in a person's long-term store and then determined if these more available concepts were evident in the evaluation the person formed of another person's behavior. To heighten the availability of certain concepts subtly, Higgins et al. led subjects to believe that they first were going to participate in a perception experiment. The procedure in this "perception" experiment entailed naming colors as quickly as possible while trying to remember certain words briefly. Although subjects did not realize it, the words they were trying to remember briefly were the crucial aspect of the study. One group of subjects received words that had positive connotations (e.g., adventurous, self-confident, independent, persistent), while another group received words with negative connotations (e.g., reckless, conceited, aloof, stubborn). After completing the "perception" experiment, subjects were then led to believe that they were going to participate in a totally unrelated "reading comprehension" study. This phase of the experiment required subjects to read a paragraph that described a person named Donald.

> Donald spent a great amount of his time in search of what he liked to call excitement. He had already climbed M. McKinley, shot the Colorado rapids in a kyack, driven in a demolition derby, and piloted a jet-powered boat—without knowing very much about boats. He had risked injury, and even death, a number of times. Now he was in search of new excitement. He was thinking, perhaps, he would do some skydiving or maybe cross the Atlantic in a sailboat. By the

way he acted one could readily guess that Donald was well aware of his ability to do many things well. Other than business engagements, Donald's contacts with people were rather limited. He felt he didn't really need to rely on anyone. Once Donald made up his mind to do something it was as good as done no matter how long it might take or how difficult the going might be. Only rarely did he change his mind even when it might well have been better if he had. (p. 145)

Immediately after reading this passage, subjects in both groups were asked four questions about Donald. One question required them to characterize Donald's personality on the basis of his contacts with other people: "Considering only Donald's attitude towards contacts with other people, how might one characterize, with a single word, this aspect of his personality?" (p. 146). Other questions asked subjects to characterize Donald on the basis of his desire to skydive and cross the Atlantic, his awareness of his own abilities, and his tendency to change his mind. It was found that the connotation of the trait words presented in the "perception" experiment had a strong effect on subjects' characterizations of Donald. Of the subjects who had received trait words having negative connotations, 70 percent used more negative than positive words to describe Donald. Of the subjects who had received trait words having positive connotations, 70 percent used more positive than negative words to describe Donald.

Higgins et al. suggest that subjects' choice of words was influenced by the different availabilities of the descriptive concepts. Concepts that had been aroused during the "perceptual" task became more available and thus more likely to be utilized both during the reading of the passage and during the judgment process. This account has much in common with both the notion of constructive processing and the availability heuristic. That is, just as in Sulin and Dooling's (1974) study, in which provision of the name Helen Keller led subjects to supplement the passage with inappropriate information and later to recognize never-presented statements, activation of information in the "perceptual" task of the Higgins et al. study may have led subjects to supplement details of the passage with this activated information and may have led to the inappropriate remembering of this biased information at the time a character judgment was made.

Thus, it seems that availability can be an important determinant of the kinds of concepts a decision maker uses to supplement the stimulus information. Perhaps we can say that the reason one changes one's opinion about another individual has to do with the changing availability of concepts that are used to help comprehend and interpret this individual's behavior. Very often this sort of supplementation is crucial to the opinion one forms of another person's behavior, because many of the behaviors that one observes are really quite ambiguous. They are ambiguous in the sense that the behavior alone, in isolation from any other ongoing behavior, is quite difficult to interpret. Thus, when seeing another person ask a question, an observer might not be able to determine if the person is being demanding or just inquisitive. It is in this kind of situation that memory of previous experiences can play a crucial role. If, in the past, this person who is being observed has behaved in an inconsiderate, demanding way, then an observer may tend to interpret a present behavior as a demand rather than an instance of curiosity. The Higgins et al. study shows that availability can influence the kinds of concepts used to help disambiguate behaviors.

Representativeness.   Availability is not the only factor that can influence the kinds of concepts used to fill in details that are missing in a decision situation. Consider the following study by Gilovich (1981). Gilovich had observed that in making decisions people often seemed to draw on past experience. For example, in decisions made by personnel directors about which college football players to draft into the National Football League, Gilovich noted that comparisons were often drawn between a college player and some current professional player. That is, personnel directors often explained their choices of college players by saying things like "[He's] a Lynn Swann type" or "he reminds me of the Steelers' corners" (*Pro Football Weekly,* June, 1979, cited in Gilovich, 1981, p. 798). Gilovich conducted a series of experiments to determine better how important a role past experience plays in certain decision-making situations.

In one study, 12 male sportswriters from various California newspapers served as subjects. Each sportswriter agreed to rate five descriptions of different hypothetical college football players according to how successful each football player would be as a professional. Unknown to the sportswriters, two descriptions of each player had been prepared. In one experimental manipulation, the two versions differed only in that one made an irrelevant reference to a successful football player while the other made no such reference. Specifically, the irrelevant reference was that the college player came from the same home town as some currently successful professional player. Gilovich found that this irrelevant reference had a reliable effect on the success judgments. The sportswriters receiving the description with the irrelevant reference to the successful player gave the college player a success rating of 7.5 on a 9-point scale (A ranking of 9 indicated superstar, while a ranking of 1 indicated waived in preseason.) The rating given to the college player whose description contained no reference to a successful professional was 5.87.

Why were the sportscasters' judgments affected by the irrelevant similarity between the college and professional player? Both the representativeness strategy and a filling-in-gaps process were likely to have contributed to this effect. Consider first the way the representativeness strategy combines with a filling-in-gaps process. Ordinarily, when the representativeness strategy is used, a decision maker evaluates the extent to which some current situation is similar to a previously encountered situation. To the extent that they are similar, the decision maker can assume that the two share additional characteristics beyond those given in the problem. Thus, if person X resembles person Y in terms of general aptitude and interests, and one knows what profession person Y entered, one may reasonably presume that person X will also eventually enter this profession. Here, of course, one is filling in missing information about X from information about a similar concept, Y, in memory. Representativeness is therefore used as a basis for selecting concepts from memory that can aid in the decision-making process. Evidently, this same process was occurring in Gilovich's study. What makes the study especially interesting is the apparant readiness with which the sportswriters used information about the well-known player in their decisions. That is, the sportswriters seemed to treat a minor similarity, such as two players' hometowns, as a sufficient basis for establishing a meaningful equivalence between the two athletes that was extended or generalized to their performance as professional football players.

Using other experimental situations and subjects, Gilovich (1981) has found this same tendency for decision makers to utilize concepts derived on the basis of marginally relevant similarities to a current problem. It seems that when people are asked to make some decision that really cannot be rationally made on the basis of information presented, they become highly susceptible to the influence of cues that allow supplementary information to be brought into the decision process.

Problem Solving

Introduction

A baker is kneading dough in a tent. There is a pole in the center of the tent and the baker's small table is next to this pole. On the other side of the pole is an open bag of flour. When the baker begins to run out of flour, he reaches around one side of the pole with one hand and around the other side with the other hand and, using both hands together, scoops some flour from the bag. He now has a problem. He can't pull his cupped hands directly back to his table because the pole is in the way. How can he get this handful of flour to the dough without spilling any?

This problem was posed by the Gestalt psychologist Max Wertheimer in the 1930s (Luchins & Luchins, 1970). It, like many other problems posed by Gestalt psychologists, calls for a rearrangement of elements specified in the problem's presentation. In this case, the flour and the dough, which are in different positions at the outset, must be rearranged so they end up in the same position. Finding a means by which this goal may be attained may require some thought. The point to be made in this section is that the thinking process in these situations, that is, a problem solver's mental rearrangement of the problem's elements, is importantly influenced by information in memory.

Early Theories of Problem Solving

The Associationist View.   In an attempt to understand better how animals reason, Thorndike (1898) constructed a number of wooden boxes measuring approximately two feet long by one foot wide by one foot high. A small door on each box was secured by a system of pulleys and weights and could be released in some cases by pulling on either a string or a wire loop hanging from the roof of the box, and in other cases by turning a knob. In one series of experiments, Thorndike placed a cat inside one of these so-called *puzzle boxes* and observed the cat's behavior. Generally, the cat struggled to get out of the box, reaching out any small opening with its paws, biting bars or wires, and clawing at everything. In the process of making these desperate and seemingly instinctive responses to escape, the cat often operated the release mechanism by accident. The door then opened and the cat was allowed to escape and eat some food that had been placed outside the box. The cat was then returned to the puzzle box, from which it attempted once again to escape. Thorndike found that cats began to escape more and more quickly from a box as the experiment progressed. He explained this in conditioning terms, saying that because an originally random response that led to escape and food was being reinforced, it tended to become increasingly more likely to be performed in the future. In his own words:

> The cat that is clawing all over the box in her impulsive struggle will probably claw the string or loop or button so as to open the door. And gradually all the other non-successful impulses will be stamped out and the particular impulse leading to the successful act will be stamped in by the resulting pleasure, until, after many trials, the cat will, when put in the box, immediately claw the button or loop in a definite way. (p. 13)

Some psychologists who adhere to the behaviorist point of view have applied and extended this analysis to human problem solving. Campbell (1960), for example, has suggested that creative thinking rests on a trial-and-error production of thoughts coupled with a decision process for determining when a suitable idea has been produced.

Memory need not be irrelevant in the associationist approach. Even though a response may originally become associated with a stimulus through a trial-and-error mechanism, once this association has been established, it will be represented in memory and will be capable of being aroused again when the organism encounters a suitable stimulus. This possibility is incorporated in a view suggested by Maltzman (1955). According to Maltzman, a problem will act as a stimulus that arouses similar representations in memory. Building on the concept of *habit family hierarchy*, proposed earlier by Hull (1934), Maltzman suggested that associated with each stimulus in memory will be a variety of responses. Some responses will be more strongly associated with the stimulus than others, due in part to their having in the past been more likely to have led to a reward. According to Maltzman, the response that a problem solver first attempts will probably be the one that was previously the most successful. If a solution cannot be achieved with the most strongly associated response, that response will tend to extinguish and the next strongest response in the habit-family hierarchy will then be emitted.

The Gestalt View.   A strong reaction against the associationist view was taken by psychologists of the Gestalt tradition. Köhler (1926), for example, objected to Thorndike's conclusions that an animal's behavior in a problem-solving situation consists of automatic, mindless responses, ones that are either of the trial-and-error nature or are elicited automatically from memory by a suitable stimulus situation. Köhler felt instead that when man and higher animals faced a problem, their correct solutions were more a matter of an intelligent understanding of the problem, that is, of an *insight* into the problem. Köhler supported his contention with some observations that he made of the behaviors of chimpanzees captured on the island of Tenerife in 1914. For one series of observations, Köhler suspended some fruit from the roof of the chimpanzees' cage at a height that was too great for the animals to reach. Inside the cage was a box. The following passage describes the behavior of the chimpanzee named Sultan.

> All six apes vainly endeavoured to reach the fruit by leaping up from the ground. Sultan soon relinquished this attempt, paced restlessly up and down, suddenly stood still in front of the box, seized it, tipped it hastily straight towards the objective, but began to climb upon it at a (horizontal) distance of half a metre, and springing upwards with all his force, tore down the banana. About five minutes had elapsed since the fastening of the fruit; from the momentary pause before the box to the first bite into the banana, only a few seconds elapsed, a perfectly continuous action after the first hesitation. (pp. 39–40)

On the basis of behaviors such as these, Köhler argued that the higher animals solved problems by a conscious, intelligent process, one that involved understanding the organization of the elements in the problem situation and how that organization could be restructured to achieve a solution to the problem.

Memory in the Associationist and Gestalt Views.   In the associationist view, memory can play an important role in problem solving. According to this associationist view, if some current problem is identical or similar to one solved successfully in the past, the current situation will be able to arouse a previously formed habit-family hierarchy and cause a previously associated response to be emitted once again. What role does memory play in the Gestalt view? Birch (1945) has noted that the Gestalt school gave very little emphasis to memory, and instead tended "to approach the problem of the mechanisms underlying problem-solving in immediate situational terms" (p. 279). There is evidence, however, that memory plays an important role in the problem-solving tasks utilized by Gestalt psychologists. Consider, for example, the "insightful" behaviors displayed by Köhler's chimpanzees. An experiment by Birch (1945) indicates that behavior that may appear to an observer to be sudden, spontaneous, and insightful is strongly influenced by an animal's previous experiences. Birch's experiment was designed to investigate further a problem situation that Köhler had previously presented to chimpanzees. The problem entailed reaching some bananas placed outside a cage beyond the reach of a chimpanzee. Köhler had noted that his chimpanzees could successfully solve this problem by using a stick to rake in the bananas. Birch wished to determine whether a chimpanzee's previous experience with the use of sticks would influence the readiness with which this "insightful" solution was achieved. He hypothesized that because Köhler had used chimpanzees that had been raised in the wild, their previous experience in playing with or using sticks may have formed the basis for their use of the sticks in the problem situation. To evaluate this possibility, Birch used six chimpanzees that had been raised from birth in captivity. Only one of the chimpanzees had been observed to have regularly played with sticks. In the first phase of the experiment, each animal was placed in a cage. Outside the cage was a hoe that was within reach and some food that was beyond reach. Of the six animals, only one solved the problem immediately—the animal that had been observed to have played with sticks routinely. Birch describes this behavior as follows: "She went to the grill, looked at the food, glanced at the stick, and at once reached for the stick, *picked the stick up,* and in one smooth sweep . . . brought the food into reach. Time for solution was 12 seconds" (p. 372). After four minutes of unsuccessful attempts, another chimpanzee also succeeded in obtaining the food, though his behavior was much less deliberate than that of the more experienced stick user. As Birch describes it, the animal's use of the stick was initiated when "in the course of . . . direct reaching for the food, his thrashing arm happened accidentally to brush against the stick, causing it to move" (p. 373). Thus, this first phase of the study showed that most of the animals did not exhibit behavior that could be considered evidence of an intelligent understanding of the situation. The only animal that appeared to exhibit an "insightful" solution had had previous experience with using sticks. To elucidate better the role of experience, and thus memory, in the production of solutions to this problem, Birch next allowed the animals to play with sticks for three days. He noted that by the end of the first day, the animals had begun to use sticks as extensions of their arms, often reaching out with a stick to touch another animal or object. By the end of the third day, Birch noted that several chimpanzees had developed "the somewhat annoying habit of poking at the experimenter through the enclosure mesh" (p. 375). What effect did this experience have on the animals' abilities to solve the bananas-beyond-reach problem? When this same problem was re-presented to the animals, all were able to solve it easily within 20 seconds. Birch concluded that the behaviors of Köhler's apes may also have been strongly influenced by their previous experiences and that Köhler's rejection of the associationist view may have been unwarranted.

The Role of Memory in Problem Solving

The conclusion to be drawn here is not that the associationist view is correct and that the Gestalt view is incorrect. Both views have made a contribution to our understanding of how problems are solved. At the same time, however, both are inadequate in certain ways. For example, it has proven very difficult for the associationist view to account for certain problem-solving behaviors, such as an animal's being able to devise an alternate route to some goal in a maze when its usual routes have been blocked (see Hull, 1934). A problem with the Gestalt view is its reliance on vague terms, such as *insight*. Rather than debate the strengths and weaknesses of the rival approaches, the suggestion to be made here is that another view, one proposed by Weisberg (1980) and anticipated earlier by Maier (1931), is useful in understanding problem-solving behavior and also accords well with the retrieval view being promoted throughout this chapter. Weisberg's proposal is that the behavior of a person in a problem-solving situation is much like that of a person trying to understand any spoken message. In both situations, a person must use general knowledge to fill in information missing from the environmental stimulus. In problem-solving situations, this missing information is, most importantly, some critical aspect of the situation that prevents the problem from being solved. In Weisberg's words:

Verbal messages are usually lacking in much specific information, and this information must be "filled in" by using a [schema], which is the hearer's knowledge concerning the situation being discussed. In the same way, many events which occur in problem-solving experiments are also in need of interpretation, and problem solvers use [schemas] to interpret these events. . . . Much of what people do in certain experimental situations is a function of their interpretation of the situation; that is, of the [schema] that they are using. . . . These notions provide a straightforward explanation of behavior on "insight" problems, and no recourse to other sorts of explanatory constructs is necessary. (pp. 249–250)

It is easy for this view to accommodate Birch's (1945) results. The experience the chimpanzees gained by playing with sticks can be thought of as forming a schema, one depicting the concept of stick use. When the chimpanzees were faced with the problem of obtaining the food that was out of reach and were presented with the stick, this schema was aroused from memory. Even though this schema may actually have been composed of a collection of specific experiences, these experiences as a whole formed a rather abstract, general concept, that of stick use. Thus, even though the chimpanzees had never been observed to have previously used a stick to sweep objects about, the general knowledge of sticks as extensions of the arm was sufficient to allow them to apply this past experience to the current problem.

If memory plays a central role in problem solving, we should expect to find that retrieval cues can influence the discovery of creative solutions. Specifically, we should find that, just as in decision-making situations, concepts that are primed by retrieval cues should tend to become incorporated in the solutions a problem solver attempts to apply to the problem. Let us look first at problem-solving behavior that occurs under the influence of appropriate retrieval cues, that is, cues that arouse or prime concepts that can be used to solve a problem successfully.

The Influence of Appropriate Retrieval Cues. In a well-known study by Maier (1931), subjects were placed individually in a large room that had two cords hanging from the ceiling to near the level of the floor. The task given each subject was to tie the ends of the two cords together. What made the task difficult was the separation between the two cords. The cords were hanging far enough apart to prevent a person who was holding onto the end of one from walking over and grasping the other. Subjects were permitted to make use of any object in the room in solving the problem. The objects included tables, chairs, extension cords, poles, clamps, and pliers.

Many subjects quickly found a number of fairly easy ways to solve the problem. Some tied the end of one cord to a large object, such as a chair, and pulled the chair towards the other cord. This allowed the distance between the two cords to be reduced so that a subject holding on to the end of the cord hanging freely from the ceiling could walk over and grasp the end of the other cord tied to the large object. Other simple solutions included lengthening a cord with the extension cord and raking in one cord with a pole. When a subject used one of these simple solutions, however, Maier encouraged the subject to find an alternate solution. Maier had a particular alternate solution in mind. The solution he wanted subjects to discover involved their using one cord as a pendulum. Specifically, he wanted subjects to tie a weight to one cord, set it in motion, then catch it as it swung close to them while they stood holding onto the end of the other cord.

A number of subjects did discover this pendulum solution. Of the 61 subjects participating in the study, 24 solved the problem in this way within about 10 minutes. Maier, however, was more interested in subjects who were unable to arrive at this solution on their own. For these subjects, he attempted to assess the effect of a subtle hint. Here is how Maier described this hint.

> The experimenter walked about the room, and, in passing the cord which hung from the center of the room, he put it in slight motion a few times. This was done without the subject knowing that a suggestion was being given. The experimenter merely walked to the window and had to pass the cord. It was noted whether or not the moving cord was in the subject's line of vision. If the subject was facing in a different direction, the action was repeated. (p. 183)

This hint, given to subjects who had worked for about 12 minutes on the problem without discovering the pendulum solution, had a rather sudden effect. About 40 percent of these subjects solved the problem within approximately 43 seconds. It seems that the hint acted as a retrieval cue that primed a suitable "pendulum" concept in these subjects' long-term stores. Interestingly enough, about 70 percent of these subjects who solved the problem did not mention the hint in their description of how they had arrived at the pendulum solution, and "further questioning did not reveal that the hint played a part in bringing about the solution" (Maier, 1931, p. 186). Evidently, the subjects were not always aware of what cue triggered retrieval of the idea from memory. This is not unusual. In Anderson and Pichert's (1978) study, in which a subject was asked to switch between a homebuyer and a burglar perspective, subjects described new memories as suddenly popping into their minds after their perspective change. An even more dramatic demonstration of the subtleness of a retrieval cue's effectiveness comes from a finding of Bargh and Pietromonaco (1982). These researchers found that subliminal stimuli—very briefly presented hostile words—caused subjects to form a more negative impression of another individual. Thus, people need not be, and often are not, aware of the stimulus that acted as a retrieval cue for some idea.

The effects of cues in the problem situation that prime appropriate concepts are also evident in some studies of anagram solving. An anagram is a word in which the letters are incorrectly arranged. The subject's task is to provide the name of the word when shown the anagram. Thus, a subject might be presented with the anagram *lbcak* and have to supply an English word that can be spelled with these letters. A study by Safren (1962) demonstrated that words generated by a subject in solving anagrams can act as retrieval cues that prime other appropriate solutions for the task. In Safren's experiment subjects were given lists of anagrams to solve. Each anagram list consisted of six words. For a control group, the six anagrams in each list represented unrelated words. For the experimental group, on the other hand, the anagrams in each list represented words that were conceptually related to each other. For example, the anagrams in one list represented the words *doctor, nurse, health, sick, medicine,* and *cure.* Examples of three other lists are given in Table 11–2. Safren presented the anagram lists to the two groups of subjects and recorded how long it took each subject to solve them. The solution times for the two groups were found to differ. Overall, the experimental group solved their anagrams faster than the control group. It took the experimental subjects an average of only 7.4 seconds to solve each anagram, as opposed to 12.2 seconds for the control subjects. More specifically, within each list, the experimental group, unlike the control group, showed a significant tendency to solve the words faster; that is, they were slowest to solve the first word in each list and fastest to solve the

Table 11–2
Three lists of anagrams from Safren's (1962) study, each representing words from a conceptual category.

List 1	List 2	List 3
candomm	whelist	limk
redor	tarni	recam
ramy	nesoi	usgra
oyeb	undos	efecof
vany	shlirl	sewte
sodleri	oldu	dinrk

From M. Safren, "Associations, sets, and the solution to word problems." *Journal of Experimental Psychology,* 1962, *64,* 40–45. Copyright 1962 by the American Psychological Association. Reprinted by permission of publisher.

last word in each list. Safren's explanation of these results is similar to the priming account suggested here.

> When subjects solve a list of anagrams, at least in part, they are calling up words to match the letters presented and sampling from a momentary response pool of available words. After subjects have determined some of the words from which the problems were made, these words implicitly evoke others which are associatively related. These associations become part of the momentary available pool of words from which subjects are sampling. Thus, implicitly evoked associations from the solution of preceding problems can facilitate the solution of subsequent problems by converging upon words on the list from which the anagrams were made. (p. 44)

The Influence of Inappropriate Retrieval Cues.　In the discussion of decision making it was mentioned that a concept may be used to supplement some currently considered problem. Two factors, a concept's availability and its similarity to the current situation (i.e., representativeness), were shown to influence the probability that the concept functions in this manner. These same considerations apply to problem solving. That is, a person will be more likely to apply previous knowledge to solving a problem when the prior knowledge is highly available and when it is similar in some aspect to the present problem.

Unfortunately, prior knowledge that is applied to a current problem will not always be appropriate. Consider a problem posed by Luchins (1942). Luchins asked subjects to determine how a person could obtain a certain amount of water using three jars as measures. For example, in one problem, subjects were asked to use a 23-unit jar, a 49-unit jar, and a 3-unit jar to obtain 20 units of water. How would you solve this problem? The obvious way is to fill the 23-unit jar, then to scoop out 3 units with the 3-unit jar. Would it surprise you to know that in Luchins' study, out of 11 people, many with a Ph.D. or an M.D. degree, none proposed this solution? Instead, all recommended that a person fill the 49-unit jar, then scoop out 23 units so that 26 units remain; then, using the 3-unit jar twice, remove 6 additional units.

The reason these subjects failed to discover the simple solution can be understood by examining their previous experiences. Immediately before receiving this problem, the subject had solved six other water jar problems, all requiring a complex solution similar to the one just described. For example, one problem asked subjects to find a way to obtain 100 units of water using a 21-, a 127-, and a 3-unit jar. In both cases, if we refer to the three jars using the letters, A, B, and C, respectively, the solution is to fill jar B, then use jar A once and jar C twice to remove excess water. It should not be surprising, now, that a problem that could be solved using a simple, direct procedure was solved instead with the more complicated procedure.

The phenomenon of automatically employing a previously used but, perhaps, less than optimal solution is known as *Einstellung,* or *problem-solving set.* Another demonstration of it comes from a study by Rees and Israel (1935, experiment 4). In this study, subjects were given a series of anagrams to solve. An experimental group received 30 anagrams, of which, unknown to the subjects, the first 15 had to be solved by making exactly the same pattern of letter transformations. For example, the anagrams *nelin, nedoz,* and *ensce* could be made to correspond to the words *linen, dozen,* and *scene,* respectively, through exactly the same pattern of letter rearrangements. The second 15 anagrams in the list—the critical items—had at least two solutions. For example, the anagrams *klsta, eltab,* and *tnsai* could be made to correspond to *stalk* or *talks; table* or *bleat;* and *saint, stain,* or *satin,* respectively. Here, one solution for each anagram is obtained by making exactly the same pattern of letter transformations required by the first 15 anagrams. The control subjects in this experiment also received this same set of 15 critical anagrams that had more than one solution. However, unlike the list for the experimental subjects, the first 15 items in the control list consisted of anagrams that were not solveable in exactly the same way. Rees and Israel found that the first 15 set-producing items in the experimental list strongly influenced the kind of solution proposed for the remaining 15 critical items. This was true even for the 60 percent of the experimental subjects who did not realize that there was any regular pattern of letter rearrangements involved in the first 15 items. These unaware subjects in the experimental group utilized the same pattern of letter rearrangements they had employed for the set-producing anagrams on about 91 percent of the critical items. Subjects in the control group used these same solutions on only about 47 percent of the critical items. Rees and Israel concluded that "the most significant feature of this experiment was its demonstration that the set could operate at such a high level of effectiveness without the subject's being aware of its existence" (p. 15).

Another phenomenon that is quite similar to Einstellung or problem-solving set is *functional fixedness.* Functional fixedness is an inability to perceive an object as having some function other than its usual, present function. This phenomenon has been demonstrated in a number of studies, most notably in Duncker's (1945) "candle problem." In the candle problem, subjects are asked to mount three candles onto a wall so that the candles can burn properly. The objects that are available to subjects are several tacks, three small boxes, matches, and a number of other objects. For one group of subjects, the experimental group, the three boxes initially contain objects; that is, when the subject is introduced to the problem situation, the boxes contain candles, matches, or tacks. For the control group, the three boxes are initially empty. The solution that Duncker was looking for was for subjects to tack the empty boxes to the wall so that the boxes would function as platforms for the candles. Duncker found that all the subjects in the control group were eventually able to solve the problem in the prescribed way. However, in the experimental group, only about 43 percent of the subjects were able to discover this "platform" solution. Similar results have been obtained by other experimenters (e.g., Adamson, 1952; Weisberg & Suls, 1973). Duncker interpreted this finding as supporting the notion that people are prone to perceiving an object in terms of its usual, everyday function. This functional fixedness, Duncker believed, leads to an inability to conceive of an object serving some other, novel purpose, one that might serve as a solution to a problem.

Why did subjects in the experimental group so often fail to use the boxes as platforms, while subjects in the control group did not? One possibility that Duncker and others (e.g., Weisberg, 1980) have considered is that the subjects in the experimental group believed that the experimenter did not wish them to use the boxes in the solution to the problem. According to this account, because the subjects in the experimental group received boxes that contained objects at the beginning of the experiment, they believed the experimenter intended boxes to serve only as containers. This account assumes that the subjects actually did think of using the boxes in the solution or could have thought of using the boxes in the solution, but did not pursue this possibility because of their assumption that the experimenter did not wish the boxes to be used in this way. Duncker, however, rejected this account. He claimed that "there were many among our subjects for whom it was as if 'the scales had fallen from their eyes' when the crucial object was afterwards pointed out. They did not have the feeling of having been victims of a false interpretation of the experimental conditions" (p. 88).

If this possibility is dismissed, what then is responsible for the difference in the control and experimental groups' abilities to solve the problem? While Duncker did not propose a retrieval mechanism as being responsible for functional fixedness, such a mechanism seems likely to have played an important role. That is, in the candle problem, the experimental group is presented with boxes that are filled. These filled boxes can be thought of as retrieval cues, cues that activate the concept of box in a subject's long-term store. This concept, however, will probably not arouse any platform-like solutions in these subjects' long-term stores. On the other hand, a subject in the control group who receives an empty box will not be as ready to interpret such an object as a box. The object may instead be loosely identified as a container of sorts and as such be less likely to be dismissed from further consideration in solution attempts.

Gestalt psychologists (e.g., Scheerer, 1963) have often referred to a more general form of fixation in accounting for a problem solver's inability to discover certain solutions. For example, in the nine-dot problem (see Figure 11–1A), a subject is asked to connect all the dots using four straight lines drawn without raising the pencil from the paper. In the triangle problem (see Figure 11–1B), six matches are to be used to make four equilateral triangles. Scheerer (1963) has suggested that subjects who are unable to solve these problems fail to perceive the correct solutions because they become fixated on some inappropriate assumptions. In the nine-dot problem the fixation is proposed to involve the inappropriate assumption that the four lines must stay within the boundaries of the square formed by the nine dots. In the triangle problem, the fixation is proposed to involve the inappropriate assumption that the triangles must be formed on the same horizontal surface. These mistaken assumptions will be better understood by examining the problem solutions shown in Figure 11–2. It can be seen that in the nine-dot problem, the solution involves drawing straight lines that extend beyond the borders of the square, and in the triangle problem, the solution involves working in three dimensions.

Why do people make the inappropriate assumptions in these problems? Probably it is because these assumptions are ones people usually have correctly developed in other, analogous situations. For example, in children's puzzle books where numbered dots are to be connected, the procedure normally involves connecting the consecutively numbered points using

Figure 11–1.
Part A shows the stimuli presented to subjects in the nine-dot problem. Part B shows the stimuli presented for the triangle problem.

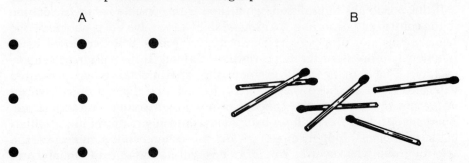

Figure 11-2.
Solutions to the nine-dot and triangle problem.

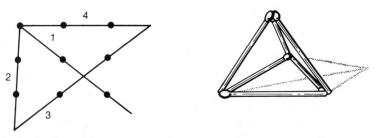

straight lines. Here, one does not go beyond each point as is required in the nine-dot problem. The stimuli presented in the nine-dot problem are likely to cue these sorts of experiences. Similarly, in the triangle problem, the cues provided by the problem situation are likely to exclude experiences involving building three-dimensional structures, for one is not provided with the ideal materials for these sorts of constructs. Thus, the retrieval of inappropriate concepts may again be involved in these failures to arrive at particular problem solutions.

It should be noted that Weisberg and Alba (1981) have reexamined these and other "insight" problems and have concluded that fixation is not a factor in making these problems difficult. They base this conclusion on the finding that provision of the appropriate assumption to subjects does not remove all difficulty in solving the problem. For example, in one experiment (experiment 7) Weisberg and Alba gave three groups of subjects the triangle problem. One group, the uninformed control group, was given six small sticks and asked to "construct four equilateral triangles, with one complete match making up one side of each triangle" (p. 170). An experimental group was given the additional instruction: "You will have to go into three dimensions. In other words, you will have to make a three-dimensional figure" (p. 186). Finally, a fully informed control group was told that in addition to having to go into three dimensions in order to solve the problem, the solution required making a pyramid. Weisberg and Alba found that in 10 minutes, none of the subjects in the uninformed control group solved the problem, 87 percent of the subjects in the experimental group solved the problem, and 100 percent of the subjects in the fully informed control group solved the problem. Because the experimental group was not as successful in solving the problem as the fully informed control group either in terms of the percent of subjects solving the problem or in terms of average solution times (3.0 minutes versus 1.17 minutes for the experimental and fully informed control groups, respectively), Weisberg and Alba concluded that fixation was not responsible for the problem's difficulty. This conclusion, however, does not seem appropriate. The ability of subjects in the experimental group to solve this problem was clearly facilitated by their being disabused of the inappropriate assumption. The fact that this manipulation did not fully remove all difficulties in solving the problem does not indicate that fixation was not an important factor in the problem-solving process, only that it may not have been the only relevant factor.

Avoiding Inappropriate Concepts.   How does one prevent inappropriate concepts from interfering with solving a problem? The Gestalt psychologists stressed the need for flexibility and for questioning all assumptions rather than blindly and automatically assuming that certain objects had to function in particular ways or that certain previously used solutions were always optimal. This approach, which involves flexibility and a careful consideration of all assumptions concerning a problem, contributes to what the Gestalt psychologists called *productive* thinking, in contrast to *reproductive* thinking. Reproductive thinking, according to the Gestalt view, involves attempts to solve a new problem by automatically applying seemingly appropriate procedures used previously in other similar situations, without considering the possibility that a novel, more appropriate solution may be adopted.

Another suggestion that has been made for avoiding inappropriate concepts is simply for the problem solver to take a rest after working unsuccessfully on the problem for some time. This suggestion forms the basis of a hypothetical process known as *incubation.* In the incubation process, a period of rest that follows a period of intense work on a problem is supposed to produce an improved chance of arriving at a successful solution to the problem. During the incubation process, no conscious effort is supposed to be directed to the problem; all the facilitation in problem solving that takes place is supposed to occur effortlessly. Although there is much anecdotal evidence that accords with the notion of incubation (e.g., Koestler, 1964; Poincare, 1929; Woodworth & Schlosberg, 1954), not a great deal of experimental support has been gathered for it (Posner, 1973). Among the processes that have been suggested to contribute to incubation's supposed effects are a decrease in mental fatigue (Woodworth & Schlosberg, 1954), unconscious work on the problem (Poincare, 1929), the opportunity to encounter relevant hints in the environment (Posner, 1973), and a dissipation of interference from inappropriate assumptions or ideas (Woodworth & Schlosberg, 1954). The phenomenon of blocking may be relevant to this last suggestion. That is, when a person has fixated on some inappropriate assumption in a problem, that assumption may be continually aroused by the problem situation and thus block the retrieval of a more appropriate idea. Maier (1931), in his analysis of subjects' attempts to solve the two-string problem, noted: "There was a great tendency (for subjects) to think of variations of previous solutions. . . . This tendency was most marked in subjects who had great difficulty with the problem" (p. 189). Part of the suggested effects of incubation may thus result from a rest period's decreasing the availability of such unsuccessful ideas, which diminishes the tendency of these inappropriate ideas to block alternate, more appropriate ones.

The Role of Concepts in Different Types of Problems. Concepts in memory do not play an equally critical role in solving all types of problems. Greeno (1978) has distinguished among three basic types of problems that have been studied in the laboratory. One problem type Greeno calls transformation problems. In this category of problem, a person is presented with a situation, rules, or operations that can be used to change this given situation, and a goal that must be achieved. For example, in the disk puzzle (also known as the Tower of Hanoi problem), a person is given a set of three vertical pegs, one of which has a set of different-sized disks stacked on it in order of decreasing size. (See Figure 11–3.) The goal of the problem is to get the set of disks stacked on a different peg. The only operation that may be performed is transporting one disk at a time from one peg to another with the restriction that the disk cannot be placed on a peg already containing a smaller disk. Another example of a transformation problem is the missionaries and cannibals problem (also known as the Hobbits and Orcs problem). In one version of this problem (Thomas, 1974), there are three missionaries (or Hobbits) and three cannibals (or Orcs) on one side of a river. The goal is to have all six on the opposite bank. The operation that may be used in this task is transporting up to two people at once

Figure 11–3.
The given state for the disk (Tower of Hanoi) problem.

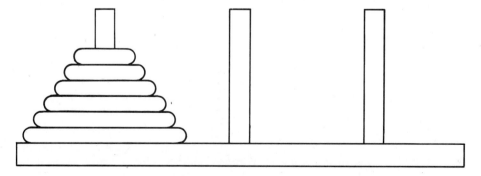

across the river in a boat with the restriction that at least one person must be in the boat during a crossing and with the additional restriction that at no time can the cannibals outnumber the missionaries.

How do people solve these transformation problems? Although studies of the problems mentioned above have not always obtained clear and consistent results (e.g., Egan & Greeno, 1974; Greeno, 1974; Thomas, 1974), it has been suggested (Greeno, 1978) that some form of means–ends analysis underlies the solution strategy. The means–ends strategy involves analyzing the discrepancy between the current and desired situation and selecting an operator to reduce this discrepancy. As a simple illustration of this strategy, imagine that you are faced with the problem of crossing a four-foot-wide stream without getting wet. To solve the problem you must perform some action or operation that will result in placing you either on the other bank or closer to the other bank. A reasonable operation to select under these circumstances is jumping. Here, you will have used information in the problem to generate suitable cues to retrieve various operations from memory (e.g., jumping, stepping, swimming) and will have selected the one that will best reduce the difference between where you are and where you want to be. This basic strategy has been incorporated in the "General Problem Solver," a well-known computer problem-solving program (Ernst & Newell, 1969) capable of performing tasks such as proving mathematical theorems. It should be noted that because transformation problems often involve making some temporary moves away from the goal, the means–ends strategy will generally be supplemented by some additional strategies, such as forming subgoals (Ernst & Newell, 1969). As an example of having to move further away from a goal to solve a problem, imagine that in order to jump a stream successfully, a person has to take a running start and thus first move a few steps further back from the goal before initiating the operation that will achieve the goal.

Concepts in memory can play an important role in the means–ends strategy when the problem situation does not include a specification of which concepts the problem solver should consider using to achieve the goal. However, in many transformation problems, the individual operations permitted in the problem are all provided. The task of the problem solver is to find ways to combine these already-specified operations to achieve the goal. Greeno (1978) has suggested that the cognitive skills required include the ability to evaluate the discrepancies between the current and goal situations, the ability to develop ways to combine simple operations to achieve complex transformations, and the ability to select operators that will produce a useful change. While memory will be important in these skills, its role will not be as dramatic as in other types of problems, because important information about the solution will already have been provided in the statement of the problem.

There are other types of problems in which concepts stored in the problem solver's long-term store can play a more critical role. Consider, for example, the type of problems that Greeno (1978) calls problems of inducing structure. This category of problem requires a problem solver to see some pattern or relation in the problem's elements. Analogy problems exemplify this type of task. A typical analogy problem requires a person to select a word from a list that makes the relation between the members of a second word pair analogous to that between the members of a given word pair. For example, in the problem apple:tree::grape:_____, a person might be asked to choose the missing word from the list a) bush, b) vine, c) barrel, d) ground. Here, of course, the correct choice is vine. Memory is acknowledged to play an important role in solving this kind of problem (Greeno, 1978; Rumelhart & Abrahamson, 1973), for the basic patterns and relations that provide the answers to these problems (i.e., the semantic relations among words) are stored in memory. The importance of memory in solving these problems is reflected in Greeno's (1978) suggestion that the solution process is very much like the process of understanding a sentence. As mentioned earlier, this understanding process is strongly dependent on supplementing given information with conceptual information in the long-term store.

Not all problems that involve inducing structure are critically dependent on conceptual information in memory, however. Consider, for example, series extrapolation problems. A typical series extrapolation problem requires a person to complete a list of symbols, such as 1 2 8 3 4 6 5 6 __. Another example of this sort of problem is c e g e d e h e e e i e f e __. The relevant information in memory for solving this sort of problem is knowledge of the alphabet and the sequence of numbers in forward and reverse order (Simon & Kotovsky, 1963), knowledge that is rather obvious and readily retrieved by the problem solver. The task involved here is more one of perceiving patterns in the symbols rather than of retrieving critical conceptual information from memory.

Problems of arrangement constitutes a third problem type that Greeno (1978) has distinguished. Memory will often be importantly involved in these problems because the critical information missing from these problems is generally contained in the long-term store. For example, in anagrams, the missing information is the word that the letters spell. The problem solver must use the letters to generate cues to retrieve suitable words from memory. It seems that this process involves the generation of small combinations of letters that form pronounceable units, which are used as cues to retrieve test words from memory (Greeno, 1978). Another example of an arrangement problem is known as cryptarithmetic. The task here is to substitute the numbers zero to nine for letters in given words in a way that produces correct arithmetic. A well-known example of this type of problem is

$$Donald$$
$$+ \underline{Gerald}$$
$$Robert$$

The only hint given is that $D = 5$. A solution to this problem can often be achieved in 10 minutes or less (Simon & Newell, 1971) if one realizes that certain mathematical rules and facts about numbers can be applied to limit the otherwise enormous number of possibilities (362,880) that could be considered. These include the rule that the sum of two identical whole numbers is always an even number. Part of the process of solving this sort of problem, then, is using the letters as retrieval cues for known facts about numbers. Thus, the column involving the sum $L + L = R$ should enable the problem solver to conclude something about the possible values of the letter R. Similarly, the column having the sum $0 + E = 0$ could be used to retrieve (or derive) another general fact about numbers that obey this general pattern.

In general, then, it seems that concepts will play an important role in solving problems when the solution requires that the problem solver supplement the given information with information from the long-term store. This process will not readily occur, and thus makes for a difficult problem when the information provided in the problem situation does not present the solver with effective cues for retrieving the missing information.

Summary

The term *thinking* refers to a wide range of behaviors. Three rather broad categories of thought-inducing situations were considered in this chapter. All the situations required thought in the sense that they called for responses that could not readily be provided with the information given in the problem situation. The chapter began with a discussion of question answering. It was suggested that when a person is asked a question that can ultimately, but not immediately, be answered on the basis of information stored in memory, the person has, in effect, been provided with an inappropriate or less-than-optimal retrieval cue. The point made in discussing this situation, as well as in the other problem situations described in the chapter, was that conditions that induce thought often provide the problem solver with inadequate or misleading retrieval cues and that to achieve a solution, the problem solver may find it necessary to supplement the information given in the problem with information stored in memory. In the case of answering questions, it was shown that the problem solver tends to use the cues given in the question to generate other cues, ones containing information that may possibly have been associated with the target trace in memory.

Decision situations often invite memory to play an important role, especially when the decision situation does not provide the decision maker with sufficient information on which to base a response. It was pointed out that under these circumstances, the decision maker supplements the information given in the problem with information found in memory. The influence of memory in decision making was illustrated with situations that induced subjects to utilize the availability or representativeness strategy. Both strategies were analyzed in terms of retrieval processes; that is, in both strategies, information given in the decision problem was said to function as a retrieval cue. It was shown that when these strategies produce biases, the errors can be understood in terms of retrieval mechanisms. Thus, when assessing the probability of events A and B occurring using the availability strategy, if A is a better retrieval cue of A events stored in memory than B is of B events stored in memory, even though A and B may be equally frequently represented in memory, A will be judged more likely. The role of memory in decisions was also illustrated with some demonstrations of how availability and representativeness can subtly influence the kinds of concepts a decision maker uses to fill in missing information in a decision-making situation.

Memory was shown also to be capable of affecting a problem solver's ability to resolve various "insight" problems. Again, it was suggested that a problem may be difficult to solve when the stimuli available in the problem situation do not arouse suitable concepts in memory that may be used to overcome some difficulty. The role of memory in these situations was demonstrated in two ways. First, experimental studies were described (e.g., Maier's two-string problem) in which the provision of suitable cues helped subjects to achieve a solution. Here, it was suggested that the cues helped arouse concepts in memory that could be utilized in the problem solution. A second demonstration of the role of memory involved the effects of inappropriate cues. It was demonstrated that phenomena such as problem solving set, functional fixedness and fixation on inappropriate assumptions are made more likely by the presentation of cues that arouse concepts unsuited for use in the solution.

References

Adamson, R. E. (1952). Functional fixedness as releted to problem solving: A repetition of three experiments. *Journal of Experimental Psychology, 44,* 288–291.

Adelson, E. H. (1978). Iconic storage: The role of rods. *Science, 201,* 544–546.

Alba, J. W., Alexander, S. G., Hasher, L., and Caniglia, K. (1981). The role of context in the encoding of information. *Journal of Experimental Psychology: Human Learning and Memory, 7,* 283–292.

Allais, M. (1953). Le comportement de l'homme rationnel devant le risque: Critique des postulats et axiomes de l'ecole americaine. *Econometrica, 21,* 503–546.

Allik, J. P., and Siegel, A. W. (1976). The use of the cumulative rehearsal strategy: A developmental study. *Journal of Experimental Child Psychology, 21,* 316–327.

Allport, G. W. (1954). *The nature of prejudice.* Cambridge, Mass.: Addison-Wesley.

Anderson, J. R. (1976). *Language, memory, and thought.* Hillsdale, N.J.: Erlbaum.

Anderson, J. R. (1978). Arguments concerning representations for mental imagery. *Psychological Review, 85,* 249–277.

Anderson, J. R., and Bower, G. H. (1973). *Human associative memory.* Washington, D.C.: Winston.

Anderson, J. R., and Reder, L. M. (1979). An elaborative processing explanation of depth of processing. In L. S. Cermack and F. I. M. Craik (Eds.), *Levels of processing in human memory.* Hillsdale, N.J.: Erlbaum.

Anderson, J. R., and Ross, B. H. (1980). Evidence against a semantic-episodic distinction. *Journal of Experimental Psychology: Human Learning and Memory, 6,* 441–465.

Anderson, R. C., and Watts, G. H. (1971). Response competition in the forgetting of paired associates. *Journal of Verbal Learning and Verbal Behavior, 10,* 29–34.

Anderson, R. C., and Pichert, J. W. (1978). Recall of previously unrecallable information following a shift in perspective. *Journal of Verbal Learning and Verbal Behavior, 17,* 1–12.

Anisfeld, M., and Knapp, M. E. (1968). Association, synonymity, and directionality in false recognition. *Journal of Experimental Psychology, 77,* 171–179.

Atkinson, R. C. (1975). Mnemonotechnics in second-language learning. *American Psychologist, 30,* 821–828.

Atkinson, R. C., Herrmann, D. J., and Wescourt, K. T. (1974). Search processes in recognition memory. In R. L. Solso (Ed.) *Theories in cognitive psychology: The Loyola Symposium.* Potomac, Md.: Erlbaum.

Atkinson, R. C., and Juola, J. F. (1973). Factors Influencing speed and accuracy of word recognition. In S. Kornblum (Ed), *Attention and performance,* Vol. 4. New York: Academic Press.

Atkinson, R. C., and Juola, J. F. (1974). Search and decision processes in recognition memory. In D. H. Krantz, R. C. Atkinson, R. D. Luce, and P. Suppes (Eds.), *Contemporary developments in mathematical psychology.* San Francisco: W. H. Freeman.

Atkinson, R. C., and Raugh, M. R. (1975). An application of the mnemonic keyword method to the acquisition of a Russian vocabulary. *Journal of Experimental Psychology: Human Learning and Memory, 1,* 126–133.

Atkinson, R. C., and Shiffrin, R. M. (1968). Human memory: A proposed system and its control processes. In K. W. Spence and J. T. Spence (Eds.), *The psychology of learning and motivation: Advances in research and theory,* Vol. 2, New York: Academic Press.

Averbach, E., and Coriell, A. S. (1961). Short-term memory in vision. *Bell System Technical Journal, 40,* 309–328.

Baddeley, A. D. (1966). Short-term memory for word sequences as a function of acoustic, semantic, and formal similarity. *Quarterly Journal of Experimental Psychology, 18,* 362–365.

Bahrick, H. P., Clark, S., and Bahrick, P. (1967). Generalization gradients as indicants of learning and retention of a recognition task. *Journal of Experimental Psychology, 75,* 464–471.

Banks, W. P., and Barber, G. (1977). Color information in iconic memory. *Psychological Review, 84,* 536–546.

Barclay, J. R., Bransford, J. D., Franks, J. J., McCarrell, N. S., and Nitsch, K. (1974). Comprehension and semantic flexibility. *Journal of Verbal Learning and Verbal Behavior, 13,* 471–481.

Bargh, J. A., and Pietromonaco, P. (1982). Automatic information processing and social perception: The influence of trait information presented outside of conscious awareness on impression formation. *Journal of Personality and Social Psychology, 43,* 437–449.

Bartlett, F. C. (1932). *Remembering: A study in experimental and social psychology.* Cambridge, England: Cambridge University Press.

Bekerian, D. A., and Baddeley, A. D. (1980). Saturation advertising and the repetition effect. *Journal of Verbal Learning and Verbal Behavior, 19*, 17–25.

Birch, H. G. (1945). The relation of previous experience to insightful problem solving. *Journal of Comparative Psychology, 38*, 367–383.

Bjork, R. A., and Jongeward, R. J., Jr. (1975). Rehearsal and mere rehearsal. Cited in Bjork, R. A. Short-term storage: The ordered output of a central processor. In F. Restle, R. M. Shiffrin, N. J. Castellan, H. R. Lindman, and D. B. Pisoni (Eds.), *Cognitive theory*, Vol I. New York: Wiley.

Bleuler, E. (1950). *Dementia praecox or the group of schizophrenias.* New York: International Universities Press.

Bourne, L. E., Jr. (1970). Knowing and using concepts. *Psychological Review, 77*, 488–494.

Bourne, L. E., Jr., and Guy, D. E. (1968). Learning conceptual rules. II: The role of positive and negative instances., *Journal of Experimental Psychology, 77*, 488–494.

Bourne, L. E., Jr., Ekstrand, B. R., Lovallo, W. R., Kellog, R. T., Hiew, C. C., and Yaroush, R. A. (1976). Frequency analysis of attribute identification., *Journal of Experimental Psychology: General, 3*, 294–312.

Bousfield, W. A. (1953). The occurrence of clustering in the recall of randomly arranged associates. *Journal of General Psychology, 49*, 229–240.

Bower, G. H. (1970). Imagery as a relational organizer in associative learning. *Journal of Verbal Learning and Verbal Behavior, 9*, 529–533.

Bower, G. H. (1972). Mental imagery and associative learning. In L. W. Gregg (Ed.), *Cognition in learning and memory.* New York: Wiley.

Bower, G. H. (1981). Mood and memory. *American Psychologist, 36*, 129–148.

Bower, G. H., Karlin, M. B., and Dueck, A. (1975). Comprehension and memory for pictures. *Memory & Cognition, 3*, 216–220.

Bower, G. H., and Springston, F. (1970). Pauses as recoding points in letter series. *Journal of Experimental Psychology, 83*, 421–430.

Bower, G. H., and Trabasso, T. (1963). Reversals prior to solution in concept identification. *Journal of Experimental Psychology, 66*, 409–418.

Bower, G. H., and Winzenz, D. (1970). Comparison of associative learning strategies. *Psychonomic Science, 20*, 119–120.

Bransford, J. D., and Johnson, M. K. (1972). Contextual prerequisites for understanding: Some investigations of comprehension and recall. *Journal of Verbal Learning and Verbal Behavior, 11*, 717–726.

Bransford, J. D., and Johnson, M. K. (1973). Considerations of some problems of comprehension. In W. G. Chase (Ed.), *Visual information processing.* New York: Academic Press.

Bransford, J. D., and McCarrell, N. S. (1974). A sketch of a cognitive approach to comprehension. In W. Weimer and D. Palermo (Eds.), *Cognition and the symbolic processes.* Hillsdale, N.J.: Erlbaum.

Brewer, W. F., and Treyens, J. C. (1981). Role of schemata in memory for places. *Cognitive Psychology, 13,* 207–230.

Brigden, R. (1933). A tachistoscopic study of the differentiation of perception. *Psychological Monographs, 44,* 153–166.

Broadbent, D. E. (1966). The well ordered mind. *American Educational Research Journal, 3,* 281–295.

Broadbent, D. E. (1975). The magic number seven after fifteen years. In A. Kennedy and A. Wilkes (Eds.), *Studies in long-term memory.* New York: Wiley.

Brown, A. S. (1979). Priming effects in semantic memory retrieval processes. *Journal of Experimental Psychology: Human Learning and Memory, 5,* 65–77.

Brown, A. S. (1981). Inhibition in cued retrieval. *Journal of Experimental Psychology: Human Learning and Memory, 7,* 204–215.

Brown, J. A. (1958). Some tests of the decay theory of immediate memory. *Quarterly Journal of Experimental Psychology, 10,* 12–21.

Brown, J. A. (1968). Reciprocal facilitation and impairment of free recall. *Psychonomic Science, 10,* 41–42.

Brown, R., and Kulik, J. (1977). Flashbulb memories. *Cognition, 5,* 73–99.

Brownell, H. H., and Caramazza, A. (1978). Categorizing with overlapping categories. *Memory & Cognition, 6,* 481–490.

Bruce, D., and Gaines, M. T. (1976). Tests of an organizational hypothesis of isolation effects in free recall. *Journal of Verbal Learning and Verbal Behavior, 15,* 59–72.

Buckhout, R., Alper, A., Chern, S., Silverberg, G., and Slomovits, M. (1974). Determinants of eyewitness performance in a lineup. *Bulletin of the Psychonomic Society, 4,* 191–192.

Bugelski, B. R. (1968). Images as mediators in one-trial paired-associate learning. II: Self-timing in successive lists. *Journal of Experimental Psychology, 77,* 328–334.

Bugelski, B. R., Kidd, E., and Segman, J. (1968). Image as the mediator in one-trial paired-associate learning. *Journal of Experimental Psychology, 76,* 69–73.

Burns, B. D. (1958). *The mammalian cerebral cortex.* London: Arnold.

Burtt, H. E. (1941). An experimental study of early childhood memory. *Journal of Genetic Psychology, 58,* 435–439.

Campbell, D. T. (1960). Blind variation and selective retention in creative thought and other knowledge processes. *Psychological Review, 67,* 380–400.

Cantor, N., and Mischel, W. F. (1979). Prototypes in person perception. In L. Berkowitz (Ed.), *Advances in experimental social psychology.* New York: Academic Press.

Carmichael, L. C., Hogan, H. P., and Walters, A. A. (1932). An experimental study of the effect of language on the reproduction of visually perceived form. *Journal of Experimental Psychology, 15,* 73–86.

Cermack, L. S., Butters, N., and Gerrein, J. (1973). The extent of the verbal encoding ability of Korsakoff patients. *Neuropsychologia, 11,* 85–94.

Cermack, L. S., and Reale, L. (1978). Depth of processing and retention of words by alcoholic korsakoff patients. *Journal of Experimental Psychology: Human Learning and Memory, 4,* 165–174.

Chase, W. G., and Simon, H. A. (1973). Perception in chess. *Cognitive Psychology, 4,* 55–81.

Clark, L. F., and Woll, S. B. (1981). Stereotype biases: A reconstructive analysis of their role in reconstructive memory. *Journal of Personality and Social Psychology, 41,* 1064–1072.

Collins, A. M., and Loftus, E. F. (1975). A spreading activation theory of semantic processing. *Psychological Review, 82,* 407–428.

Collins, A. M., and Quillian, M. R. (1969). Retrieval time from semantic memory. *Journal of Verbal Learning and Verbal Behavior, 8,* 240–247.

Conrad, R. (1964). Acoustic confusions in immediate memory. *British Journal of Psychology, 55,* 75–84.

Conrad, R. (1972). Short-term memory in the deaf: A test for speech coding. *British Journal of Psychology, 63,* 173–180.

Coombs, C. H., Dawes, R. M., and Tversky, A. (1970). *Mathematical Psychology: An elementary Introduction.* Englewood Cliffs, N.J., Prentice–Hall, Inc..

Cooper, L. A., and Shepard, R. N. (1973). Chronometric studies of the rotation of mental images. In W. G. Chase (Ed.), *Visual information processing.* New York: Academic Press.

Cooper, L. A., and Shepard, R. N. (1975). Mental transformations in the identification of left and right hands. *Journal of Experimental Psychology: Human Perception and Performance, 1,* 48–56.

Craik, F. I. M. (1968). Two components in free recall. *Journal of Verbal Learning and Verbal Behavior, 7,* 996–1004.

Craik, F. I. M. (1970). The fate of primary memory items in free recall. *Journal of Verbal Learning and Verbal Behavior, 9,* 143–148.

Craik, F. I. M., and Birtwistle, J. (1971). Proactive inhibition in free recall. *Journal of Experimental Psychology, 91,* 120–123.

Craik, F. I. M., and Lockhart, R. S. (1972). Levels of processing: A framework for memory research. *Journal of Verbal Learning and Verbal Behavior, 11,* 671–684.

Craik, F. I. M., and Tulving, E. (1975). Depth of processing and the retention of words in episodic memory. *Journal of Experimental Psychology: General, 104,* 268–294.

Craik, F. I. M., and Watkins, M. J. (1973). The role of rehearsal in short-term memory. *Journal of Verbal Learning and Verbal Behavior, 12,* 599–607.

Crowder, R. G. (1976). *Principles of learning and memory.* Hillsdale, N.J.: Lawrence Erlbaum Associates.

Daw, P. S., and Parkin, A. J. (1981). Observations on the efficiency of two different processing strategies for remembering faces. *Canadian Journal of Psychology, 35,* 351–355.

DeGroot, A. D. (1965). *Thought and choice in chess.* The Hague: Mouton.

Den Heyer, K., and Barrett, B. (1971). Selective loss of visual and verbal information in STM by means of visual and verbal interpolated tasks. *Psychonomic Science, 25,* 100–102.

Dick, A. O. (1974). Iconic memory and its relation to perceptual processing and other memory mechanisms. *Perception and Psychophysics, 16,* 575–596.

Didner, R., and Sperling, G. (1980). Perceptual delay: A consequence of metacontrast and apparent motion. *Journal of Experimental Psychology: Human Perception and Performance, 6,* 235–243.

Dooling, D. J., and Christiaansen, R. E. (1977). Episodic and semantic aspects of memory for prose. *Journal of Experimental Psychology: Human Learning and Memory, 3,* 428–436.

Dooling, D. J., and Lachman, R. (1971). Effects of comprehension on retention of prose. *Journal of Experimental Psychology, 88,* 216–222.

350

Duncan, B. L. (1976). Differential social perception and attribution of intergroup violence: Testing the lower limits of stereotyping of blacks. *Journal of Personality and Social Psychology, 34,* 590–598.

Duncker, K. (1945). On problem-solving. *Psychological Monographs, 58,* No. 5 (Whole No. 270).

Dyer, F. N. (1973). The Stroop phenomenon and its use in the study of perceptual, cognitive, and response processes. *Memory & Cognition, 1,* 106–120.

Edwards, W. (1955). The prediction of decisions among bets. *Journal of Experimental Psychology, 50,* 201–214.

Egan, D. E., and Greeno, J. G. (1974). Theory of rule induction: Knowledge acquired in concept learning, serial pattern learning, and problem solving. In L. Gregg (Ed.), *Knowledge and cognition.* Potomac, Md.: Erlbaum.

Eich, J. E. (1976, August). Dissociation of memory: A state of the research-art report. Paper presented at the conference on alcohol and human memory, Laguna Beach, California.

Eich, J. E. (1980). The cue-dependent nature of state-dependent retrieval. *Memory & Cognition, 8,* 157–173.

Epstein, W., Rock, I., and Zuckerman, C. B. (1960). Meaning and familiarity in associative learning. *Psychological Monographs, 74,* No. 4 (Whole No. 491).

Ericsson, K. A., Chase, W. G., and Faloon, S. (1980). Acquisition of a memory skill. *Science, 208,* 1181–1182.

Eriksen, C. W., and Collins, J. F. (1967). Some temporal characteristics of visual pattern perception. *Journal of Experimental Psychology, 74,* 476–484.

Ernst, G. W., and Newell, A. (1969). *GPS: A case study in generality and problem solving.* New York: Academic Press.

Eysenck, M. W. (1979). Depth, elaboration, and distinctiveness. In L. S. Cermack and F. I. M. Craik (Eds.), *Levels of processing in human memory.* Hillsdale, N.J.: Lawrence Erlbaum Associates.

Finke, R. A., and Pinker, S. (1982). Spontaneous imagery scanning in mental extrapolation. *Journal of Experimental Psychology: Learning, Memory & Cognition, 8,* 142–147.

Fischler, I. (1977). Semantic facilitation without association in a lexical decision task. *Memory & Cognition, 5,* 335–339.

Fischler, I., and Goodman, G. O. (1978). Latency of associative activation in memory. *Journal of Experimental Psychology: Human Perception and Performance, 4,* 455–470.

Fischoff, B., Slovic, P., and Lichtenstein, S. (1977). Knowing with certainty: The appropriateness of extreme confidence. *Journal of Experimental Psychology: Human Perception and Performance, 3,* 552–564.

Franks, J. J., and Bransford, J. D. (1971). Abstarction of visual patterns. *Journal of Experimental Psychology, 90,* 65–74.

Freedman, B., and Chapman, L. J. (1973). Early subjective experience in schizophrenic episodes. *Journal of Abnormal Psychology, 82,* 46–54.

Friedman, A. (1979). Framing pictures: The role of knowledge in automatized encoding and memory for gist. *Journal of Experimental Psychology: General, 108,* 316–355.

Frost, N. (1971). Clustering by visual shape in the free recall of pictorial stimuli. *Journal of Experimental Psychology, 88,* 409–431.

Frost, N. (1972). Encoding and retrieval in visual memory tasks. *Journal of Experimental Psychology, 95,* 317–326.

Gardiner, J. M., Craik, F. I. M., and Birtwistle, J. (1972). Retrieval cues and release from proactive inhibition. *Journal of Verbal Learning and Verbal Behavior, 11,* 778–783.

Geiselman, R. E., and Bjork, R. A. (1980). Primary versus secondary rehearsal in imagined voices: Differential effects on recognition. *Cognitive Psychology, 12,* 188–205.

Gilovich, T. (1981). Seeing the past in the present: The effect of associations to familiar events on judgments and decisions. *Journal of Personality and Social Psychology, 40,* 797–808.

Glanzer, M., Gianutsos, R., and Dubin, S. (1969). The removal of items from short-term storage. *Journal of Verbal Learning and Verbal Behavior, 8,* 435–447.

Glanzer, M., and Razel, M. (1974). The size of the unit in short-term storage. *Journal of Verbal Learning and Verbal Behavior, 13,* 114–131.

Glass, A. L., and Holyoak, K. J. (1975). Alternative conceptions of semantic memory. *Cognition, 3,* 313–339.

Godden, D. R., and Baddeley, A. D. (1975). Context-dependent memory in two natural environments: On land and underwater. *British Journal of Psychology, 66,* 325–331.

Goldman, D., and Homa, D. (1977). Integrative and metric properties of abstracted information as a function of category discriminability, instance variability, and experience. *Journal of Experimental Psychology: Human Learning and Memory, 3,* 375–385.

Graf, P. (1980). Two consequences of generating: Increased inter- and intra-word organization of sentences. *Journal of Verbal Learning and Verbal Behavior, 19,* 316–327.

Greeno, J. G. (1974). Hobbits and Orcs: Acquisition of a sequential concept. *Cognitive Psychology, 6,* 270–292.

Greeno, J. G. (1978). Natures of problem solving abilities. In W. K. Estes (Ed.), *Handbook of learning and cognitive processes* (Vol. 5). Hillsdale, N.J.: Erlbaum.

Griffith, D. (1981). An evaluation of the key-word technique for the acquisition of Korean vocabulary by military personnel. *Bulletin of the Psychonomic Society, 17,* 12–14.

Grossman, L., and Eagle, M. (1970). Synonymity, antonymity, and association in false recognition responses. *Journal of Experimental Psychology, 83,* 244–248.

Gruneberg, M. M., and Sykes, R. N. (1978). Knowledge and retention: The feeling of knowing and reminiscence. In M. M. Gruneberg, P. E. Morris, and R. N. Sykes (Eds.), *Practical aspects of memory.* London: Academic Press.

Gumenik, W. E., and Slak, S. (1970). Denotative meaning isolation effect in multitrial free recall. *Journal of Experimental Psychology, 75,* 434–435.

Hall, D. C. (1974). Eye movements in scanning iconic imagery. *Journal of Experimental Psychology, 103,* 825–830.

Hamilton, D. L. (1979). A cognitive-attributional analysis of stereotyping. In L. Berkowitz (Ed.), *Advances in experimental and social psychology.* New York: Academic Press.

Harris, G. J., and Burke, D. (1972). The effects of grouping on short-term serial recall of digits by children: Developmental trends. *Child Development, 43,* 710–716.

Harris, J. E. (1980). Memory aids people use: Two interview studies. *Memory & Cognition, 8,* 31–38.

Hart, J. T. (1965). Memory and the feeling-of-knowing experience. *Journal of Educational Psychology, 56,* 208–216.

Hart, J. T. (1967). Memory and the memory-monitoring process. *Journal of Verbal Learning and Verbal Behavior, 6,* 685–691.

Hasher, L., and Griffin, M. (1978). Reconstructive and reproductive processes in memory. *Journal of Experimental Psychology: Human Learning and Memory, 4,* 318–330.

Haviland, S. E., and Clark, H. H. (1974). What's new? Acquiring new information as a process in comprehension. *Journal of Verbal Learning and Verbal Behavior, 13,* 512–521.

Hebb, D. O. (1949). *The organization of behavior: a neuropsychological theory.* New York: Wiley.

Hebb, D. O. (1961). Distinctive features of learning in the higher animal. In J. F. Delafresnaye (Ed.), *Brain mechanisms and learning.* New York: Oxford University Press.

Hebb, D. O. (1963). The semi-autonomous process: Its nature and nurture. *American Psychologist, 18,* 16–27.

Heidbreder, E. (1946a). The attainment of concepts: I. Terminology and methodology. *Journal of General Psychology, 35,* 173–189.

Heidbreder, E. (1946b). The attainment of concepts: II. The problem. *Journal of General Psychology, 35,* 191–223.

Hemsley, D. R., and Zawada, S. L. (1976). "Filtering" and cognitive deficit in schizophrenia. *British Journal of Psychiatry, 128,* 456–461.

Higgins, E. T., Rholes, W. S., and Jones, C. R. (1977). Category acessibility and impression formation. *Journal of Experimental Social Psychology, 13,* 141–154.

Hintzman, D. L. (1976). Repetition and memory. In G. H. Bower (Ed.), *The psychology of learning and motivation.* New York: Academic Press.

Hintzman, D. L. (1978). *The psychology of learning and memory.* San Francisco: W. H. Freeman and Company.

Hintzman, D. L., and Block, R. A. (1971). Repetition and memory: Evidence for a multiple-trace hypothesis. *Journal of Experimental Psychology, 88,* 297–306.

Hintzman, D. L., and Ludlam, G. (1980). Differential forgetting of prototypes and old instances: Simulation by an exemplar-based classification model. *Memory & Cognition, 8,* 378–382.

Hintzman, D. L., and Stern, L. D. (1978). Contextual variability and memory for frequency. *Journal of Experimental Psychology: Human Learning and Memory, 4,* 539–549.

Hollan, J. D. (1975). Features and semantic memory: Set-theoretic or network model? *Psychological Review, 82,* 154–155.

Hoyt, W. G. (1976). *Lowell and Mars.* Tuscon, Arizona: The University of Arizona Press.

Hull, C. L. (1920). Quantitative aspects of the evolution of concepts. *Psychological Monographs, 28,* No. 123.

Hull, C. L. (1934). The concept of the habit-family hierarchy and maze learning. Part I. *Psychological Review, 41,* 33–54.

Hunt, E., and Love, T. (1972). How good can memory be? In A. W. Melton and E. Martin (Eds.), *Coding processes in human memory.* Washington, D.C.: V. H. Winston and Sons.

Hunter, I. M. L. (1962). An exceptional talent for calculative thinking. *British Journal of Psychology, 53,* 243–258.

Hunter, I. M. L. (1978). The role of memory in expert mental calculations. In M. M. Gruneberg, P. E. Morris, and R. N. Sykes (Eds.), *Practical aspects of memory.* London: Academic Press Inc..

Huppert, F. A., and Piercy, M. (1976). Recognition memory in amnesic patients: Effect of temporal context and familiarity of material. *Cortex, 4,* 3–20.

Intons–Peterson, J. J. (1983). Imagery paradigms: How vulnerable are they to experimenters' expectations? *Journal of Experimental Psychology: Human Perception and Performance, 9,* 394–412.

Jenkins, J. G., and Dallenbach, K. M. (1924). Oblivescence during sleep and waking. *American Journal of Psychology, 35,* 605–612.

Johnson, M. K., Bransford, J. D., and Solomon, S. (1973). Memory for tacit implications of sentences. *Journal of Experimental Psychology, 98,* 203–205.

Johnson, M. K., Raye, C. L., Wang, A. Y., and Taylor, T. H. (1979). Fact and fantasy: The roles of accuracy and variability in confusing imaginations with perceptual experiences. *Journal of Experimental Psychology: Human Learning and Memory, 5,* 229–240.

Kahneman, D. (1968). Methods, findings, and theory on studies of visual masking. *Psychological Bulletin, 70,* 404–425.

Kahneman, D., and Tversky, A. (1973). On the psychology of prediction. *Psychological Review, 80,* 237–251.

Kahneman, D., and Tversky, A. (1979). Prospect theory: An analysis of decision under risk. *Econometrica, 47,* 263–275.

Karchmer, M. A., and Winograd, E. (1971). Effects of studying a subset of familiar items on the recall of the remaining items: The John Brown effect. *Psychonomic Science, 25,* 224–225.

Keppel, G., and Underwood, B. J. (1962). Proactive inhibition in short-term retention of single items. *Journal of Verbal Learning and Verbal Behavior, 1,* 153–161.

Kintsch, W. (1976). Memory for prose. In C. N. Cofer (Ed.), *The structure of human memory.* San Francisco: Freeman.

Klatzky, R. L. (1980). *Human memory: Structures and processes.* San Francisco: W. H. Freeman and Co..

Klein, G. S. (1964). Semantic power measured through the interference of words with color-naming. *American Journal of Psychology, 77,* 576–588.

Koestler, A. (1964). *The act of creation.* New York: The Macmillian Co..

Köhler, W. (1926). *The mentality of apes.* New York: Harcourt, Brace and Co., Inc..

Kosslyn, S. M. (1975). Information representation in visual images. *Cognitive Psychology, 7,* 341–370.

Kosslyn, S. M. (1980). *Image and mind.* Cambridge, Mass.: Harvard University Press.

Kosslyn, S. M., Ball, T. M., and Reiser, B. J. (1978). Visual images preserve matric spatial information: Evidence from studies of image scanning. *Journal of Experimental Psychology: Human Perception and Performance, 4,* 47–60.

Kosslyn, S. M., and Pomerantz, J. R. (1977). Imagery, propositions, and the form of internal representations. *Cognitive Psychology, 9,* 52–76.

Krechevsky, I. (1938). A study of the continuity of the problem-solving process. *Psychological Review, 45,* 107–133.

Kroll, N. E. (1972). The von Restorff effect as a function of method of isolation. *Psychonomic Science, 26,* 333–334.

Kuhn, T. (1962). *The structure of scientific revolutions.* Chicago: University of Chicago Press.

Lachman, R., Lachman, J. L., and Butterfield, E. C. (1979). *Cognitive psychology and information processing: An introduction.* Hillsdale, N.J.: Lawrence Erlbaum Associates.

LeDoux, J. E., Barclay, L., and Premack, A. (1978). The brain and cognitive sciences. *Annals of Neurology, 4,* 391–398.

Leeper, R. (1935). A study of a neglected portion of the field of learning—the development of sensory organization. *Journal of Genetic Psychology, 46,* 41–75.

Levine, M. J. (1975). *A cognitive theory of learning.* Hillsdale, N.J.: Lawrence Erlbaum Associates.

Lichtenstein, S., Slovic, P., and Zink, D. (1969). Effect of instruction in expected value on optimality of gambling decisions. *Journal of Experimental Psychology, 79,* 236–240.

Locke, J. L., and Fehr, F. S. (1970a). Subvocal rehearsal as a form of speech. *Journal of Verbal Learning and Verbal Behavior, 9,* 495–498.

Locke, J. L., and Fehr, F. S. (1970b). Young children's use of the speech code in a recall task. *Journal of Experimental Child Psychology, 10,* 367–373.

Loftus, E. F. (1974). Reconstructing memory. The incredible eyewitness. *Psychology Today, 8,* 116–119.

Loftus, E. F. (1975). Leading questions and the eyewitness report. *Cognitive Psychology, 7,* 560–572.

Loftus, E. F. (1977). Shifting human color memory, *Memory & Cognition, 5,* 696–699.

Loftus, E. F. (1979). *Eyewitness testimony.* Cambridge: Harvard University Press.

Loftus, E. F., and Burns, T. E. (1982). Mental shock can produce retrograde Amnesia. *Memory & Cognition, 10,* 318–323.

Loftus, E. F., and Loftus, G. R. (1980). On the permanence of stored information in the human brain. *American Psychologist, 35,* 409–420.

Loftus, E. F., and Palmer, J. C. (1974). Reconstruction of automobile destruction: An example of the interaction between language and memory. *Journal of Verbal Learning and Verbal Behavior, 13,* 585–589.

Loftus, E. F., Miller, D. G., and Burns, H. J. (1978). Semantic integration of verbal information into a visual memory. *Journal of Experimental Psychology: Human Learning and Memory, 4,* 19–31.

Long, G. M., and Sakitt, B. (1980). Target duration effects on iconic memory: The confounding role of changing stimulus dimensions. *Quarterly Journal of Experimental Psychology, 32,* 269–285.

Lorayne, H., and Lucas, J. (1974). *The memory book.* New York: Ballantine Books.

Lorch, R. F. (1981). Effects of relation strength and semantic overlap on retrieval and comparison processes during sentence verification. *Journal of Verbal Learning and Verbal Behavior, 20,* 593–610.

Luchins, A. S. (1942). Mechanization in problem solving: The effect of Einstellung. *Psychological Monographs, 54,* No. 6 (Whole No. 248).

Luchins, A. S., and Luchins, E. H. (1970). Wertheimer's seminars revisited: Problem solving and thinking. Albany, N.Y.: State University of New York.

Luria, A. R. (1968). *The mind of a mnemonist.* New York: Basic Books.

Luszcz, M. A., and Bacharach, V. R. (1980). Preschoolers' picture recognition memory: The pitfalls of knowing how a thing shall be called. *Canadian Journal of Psychology, 34,* 155–160.

Maier, N. R. F. (1931). Reasoning in humans: Part II. The solution of a problem and its appearance in consciousness. *Journal of Comparative Psychology, 11,* 181–194.

Malpass, R. S., and Kravitz, J. (1969). Recognition for faces of own and other race. *Journal of Personality and Social Psychology, 13,* 330–334.

Maltzman, I. (1955). Thinking: From a behavioristic point of view. *Psychological Review, 66,* 367–386.

McCarty, D. L. (1980). Investigation of a visual imagery mnemonic device for acquiring face–name associations. *Journal of Experimental Psychology: Human Learning and Memory, 6,* 145–155.

McCloskey, M., and Glucksberg, S. (1979). Decision processes in verifying category membership statements: Implications for models of semantic memory. *Cognitive Psychology, 11,* 1–37.

McCloskey, M., and Watkins, M. J. (1978). The seeing-more-than-is-there phenomenon: Implications for the locus of iconic storage. *Journal of Experimental Psychology: Human Perception and Performance, 4,* 553–564.

McCulloch, T. L., and Pratt, J. G. (1934). A study of the pre-solution period in weight discrimination by white rats. *Journal of Comparative Psychology, 18,* 271–290.

McGhie, A., and Chapman, J. (1961). Disorders of attention and perception in early schizophrenia. *British Journal of Medical Psychology, 34,* 103–116.

McKoon, G. (1981). The representation of pictures in memory. *Journal of Experimental Psychology: Human Learning and Memory, 7,* 216–221.

McKoon, G., and Ratcliff, R. (1979). Priming in episodic and semantic memory. *Journal of Verbal Learning and Verbal Behavior, 18,* 463–480.

Medin, D., and Schaffer, M. M. (1978). Context theory of classification learning. *Psychological Review, 85,* 207–238.

Melton, A. W. (1963). Implications of short-term memory for a general theory of memory. *Journal of Verbal Learning and Verbal Behavior, 2,* 1–21.

Melton, A. W., and Martin, E. (1972). *Coding processes in human memory.* Washington, D.C.: V. H. Winston and Sons.

Merikle, P. M., Coltheart, M., and Lowe, D. G. (1971). On the selective effects of a patterned masking stimulus. *Canadian Journal of Psychology, 25,* 264–279.

Mervis, C. B., and Pani, J. R. (1980). Acquisition of basic object categories. *Cognitive Psychology, 12,* 496–522.

Meyer, D. E., Schvaneveldt, R. W., and Ruddy, M. G. (1972, November).

358

Activation of lexical memory. Paper presented at the meeting of the Psychonomic Society, St Louis.

Meyer, D. E., Schvaneveldt, R. W., and Ruddy, M. G. (1975). Loci of contextual effects on visual word recognition. In P. M. A. Rabbitt and S. Dornic (Eds.), *Attention and performance V.* London: Academic Press.

Miller, G. A. (1956). The magical number seven plus or minus two: Some limits on our capacity for processing information. *Psychological Review, 63,* 81–97.

Miller, G. A., and Isard, S. (1963). Some perceptual consequences of linguistic rules. *Journal of Verbal Learning and Verbal Behavior, 2,* 217–228.

Miller, J. R., and Kintsch, W. (1980). Readability and recall of short prose passages: A theoretical analysis. *Journal of Experimental Psychology: Human Learning and Memory, 6,* 335–354.

Milner, B. (1968). Disorders of memory after brain lesions in man. Preface: Material-specific and generalized memory loss. *Neuropsychologia, 6,* 175–179.

Milner, B. (1970). Memory and the medial temporal regions of the brain. In K. H. Pribraum and D. E. Broadbent (Eds.), *Biology of memory.* New York: Academic Press.

Milner, B., Corkin, S., and Teuber, H. L. (1968). Further analysis of the hippocampal amnesic syndrome: 14-year follow-up study of H. M. *Neuropsychologia, 6,* 215–234.

Milner, P. M. (1970). *Physiological psychology.* New York: Holt, Rinehart & Winston.

Morris, C. D., Bransford, J. D., and Franks, J. J. (1977). Levels of processing versus transfer appropriate processing. *Journal of Verbal Learning and Verbal Behavior, 16,* 519–534.

Morris, P. E., Jones, S., and Hampson, P. (1978). An imagery mnemonic for the learning of people's names. *British Journal of Psychology, 69,* 335–336.

Morris, P. E., and Reid, R. L. (1970). The repeated use of mnemonic imagery. *Psychonomic Science, 20,* 337–341.

Morton, J. (1969). Interaction of information in word recognition. *Psychological Review, 76,* 165–178.

Moscovitch, M., and Craik, F. I. M. (1976). Depth of processing, retrieval cues, and uniqueness of encoding as factors in recall. *Journal of Verbal Learning and Verbal Behavior, 15,* 447–458.

Mueller, C. W., and Watkins M. J. (1977). Inhibition from part-set cuing:

A cue overload interpretation. *Journal of Verbal Learning and Verbal Behavior, 16,* 699–709.

Müller, G. E., and Pilzecker, A. (1900). Experimentalle beitrage zur lehre vom gedachtnis. *Zeitschrift fur Psychologie, 1,* 1–300.

Murdock, B. B. (1962). The serial position effect of free recall. *Journal of Experimental Psychology, 64,* 482–488.

Naish, P. (1980). The effects of graphemic and phonemic similarity between targets and masks in a backward visual masking paradigm. *Quarterly Journal of Experimental Psychology, 32,* 57–68.

Naus, M. J., Ornstein, P. A., and Aivano, S. (1977). Developmental changes in memory. The effects of processing time and rehearsal instructions. *Journal of experimental child psychology, 23,* 237–251.

Neisser, U. (1967). *Cognitive Psychology.* New York: Appleton–Century–Crofts.

Nelson, T. O., and Rothbart, R. (1972). Acoustic savings for items forgotten from long-term memory. *Journal of Experimental Psychology, 93,* 357–360.

Neumann, P. G. (1977). Visual prototype formation with discontinuous representation of dimensions or variability. *Memory & Cognition, 5,* 187–197.

Norman, D. A., and Bobrow, D. G. (1975). On data-limited and resource-limited processes. *Cognitive Psychology, 7,* 44–64.

Noton, D., and Stark, L. (1971). Scanpaths in eye movements during pattern perception. *Science, 171,* 308–311.

Oh say can you see. (1973). *Time,* April 2, 59.

Oltmanns, T. F. (1978). Selective attention in schizophrenic and manic psychoses: The effect of distraction on information processing. *Journal of Abnormal Psychology, 87,* 212–225.

Ornstein, P. A., Naus, M. J., and Liberty, C. (1975). Rehearsal and organizational processes in children's memory. *Child Development, 46,* 818–830.

Owens, J., Bower, G. H., and Black, J. B. (1979). The "soap opera" effect in story recall. *Memory & Cognition, 7,* 185–191.

Paivio, A. (1971). *Imagery and verbal processes.* New York: Holt, Rinehart, & Winston.

Paivio, A. (1977). Images, propositions and knowledge. In J. M. Nicholas (Ed.), *Images, perception, and knowledge.* Dordrech, Holland: Reidel.

Palmer, S. E. (1975). The effects of contextual scenes on the identification of objects. *Memory & Cognition, 3,* 519–526.

Parkinson, S. R. (1982). Performance deficits in short-term memory tasks: A comparison of amnesic Korsakoff patients and the aged. In L. S. Cermak (Ed.), *Human memory and amnesia.* Hillsdale, N.J.: Lawrence Erlbaum Associates.

Payne, J. W. (1973). Alternative approaches to decision making under risk: Moments versus risk dimensions. *Psychological Bulletin, 80,* 439–453.

Penfield, W. (1955). The permanent record of the stream of consciousness. *Acta Psychologica, 11,* 47–69.

Penfield, W. (1969). Consciousness, memory, and man's conditioned reflexes. In K. H. Pribram (Ed.), *On the biology of learning.* New York: Harcourt, Brace and World, Inc..

Peterson, L. R., and Peterson, M. J. (1959). Short-term retention of individual verbal items. *Journal of Experimental Psychology, 58,* 193–198.

Pichert, J. W., and Anderson, R. C. (1977). Taking different perspectives on a story. *Journal of Educational Psychology, 69,* 309–315.

Place, E. J. S., and Gilmore, G. C. (1980). Perceptual organization in schizophrenia. *Journal of Abnormal Psychology, 89,* 409–418.

Pogue–Geile, M. F., and Oltmanns, T. F. (1980). Sentence perception and distractibility in schizophrenic, manic, and depressed patients. *Journal of Abnormal Psychology, 89,* 115–124.

Poincare, H. (1929). *The foundations of science.* New York: Science House, Inc..

Pollack, I., Johnson, L. B., and Knaff, P. R. (1959). Running memory span. *Journal of Experimental Psychology, 57,* 137–14.

Posner, M. I. (1973). *Cognition: An introduction.* Glenview, Illinois: Scott, Foresman and Co..

Posner, M. I., Goldsmith, R., and Welton, K. E. (1967). Perceived distance and the classification of distorted patterns. *Journal of Experimental Psychology, 73,* 28–38.

Posner, M. I., and Keele, S. W. (1968). On the genesis of abstract ideas. *Journal of Experimental Psychology, 77,* 353–363.

Posner, M. I., and Keele, S. W. (1970). Retention of abstract ideas. *Journal of Experimental Psychology, 83,* 304–308.

Postman, L. (1975). Verbal learning and memory. *Annual Review of Psychology, 26,* 291–335.

Pressley, M., Levin, J. R., Hall, J. W., Miller, G. E., and Berry, J. K. (1980).

The keyword method and foreign word acquisition. *Journal of Experimental Psychology: Human Learning and Memory, 6,* 163–173.

Pylyshyn, Z. W. (1981). The imagery debate: Analogue media versus tacit knowledge. *Psychological Review, 88,* 16–45.

Pylyshyn, Z. W. (1973). What the mind's eye tells the mind's brain: A critique of mental imagery. *Psychological Bulletin, 80,* 1–24.

Quillian, M. R. (1967). Word concepts: A theory and simulation of some basic semantic capabilities. *Behavioral Science, 12,* 410–430.

Raaijmakers, J. G. W., and Shiffrin, R. M. (1981). Search of associative memory. *Psychological Review, 88,* 93–134.

Rand, G., and Wapner, S. (1967). Postural states as a factor in memory. *Journal of Verbal Learning and Verbal Behavior, 6,* 268–271.

Raugh, M. R., and Atkinson, R. C. (1975). A mnemonic method for learning a second-language vocabulary. *Journal of Educational Psychology, 67,* 1–16.

Rayner, K. (1975). The perceptual span and peripheral cues in reading. *Cognitive Psychology, 7,* 65–81.

Razran, G. (1971). *Mind in evolution.* Boston: Houghton Mifflin.

Read, J. D., and Bruce, D. (1982). Longitudinal tracking of difficult memory retrievals. *Cognitive Psychology, 14,* 280–300.

Reder L. M., Anderson, J. R., and Bjork, R. A. (1974). A semantic interpretation of encoding specificity. *Journal of Experimental Psychology, 102,* 648–656.

Reed, S. K. (1972). Pattern recognition and categorization. *Cognitive Psychology, 3,* 382–407.

Reed, S. K., Hock, H. S., and Lockhead, G. R. (1983). Tacit knowledge and the effect of pattern configuration on mental scanning. *Memory & Cognition, 11,* 137–143.

Rees, H. J., and Israel, H. E. (1935). An investigation of the establishment and operation of mental sets. *Psychometric Monographs, 46,* No. 210.

Reitman, J. S. (1970). Computer simulation of an information processing model of short-term memory. In D. A. Norman (Ed.), *Models of human memory.* New York: Academic Press.

Reitman, J. S. (1971). Mechanisms of forgetting in short-term memory. *Cognitive Psychology, 2,* 185–195.

Reitman, J. S. (1974). Without surreptitious rehearsal, information in short-term memory decays. *Journal of Verbal Learning and Verbal Behavior, 13,* 365–377.

Reutener, D. B. (1969). Background, symbolic and class shift in short-term memory. Unpublished doctoral dissertation, Ohio State University.

Reutener, D. B. (1972). Background, symbolic, and class shift in short-term verbal memory. *Journal of Experimental Psychology, 93,* 90–94.

Rips, L. J., Shoben, E. J., and Smith, E. E. (1973). Semantic distance and the verification of semantic relations. *Journal of Verbal Learning and Verbal Behavior, 12,* 1–20.

Roediger, H. L., and Schmidt, S. R. (1980). Output interference in the recall of categorized and paired-associate lists. *Journal of Experimental Psychology: Human Learning and Memory, 6,* 91–105.

Rosch, E. (1973). On the internal structure of perceptual and semantic categories. In T. W. Moore (Ed.), *Cognitive development and the acquisition of language.* New York: Academic Press.

Rosch, E. (1975). Cognitive representations of semantic categories. *Journal of Experimental Psychology: General, 104,* 192–233.

Rosch, E. (1977). Human categorization. In N. Warren (Ed.), *Studies in cross-cultural psychology.* London: Academic Press.

Rosch, E., and Mervis, C. B. (1975). Family resemblances: Studies in the internal structure of categories. *Cognitive Psychology, 7,* 573–605.

Rosch, E., Mervis, C. B., Gray, W. D., Johnson, D. M., and Boyes–Braem, P. (1976). Basic objects in natural categories. *Cognitive Psychology, 8,* 382–439.

Roth, D. M. (1957). *Roth memory course* (Rev. ed.). Cleveland, Ohio: Ralston.

Rozin, P. (1976). The psychobiological approach to human memory. In M. R. Rosenzweig and E. L. Bennett (Eds.), *Neural mechanisms of learning and memory.* Cambridge, Mass: M. I. T. Press.

Rubenstein, H., Garfield, L., and Millikan, J. A. (1970). Homographic entries in the internal lexicon. *Journal of Verbal Learning and Verbal Behavior, 9,* 487–494.

Rumelhart, D. E., and Abrahamson, A. A. (1973). A model for analogical reasoning. *Cognitive Psychology, 5,* 1–28.

Rumelhart, D. E., Lindsay, P. H., and Norman, D. A. (1972). A process model for long-term memory. In E. Tulving and W. Donaldson (Eds.), *Organization of memory.* New York: Academic Press.

Rundus, D. (1973). Negative effects of using list items as recall cues. *Journal of Verbal Learning and Verbal Behavior, 12,* 43–50.

Russell, W. R., and Nathan, P. W. (1946). Traumatic amnesia. *Brain, 69,* 280–300.

Safren, M. (1962). Associations, sets, and the solution to word problems. *Journal of Experimental Psychology, 64,* 40–45.

Sakitt, B. (1976). Iconic memory. *Psychological Review, 33,* 257–276.

Sakitt, B., and Long, G. M. (1979). Spare the rod and spoil the icon. *Journal of Experimental Psychology: Human Perception and Performance, 5,* 19–30.

Scheerer, M. (1963). Problem solving. *Scientific American, 208,* 118–128.

Schneider, D. J., Hastorf, A. H., and Ellsworth, P. C. (1979). *Person perception.* Reading, Mass.: Addison-Wesley.

Schonfield, D., and Stones, M. J. (1979). Remembering and aging. In J. F. Kihlstrom and F. J. Evans (Eds.), *Functional disorders of memory.* Hillsdale, N.J.: Erlbaum.

Shand, M. A. (1982). Sign-based short-term coding of American sign language signs and printed English words by congenitally deaf signers. *Cognitive Psychology, 14,* 1–12.

Shannon, C. E. (1948). A mathematical theory of communication. *Bell System Technical Journal, 27,* 379–423; 623–656.

Shaughnessy, J. J., and Mand, J. L. (1982). How permanent are memories for real life events? *American Journal of Psychology, 95,* 51–65.

Shepard, R. N., and Metzler, J. (1971). Mental rotations of three-dimensional objects. *Science, 171,* 701–703.

Shiffrin, R. M., and Atkinson, R. C. (1969). Storage and retrieval processes in long-term memory. *Psychological Review, 76,* 179–193.

Shoben, E. J., Wescourt, K. T., and Smith, E. E. (1978). Sentence verification, sentence recognition, and the semantic/episodic distinction. *Journal of Experimental Psychology: Human Learning and Memory, 4,* 304–317.

Shulman, H. G. (1970). Encoding and retention of semantic and phonemic information in short-term memory. *Journal of Verbal Learning and Verbal Behavior, 9,* 499–508.

Sichel, J. L., and Chandler, K. A. (1969). The color-word interference test: The effects of varied color-word combinations upon verbal response latency. *Journal of Psychology, 72,* 219–231.

Simon, H. A. (1974). How big is a chunk? *Science, 183,* 482–488.

Simon, H. A., and Kotovsky, K. (1963). Human acquisition of concepts for sequential patterns. *Psychological Review, 70,* 534–546.

Simon, H. A., and Newell, A. (1971). Human problem solving: The state of the theory in 1970. *American Psychologist, 26,* 145–159.

Skinner, B. F. (1979). *The shaping of a behaviorist*. New York: Alfred A. Knopf.

Slamecka, N. J. (1968). An examination of trace storage in free recall. *Journal of Experimental Psychology, 76,* 504–513.

Slovic, P., Fischoff, B., and Lichtenstein, S. (1976). Cognitive processes and social risk taking. In J. S. Carroll and J. W. Payne (Eds.), *Cognition and social behavior*. Potomac, Md.: Erlbaum.

Smith, A. D. (1971). Output interference and organized recall from long-term memory. *Journal of Verbal Learning and Verbal Behavior, 10,* 400–408.

Smith, A. D., D'Agostino, P. R., and Reid, L. S. (1970). Output interference in long-term memory. *Canadian Journal of Psychology, 24,* 85–89.

Smith, A. D., and Winograd, E. (1978). Adult age differences in remembering faces. *Developmental Psychology, 14,* 443–444.

Smith, E. E., Shoben, E. J., and Rips, L. J. (1974). Structure and process in semantic memory: A featural model for semantic decisions. *Psychological Review, 81,* 214–241.

Smith, S. M., Glenberg, A., and Bjork, R. A. (1978). Environmental context and human memory. *Memory & Cognition, 6,* 342–353.

Snyder, M., and Uranowitz, S. W. (1978). Reconstructing the past: Some cognitive consequences of person perception. *Journal of Personality and Social Psychology, 36,* 941–950.

Spence, K. W. (1945). An experimental test of the continuity and non-continuity theories of discrimination learning. *Psychological Review, 35,* 253–266.

Spencer, J. J., and Shuntich, R. (1970). Evidence for an interruption theory of backward masking. *Journal of Experimental Psychology, 85,* 198–203.

Sperling, G. (1960). The information available in brief visual presentations. *Psychological Monographs: General and Applied, 74,* 1–28.

Sperling, G. (1963). A model for visual memory tasks. *Human Factors, 5,* 19–31.

Sperling, G. (1970). Short-term memory, long-term memory, and scanning in the processing of visual information. In F. A. Young and D. B. Lindsley (Eds.), *Early experience and visual information processing in perceptual and reading disorders*. Washington: National Academy of Sciences.

Spiro, R. L. (1980). Accommodative reconstruction in prose recall. *Journal of Verbal Learning and Verbal Behavior, 19,* 84–95.

Squire, L. R., Slater, P. C., and Chace, P. M. (1975). Retrograde amnesia: Temporal gradient in very long term memory following electroconvulsive therapy. *Science, 187,* 77–79.

Stern, L. D. (1981). A review of theories of human amnesia. *Memory & Cognition, 9,* 247–262.

Sternberg, S. (1966). High-speed scanning in human memory. *Science, 153,* 652–654.

Straube, E. R., and Germer, C. K. (1979). Dichotic shadowing and selective attention to word meaning in schizophrenia. *Journal of Abnormal Psychology, 88,* 346–353.

Strauss, M. (1979). Abstraction of prototypical information by adults and 10-month-old infants. *Journal of Experimental Psychology: Human Learning and Memory, 5,* 618–632.

Stroop, J. R. (1935). Studies of interference in serial verbal reaction. *Journal of Experimental Psychology, 18,* 643–662.

Sulin, R. A., and Dooling, D. J. (1974). Intrusion of a thematic idea in retention of prose. *Journal of Experimental Psychology, 103,* 255–262.

Suzuki, N. S., and Rohwer, W. D. (1968). Verbal facilitation of paired-associate learning: Type of grammatical unit vs. connective form class. *Journal of Verbal Learning and Verbal Behavior, 7,* 584–588.

Swanson, J. M., and Kinsbourne, M. (1979). State-dependent learning and retrieval: Methodological cautions and theoretical considerations. In J. F. Kihlstrom and F. J. Evans (Eds.), *Functional disorders of memory.* Hillsdale, N.J.: Erlbaum.

Tajfel, H., and Wilkes, A. L. (1963). Classification and quantitative judgement. *British Journal of Psychology, 54,* 101–114.

Taylor, S. E., Fiske, S. T., Etcoff, N. L., and Ruderman, A. J. (1978). Categorical and contextual bases of person memory and stereotyping. *Journal of Personality and Social Psychology, 36,* 778–793.

Thomas, J. C. (1974). An analysis of behavior in the Hobbits-Orcs problem. *Cognitive Psychology, 6,* 257–269.

Thompson, C. P., and Barnett, C. (1981). Memory for product names: The generation effect. *Bulletin of the Psychonomic Society, 18,* 241–243.

Thomson, D. M., and Tulving, E. (1970). Associative encoding and retrieval: Weak and strong cues. *Journal of Experimental Psychology, 86,* 255–262.

Thorndike, E. L. (1898). Animal intelligence: An experimental study of the associative processes in animals. *Psychological Monographs, 2,* No. 8.

Thurm, A. T., and Glanzer, M. (1971). Free recall in children: Long-term store vs short-term store. *Psychonomic Science, 23,* 175–176.

Titus, T. G., and Robinson, J. A. (1973). Pseudo-primacy effects in free-recall. *Perceptual and Motor Skills, 37,* 891–899.

Tulving, E. (1968). When is recall higher than recognition? *Psychonomic Science, 10,* 53–54.

Tulving, E. (1972). Episodic and semantic memory. In E. Tulving and W. Donaldson (Eds.), *Organization of memory.* New York: Academic Press.

Tulving, E., and Pearlsone, Z. (1966). Availability versus accessibility of information in memory for words. *Journal of Verbal Learning and Verbal Behavior, 5,* 381–391.

Tulving, E., and Psotka, J. (1971). Retroactive inhibition in free recall: Inaccessibility of information available in the memory store. *Journal of Experimental Psychology, 87,* 1–8.

Tulving, E., and Thomson, D. M. (1973). Encoding specificity and retrieval processes in episodic memory. *Psychological Review, 80,* 352–373.

Turvey, M. T. (1973). On peripheral and central processes in vision: Inferences from an information-processing analysis of masking and patterned stimuli. *Psychological Review, 80,* 1–52.

Tversky, A., and Kahneman, D. (1973). Availability: A heuristic for judging frequency and probability. *Cognitive Psychology, 5,* 207–232.

Tversky, A., and Kahneman, D. (1981). The framing of decisions and the psychology of choice. *Science, 211,* 453–458.

Tversky, B. G. (1969). Pictorial and verbal encoding in a short-term memory task. *Perception and Psychophysics, 6,* 225–233.

Underwood, B. J. (1945). The effect of successive interpolations on retroactive and proactive inhibition. *Psychological Monographs, 59,* No. 3 (Whole No. 273).

Warren, R. E. (1972). Stimulus encoding and memory. *Journal of Experimental Psychology, 94,* 90–100.

Warren, R. M. (1970). Perceptual restoration of missing speech sounds. *Science, 167,* 392–393.

Watkins, M. J. (1974a). When is recall spectacularly higher than recognition? *Journal of Experimental Psychology, 102,* 161–163.

Watkins, M. J. (1974b). Concept and measurement of primary memory. *Psychological Bulletin, 81,* 695–711.

Watkins, M. J. (1975). Inhibition in recall with extralist "cues." *Journal of Verbal Learning and Verbal Behavior, 14,* 294–303.

Watkins, M. J. (1977). The intricacy of memory span. *Memory & Cognition, 5,* 529–534.

Watkins, M. J., Watkins, O. C., Craik, F. I. M., and Mazuryk, G. (1973). Effect of nonverbal distraction on short-term storage. *Journal of Experimental Psychology, 101,* 296–300.

Watkins, M. J., and Tulving, E. (1975). Episodic memory: When recognition fails. *Journal of Experimental Psychology: General, 104,* 5–29.

Watkins, M. J., and Watkins, O. C. (1976). Cue-overload theory and the method of interpolated attributes. *Bulletin of the Psychonomic Society, 7,* 289–291.

Watkins, O. C., and Watkins, M. J. (1975). Build-up of proactive inhibition as a cue-overload effect. *Journal of Experimental Psychology: Human Learning and Memory, 1,* 442–452.

Waugh, N. C. (1969). Free recall of conspicuous items. *Journal of Verbal Learning and Verbal Behavior, 8,* 448–456.

Waugh, N. C., and Norman, D. A. (1965). Primary memory. *Psychological Review, 72,* 89–104.

Weisberg, R. (1980). *Memory, thought, and behavior.* New York: Oxford University Press.

Weisberg, R., and Alba, J. W. (1981). An examination of the alleged role of "fixation" in the solution of several "insight" problems. *Journal of Experimental Psychology: General, 110,* 169–192.

Weisberg, R., and Suls, J. M. (1973). An information-processing model of Duncker's candle problem. *Cognitive Psychology, 4,* 255–276.

Weiskrantz, L., and Warrington, E. K. (1979). Conditioning in amnesic patients. *Neuropsychologia, 17,* 187–194.

Wickelgren, W. A. (1964). Size of rehearsal group and short-term memory. *Journal of Experimental Psychology, 68,* 413–419.

Wickelgren, W. A. (1974). Single-trace fragility theory of memory dynamics. *Memory & Cognition, 2,* 775–780.

Wickelgren, W. A. (1975a). Age and storage dynamics in continuous recognition memory. *Developmental Psychology, 11,* 165–169.

Wickelgren, W. A. (1975b). Alcoholic intoxication and memory storage dynamics. *Memory & Cognition, 3,* 385–389.

Wickelgren, W. A. (1977). *Learning and memory.* Englewood Cliffs, N.J.: Prentice-Hall.

Wickelgren, W. A. (1979a). *Cognitive psychology.* Englewood Cliffs, N.J.: Prentice-Hall.

Wickelgren, W. A. (1979b). Chunking and consolidation: A theoretical synthesis of semantic networks, configuring in conditioning, S-R versus cognitive learning, normal forgetting, the amnesic syndrome and the hippocampal arousal system. *Psychological Review, 86,* 44–60.

Wickens, D. D. (1972). Characteristics of word encoding. In A. W. Melton and E. Martin (Eds.), *Coding processes in human memory.* Washington, D.C.: V. H. Winston and Sons.

Williams, M. D. (1976). Retrieval from very long-term memory. Unpublished doctoral dissertation. University of California, San Diego.

Wingfield, A., and Byrnes, D. L. (1981). *The psychology of human memory.* New York: Academic Press.

Winocur, G., and Weiskrantz, L. (1976). An investigation of paired-associate learning in amnesic patients. *Neuropsychologia, 14,* 97–110.

Winograd, E. (1978). Encoding operations which facilitate memory for faces across the life span. In M. M. Gruneberg, P. E. Morris, and R. N. Sykes (Eds.), *Practical aspects of memory.* New York: Academic Press.

Winograd, E. (1981). Elaboration and distinctiveness in memory for faces. *Journal of Experimental Psychology: Human Learning and Memory, 7,* 181–190.

Wollen, K. A., Weber, A., and Lowry, D. H. (1972). Bizarreness versus interaction of mental images as determinants of learning. *Cognitive Psychology, 3,* 518–523.

Woodward, A. E., Bjork, R. A., and Jongeward, R. H. (1973). Recall and recognition as a function of primary rehearsal. *Journal of Verbal Learning and Verbal Behavior, 12,* 608–617.

Woodworth, R., and Schlosberg, H. (1954). *Experimental psychology.* New York: Holt, Rinehart and Winston.

Yates, F. A. (1966). *The art of memory.* Middlesex, England: Penguin.

Zangwill, O. L. (1966). The amnesic syndrome. In C. W. H. Whitty and O. L. Zangwill (Eds.), *Amnesia,* London: Butterworth.

Name index

Subject index

A

Acoustic codes, 44–45, 47, 163–69
Activation of memories, 105–7, 132, 142–43; *see also* Priming
Age and memory, 93, 135–38, 176–79, 188
Aitken, A. C., 4–5
Alcohol and memory, 94, 111
Amnesia, 6–7, 49, 95, 189, 191
Analog encoding of visual information, 61–76
Associations; *see also* Priming
  contextual, 183–85, 189–90
  and evolution, 190–92
  interitem, 185–88
  and levels of processing, 228–29
  and visual stimuli, 201–3
Asymptote of the serial position curve, 134–35
Availability strategy, 313–17, 321–24

B

Bit, 77–78
Blocking, 116–28, 126–30, 226–27, 338–39
Brown-Peterson task, 158–61, 213, 215
Buildup of proactive interference, 124–26, 159–61, 213

C

Cell assembly, 79, 90, 108
Chunk, 140, 142, 181–83
Clustering, 40, 42–43
Concept formation procedure, 255–56
Concept identification procedure, 255–56
Concepts
  acquisition of, 233–39, 250–51
  conditioning view of, 252–53
  definition, 233
  and hypotheses, 252–63
  representation in memory, 242–51
  and retrieval, 23–34, 237–40, 242, 251, 258–63, 271–73
  role in
    comprehension, 281
    inferences, 286–89
    perception, 274–81
    perceptual distortions, 278–81
  types of
    basic, 266–71
    biconditional, 260–61
    conditional, 261
    conjunctive, 261
    fuzzy, 265
    ill defined, 265
    inclusive disjunctive, 261
    natural, 263–72

This book has been set in 10 and 9 point Caledonia, leaded 2 points. Part numbers are 24 pt Helvetica and part titles are 24 point Helvetica Bold. Chapter numbers are 20 point Helvetica, chapter titles are 20 point Helvetica Bold. The size of the type page is 36 by 48 picas.